AF693014

RXpert SERIES

Student's Companion

Regulatory Affairs

Basic Protocols

RXpert SERIES

Student's Companion

Regulatory Affairs

Basic Protocols

Sankar Veintramuthu
Professor and Head,
Department of Pharmaceutics,
P.S.G College of Pharmacy, Coimbatore, Tamil Nadu.

S. Pranav Ragavendra
Research Scholar,
Department of Pharmaceutics,
P.S.G College of Pharmacy, Coimbatore, Tamil Nadu.

Pharma Med PRESS
An Imprint of BSP Books Pvt. Ltd.

PharmaMed Press
An imprint of BSP Books Pvt. Ltd
4-4-309/316, Giriraj Lane,
Sultan Bazar, Hyderabad - 500 095.

Regulatory Affairs: ***Basic Protocols***
by **Sankar Veintramuthu and S. Pranav Ragavendra**

Disclaimer: The authors and the publishers have taken due care to provide the authentic, reliable and up to date information related to the subject. However, neither the authors nor the publisher shall be responsible for any liability for any damage caused as a result of use of this book. The respective user must check the accuracy from other sources too.

Published by:

Pharma Med PRESS
An Imprint of BSP Books Pvt. Ltd.

PharmaMed Press

An imprint of BSP Books Pvt. Ltd.
4-4-309/316, Giriraj Lane, Sultan Bazar, Hyderabad - 500 095.
Phone: 040-23445688; Fax: 91+40-23445611
e-mail: info@pharmamedpress.com
www.pharmamedpress.com/pharmamedpress.net

ISBN: 978-93-95039-57-4 (Hardback)

PSG COLLEGE OF PHARMACY

(An ISO 9001 : 2015 Certified Institution)
Accredited with 'B++' Grade by NAAC (2nd Cycle)
Affiliated to The Tamil Nadu Dr. M.G.R. Medical University, Chennai
Approved by Pharmacy Council of India and All India Council for Technical Education, New Delhi
AVINASHI ROAD, PEELAMEDU, COIMBATORE 641 004, TAMILNADU, INDIA

Phone 0422-4345841
0422-2570170 (6 Lines)
Fax 0422-2594400
E mail principal@psgpharma.ac.in

Foreword

Globalization of the market resulted in stringent regulatory requirements to market the product globally. In the health sector, promotion and sale of pharmaceutical products in India and abroad experiencing stringent regulatory requirements as per the respective drug regulatory authorities. Considering this fact, recently the Pharmacy Council of India introduced a new Course Regulatory Affairs. Many institutions at National level offering M. Pharm Regulatory Affairs program. The job potential in the regulatory sector is wider and it is popularly known as RA. Many Pharma students as well as science graduates take-up this as a career. Considering this fact the authors have written a book in Regulatory Affairs as per the PCI regulations 2016 for M. Pharm first semester.

The book covers various units referring documents required to preserve for auditing and definitions as per the regulatory bodies. They also discussed the Code for Federal Regulations (CFR). ANDA application process including product approvals. The book contents includes regulatory requirements for conducting BA/BE studies. It addresses the regulatory requirement for registration of drug molecules and biologicals in European Union and US market. The clinical research aspects referring the development of safe and affordable product have been presented as per the international standards.

Topics in the book are discussed on student's point of view with figures and illustrative examples. Explicit and easy to read. Industrial perspectives are also included. I congratulate the authors for providing quality contents. Wish them all success.

Dr. M. Ramanathan
Principal

Dr. M. Ramanathan, D.Sc.,
Principal
PSG College of Pharmacy
Peelamedu, Coimbatore - 4

PSG COLLEGE OF PHARMACY
PEELAMEDU
COIMBATORE-641 004.

Recognized as Industrial Scientific Research Organization by DSIR • DST FIST Sponsored Institution
Website: www.psgpharma.in

Preface

Regulatory Affairs is the most fascinating branch of pharmaceutical sciences, it plays a key role throughout the product lifecycle to demonstrate the quality, control, conformity, safety, and efficacy of the product in the documentation submitted to the competent authorities for review and approval.

The first edition of this book entitled "Regulatory Affairs – Basic Protocols" Consists of 4 chapters covering basic regulatory aspects of pharmaceuticals with respect to documentation in pharmaceutical industry.

It gives us great pleasure in presenting this book to the students of Master of Pharmacy with the latest Pharmacy Council of India syllabus.

This book covers ICH guidelines, Investigational medicinal product dossier, Investigator's brochure, Development of clinical trial protocol, Institutional review board , Regulatory requirements in clinical trials, Safety monitoring and reporting, Health insurance and portability and liability act, Informed consent process and Pharmacovigilance, Regulatory requirements for product approval, SUPAC, Outsourcing BA & BE to CRO, Regulatory requirements for registration of API in US and EU, Biologics, U.S registration for foreign drugs also discussed.

We would be grateful to the members of pharmaceutical profession for any suggestion and criticism towards the improvement of this book.

The authors are highly thankful to the following members who were helped in the successful completion of this book.

Our heartfelt thanks to Mrs. Loganathan Thilagavathi M. Pharm, Lecturer, Department of Pharmaceutics, Sri Ramakrishna Institute of Paramedical sciences, Coimbatore.

Our sincere thanks to Mrs. Baby Roselin. R, Research Scholar, Department of Pharmaceutics, PSG College of Pharmacy, Coimbatore.

Our special thanks to Shankar. T, Karunambigai. B, Goutham Ragavendra. S, Yamuna TG, Kousalya Rajendran, Sree V, Balaji Arunachalam, Sathya Priya O and Priyadharshni Arul.

Our special acknowledgement to S veintramuthu, S Narayanan, V Easwaram, S Eswari, G Jayasundari.

Our sincere gratitude to Dr. M. Ramanathan D.Sc. Principal PSG College of Pharmacy Coimbatore for his constant support and encouragement.

We express our sincere thanks to the management of PSG College of Pharmacy, Coimbatore.

Above all we thank the almighty for the successful completion of the book.

- Authors

Contents

Chapter – 1.4

Generic Drugs Product Development

Chapter – 1.5

Hatch-Waxman Act

Chapter – 1.6

Code of Federal Regulations (CFR)[1-4]

Chapter – 1.7

Drug Product Performance, *IN VITRO*

Chapter – 1.8

ANDA Regulatory Approval Process

Chapter – 1.9

Regulatory Requirements for Product Approval

Chapter – 1.10

SUPAC

Chapter – 1.11

Outsourcing BA & BE to CRO

Chapter – 1.12

Regulatory Requirements for Registration of API in US and EU

Chapter – 1.13

Biologics

Chapter – 1.14

U.S Registration for Foreign Drugs

Chapter – 1.15

Bioequivalence and Drug Product Assessment

Chapter – 1.16

Post Marketing Surveillance

Chapter – 2.1

Chemistry, Manufacturing and Controls (CMC)

Chapter – 2.2

CTD and E CTD

Chapter – 2.3

ICH Guidelines

Chapter – 2.4

Regulatory Requirement of EU, MHRA and TGA

Chapter – 3.1

Investigational Medicinal Product Dossier (IMOD)

Chapter – 3.2

Investigator's Brochure

Chapter – 4.1

Development of Clinical Trial Protocol

Chapter – 4.2

Institutional Review Board (IRB)

Chapter – 4.3

Regulatory Requirements in Clinical Trails

Chapter – 4.4

Safety Monitoring and Reporting on Clinical Trails

Chapter – 4.5

Health Insurance and Portability and Liability Act

Chapter – 4.6

Informed Consent Process and Procedures

Chapter – 4.7

Pharmacovigilance

CHAPTER 1.1

Documentation in Pharmaceutical Industry

1.1.1 Master Formula Record - Definition

"A document or set of documents describing the raw materials and quantities, as well as the procedures and precautions required to manufacture a specific quantity of a final product, as well as the processing instructions, including in-process controls." For each product and batch size to be generated, Master Formula papers referring to all production methods must be kept. These must be created and approved by qualified technical personnel, such as the head of manufacturing and quality control. MFR is a key regularity in each batch of production.

1.1.2 Master Formula Record

- A master formula record (MFR) is a document that includes all of the details about a pharmaceutical product.
- The MFR contains all information about the manufacturing process of the product.
- The MFR is prepared by the company's research and development staff.
- When establishing batch manufacturing records, manufacturing units use MFR as a reference standard (BMR).
- Master Manufacturing Record, often known as MFR, is a type of manufacturing record.

1.1.3 MFR - Product Details

✓ Name, logo and address of the manufacturing company.

✓ Dosage form name.

✓ Brand name.

- ✓ Generic name.
- ✓ Product code
- ✓ Label claim of all ingredients
- ✓ Product description and quality of raw materials
- ✓ Batch size
- ✓ Pack size and packing style
- ✓ Shelf life
- ✓ Storage conditions
- ✓ MFR number and date
- ✓ Supersede MFR number and date
- ✓ Effective batch number
- ✓ Authorization by the production and quality assurance head

Flow Chart: The steps that will be tracked in the manufacturing process. Material flow from dispensing to final product distribution to stores is depicted in this flowchart.

Equipment: Make a list of all the necessary equipment and machines for the production process, along with their capacities.

Special instructions: Make a list of any precautions or special instructions that must be followed during the product's manufacturing and packaging, and include them in the batch manufacturing formula.

Calculations: To acquire 100 percent of the active ingredient, include the calculation procedures for all active materials. To reach 100 percent potency, the calculation should be done with water or LOD.

Manufacturing Process: Every stage of the manufacturing process must be recorded. Shifting, milling, lubrication, granulation, compression, and coating should all be meticulously documented, as should the process duration and yield. For each phase, it also incorporates environmental parameters such as temperature, humidity, and storage conditions.

Packing Process: All packing materials, as well as their quantities, are listed. The details should include line clearance and reconciliation of printed and unprinted packing goods.

Include the batch's theoretical, real, and acceptable constraints in the yield.

1.1.4 Procedure to Prepare a Master Formula Record

The knowledge of seasoned specialists, such as manufacturing or analytical chemists, is combined with the manufacturing history of a batch size to create a Master Formula Record. At any level, we cannot overlook the Master formula record.

All prior and new employees are then handed the Master Formula Record. In batch processing, it's a common document. The Master Formula record is the gold standard when it comes to creating a Batch Manufacturing Record.

1.1.5 SOP for Preparation of the Master Formula Record

RESPONSIBLE DEPARTMENTS:

Primary Responsibility:

F&D and Production Department

Secondary Responsibility:

Quality Assurance Department

ACCOUNTABILITY:

Head-Quality Assurance shall be responsible for Implementation of SOP.

1.1.6 Steps to Prepare a Master Formula Record

- Production Department in association with F&D shall prepare MFR.
- MFR shall prepare as per the format attached with this SOP.
- MFR shall be divided into two parts:
- Packaging part
- Manufacturing part

1.1.7 The First Page of both the Sections Shall have Following Details

- Name, address and logo of the company
- Dosage form
- Brand name
- Generic name

- Product code
- Label claim: This should include all ingredients and text included in product permission
- Product Description
- Batch Size
- Pack Size
- Shelf Life
- Storage conditions
- Drug Schedule: whether schedule H or schedule G drug.
- Superseded Master card number and Date.
- Present Master card number and Date.
- Present Master card effective Batch number.
- Reference of changed control number.
- There shall be authorization of Master Formula Record by all the responsible members
- The secondary page of manufacturing section shall include-Process steps to be monitored.
- Subsequent pages shall include the processes to be monitored. The stage wise movement of material in a form of flow chart.
- The list of equipment, machines, utensils to be used, shall be described.
- Any particular measures to be taken for the product during manufacture and packing will be listed on the next page. Batch Manufacturing Formula should be included on the same page.

1.1.8 Batch Formula should have the following columns

- Serial number
- Name of ingredients
- Reference of specifications of ingredients
- Quantity to be added (in mg/ml or per tablet or per capsule or per gm. as the case may be)
- Overages to be added (in %)
- Quantity to be added per batch or per lot below that give the calculation step for every active

- Material, ensuring that the active material shall be compensated for assay values less than 100% which could be due to less potency or higher moisture content.

1.1.9 At the End of Every Important Stage, include a Statement of the Yield with the Acceptable Limits

Include quality checks at the beginning and end of essential processes and stages, as well as at the process's boundaries.

The tools that will be utilised must be included in the technique. Methods or references to methods/procedures for preparing, cleaning, assembling, and operating diverse equipment must be provided.

Include clear, step-by-step directions for processing (example: checks on materials, pretreatments, sequence for adding materials, mixing times, temperatures, humidity etc.)

Product storage conditions must meet certain criteria.

1.1.10 The Packaging Part of MFR

Check for line clearance during batch coding and batch packaging activities.

Includes appropriate packaging element reconciliation (printed and unprinted).

Extra or rejected and printed packaging materials are discarded.

Describes the packing operation, as well as any relevant supporting operations and equipment.

Master Formulation Record

Isopropyl alcohol antiseptic 75% topical solution			
Name:	**isopropyl alcohol**	Batch Volume:	50,000 mL (50 L)
Concentration:	75%	Dispensed Product:	50 mL or 1,000 mL
Route:	Topical	Beyond-Use Date:	1-year
Form:	Solution	Storage:	Room Temperature
Auxiliary Labeling:	Flammable, external use only, avoid contact with eyes		

INGREDIENTS	AMOUNT	FINAL CONCENTRATION
Isopropyl alcohol 99.8%, USP	37,575 mL	75% (v/v) *(active ingredient)*
Hydrogen peroxide 3%, USP	2,085 mL	0.125% (v/v)
Glycerin 98%, USP	725 mL	1.45% (v/v)
Sterile Water for Irrigation, USP	~9,615 mL	*(qs to final volume)*
Total Batch Volume:	**50,000 mL**	

EQUIPMENT AND SUPPLIES
15-gallon stainless steel pot w/ spigot and fitted lid with opening
Large plastic stir
1,000 mL graduated cylinder
500 mL graduated cylinder
250 mL graduated conical beaker
Silicone adapter for dispenser
50 mL plastic bottle with flip top dispensing lid
1,000 mL plastic bottle with spray apparatus
PPE: R-95 mask, lab goggles, gown, gloves

LABEL

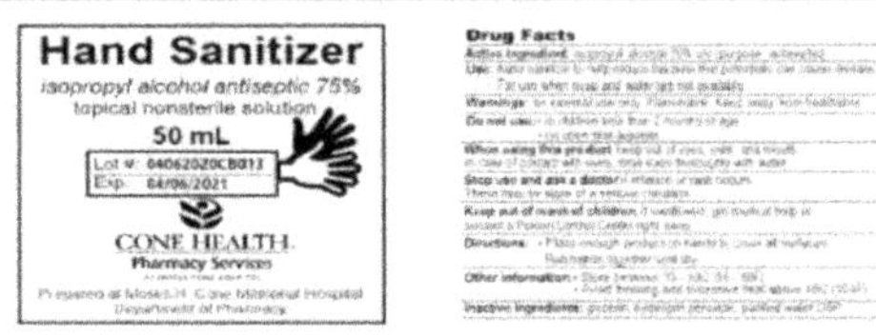

METHOD OF PREPARATION

Note: Preparation to occur only in the negative pressure nonsterile compounding room. PPE required during preparation. Remove any sources of potential flame or spark to minimize fire risk.

1. Measure quantities of isopropyl alcohol and hydrogen peroxide in separate graduated cylinders and combine them in a 15-gallon stainless steel pot.
2. Measure glycerin in a conical graduated cylinder and add to mixture in stainless steel pot. As glycerin is very viscous and sticks to the wall of the measuring cylinder, it should be rinsed with some sterile water for irrigation and then emptied into the kettle.
3. Measure quantities of sterile water for irrigation sufficient to final volume of 50,000 mL and add to the mixture in the pot.
4. Carefully stir solution in kettle and place stainless steel lid on kettle to minimize vapors while dispensing.
5. Using stainless steel spigot and empty plastic bottle, slowly open flow to fill 1,000 mL empty plastic bottle to approximately 1,000 mL.
6. Product can further be unit dosed into either: (1) 50 mL bottles with dispensing lid, or (2) 1,000 mL spray bottle.

FINAL PRODUCT DESCRIPTION / QUALITY ASSURANCE

- Clear colorless low viscosity liquid
- Verify final alcohol concentration of hand sanitizer using an alcohol meter. Isopropyl 75% will be shown as 77% (+/- 1%) on the scale.
- Due to the high alcohol content of this formula, it is considered self-preserved. Filled, bottles should be quarantined for 72-hours to eliminate any spores present.

REFERENCES

1. World Health Organization. (2010). Guide to local production: WHO-recommended hand rub formulations. Geneva: WHO.
2. Food and Drug Administration (FDA) – Policy for Temporary Compounding of Certain Alcohol-Based Hand Sanitizer Products During the Public Health Emergency. March 2020.

Figure 1

References

1. A Textbook of Pharmaceutical Quality assurance by Mr. Sanjay A. Nagdev, Mr. Mayur R. Bhurat, Dr. Md. Rageeb Md. Usman Dr. Krishna R. Gupta, Dr. Upendra B. Gandagule.
2. https://www.slideshare.net/NavaneethakrishnanPa4/documentation-in-pharmaceutical-industry-144312056.

CHAPTER 1.2

Drug Master File (DMF)

Definition

DMFs (Drug Master Files) are FDA filings that contain sensitive information regarding a drug product's Chemistry, Manufacturing, and Controls (CMCs), as well as non-CMC related information (such as packaging)

1.2.1 Table of Contents

I. Introduction

II. Definitions

III. Types of drug master files

IV. Submissions to drug master files

A. Transmittal Letters

1. Original Submissions
2. Amendments

B. Administrative Information

1. Original Submissions
2. Amendments

C. Drug Master File Contents

1. Types of Drug Master Files

(a) *Type I*: Manufacturing Site, Facilities, Operating Procedures, and Personnel

(b) *Type II*: Drug Substance, Drug Substance Intermediate, and Material Used in Their Preparation, or Drug Product

(c) *Type III*: Packaging Material

(d) *Type IV*: Excipient, Colorant, Flavor, Essence, or Material Used in Their Preparation

(e) *Type V*: FDA Accepted Reference Information

2. General Information and Suggestions

A. Environmental Assessment

B. Stability

C. Format, Assembly, and Delivery

V. Authorization to Refer to A Drug Master File

A. Letter of Authorization to FDA

B. Copy to Applicant, Sponsor, or Other Holder

VI. Processing and Reviewing Policies

A. Policies Related to Processing Drug Master Files

B. Drug Master File Review

VII. Holder Obligations

A. Notice Required for Changes to a Drug Master File

B. Listing of Persons Authorized To Refer to a Drug Master File

C. Annual Update

D. Appointment of an Agent

E. Transfer of Ownership

IX. Closure of a Drug Master File

1.2.2 Guideline for Drug Master Files

I. Introduction

A Drug Master File is a top-secret submission to the FDA that comprises complete information regarding the facilities, processes, or materials used in the production, processing, packing, and storage of one or more human pharmaceuticals (DMF). There is no legal or FDA requirement for a DMF.

A DMF is given to the bearer on his or her own terms. The information in the DMF can be used in an IND, a New Drug Application (NDA), an Abbreviated New Drug Application (ANDA), another DMF, an Export Application, or changes and supplements to any of these applications. A DMF cannot be replaced by an IND, NDA, ANDA, or Export Application. It hasn't been accepted or rejected yet. Only when an IND, NDA, ANDA, or Export Application is being reviewed is the technical content of a DMF considered. There are no requirements in this guideline. It does, however, provide guidance on how to effectively comply with regulatory standards.

Different approaches may be used, but it is recommended that the applicant meet with FDA reviewers ahead of time to avoid spending time and effort on a submission that the FDA may later find unsatisfactory. The standards for Drug Master Files are laid out in 21 CFR 314.420. The purpose of this guideline is to show DMF holders how to prepare and submit DMFs that the agency will approve. The guideline discusses the many types of DMFs, the data necessary for each, the structure of DMF submissions, the administrative procedures that oversee DMF evaluation, and the duties of the DMF holder.

DMFs were established to allow parties other than the DMF holder to access information without revealing the file's contents. Rather than producing a new DMF, an applicant should specifically cite the information supplied in its existing IND, NDA, or ANDA when referring to its own material.

Who must file a dmf?

Nobody

There is no legal or regulatory requirement to file a DMF. CMC data can be submitted to the FDA for assessment via a DMF. An IND/NDA/ANDA, another DMF, an export application, or amendments and supplements to any of these papers can all benefit from DMF data.

Remember that,

DMF is **NOT a substitute** for IND / NDA / ANDA or export application.

Technical contents of a DMF are reviewed only in connection with the review of IND /NDA /ANDA or an export application.

Some basic Terminologies

Holder: The person /company **who submits** DMF.

Agent: The person / company **who represents** a DMF HOLDER. (*Also called Representative.*)

Applicant/Customer/Authorised Party (AP): The person / company **who Reference** the DMF.

Application: Investigational New Drug Application (IND), New Drug Application (NDA), Abbreviated New Drug Application (ANDA)

Supplement to an ANDA / NDA: A report of change in an **approved** ANDA / NDA.

Amendment to an Application: Additional information to... An existing IND, a pending ANDA / NDA a pending ANDA / NDA supplement

II. Definitions

For the purposes of this guideline, the following definitions apply:

1. *Agency* means the Food and Drug Administration.
2. *Agent or representative* means any person who is appointed by a DMF holder to serve as the contact for the holder.
3. *Applicant* means any person who submits an application or abbreviated application or an amendment or supplement to them to obtain FDA approval of a new drug or an antibiotic drug and any other person who owns an approved application (21 CFR 314.3 (b)).
4. *Drug product* means a finished dosage form, for example, tablet, capsule, or solution, that contains a drug substance, generally, but not necessarily, in association with one or more other ingredients (21 CFR 314.3 (b)).
5. *Drug substance* means an active ingredient that is intended to furnish pharmacological activity or other direct effect in the diagnosis, cure, mitigation, treatment, or prevention of disease or to affect the structure or any function of the human body, but does not include intermediates used in the synthesis of such ingredient (21 CFR 314.3 (b)).
6. *Export application* means an application submitted under section 802 of the Federal Food, Drug, and Cosmetic Act to export a drug that is not approved for marketing in the United States.
7. *Holder* means a person who owns a DMF.
8. *Letter of authorization* means a written statement by the holder or designated agent or representative permitting FDA to refer to information in the DMF in support of another person's submission.
9. *Person* includes individual, partnership, corporation, and association. (Section 201(e) of the Federal Food, Drug, and Cosmetic Act.)
10. *Sponsor* means a person who takes responsibility for and initiates a clinical investigation. The sponsor may be an individual or pharmaceutical company, governmental agency, academic institution, private organization, or other organization (21 CFR 312.3 (b)).

III. Types of Drug Master Files

There are five types of DMF's:

Type I Manufacturing Site, Facilities, Operating Procedures, and Personnel

Type II Drug Substance, Drug Substance Intermediate, and Material Used in Their Preparation, or Drug Product

Type III Packaging Material

Type IV Excipient, Colorant, Flavor, Essence, or Material Used in Their Preparation

Type V FDA Accepted Reference Information

Each DMF should contain only one type of information and all supporting data.

IV. Submissions to Drug Master Files

A transmittal letter, administrative information concerning the submission, and the precise information to be included in the DMF as described in this section should be included in each DMF submission.

The DMF must be written entirely in English. A certified English translation must be included with any submission that incorporates material in another language.

Each page of each DMF copy should be dated and numbered in order. Each submission should include a table of contents.

Transmittal Letters

The following should be included:

Original Submissions

a. Submission identification: Original, DMF type (as defined in Section III), and subject.
b. Identification of the applications that the DMF is intended to support, including the sponsor, applicant, or holder's name and address, as well as all relevant document numbers, if known.
c. The holder's or authorised representative's signature
d. The signer's typewritten name and title.

Amendments

a. Identification of submission: Amendment, the DMF number, type of DMF, and the subject of the amendment.
b. A description of the purpose of submission, e.g., update, revised formula, or revised process.
c. Signature of the holder or the authorized representative.
d. Typewritten name and title of the signer.

Administrative Information

Administrative information should include the following:

Original Submissions

a Names and addresses of the following:

1. DMF holder.
2. Corporate headquarters.
3. Manufacturing/processing facility.
4. Contact for FDA correspondence.
5. Agent(s), if any.

b. The specific responsibilities of each person listed in any of the categories in Section a.

c. Statement of commitment.

A signed statement by the holder certifying that the DMF is current and that the DMF holder will comply with the statements made in it.

Amendments

a. Name of DMF holder.
b. DMF number.
c. Name and address for correspondence.
d. Affected section and/or page numbers of the DMF.
e. The name and address of each person whose IND, NDA, ANDA, DMF, or Export Application relies on the subject of the amendment for support.
f. The number of each IND, NDA, ANDA, DMF, and Export Application that relies on the subject of the amendment for support, if known.
g. Particular items within the IND, NDA, ANDA, DMF, and Export Application that are affected, if known.

Drug Master File Contents

Types of Drug Master Files

***Type I*: Manufacturing Site, Facilities, Operating Procedures, and Personnel**

A Type I DMF should be obtained by someone who lives outside of the United States and wants to assist the FDA in evaluating their manufacturing facilities on the spot. The DMF should include information regarding the manufacturing facility, its equipment, and its operational structure. Unless there are special circumstances, such as when a person is not registered and inspected on a regular basis, a Type I DMF is usually not required to display household amenities. The acreage, true site address, and a map demonstrating the property's location in relation to the nearest city should all be included in the site description. Aerial photographs and a site map could be extremely useful.

Understanding the operating structure is aided by a visual representation of major production and processing zones. The capabilities, applications, and locations of major equipment should all be stated. Unless the equipment is new or distinctive, the make and model are usually not required. A representation of the primary corporate organisational components at both the production site and the corporate headquarters, with key manufacturing, quality control, and quality assurance positions indicated, is also useful.

***Type II*: Drug Substance, Drug Substance Intermediate, and Material Used in Their Preparation, or Drug Product**

A single drug intermediary, drug substance, drug product, or kind of material employed in their synthesis should be the focus of a Type II DMF.

Drug Substance Intermediates, Drug Substances, and Material Used in Their Preparation

Make a list of all the steps involved in creating and testing the drug intermediate or substance. The following guidelines provide precise information on what should be included in a Type II DMF for therapeutic compounds and intermediates:

Guideline for Submitting Supporting Documentation in Drug Applications for the Manufacture of Drug Substances.

Guideline for the Format and Content of the Chemistry, Manufacturing, and Controls Section of an Application.

Drug Product

Manufacturing processes and controls for completed dosage forms should normally be included in an IND, NDA, ANDA, or Export Application. If this information cannot be included in an IND, NDA, ANDA, or Export Application, it should be included in a DMF. The applicant/sponsor should follow the steps in the following recommendations when submitting a Type II DMF for a medicine:

A guide to the format and content of an application's Chemistry, Manufacturing, and Controls section.

Guidelines for Submitting Documentation for Drug Product Manufacturing and Controls

Submission of Samples and Analytical Data for Method Validation Guidelines

***Type III*: Packaging Material**

The intended use, components, composition, and release controls for each packing material should all be determined. Include the names of the component suppliers or fabricators who assisted with the packing material preparation, as well as the acceptance criteria.

According to the "Guideline for Submitting Documentation for Packaging for Human Drugs and Biologics," data proving the appropriateness of the packaging material for its intended application should also be submitted. If toxicological data on these materials wasn't previously available via a cross reference to another document, this sort of DMF would supply it.

***Type IV*: Excipient, Colorant, Flavor, Essence, or Material Used in Their Preparation**

The production process, release specifications, and testing techniques for each additive should all be documented.

If toxicological data on these materials wasn't previously available by a cross reference to another document, this sort of DMF would supply it.

Color additives (21 CFR Parts 70–82), direct food additives (21 CFR Parts 170–173), indirect food additives (21 CFR Parts 174–178), and food substances (21 CFR Parts 181–186) are all examples of release testing, standard, and safety sources. Type IV DMFs may be subject to the same standards as Type II DMFs. Any extra supporting materials or data not identified by cross-referencing another document should be included in the DMF.

***Type V*: FDA Accepted Reference Information**

Type V DMFs should not be used for information that belongs in one of the other DMF categories, such as miscellaneous data, redundant data, or data that belongs in one of the other types of DMFs, according to the FDA. Holders who want to transmit information and supporting data to the Drug Master File Staff for a DMF that isn't covered by Types I through IV must first send a letter of intent to the Drug Master File Staff (for address, see D.5.a. of this section). The holder will be contacted by FDA to discuss the proposed submission.

General Information and Suggestions

Environmental Assessment

The firm shall agree to operating its facilities in accordance with applicable environmental legislation in Type II, Type III, and Type IV DMFs. See 21 CFR Part 25 if a completed environmental assessment is required.

Stability

Stability study design, data, interpretation, and other information should be submitted, when applicable, as outlined in the "*Guideline for Submitting Documentation for the Stability of Human Drugs and Biologics.*"

Format, Assembly, and Delivery

An original and duplicate are to be submitted for all DMF submissions

Holders of Drug Master Files and their agents/representatives should keep a comprehensive reference copy that is similar to their FDA filings and kept in the same chronological order.

The original and duplicate copies must be collated, fully assembled, and individually jacketed.

Each volume of a DMF should be little more than 2 inches thick in general. In a multivolume submission, number each volume. For a three-volume submission, the volumes would be labelled 1 of 3, 2 of 3, and 3 of 3.

U.S. standard paper size (8-1/2 by 11 inches) is preferred.

The paper should be no less than 10 inches long and no longer than 12 inches long. Individual pages bigger than standard paper size may be required on occasion for a floor plan, synthesis flowchart, batch formula, or production instructions. Those pages should be folded and mounted so that they can be examined without having to remove the jacket, and then refolded without causing damage to the book.

The agency's DMF filing method allows for assembly on the left side of the page. The left margin should be at least three fourths of an inch to ensure that text in the associated area is not covered. On the right margin, at least a half-inch should be left. Each page should have 8 1/2 inch holes punched in it.

Delivery to FDA

Drug Master File submissions and correspondence should be addressed as follows:

Drug Master File Staff

Food and Drug Administration

5901-B Ammendale Rd.

Beltsville, MD 20705-1266

Delivery charges to the above address must be prepaid.

V. Authorization to Refer to A Drug Master File

Letter of Authorization to FDA

Before FDA can consider DMF information in support of an application, the DMF holder must furnish a letter of authorization allowing FDA to reference the DMF in triplicate to the DMF. If the holder wishes to cross-reference its own DMF, the information supplied in items 3, 5, 6, 7, and 8 of this section should be included in a letter of authorization. A transmittal letter is not required from the holder of the letter of authorization.

The following should be included in the authorization letter:

1. The date.
2. Name of DMF holder.
3. DMF number.
4. Name of person(s) authorized to incorporate information in the DMF by reference.
5. Specific product(s) covered by the DMF.
6. Submission date(s) of 5, above.
7. Section numbers and/or page numbers to be referenced.
8. Statement of commitment that the DMF is current and that the DMF holder will comply with the statements made in it.
9. Signature of authorizing official.
10. Typed name and title of official authorizing reference to the DMF.

Copy to Applicant, Sponsor, or Other Holder

The impacted application, sponsor, or other holder who is entitled to use the specified information in the DMF by reference shall also get a copy of the letter of authorization. The applicant, sponsor, or other holder must submit a copy of the DMF holder's letter of authorization when citing a DMF in an application.

VI. Processing and Reviewing Policies

Policies Related to Processing Drug Master Files

Public availability of the information and data in a DMF is determined under 21 CFR Part 20, 21 CFR 314.420(e), and 21 CFR 314.430.

An original DMF submission will be examined on receipt to determine whether it meets minimum requirements for format and content. If the submission is administratively acceptable, FDA will acknowledge its receipt and assign it a DMF number.

The submitter will receive a letter from the Drug Master File Staff outlining the issue if the submission is administratively incomplete or deficient, and the submission will not be given a DMF number.

Drug Master File Review

At any time, a DMF cannot be rejected or approved. Only materials mentioned in the DMF by an IND sponsor, an NDA, ANDA, or Export Application applicant, or another DMF holder will be taken into account. A copy of the DMF holder's letter of authorization must be supplied with the incorporation by reference, as previously mentioned.

When FDA investigators find problems with a DMF's data, the DMF's owner is told in writing. Those that rely on the information in the faulty DMF will be alerted that they will require extra information from the supporting DMF. The defect's general problem is raised, but only the DMF holder has access to the flaw's specifics. When delivering the relevant data to the DMF in response to the agency's deficiency notice, the holder must include a copy of the accompanying transmittal letter for anybody who relies on the DMF, as well as the FDA reviewing division that discovered the inaccuracies. If the issues have been resolved, the transmittal letter will mention so.

VII. Holder Obligations

For example, any change in individual customer authorization should be recorded twice and cross-referenced with previous contributions (s). The reference should include the affected date(s), volume(s), section(s), and/or page number (s).

Notice Required for Changes to a Drug Master File

Every affected applicant or sponsor who has mentioned the DMF must be notified of any relevant changes in the DMF (21 CFR 314. 420(c)).

The sponsor/applicant should be notified well in advance of the change so that any affected application(s) can be supplemented or altered as needed.

Listing of Persons Authorized to Refer to a Drug Master File

Any change in individual customer authorization, for example, should be reported twice and cross-referenced with earlier contributions (s). The affected date(s), volume(s), section(s), and/or page number should all be included in the reference (s).

Any person whose authorization has been withdrawn during the previous year should be identified under a suitable caption.

The DMF holder should also provide a statement confirming the list is current if the list is unaltered on the anniversary date.

Annual Update

On the anniversary of the original filing, the holder must file an annual report. The required list (see B.1), as well as any modifications or new information added to the DMF since the prior annual report on the DMF's subject matter, should be included in this report. If the subject content of the DMF remains unchanged, the DMF holder should declare that it is current.

If previously submitted material and listings in the DMF are not updated on an annual basis, FDA inspection of an ongoing IND, NDA, ANDA, Export Application, or any amendment or addition to such application may be delayed, and FDA may initiate DMF closure proceedings (see Section IX).

Appointment of an Agent

The holder must submit a signed letter of appointment to the DMF stating the agent's name, address, and responsibilities (administrative and/or scientific). Although it is preferred for international DMF holders to work through a US agency, domestic DMF holders are not required to do so.

Transfer of Ownership

To transfer ownership of a DMF to another party, the holder should so notify FDA and authorized persons in writing. The letter should include the following:

1. Name of transferee
2. Address of transferee
3. Name of responsible official of transferee
4. Effective date of transfer

5. Signature of the transferring official
6. Typewritten name and title of the transferring official.

Where applicable, the new holder should submit a letter of acceptance of the transfer as well as an update to the information contained in the DMF. Any new ownership-related changes (e.g., plant location and techniques) should be included.

VIII. Major Reorganization of A Drug Master File

A holder who wishes to restructure a DMF should submit a detailed plan of the changes to the Drug Master File Staff for review. Prior to a big restructuring, employees should have enough opportunity to discuss and express suggestions.

IX. Closure of a Drug Master File

A holder must submit a request to the Drug Master File Staff explaining why a DMF should be closed. The address is found in section IV.D.5.a. A statement indicating that the holder's Section VII requirements have been met should be included in the request. The Agency has the authority to close a DMF if it does not include an annual update of persons authorised to integrate information in the DMF by reference, as well as a summary of changes since the previous annual report. The holder will be informed of the FDA's decision to close the DMF.

References

1. https://www.fda.gov/drugs/guidances-drugs/drug-master-files-guidelines.

CHAPTER 1.3

Distribution of Records

1.3.1 Introduction

In the integrated supply-chain management of pharmaceutical products, distribution is critical. The administration, storage, and distribution of such artefacts is usually the responsibility of a large number of people and organizations. However, in some circumstances, a person or entity is only in charge of a portion of the distribution process.

These regulations are intended to aid in the quality control and identification of pharmaceutical items along the distribution chain. Procurement, purchasing, storage, distribution, transportation, repackaging, relabeling, documentation, and record-keeping systems are among these factors. Pharmaceuticals are kept, sold, and distributed by a wide range of organisations, institutions, and people.

The methods to be followed in order to meet the duties associated with various components of the supply chain's distribution process, as well as to prevent counterfeit items from accessing the market through the distribution chain, are covered in this article.

The relevant portions should be considered by various players in relation to their individual function in pharmaceutical distribution. Mix-ups, adulteration, contamination, and cross-contamination are likely to occur in the home, just as they do in the workplace. Good manufacturing practises (GMP) should be observed during manufacturing procedures such as repackaging and relabeling when the distribution chain is disrupted.

1.3.2 Why Distribution of Records is Necessary?

The product's name and strength, as well as a description of the dosage form, the consignee's name and address, the date and quality of the shipment, and the drug's lot or control number, must all be included in the distribution records. Compressed medical gas products do not require lot or control numbers in distribution records.

The primary purpose is to guarantee that enough information is available in the case of a recall to reach trade customers. This goal will surely be met by assigning a lot number to each order. Distribution data and standards must be developed to make the recall of a defective product easier. Before a quantity of medicine may be supplied, the system requires approval and specific release from the quality control function. Under this completed products shipping law, only medications that have been examined and found to meet all applicable requirements are admitted into commerce.

All distribution transactions involving in-process or finished items must be tracked by the manufacturer. As a form of accountability, all records should be indexed by either the production batch-lot number or the packaging control number until the shipment leaves the manufacturer's direct control.

Because only one shipment record needs to be inspected, this sort of indexing allows for a speedy determination of the receiver of a recalled item. Distribution records may reflect shipments to consignees for packing or labelling, or to an independent distributor, wholesaler, retail pharmacy, physician, or possibly the ultimate client, depending on the marketing approach utilised by the firm. A variety of distribution recording technologies are available. Two of the most widely used approaches are as follows:

1. To record the **lot or control number** on the retained copies of the shipping invoices
2. To record the **dates** on which each lot commenced distribution.

   The disadvantages of this strategy include the inability to handle minor amounts of returned items and the requirement to distribute component lots out of order on occasion. Many American companies also supply their international operations with goods.

   These transactions should also be included in the distribution records. If distribution from the United States is to a central worldwide distribution centre and the US business has no records of the ultimate distribution, this can become complex. The US QA function will examine and audit the functioning of the central international distribution centre, as well as the system and control sufficiency, in these conditions.

1.3.3 Objectives

- Other factors are also taken into account throughout the distribution process. It must be set up in such a way that merchandise is moved first in, first out. This criterion is in line with the stability and expiration dating policy's aim.

- In order to achieve this movement, the distribution system must have provisions. Written procedures should be used to describe any exceptions to this rule that may be allowed.
- After the distribution process for each control number has been completed, all distribution records should be kept for at least three years.
- If a product's expiration date is used, distribution records must be kept for at least one year after the product's expiration date.
- It's possible to use the dates on which a given lot of merchandise started and stopped being distributed. Between these dates, any customers who received the product could be reached.
- Obviously, some consumers may have received product from the end of the previous lot or the beginning of the following lot on the first and last days of delivery.
- This overlap should have no negative influence on the recall's effectiveness.
- Whatever mechanism is utilised, it must allow returned goods to be reintroduced into the distribution network.
- Invoices, bills of lading, customers' receipts, internal warehouse storage, and inventory records are all examples of documentation that must be included in distribution records.
- The required information does not have to be included on every paper. Alternatives to client names, addresses, and product names include customer codes and product codes.

1.3.4 Documentation in Pharmaceutical Industry

(a) Standard Operating Procedure

A standard operating procedure (SOP) is a set of step-by-step instructions developed by a company to help employees do tough routine tasks. Workers follow this phase of instruction regularly or repeatedly.

(b) Goals of the SOP:

1. Create the culture where quality objective is transparent and well understand
2. They form the backbone of the pharmaceutical
3. To achieve efficiency
4. To achieve quality output
5. To achieve uniformity of performance
6. To achieve uniformity of quality

(c) Standard Operating Procedures (SOP) for Shimadzu UV-VIS in RH385

PPE required

1. Gloves, lab glasses, lab coat

Turning on UV-VIS

1. Flip switch on the bottom left end of UVVIS
2. Open UV Probe 2.21 program
3. On the bottom, click on connect

A. V-VIS will go through a checklist of Items.

B. Click OK after checklist is finished

Taking Spectra

1. To take a background, fill 2 Cuvettes with the same solution, place them in the reference slot (R) and sample slot (S), and click on Baseline
2. The program will ask for range of wavelength. Type in 700 to 200nm, and then click ok
3. Replace the cuvette in the sample slot with your actual sample. Be sure that the cuvette is 2/3 full.
4. Click Start
5. After the scan is done, select where to save the data
6. To view data points, click on the icon that looks like a paper with writing on it. (to the right of the icon with an M in a circle)
7. To organize data, copy and paste data onto your own excel sheet
8. To save a single scan, go to file>save as

Turning Off UV-VIS

Click Disconnect.

Flip switch on UV-VIS off.

Always turn the system off when you do not Plan to use it soon to conserve the lamp life.

(d) SOP Writing Style

SOPs must be prepared in a clear, step-by-step format that is simple to read and understand.

Information should not be difficult to understand. It's best to use the active voice and the present tense.

It should be straightforward and concise.

Simple steps style can be used to write routine procedures that are short and need few decisions.

Long procedures with few decisions and more than 10 steps should be described in a graphical fashion or in hierarchical levels.

Procedures requiring a lot of decisions should be written with a flow chart.

Every SOP must include requirements for document identification and control, accountability, and traceability responsibilities; this can be accomplished by ensuring uniform Format.

While Writing SOP:

- ✓ Write in the present tense.
- ✓ Don't write in the past.
- ✓ Conditional or future tense unless you have good reason to do so.
- ✓ Avoid ambiguity.
- ✓ Be concise.
- ✓ Keep the words short and get to point.
- ✓ Move from one step to another step in logical manner.
- ✓ Highlight exception. Use a symbol to flag that this is an exception and how to handle it.
- ✓ Highlight warning. Again warn users that caution must be used in this scenario. Warning must stand out; use a larger font or a warning icon.

Figure 1

Figure 2

- ✓ Reduce the word count where possible without altering the meaning of the text.

While Writing SOP

- ✓ Introduce acronyms without explaining what it means.
- ✓ Don't use the word "may", "if possible" as it implies that the user can do something under conditions. Instead be positive and tell them what to do.

Inside The SOP

Company name and pagination. The company name and pagination (e.g. page 4 of 7) must appear on every page.

Title

The title should be descriptive. The title should use directive language to declare what is being done to what.

Identification

A unique number and version number must be used to distinguish procedures. The SOP's unique number allows it to be monitored throughout the facility and over time as it changes.

Review and approval

All SOPs shall have space for signature of:

- Initiator (the person who has written the SOP)
- Reviewer (The persons who has reviewed the SOP) and
- Approver (Quality Assurance Head of the organization).

Purpose

The procedure's purpose or goal should restate and expand on the well-written title. Expand on or qualify the title's directive language (e.g. to describe the operation procedure of compression machine)

Scope

The scope should provide limits to the use of procedure. The scope shall be written in such a way

That it answers following questions....

1. Are there certain samples that are appropriate to test by this method?
2. Do these operations apply only to certain equipment or certain departments?
3. Is there a limit to the capacity, volume, or throughout of the procedure?
4. State to what areas this procedure does apply and does not apply?

Responsibility

Who is responsible for performing the work described? Who is responsible for implementing the procedure?

Procedure

Describe the procedure in a step by step, chronological manner. Use active verbs and direct statements

(e) General Format For SOP

1. SOP Number:
2. Title:
3. Department:
4. Date:
5. Revision number:
6. Effective date:
    1. Objective:-Why?
    2. Scope-When? Where?
    3. Responsibility:-Who?
    4. Material equipment:-What?
    5. Procedure:-How?

       It includes:

       (a) Preliminary test

       (b) Safety consideration

       (c) Chronological instruction

       (d) Calculation
    6. Reporting: -What next
    7. Abbreviation
    8. Reference document- Written by ….. Edited by….. Authorize sign...

(f) Master Batch Records

Master Batch Records are version-controlled templates for your manufacturing process, also known as Master Production Records and Master Manufacturing Records. These papers must be created and kept on file by dietary supplement manufacturing facilities, but what exactly does the FDA look for in a Master Batch Record?

In addition to a list of instructions for manufacturing each unique product and Batch size, the FDA is looking for:

- A complete list of individual equipment and processing lines
- Identification of all equipment and processing lines
- Verification of cleaning and calibration activities
- Lot numbers and other control information for components, packaging and labels
- Sampling, inspection and results of testing activities
- Control of issuance and labels
- Quality control approval
- Signatures

(g) Batch Manufacturing Record BMR:

BMR stands for Batch Manufacturing Record. Batch Manufacturing Record is abbreviated as "BMR." This is a product and batch specific document that provides a complete view of the manufacturing history of each batch of each product.

The following items are included in the Batch Manufacturing Record, which is based on the master formula record.

1. Name of product
2. Trade Name
3. Specification of raw material
4. Name of raw material
5. Specification of container, closure and packing material
6. Name of item
7. Weighment sheet
8. Dispensing Instructions
9. List of equipment and machinery
10. Dispensing instructions
11. Packaging requirements
12. Packaging instructions
13. Precautions to be taken
14. Finished product specifications
15. Expiry date
16. Review due on

	Pharmaceutical Guidelines **Delhi, India** **Batch Manufacturing Record**	Page No. 1 of 16

Product	: Atorvastatin Tablets IP 40 mg	**B.M.R. No.**	XX/XXX/000
		B.M.R Revision No./ Date	00/ddmmyyyy
Batch Size	: 2,00,000 Tablets	**Ref. M.F.R. No**	XX/XXX/000
Batch No.	: XXXXX/XX	**M.F.R. Revision No. & Date**	00/ddmmyyyy

Batch Quantity	: 35.00 kg.	**COMPOSITION:** **Each Film Coated Tablet contains:** Atorvastatin Calcium IP Equivalent to Atorvastatin ------ 40 mg Color :Titanium Dioxide IP
Reworking Added (If any)	:	
Theoretical Yield	:	
Mfg. Date:		Exp. Date:
Document issued by: Date:		Document Received by: Date:

This Document Supersedes	: None	
Reason for Change	: New	
Mfg. Licence No.	: XXXX/XX/XXXX	Material code No. - XXXXXXXX
Shelf Life	: 36 Months or expiry of active ingredient whichever is less.	
Storage Condition	: Store in cool, dry & dark place.	
Marketed by	: XYZ Pharmaceuticals Ltd.	
Serial No.	:	

	Granulation	Compression	Coating
Date of Commencement:			
Date of Completion:			
Area Used:			
Previous Product Processed:			
Batch No:			
Checked by Pharmacist: Date:			

This batch has/has not been completed according to the instructions given in M.F.R. No. XX/XXX/00. Deviation sheet attached: Y/N	
Actual Yield:__________Tablets Reworking Generated:_______Kg. Total Yield: ______%	Date of Packing: Quantity:
Final BMR Checked By: Date:	Final BMR Checked By: Date:

Prepared By	**Checked By**	**Reviewed By**	**Approved By**
Quality Assurance	**Production**	**Production Head**	**QA & QC Head**
Date:	**Date:**	**Date:**	**Date:**

Figure 3

References

1. https://beinnovatives.home.blog/2020/01/08/importance-of-documentation-in-pharmaceutical-industry/. (External link)
2. https://www.slideshare.net/NavaneethakrishnanPa4/documentation-in-pharmaceutical-industry-144312056. (External link)

3. PIC/S Pharmaceutical Inspection Convention Pharmaceutical Inspection Co-operation Scheme "Guide to Good Manufacturing Practice for Medicinal Products PE 009-9 Part-I; September 2009. Available from: http://www.picscheme.org/publication.php?id=4. [Last cited on 2010 Apr 1]
4. 10. Guidance for Industry: Manufacturing, Processing or Holding Active Pharmaceutical Ingredient, Draft Guidance; USFDA, Centre for Drug Evaluation and Research CDER March 1998 [Google Scholar]

CHAPTER 1.4

Generic Drugs Product Development

1.4.1 Generic Drug

In dosage form, potency, mode of administration, quality and performance attributes, and intended purpose, a drug product that is similar to a brand/ innovator medicine. The active components must be the same as those in the original formulation.

1.4.2 What are Generic Drugs?

They are pharmaceuticals that have the same chemical composition as branded drugs and are sold under the same chemical name. For example, the generic name for pain medicines like Crocin and Calpol is paracetamol. In the United States, only the firm with the FDA patent has the legal ability to set the price, giving them a market monopoly.

India had no patent limits prior to 2005, which meant that anyone could produce any pharmaceutical without fear of legal ramifications. As a result, branded generic medications have grown in popularity and now account for 99.5 percent of the generic drug industry in the United States.

1.4.3 When Generic Drug Marketed?

I. A patent and exclusivity after protection ends

II. Patent owner waives its rights

III. FDA requirements are met

Table 1

Brand name drug NDA requirements	Generic drug ANDA Requirements
1. Labeling	1. Labeling
2. Chemistry	2. Chemistry
3. Manufacturing	3. Manufacturing
4. Controls	4. Controls

Table 1 *Contd...*

Brand name drug NDA requirements	Generic drug ANDA Requirements
5. Microbiology	5. Microbiology
6. Testing	6. Testing
7. Animal studies	7. Bioequivalence
8. Clinical studies	
9. Bioavailability	

1.4.4 Where are they Available?

Generic drugs are widely available, including at our local pharmacy. Simply request a generic version of a branded drug; however, generic versions may not be accessible for all prescriptions.

The government's pharmaceuticals department is in charge of generic medicine promotion, but they haven't done a particularly good job.

When a patent drug's patent or marketing rights expire, generic drugs are released.

They are comparable to brand-name medications in terms of dose form, potency, mode of administration, quality and performance qualities, and intended use.

Generic drugs are available at a low cost while maintaining great quality.

Interest as critical disease like cancer, AIDS etc.

1.4.5 Product Development

Product: A product is something sold by an enterprise to its customers.

Product Development: Product development is a series of operations that starts with the identification of a market opportunity and ends with the manufacture, sale, and delivery of a product.

(a) The Product Development Process

- *A process is a sequence of steps that transforms a set of inputs into a set of outputs*
- *A product development process is the sequence of steps or activities that an enterprise employs to conceive, design, and commercialize a product.*
- *Some organizations define and follow a precise and detailed product development process. While others may not even be able to describe their processes.*

(b) A Generic Product Development Process

We'll look at developing a generic product that can be employed in a market pull situation.

A mission statement is the process's input, and the process's output is the product launch.

- **Mission Statement**: identifies the target market for the product, provides a basic functional description of the product, and specifies the business goals of the effort; results from well executed product planning phase
- **Product Launch:** Occurs when the product becomes available for purchase in the market place.

(c) A Generic Product Development Process

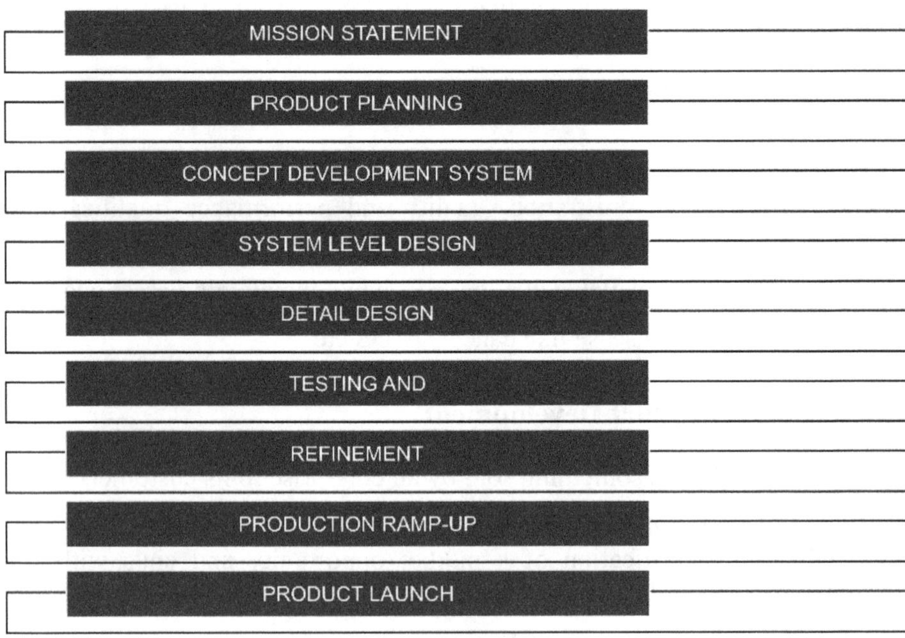

Figure 1

(d) Concept Development

The needs of the target market are identified, alternative product concepts are generated and evaluated, and only one development is selected for further development.

A concept is a description of a product's form, functions, and qualities, usually accompanied by a set of specifications, a competitive product analysis, and a project business case.

(e) System – Level Design

The product architecture is defined, as well as the split of the product into subsystems and components.

During this step, the final assembly scheme for the production system is usually defined.

This phase normally produces a geometric layout of the product, a functional specification of each of the product's subsystems, and a preliminary process flow diagram for the final assembly process.

(f) Detail Design

Any of the unique parts in the product's shape, materials, and tolerances are fully specified, as well as the identification of all standard parts to be obtained from vendors.

For each part to be fabricated inside the manufacturing system, a process plan is prepared and tooling is designed.

This phase's output is the product's control documentation.

(g) Testing and Refinement

It entails the creation and testing of several prototype product variants.

Production intent parts [parts having the same geometry and material qualities as planned for the production version of the product will work as designed and whether or not the product satisfies the primary customer needs] are frequently used in early prototypes. • Later prototypes are usually made with pieces from the intended production process, but they may not be completed using the intended final assembly technique.

Later prototypes go through extensive internal testing as well as client testing in their own settings.

The goal of beta prototypes is usually to solve performance and reliability issues so that the final product can be adjusted appropriately.

(h) Production RAMP - UP

The term "ramp up" is used in economics and business to describe a rise in firm production ahead of predicted increases in product demand. Ramp up, on the other hand, is the period of time between the completion of initial product development and reaching full capacity utilisation, which is marked by product and process testing and upgrades.

In the first sense, a company's ramp up begins when it strikes a deal with a distributor, retailer, or producer that will dramatically increase product demand.

(i) Abbreviated New Drug Application (ANDA)

An abbreviated new drug application (ANDA) is a document that must be filed to the Food and Drug Administration (FDA) in order for a generic drug product to be assessed and authorised. Once approved, a generic drug product can be manufactured and marketed as a safe, effective, and less priced alternative to the brand-name drug it replaces. In terms of dose form, strength, method of administration, quality, performance qualities, and intended application, a generic drug product is comparable to an innovator drug product.

The FDA's Authorized Drug Medicines with Therapeutic Equivalence Evaluations list all approved pharmaceuticals, including innovator and generics (Orange Book). Because preclinical (animal) and clinical (human) evidence are not required to demonstrate safety and effectiveness, generic medication applications are referred to as "abbreviated." Instead, generic applicants must show that their medication works in the same way as the original drug through scientific research. Measurement of the time it takes for a generic drug to reach the bloodstream in healthy volunteers is one method by which applicants prove that a generic product functions in the same way as the innovator drug.

This "bioequivalence" demonstration offers the generic medication's rate of absorption, or bioavailability, which may then be compared to the innovator drug. The generic version must deliver the same amount of active chemicals into a patient's bloodstream in the same amount of time as the innovator medicine in order to be approved by the FDA.

The Hatch-Waxman Amendments, sometimes known as the Hatch-Waxman Act, established bioequivalence as the cornerstone for authorising generic copies of drug commodities "In 1984, Congress passed the Drug Price Competition and Patent Term Restoration Act.

"Without expensive and time-consuming clinical trials to verify safety and efficacy, the FDA can now approve generic versions of brand-name pharmaceuticals. The Hatch-Waxman Amendments provided patent term extensions to brand-name firms to account for the time a patented product is under FDA assessment as well as certain periods of commercial exclusivity. Before selling their products, generic medication businesses now have the ability to challenge patents in court, as well as 180 days of generic drug exclusivity.

(j) Resources for ANDA Submissions

The links below give information on the statutory and regulatory requirements of an ANDA application, as well as CDER assistance in meeting those requirements and internal ANDA review principles, policies, and procedures. ANDA Submission Forms Summary tables, application forms, and other submission documents are included in the requirements.

(k) Guidance Documents for ANDAs

Guidance documents provide the Agency's current position on a topic. These publications provide instructions for the content, evaluation, and ultimate approval of applications, as well as the design, development, manufacturing, and testing of regulated products, to FDA review staff, applicants, and ANDA holders.

- Generic Drugs Guidances (Search "Generics" under topics)
- Biopharmaceutics Guidances (Search "Biopharmaceutics" under topics)
- Product-Specific Guidances for Generic Drug Development

(l) Laws, Regulations, Policies, and Procedures

The Federal Food, Drug, and Cosmetic Act is the United States' core food and drug law. The law is intended to provide consumers with assurances that foods are pure and wholesome, safe to eat, and produced in sanitary conditions; that drugs and devices are safe and effective for their intended uses; that cosmetics are safe and made from appropriate ingredients; and that all labelling and packaging is truthful, informative, and not misleading.

(m) Code of Federal Regulations

Final regulations published in the Federal Register (a daily published record of proposed rules, final rules, meeting notices, and other items) are collected in the Code of Federal Regulations (CFR). Section 21 of the CFR contains the majority of the food and drug regulations. The regulations lay out the majority of the steps that all drug applicants must do under federal law. The following rules are directly applicable to the ANDA method:

- 21CFR Part 314: Applications for FDA Approval to Market a New Drug
- 21CFR Part 320: Bioavailability and Bioequivalence Requirements

Manual of Policies and Procedures

CDER's Manual of Policies and Procedures (MAPPs) document internal practices and procedures followed by CDER staff to help standardize the drug review process and other activities, both internal and external. Chapter 5200 covers generic drugs processes and activities.

ANDA Review Process

Generic Drug (ANDA) Review Process

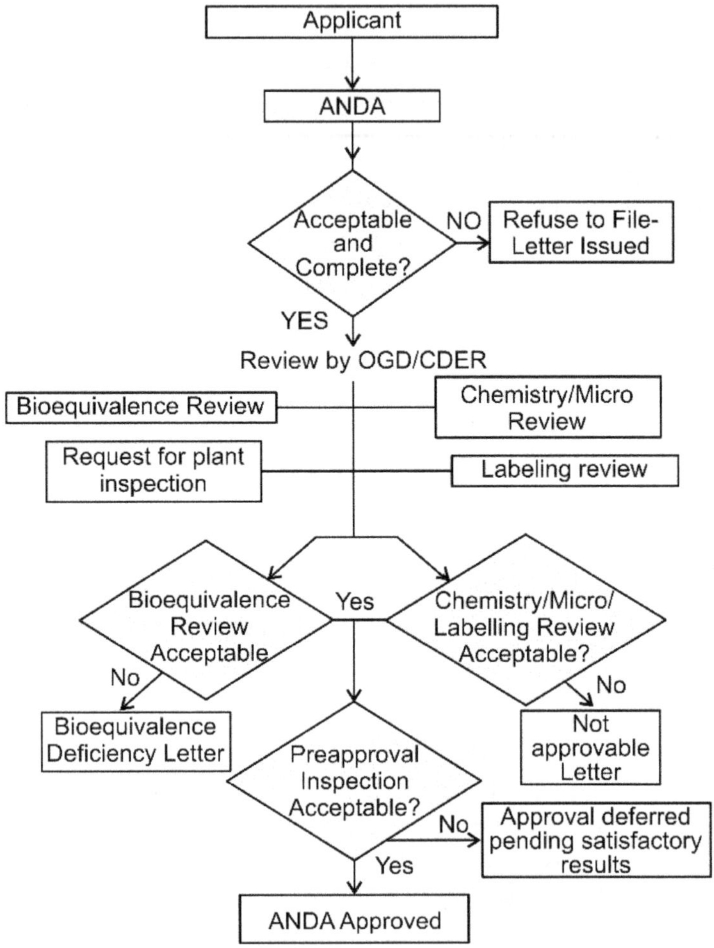

Figure 2

References (external links)

1. https://pharmachitchat.files.wordpress.com/2015/05/generic-drug-product-development-solid-oral-dosage-forms.pdf
2. https://www.slideshare.net/SachinG19/generic-drugs-product-development-176738668.

CHAPTER 1.5

Hatch-Waxman Act

The "Hatch-Waxman Act," also known as **"THE DRUG PRICE COMPETITION AND PATENT TERM RESTORATION ACT,"** was enacted in 1984, and it changed patent restrictions in place before to 1962, allowing new pharmaceuticals to be approved solely based on their safety. In 1962, proof of efficacy became a condition for a novel drug's marketing authorization. There was no way to compensate for the time lost during the marketing approval procedure prior to the Hatch-Waxman Act by extending the patent term. Generic enterprises had to submit their own comprehensive NDA, which was both costly and time-consuming. To overcome the aforementioned issues, legislation backing generic businesses was required.

1.5.1 Objectives of the Act

- Reducing the cost associated with the approval of a generic drug.
- Allowing early-experimental use.
- Compensating the branded drugs manufacturers for the time lost from the patent term because of the regulatory approval formality.
- Motivating the generic drug manufacturers.

1.5.2 Drug Approval

Every new drug, including generics, must be safe and effective, according to the FDA. Before the Hatch-Waxman Act, the FDA required both branded and generic drug businesses to submit a New Drug Application to show the safety and efficacy of their goods (NDA). Some features of the new drug application procedure and the period of new pharmaceutical patents were altered by the Hatch-Waxman Act. The Hatch-Waxman Act also made FDA approval simpler for generic medication businesses. As a result, generic pharmaceutical businesses may be able to establish their goods' safety and utility more swiftly.

New Branded Drug Approval

An NDA is required for a branded pharma firm seeking FDA clearance to launch a new medicine. The FDA can assess whether the new medicine is both safe and effective based on the facts supplied in the NDA.

Other regulatory criteria, such as those relating to labelling and excellent manufacturing practices, are met.

Obtaining and submitting this information on a regular basis is a time-consuming process that necessitates the branded drug manufacturer doing numerous lengthy and costly clinical trials.

Generic Drug Approval

The FDA reviews generic drug applications for compliance with the appropriate scientific and regulatory criteria. If an application meets those criteria, the FDA may grant either:

(a) Tentative approval

(b) Final approval

Under the Hatch-Waxman Act, generic drug companies can typically file one of two different kinds of abbreviated applications for approval of a generic drug:

(a) An Abbreviated New Drug Application (ANDA)

(b) A Section 505(b)(2) application, which is often called a paper NDA

(a) Abbreviated New Drug Applications (ANDA)

An ANDA requires a generic medicine firm to prove that the generic drug is essentially a copy of the branded, NDA drug, also known as the Reference Listed Drug (RLD). The generic drug manufacturer must specifically demonstrate that the proposed generic drug: a) Has the same active component, method of administration, dosage form, potency, and intended use as the RLD. b) If it is bioequivalent to the RLD, meaning it performs in the body in the same way.

(b) Section 505(b)(2) Applications

A proposed generic medicine could be significantly different from the RLD.

The proposed generic medication must be approved through the Section 505(b) (2) paper NDA application process, which is a hybrid of a full NDA and an ANDA. This application has fewer information than an NDA but more information than an ANDA.

1.5.3 New Drug Exclusivity

(a) Non-patent Exclusivities

1. **Orphan drug exclusivity,**

   which is granted to drugs:

   a) That treat a disease or condition that affects less than 200,000 people in the US; or

   b) For which it is unlikely that US sales of the drug will recoup its development costs. This exclusivity period is seven years, but only applies to use in treating the specific rare disease or condition.

2. **New chemical entity (NCE) exclusivity**

   The RLD and a suggested generic medication could differ significantly.

   In these cases, the proposed generic medication must be approved through the Section 505(b) (2) paper NDA application process, which is a cross between a full NDA and an ANDA. This application contains less information than an NDA, but more information than an ANDA.

3. **New clinical study exclusivity**

   When new clinical trials result in new or altered formulations, dosing regimes, or patient populations, this applies.

   If an application or supplement contains reports of additional clinical trials conducted or supported by the applicant that were necessary for approval, the applicant is entitled to exclusivity.

   For three years following the first NDA Approval, this exclusivity, also known as data exclusivity, prevents the FDA from approving a generic drug application for the new dosage form or use.

   It does not, however, prevent generic medicine applications from being approved.

4. **Pediatric exclusivity**

   This is true if the FDA has requested that the NDA holder do paediatric research using the medicine.

   Pediatric exclusivity extends any marketing or patent exclusivity by six months.

Non-Patent exclusivity [table 1]

Types	Term
New chemical entity Exclusivity	5 years
New clinical study Exclusivity	3 years
Orphan drug exclusivity	7 years
Pediatric exclusivity	6 months
180 day generic market Exclusivity	180 days

(b) Patent exclusivity & the orange book

Any patent that claims either:

a. The drug, including the active ingredient and the formulation for the active ingredient, must be reported to the FDA with the patent number and expiration date.

b. A technique of using the drug, but not additional inventions such as metabolites, synthetic intermediates, or manufacturing methods.

The patent information is published in the FDA's Approved Drug Products with Therapeutic Equivalence Determinations publication once the FDA approves the NDA (also called the Orange book).

(c) Challenging Patent Exclusivity

A generic medicine business must make one of the four certifications for each patent included in the Orange Book for an RLD when filing an ANDA or a Section 505(b) (2) application:

a. Certification in paragraph I that no relevant patents are listed in the Orange Book.

b. Certification under paragraph II that the indicated patent has expired.

c. Certification in paragraph III that the stated patent, as well as any other exclusivities, will expire before the requested permission.

d. Certification under paragraph IV that the stated patent is invalid or will not be violated by the generic drug's commercialization.

(d) Paragraph IV Certification

Because submitting an application with a paragraph IV certification is a statutory act of patent infringement, Hatch-Waxman Act patent action may be pursued.

a) The existence of the ANDA. b) A detailed summary of its rationale for concluding that the listed patents are invalid or not infringed.

(e) Section VIII Statements

A Section viii Statement, on the other hand, usually does not result in patent litigation.

Typically, the generic medicine applicant tries to chisel away anything relating to the patented technique in the RLD's label from its label.

As a result, there is no need for certification or notification. By cutting out the information that relates to the clinical studies and applicable approval, generic medication makers may be able to bypass the three-year fresh clinical study exclusivity.

For all remaining, non-protected conditions of Use, the FDA will approve these so-called skinny labels if they do not render the proposed medicine less safe or effective than the listed drug.

1.5.4 ANDA Exclusivity

If an ANDA with a paragraph IV certification for an RLD is filed first, the FDA may grant a 180-day period during which no ANDAs for a generic version of the RLD with a paragraph IV certification will be approved. The first filer may waive this exclusivity.

For 180 days, first-filer exclusivity prevents final approval of subsequent ANDAs with Paragraph IV certifications. Because it is not a paragraph IV certification, first-filer exclusivity does not apply to an applicant who has submitted a Section viii Statement.

1.5.5 Patent Term Extension

The Hatch-Waxman Act extends the length of patents for certain products and procedures, including human drug products that must be approved by the FDA. Only one extension can be granted per product, and it must be for a patent that claims one of the following:

a) Drug product, which means the active ingredient and any approved drug using that active ingredient.
b) Method of using a drug product.
c) Method of manufacturing a drug product

1.5.6 Patent Litigation Under the Hatch-Waxman Act

Various time periods relating to components of the litigation that may have an impact on the FDA's approval procedure

Drug firms may establish certain defences and counterclaims.

The parties usually seek specific remedies.

Settlement agreements present unique issues.

The generic medicine applicant has 45 days from the date of the Notice Letter to commence a declaratory judgement action against the NDA holder (45- day period).

The FDA may not award final clearance of the generic application for 30 months after the NDA holder and patentee receive the Notice Letter if the patentee sues during the 45-day time frame (30-month stay).

If either party fails to cooperate fairly in expediting the case, the court may shorten or increase the 30-month stay term in a pending patent dispute. If a court gives a final order finding the patent invalid, unenforceable, or not infringed, the 30-month stay ends.

1.5.7 Benefits for Branded Manufacturers

- Orange book provides public notice of patents.
- Allows for resolution of patent disputes prior to generic entry.
- 30-months stay of FDA approval of generic drugs
- Patent term restoration
- Allows for several market exclusivities:
  - (a) Data exclusivity
    1. 5 years for new chemical entity exclusivity
    2. 3 years for new clinical study exclusivity
  - (b) Orphan drug (7 years)
  - (c) Pediatric (PEDS) (6 months)

1.5.8 Conclusion

The Hatch-Waxman Act establishes a fast-track procedure for generic entry and market exclusivity at the USFDA.

The Hatch-Waxman Act allows for a maximum 5-year patent term extension for branded medicine manufacturers to compensate for time lost during the USFDA's NDA clearance process.

References

1. https://www.slideshare.net/AlexaJacob1/hatch-waxman-act-amp amendments-ppt.
2. https://www.fda.gov/drugs/abbreviated-new-drug-application-anda/hatch-waxman-letters.

CHAPTER 1.6

Code of Federal Regulations (CFR)

1.6.1 What is CFR?

- The Code of Federal Regulations (CFR) is the codification of the general and permanent rules and regulations (sometimes called administrative law) published in the Federal Register by the
- Executive departments and agencies of the federal government of the United States.
- The CFR is divided into 50 titles that represent broad areas subject to federal regulation.***www.ngsmips.nitte.edu.in***
- Each title is further divided into chapters, subchapters, parts, and sections.
- A regulation is cited by title, part, and section, e.g. 14 CFR 121.313 (Title 14, Part 121, Section 313).
- The soft-cover volumes of the CFR are issued each year:
- Titles 1 – 16 are updated as of January 1
- Titles 17 – 27 are updated as of April 1
- Titles 29 – 41 are updated as of July 1
- Titles 42 – 50 are updated as of October 1
- The online CFR is a joint project authorized by the publisher, the National Archives and Records Administration's (NARA) Office of the Federal Register (OFR), and the Government
- SPublishing Office (GPO) to provide the public with enhanced access to Government information.

1.6.2 History of CFR

- 1935 - Instrumental in passing the *Federal Register Act* – empowered the National Archives of the US to form an Administrative Committee – publish the *Federal Register*.
- The *Federal Register* Act - amended in 1937 to provide a "codification" of all regulations every five years – known as Code of Federal Regulations. The first edition of the CFR was published in 1938 and included all finalized regulations that were published in the *Federal Register* from March 14, 1936 to June 1, 1938
- Beginning in 1963 for some titles and for all titles in 1967, the Office of the Federal Register began publishing yearly revisions.
- Beginning in 1972 - published revisions were conducted in staggered quarters.

1.6.3 CFR Title 21

Title 21 of the CFR is reserved for rules of the Food and Drug Administration.

- Governs food and drugs within the United States for the FDA, DEA, and the ONDCP.
- In all, 21 CFR consists of 1499 parts.
- It is divided into three chapters:
- Chapter I — Food and Drug Administration
- Chapter II — Drug Enforcement Administration
- Chapter III — Office of National Drug Control Policy

1.6.4 Chapter I

Most of the Chapter I regulations are based on the Federal Food, Drug, and Cosmetic Act.

Notable sections:

- 11 Electronic records and electronic signature related.
- 50 Protection of human subjects in clinical trials.
- 54 Financial Disclosure by Clinical Investigators.
- 56 Institutional Review Boards that oversee clinical trials.
- 58 Good Laboratory Practices (GLP) for nonclinical studies.

- The 100 series are regulations pertaining to food.
- The 200 and 300 series are regulations pertaining to pharmaceuticals

- The 500 series are regulations for animal feeds and animal medications.
- The 600 series covers biological products.
- The 700 series includes the limited regulations on cosmetics.
- The 800 series are for medical devices.
- The 900 series covers mammography quality requirements enforced by CDRH.
- The 1000 series covers radiation-emitting device
- The 1100 series includes updated rules with regards to tobacco products.
- The 1200 series consists of rules primarily based in laws other than the Food, Drug, and Cosmetic Act:
  - Requirements for pasteurization of milk.
  - Sanitation on interstate conveyances.

1.6.5 Chapter II

Notable sections:

- 1308 — Schedules of controlled substances
- 1308.03 (a) — Administrative Controlled Substances Code Number
- 1308.11 — List of Schedule I drugs
- 1308.12 — List of Schedule II drugs
- 1308.13 — List of Schedule III drugs
- 1308.14 — List of Schedule IV drugs
- 1308.15 — List of Schedule V drugs

The Controlled Substances Act includes a list of SCHEDULED DRUGS, which falls within the US government's drug policy. For medications to be placed in the aforementioned schedules, the following findings must be made:

The drug or other substance has a high potential for misuse. – There is no currently recognised medical use for the drug or other substance in treatment in the United States. – There is a lack of accepted safety for using the drug or other substance under medical supervision.

Number of Administrative Controlled Substances (ACSCN)

1.6.6 CFR in Modern Times

CFR is available in a variety of electronic formats.

For example, FDsys.gov and now Gov Info, the official online document repository for the United States Government Publishing Office, are fully searchable and citation accessible.

GPO also offers an up-to-date "Electronic Code of Federal Regulations (e-CFR)" service, which displays CFR sections in their current form, including any recent Federal Register revisions. The e-CFR service is updated every day and allows you to access appendices and supplements independently.

1.6.7 Research Tools in CFR

(a) Table of Contents

- CFR titles are broken down by chapter, subchapter, and part.
- Immediately preceding each part is a table of contents for the individual regulations contained within that part.

(b) Table of CFR Titles and Chapters

- Re-designation tables to help trace new location of parts and sections of A regulation

(c) List of CFR Sections Affected in the Volume

List of CFR Sect ions Affected in Each Volume indicates the Type of Change that was made.

1.6.8 Conclusion

The former structure of two sets of regulations and legislation was superseded by the Federal Register and the Code of Federal Regulations.

The Federal Register and the CFR appear to have accomplished its initial goal of providing the public with a comprehensive publication vehicle for all regulations issued by Federal agencies and the President, notwithstanding their flaws.

The CFR provides a codified version of the rules based on title, chapters, and subjects, making it easier for the pharmaceutical industry and the general public to discover the required regulations and laws.

References

1. *"About Code of Federal Regulations". Government Publishing Office.*
2. *"A Research Guide to the Federal Register and the Code of Federal Regulations". Law Librarians' Society of Washington, D.C. July 21, 2012.*
3. *"Report to Congress on the Costs and Benefits of Federal Regulations". Office of Management and Budget. September 30, 1997.*
4. https://www.slideshare.net/SwapnilFernandes1/code-of-federal-regulations.

CHAPTER 1.7

Drug Product Performance, *In vitro*

1.7.1 Introduction

This chapter discusses the challenges of characterizing solid oral dosage forms *in vitro*. *In vitro* characterization is discussed in relation to the components that influence *in vitro* drug release, such as those inherent to the drug substance, the drug product and manufacturing process, and the dissolution test procedures that can be applied. Practical challenges that may arise during *in vitro* dissolution testing are explored, as well as *in vitro* drug product performance testing.

1.7.2 Importance of *In vitro* Drug Product Characterization

The performance characteristics of modern solid oral dosage forms must be consistent and of excellent quality. This is accomplished by careful component selection and quality control, as well as a well-defined manufacturing process that takes into account a variety of variables that can affect product appearance, potency, stability, and solubility. Making and monitoring these dosage forms using cutting-edge research methods, techniques, and technologies has grown crucial as materials, instruments, equipment, and processes have become more intricate in modern pharmaceutics. Solid oral dosage form *in vitro* characterization is significant because it offers information on the active ingredient's potency and homogeneity, as well as the rate at which the active component is released from the dosage form.

This characterization is crucial for formulation creation, comparability assessment, and quality assurance and control. To analyze the potency and release rate of active components in solid oral dosage forms *in vitro*, the United States Pharmacopoeia=National Formulary (USP=NF)(1) and different guideline papers from the Food and Drug Administration=Center for Drug Evaluation and Research (FDA=CDER) (24) are employed.

Assay or potency of the active ingredient(s) and content uniformity= weight fluctuation of dosage units are two examples of tests and standards for content and consistency of the dosage form. Dissolution and disintegration assays were used to detect the *in vitro* release of active ingredient(s) from the dosage form.

(1) Drug absorption after oral administration of a solid oral dosage form includes disintegration, dissolution, and solubilization, as well as (2,3,4) permeability across the gastrointestinal tract's membranes.

In vitro dissolution is widely utilized to predict *invivo* medicinal product performance due to the relevance of the first of these processes.

This is especially true for medications with low solubility and modified-release dosage forms, where dissolution=drug release is frequently the rate-limiting stage in *in vivo* drug absorption.

(a) Types of Solid Oral Dosage forms

The most prevalent solid oral dosage forms are tablets and capsules, which account for the majority of market share. Regular (oral), effervescent, chewable, orally disintegrating tablets are among the many types of tablets available. Soft or hard gelatin can be used to make capsules. Some of the less common solid oral dose forms include powders, granules, chewing gum, troches, and wafers. Solid oral dose forms' release qualities can also be characterised. The two types are immediate release and modified release.

In immediate-release pharmaceutical formulations, the active ingredient(s) are engineered to release fast after administration. Modified-release drug formulations include delayed-release (enteric-coated) and extended-release dosage forms (also referred to as controlled-release, sustained-release, etc.). The active component in delayed-release (DR) preparations is not released until the dose form has gone through the stomach.

This is done to protect the gastric mucosa from medicine irritation, to limit the exposure of acid-labile pharmaceuticals to stomach acid, and to guide the active ingredient's release to the lower intestine tract to improve *in vivo* absorption.

On delayed-release dosage forms, an enteric polymeric coating with unique pH-dependent solubility (or stability) is commonly used to limit active component release in the stomach at low acidic pH. As the delayed-release medication leaves the stomach, the enteric coating dissolves (or is removed), and subsequent *in vivo* drug release follows the same pattern as an immediate-release product. Extended-release (ER) drugs have an active ingredient that is available for a longer period of time. These extended-release medications, which comprise sustained-release, controlled-release, and repeat-action kinds, are believed to extend the dosage interval and reduce the dose frequency when compared to equivalent immediate-release drugs (5,6). This is done to promote patient compliance, increase therapeutic effectiveness, and/or reduce toxicity or adverse effects, particularly in therapies that need a rapidly released dose or with unwanted drug level variations.

1.7.3 Factors Affecting *In vitro* Drug Product Dissolution

A medicinal medicine must be dissolved in multiple processes. Wetting and entering the dissolving media into the dosage unit is the first of these operations. The drug material is broken and disaggregated into granules or microscopic particles in the second stage, which is essential for dissolution but not required in many traditional dosage forms. In the third step, the medication component is dissolved in a solution. These phases do not have to be completed in any certain order and can happen at any point during the dissolving process. As stated below, a number of criteria influence *in vitro* drug product dissolving, including those inherent to the drug substance, drug product formulation, manufacturing process, and dissolve testing methodology.

(a) Factors Related to Drug Substance

Dissolution is the process of solubilizing the drug into the dissolution medium. Dissolution as a fundamental process, which can be described as the diffusion of the medication into bulk liquid media, is controlled by the affinity between the solid and the dissolution medium(7). In 1897, Noyes and Whitney(8) developed a fundamental equation for solution: dm=dt14KCs—Ct1

Here, dm=dt denotes the mass rate of dissolution, Ki denotes the dissolution constant, Cs denotes the concentration at saturation or maximum solubility, and Ct denotes the concentration at time t. The concentration gradient between the diffusion layer and the bulk solution is represented by the term CsCt in the preceding equation. Brunner and Tolloczko(9) amended the preceding equation in 1900 by including the surface area, S.

dm=dt¼K0×S×ðCs—CtÞ ð2Þ

K 0 is a constant that is specific to the chemical substance and varies greatly from one medicine to the next.

Brunner expanded the scope of the above equation to include Nernst's (1904) theory(10) of a saturated and stagnant liquid lm diffusion layer of thickness around the drug particle with a diffusion coefficient.

V dC=dt1 412DS=Vh] Dinabulk dissolution volume V dC=dt1 412DS=Vh] × ðCs—CtÞ ð3Þ

Solubility, diffusivity, surface area, and solution hydrodynamics all influence drug dissolution, according to these theoretical concepts.

(a) Solubility of the Drug Substance

A medicinal drug's solubility is proportional to its dissolving rate. Compounds with high solubility have much higher dissolving rates, as seen in Eq. 1. (3). The solubility of compounds having "Ionizable groups" is determined by the pKa of the chemical and the pH of the dissolution media.

The equilibrium solubility method, which involves suspending an excess amount of solid medicine in a predetermined aqueous media, is the most common method for assessing a drug's solubility.

Estimating the equilibrium solubility of a molecule may be impossible in some cases, such as when a meta stable polymorph undergoes conversion during the solubility test. In this scenario, a dynamic approach could be used to determine the molecule's solubility. Kinetic solubility is calculated using the intrinsic dissolving rate. (11). The medicine's "dose=solubility" ratio calculates the volume of fluids needed to dissolve a single dose.

When this volume exceeds 1 litre, *invivo* dissolution becomes troublesome (12).

Griseofulvin aqueous solubility 15 mg/ml. dose of griseofulvin is 500 mg

For example, grise of ulvinhasan aqueous solubility of 15mg = m

The dose of Landata is 500mg, with a dose=solubility ratio of 33.3L.

As a result, dissolution=solubility limited oral absorption is demonstrated.

(b) Polymorphism

The drug substance may also exist in different physical forms and exhibit solid-state polymorphism. Polymorphism refers to a drug substance:

1. Existing in two or more crystalline phases that have different arrangements and conformations of the molecules in the crystal lattice,
2. Having differing hydrate (or other solvate) forms, and
3. Having amorphous phases which do not possess a distinguishable crystal lattice [13, 14].

Changes in the lattice energy of these polymorphs create differences in solubility and, as a result, dissolving speeds (15). Except for hydrates, which have a lower solubility than the anhydrous form, the changes in solubility across different crystal-line polymorphs are usually minor. The solubility of amorphous forms is hundreds of times that of crystalline forms (16). The importance of these events is demonstrated by polymorphism in chloramphenicol palmitate. Form A and Form B are two polymorphic variants of chloramphenicol palmitate. Because of its increased solubility, Form B has been demonstrated to have better oral absorption than Form A. (17).

(c) Salt Factor and 'pH' of the Diffusion Layer

Organic salts are more water-soluble than their unionized counterparts, allowing for quicker dissolution. This is why weak acid salts like sodium and potassium, as well as hydrochloride and other strong acid salts of weak bases, are widely used in pharmaceutical research. In the literature, a multi-tier technique for selecting salts for maximum product performance has been recorded (18).

Furthermore, even though the parent drug and the salt in the dissolving environment have the same equilibrium solubility, the dissolve rate of the weak acid or basic salt is commonly increased. Differences in the pH of the thin diffusion layer surrounding the drug particle can explain this phenomenon (19). The acid's salt diffusion layer will have a higher pH than the acid's diffusion layer.

Similarly, the diffusion layer pH for free base salts will be lower than free base. As a result, the effective solubilities of these salts in the diffusion layer will be higher than those of their parent unionised compounds, resulting in faster dissolution. In other situations, the salt may be used for a different therapeutic purpose.

To treat rheumatoid or osteoarthritis, the non-steroidal anti-inflammatory medication naproxen (20) was first made available as a free acid. The sodium salt, which is absorbed faster than the acid, was found to be more effective than the parent molecule in relieving post-partum discomfort.

(d) Surface Area and Particle Size

As Eq. (3) shows, a compound's dissolution rate is also proportional to its exposed surface area. As a result, drug particle size reduction, which results in more surface area exposed to the dissolution medium, should speed up dissolution. As a result, when compared to non-micronized formulations, micronized formulations of poorly soluble pharmaceuticals may have significantly higher dissolving rates (19). This can be seen in marketed glyburide tablet compositions. Glynase®tablets dissolve considerably faster than non-micronized Micronase ® tablets.

(e) Formulation Factors

Excipients (inactive ingredients) in the formulation may impact the medicinal product's solubility. Excipients are commonly utilized in immediate-release dose forms to increase dissolving rates. Disintegrants such as croscarmellose sodium and sodium starch glycolate are used to aid in the disaggregation of tablet dosage forms into granules or small particles (21).

The dis-integrant helps break down tablets by promoting disaggregation and increasing the surface area of the medication particles. Surfactants like sodium laurel sulphate and polysorbate can help in dissolution. Surfactants do so by improving the solubility of hydrophobic pharmaceuticals in water by creating micelles, or by promoting drug wetting by reducing the surface tension of the hydrophobic drug particle with the dissolution media, leading in a greater drug-solvent surface contact for dissolution (22,23).

Hydrophilic binders and fillers are used in the formulation to promote wetting of hydrophobic medicine particles, which improves dissolving rates (22). Excipients, on the other hand, can make it take longer for a drug to break down. During formulation development, for example, attention must be taken to ensure that the drug does not bind to an excipient, resulting in the creation of insoluble metal chelate that could change the medication's dissolving profile. Lubricants like sterate are routinely used in dies to reduce friction. Medication wetability may be impeded at high doses (>1%) due to the hydrophobic nature of wall cavities. (22-24).

Lower dissolving rates are caused by longer breakdown times or a less effective contact area between medication particles and the solvent media. When aldehydes or keto groups are present, gelatin capsule shells are prone to cross-linking. This could result in the formation of pellicle and a substantially slower rate of disintegration. This type of incident has been connected to gelatin capsule and gelatin-coated tablet failures packaged with rayon fillers (25).

Excipients for modified-release medicine products are chosen to have a regulated effect on the rate of drug release from the dosage form, allowing for targeted distribution to gastrointestinal "absorption windows." This can be accomplished by coating pharmaceutical particles or dose units with a polymeric or wax film, or by spreading or integrating the active ingredient inside a hydrophilic or hydrophobic matrix, ion-exchange resin, or osmotic pump.

The properties of the active ingredient, the type of release mechanism to be used, the characteristics of the modifying release excipients to be used, and the intended drug release profile are used to construct these modified-release dosage forms. (26).

(f) Manufacturing Process Factors

The dissolving qualities of a pharmaceutical drug can be influenced by a variety of production variables. Manufacturing processes could help speed up the dissolving process.

Spray drying or melt extrusion of the active component with excipients like Polyvinyl Pyrrolidine (PVP) can be utilized to produce stable amorphous dispersions with much higher dissolving rates (19,27). Wet granulation vs. dry granulation procedures are occasionally used during product production to optimize wetting of hydrophobic medicinal surfaces and increase dissolving rates (28).

Due to the tendency of directly compressed tablets to de-aggregate into finer drug particles, direct compression may be preferred to granulation for increasing solubility (29). Manufacturing variables, on the other hand, may have a retarding effect when dissolved. Excessive mixing with lubricants, for example, might reduce the wettability of medications, leading to increased disintegration and dissolution (19).

To achieve ideal disintegration rates, tablet punch pressures must also be optimized (30). Liquid entry into the tablet will be simple with low punch pressure, but tablet de-aggregation may not occur due to the tablet's large porosity; on the other hand, excessive punch pressure may prevent liquid penetration into the tablet, resulting in slower disintegration rates.

To ensure constant drug release from batch to batch, the production technique for modified-release goods must be meticulously constructed and highly durable.

The procedure of distributing the drug into the matrix or covering it with modified-release excipients must be carefully managed in this case. Unless the manufacturing process has precisely defined "endpoints" and modified-release excipients are positioned consistently around the active component, dissolving efficacy will vary. (31). Dissolution=Drug Release Test Conditions

How quickly a solid oral dosage form dissolves depends on the dissolving device type and rotational speed (32), as well as the dissolution media Hand volume (22). The dissolution test conditions are discussed in greater detail in Sections 5.2 and 5.3. The right dissolution test method and apparatus are required for accurate data on the dissolution process.

(b) *Invitro* Drug Product Performance Evaluation

(a) Disintegration Test

The USP General Chapter 701 Disintegration describes the disintegration test. When a relationship to dissolution has been established, or when disintegration has been shown to be more discriminating than dissolution, disintegration testing is regarded appropriate.

It's a qualitative test that doesn't have anything to do with drug absorption. The USP baske track assembly, an approved disintegration device generally designated for immediate-release items, is used in the test. In its Q6A Guidance document, the International Conference on Harmonization (ICH) recommended a decisiontree for the implementation of the disintegration test (33). Disintegration testing may be useful when product dissolution is quick (defined by the ICH as dissolution NLT 80 percent in 15 minutes at pH 1.2, 4.0, and 6.8) and the dosage form comprises medicines that are highly soluble throughout the physiological range.

According to the ICH Guidance, a medicinal constituent is very soluble when the highest doses are soluble in 250 mL of aqueous media with a pH range of 1.2 to 6.8. Fasting human participants are given a medical medication along with a glass of water in a typical bioequivalence trial (approximately 8 oz). A volume estimate of 250 mL was obtained using this method.

(b) Dissolution Test—Immediate-Release Solid Oral Dosage Forms

The dissolving test is referenced in USP General Chapter 711 Dissolution. The test assesses the amount of active medication that dissolves from the dosage form in a liquid dissolution medium using standard dissolution apparatus and techniques.

The FDA's Guidance describes the agency's broad recommendations for dissolving testing. Immediate Release Dissolution Testing of Oral Solid Dosage Forms (2). A dissolving test is required for practically all solid oral dose forms before they may be approved. The International Conference on Harmonization (ICH) Q6A Guidance document(33) includes three decision trees to aid in the formulation of appropriate dissolution test conditions and tolerances.

Dissolving testing settings are commonly employed to offer a sensitive and selective assessment of medicine product performance (34). Dissolution data can be used to support some post-approval manufacturing and/or formulation modifications, as well as to waive the need for *in vivo* bioequivalence studies in some situations, as described later in the chapter.

(c) Apparatus

Chapter 711 of the USP is being dissolved. The Apparatus1 (basket) and Apparatus2 (paddle), the two most often used instruments for assessing the dissolution of solid oral dosage forms, have specific equipment and operational requirements.

The basket rotates at 100 revolutions per minute, while the paddle rotates at 50. The rate of dissolution increases in lockstep with the rate of stirring or dissolution speed. On the other hand, this expansion may or may not follow a specific mathematical formula (32). In addition to extended-release medication products, the USP Apparatus 3 (see USP General Chapter 724 Medicine Release) is often used to evaluate the dissolution of immediate-release medication products (34, 35). With apparatus4and7, only oral pills and capsules are used. The permitted use of the USP equipment for dissolution=drug release testing of solid oral dosage forms is listed in the table below. target medication products and operational parameter.

Table 1

USP.APPARATUS	DESCRIPTION	ROT.SPEED	DOSAGE FORM
TYRE 1	Basket apparatus	50-120 rpm	IR, DR, ER
TYRE 2	Paddle apparatus	25-50 rpm	IR, DR, ER
TYRE 3	Reciprocating cylinder	6-35 rpm	IR, ER
TYRE 4	Flow through cell	N/A	ER, Poorly soluble API
TYRE 5	Paddle over disk	25-50 rpm	TRASDERMAL
TYRE 6	Rotating cylinder	N/A	TRASDERMAL
TYRE 7	Reciprocating holder	30 rom	ER

(d) Media

The dissolving test media is selected based on the physic-chemical properties of the medicinal substance as well as the dose form parameters. When choosing a media, try to simulate physiological settings as closely as feasible. As a result, most people employ a medium with a pH range of 1.2 (gastric pH) to 6.8 (intestinal pH).

Water, 0.1N hydrochloric acid, pH4.5 acetate buffers, and pH6.8phosphatebuffer are the most popular media used in dissolving studies. As the pH rises, the rate of solubility of weak base pharmaceuticals rises, whereas the rate of dissolution of weak acid medications falls. The most important factor in determining the ideal medium volume is drug solubility (typically 500, 1000mL, with 900mL being the most common). If the medicine has a poor water solubility, a larger amount of water may be needed to generate sink conditions that allow the drug to dissolve completely in an acceptable amount of time. Surfactants may be present in the solution media. Surfactants in the dissolution media lower interfacial tension and stimulate micelle production, increasing solubility and dissolve rate.

Ionic salts can be added to the dissolution medium to speed up the process, but utilising hydro alcoholic or other organic solvent-containing media is not recommended. Specific enzyme doses can be added to the dissolution medium for hard and soft gelatin capsules, as well as gelatin-coated tablets, to prevent the production of pelicles caused by gelatin cross-linking (1).

Small air bubbles in the fluid can jeopardise the hydrodynamic uniformity of the test. Use the de-aeration procedure indicated in USP 711 Dissolution, or another validated method, to remove the air from the medium. The dissolving bath is normally kept around 370.5°C to mimic the warmth of the human body. A new study is looking into the usage of "bio-relevant" medium to forecast the dissolution of poorly soluble drugs and the quantities of lipophilic pharmaceuticals in plasma. (36,37).

(e) Tolerance

The acceptance criterion, or tolerance, for a dissolving test is expressed in terms of the amount ("Q") dissolved in a specific time frame. The amount is indicated as a percentage of the dosage form's declared active ingredient claim (rather than the actual amount). 75 percent or 80 percent ("Q") of the recommended amount of the active medicinal component must be dissolved within a particular time period for most immediate-release oral dosage formulations (test times between 15 and 60 min are most common).

The Acceptance Table in USP 711 is used to evaluate the dissolution test results, which sets criteria for mean and individual sample dissolution findings through three stages of testing

(S1,S2,and S3, specifying 6, 12, and 24 samples tested, respectively). The "Q" number should be utilised "as is," rather than in conjunction with the "Q 5% " value provided for the S1 testing stage. Drug products may meet the dissolving criteria at any level of testing; nevertheless, stage S2 testing (12 units tested) is advised for bioequivalence purposes. To begin, dissolution tolerances are calculated based on dissolutionprofiles generated from the drugproductlot(s) used in the *in vivo* bio-availability = equivalence investigation.

If more information becomes available, the essential specifications can be changed. In general, the dissolution standards described in the USP monograph should be met by a generic immediate-release medication product. If no USPrerequisites are available, the product should be prepared to meet or surpass the *in vitro* dissolving performance of the Reference Listed Drug (RLD), as indicated in the FDA's "Orange Book" (6).

In order for the dissolve test to be useful in establishing product similarity= equivalency, characteristics such as drug solubility, permeability, dissolving rate, and pharmacokinetics should be addressed while defining dissolve test requirements. To recommend release tolerances, the *in vitro* drug release performance of the bio-study batch or lots is used. Tolerances should be measured during at least three time periods that fall within the dosing interval.

The first tolerance range is commonly set at one hour to minimise "dose-dumping." The time points after that are described as ranges, with the final time point being defined as the labelled quantity released's minimum value [for example, NLT80 percent (Q)]. Consult acceptance table 4 from USP General Chapter 724 to understand the tolerances. There are three steps of testing, identical to those used for immediate-release drugs. Dissolution=Drug Release Profiles Comparisons

In addition to achieving a single-point tolerance ("Q") criteria for proper and comprehensive dissolution characterization, certain FDA "Guidances" require submission of multi-time point dissolution profile data (2, 3, 38, 39,).

Several alternative profile comparison approaches (such as model-dependent, model-independent-multivariate, and model-independent-index) have been developed and analysed by the Agency (40). These methods can be used to compare the solubility properties of different therapeutic product batches and examine the impact of scale-up and post-approval changes.

1.7.4 Applications of *In vitro* Dissolution

(a) Product Development

For the design of a dosage form, *in vitro* dissolution is a significant and valuable tool. *In vitro* dissolution is commonly used to aid in the selection of prototype formulations and the determination of appropriate constituent levels for establishing drug release profiles, especially for extended-release formulations. *In vitro* testing can also aid in the selection of a "market-image" product for bioavailability and bioequivalence investigations in humans.

(b) Quality Assurance

The *in vivo* bioavailability or bioequivalence performance parameters of a dosage form must be acceptable. Following key *in vivo* research, *in vitro* dissolution testing procedures and acceptance criteria were developed based on dissolution testing of these bio-lots, as well as current understanding of drug solubility, permeability, dissolution, and pharmacokinetics. The results of *in vitro* dissolution testing are then used to analyse the drug product's lot-to-lot performance characteristics, ensuring product integrity=similarity on future production lots.

(c) Product Stability

A typical method for assessing the stability and shelf life of pharmaceuticals is *in vitro* dissolution. Physicochemical changes to the dose form as the medicine matures may impact the drug's dissolving properties.

When the moisture content in the tablet grows or decreases over time, for example, the tablet hardness may change, resulting in changes in dissolving capabilities. Polymorph shifts to more stable, and thus less soluble crystalline forms may induce slower dissolving rates. In gelatin-encapsulated pharmaceuticals, aldehyde-amino cross-linking can enhance pellicle formation, which slows dissolution. Throughout the shelf life of an item, *in vitro* dissolution testing is performed to ensure optimal product performance during the expiration period.

(d) Comparability Assessment

In vitro dissolution can be employed before or after approval to assess the impact of changes to the drug product, such as formulation or manufacturing procedure changes. Various "SUPAC Guidance" describe the use of either a single point or dissolution profile comparison(s) technique to evaluate the impact of these differences, depending on the form and magnitude of the adjustments. *In vitro* comparative testing is required to ensure performance equivalency and product similarity.

1.7.5 Waivers of *In vivo* Bioequivalence Requirements

In vitro dissolution or drug release testing may be used to get a waiver from the obligation to do *in vivo* bioavailability or bioequivalence studies in conjunction with the following.

(a) Formulation Proportionality

In vivo bioavailability and bioequivalence testing on lower strengths of the same dosage form may be waived if the lower strength(s) are proportionally equivalent in their active and inactive components, and their dissolving characteristics are sufficiently similar (3,). There are two types of proportionalities in formulations. The first is constant proportion, in which active and inactive ingredients are changed proportionately across strengths, and the second is constant weight, which is seen particularly in products with small amounts of active drug and in which the total weight rather than proportion is held constant across strengths.

(b) Biopharmaceutics Classification System

Class I: High Solubility = High Permeability; Class II: Low Solubility = HIgh Permeability; Class III: High Solubility=Low Permeability; and Class IV: Low Solubility=Low Permeability. Highly soluble means that a medicine's greatest dose strength is soluble in aqueous solutions with a pH range of 17.5 or the more physiological pH 6.8 in less than or equal to 250mL.

When the quantity of absorption (as assessed by the area under the plasma concentration time curve) in humans is greater than 90% of the given dose, the drug is called extremely permeable. When employing USP Apparatus I at 100 rpm or USP Apparatus II at 50 rpm in a volume of 900mL, an immediate-release medicine product dissolves at least 85 percent of the prescribed amount of the medicinal component in 30 minutes. a)acidic media, such as 0.1NHCl or USP simulated gastric fluid without enzymes (SGF); b)apH 4.5 buffers; c)apH6.8 buffer or USP simulated intestinal fluid without enzymes (SIF) (SIF).

If the drug product fits the BCS criteria for Class I, which means the drug ingredient is highly soluble and permeable and the drug product dissolves quickly, stomach emptying is most likely the rate-limiting phase for drug absorption. In this case, there are no *in vivo* bioavailability or bioequivalence studies required for this product. The BCS has shown to be a fascinating method in its early stages. The maximum absorbable dose was calculated using data such as solubility, trans-intestinal absorption rate constant, small intestinal water volume, and transit time.

(c) *In vitro=In vivo* Correlations

An *in vitro – in vivo* correlation (IVIVC) is defined by the U.S Food and Drug Administration (FDA) as "a predictive mathematical model describing the relationship between the *in vitro* property of an oral dosage form and relevant *in vivo* response".

Following the development of a formulation, significant *in vitro* dissolution can be utilised in conjunction with techniques like de-convolution to predict *in vivo* dissolution and absorption and construct an *in vitro = in vivo* relationship.

Drugs with low solubility and high permeability (BCS Class II) and extended-release products are more likely to have these associations (level "A", "B", or "C" correlation). *In vivo* bioavailability or bioequivalence studies, which are generally necessary, may be waived once these *in vitro = in vivo* correlations have been established (4). Pollie has proposed the creation of an objective criterion for identifying models prior to *in vitro= in vivo* correlation research.

(d) Limitations of *In vitro* Dissolution

So far, the chapter has concentrated on the general use of dissolution testing. Nonetheless, the technique's flaws must be acknowledged. Small operational characteristics including stirring element eccentricity, agitation alignment, torsional vibration, dosage form position, sample location, dissolved gases, flow patterns, and heat transfer might have a major impact on dissolution measurement if they're disregarded. This was proved in a recent study, which discovered that different pill orientations result in drastically different dissolving speeds. The segregation of solution hydrodynamics in the dissolve testing device causes dissolving rate disparities. To produce reliable and repeatable test results, careful consideration of these various difficult variables is required.

Relevance is another restriction of disintegration.

Dissolution testing may not be highly relevant to therapeutic product performance in the absence of a satisfactory invitro=invivo relationship.

Dissolution testing may be "over-discriminatory" in the case of IR products containing BCS Class I and Class III drugs because oral absorption is likely to be limited by gastric empty in gastrointestinal permeability.

Single point dissolution testing for IR items, such as BCS Class II and IV medications, may be "non-discriminatory," failing to detect lots with poor *in vivo* performance. Furthermore, even if an *in vitro-in vivo* link for one product has been discovered, it is unlikely to apply to other commodities.

Despite these disadvantages, dissolution testing is still one of the most important and effective *in vitro* methods for determining product quality since these connections are usually "product specific." Only by appreciating these limitations may reasonable judgments be drawn about the relevance (or lack thereof) of a dissolution test result to product performance. Recognizing these flaws could help in the development of a more helpful and relevant solution testing technique.

1.7.6 Summary

Extensive *in vitro* characterization is essential to provide sufficient *in vivo* performance of a solid dosage form in terms of product quality. A variety of tests and methodologies can be used to study the *in vitro* dissolution of solid oral dosage forms. This form of examination is beneficial to product development, quality assurance and control, product stability testing, and comparability assessment. When the dosage form exhibits formulation proportionality to the bio-studied lot, or when the drug meets the criteria for BCS Class I and exhibits rapid dissolution, or when a meaningful *invitro* = *in vivo* relationship has been established, *in vitro* dissolution testing may also be useful for forgetting waivers of *in vivo* bioavailability or bioequivalence studies. Fibre optics for monitoring medicine concentration in the dissolution medium, artificial neural networks for dissolve prediction, and Process Analytical Technology are some of the most recent breakthroughs in offering successful invitro performance testing (PAT).

Websites

1. http:==www.fda.gov=cder=: FDA Center for Drug Evaluation and Research (CDER)Homepage.
2. http:==www.fda.gov=cder=ob=default.htm: FDA=CDER''OrangeBook''.
3. http:==www.fda.gov=cder=approval=index.htm: CDER New and GenericDrugApprovalsListingsfor1998^2002.
4. http:==www.fda.gov=cder=guidance=index.htm: CDERGuidanceDocuments.
5. http:==www.fda.gov=cder=ogd=:CDERO⁄ceofGenericDrugsHomepag e.
6. http:==www.accessdata.fda.gov=scripts=cder=iig=index.cfm: InactiveIngredientGuide12=30=02.
7. http:==www.webmd.com=:WEB-MD.
8. http:==www.usp.org=: United States PharmacopeialConventionInc.(USP).

References

1. The US Pharmacopeia=National Formulary, USP 26-NF 21. Rockville, MD: UnitedStatesPharmacopeialConventionInc.,2002.
2. Guidance for Industry: Dissolution Testing of Immediate Release Solid Oral Dosage Forms. Rockville, MD: Food and Drug Administration = Center for DrugEvaluationandResearch,1997.
3. Guidance for Industry: Bioavailability and Bioequivalence Studies for Orally Administered Drug Products—General Considerations. Rockville, MD: Food and Drug Administration = Center for Drug Evaluation and Research, 2003.
4. Guidance for Industry: Extended Release Oral Dosage Forms: Development, Evaluation and Application of *In vitro* = *In vivo* Correlations. Rockville, MD: Food and Drug Administration=Center for Drug Evaluation andResearch,1997.
5. Food and Drug Administration = Center for Drug Evaluation and Research Data Standards Manual. Rockville, MD: Food and Drug Administration = Center for Drug Evaluation and Research,1992:18.
6. Approved Drug Products with Therapeutic Equivalence Evaluations (Orange Book). 23rd ed. Rockville, MD: US Department of Health and Human Services=Food and Drug Administration, 2003.
7. Abdou HM. Evolution of Dissolution Testing, Theory of Dissolution, Theoretical Concepts for the Release of a Drug from Dosage Forms and Factors Ajecting Rate of Dissolution. Dissolution Bioavailability & Bioequivalence. Easton, PA:MackPublishingCompany,1989:1^105.
8. Noyes A, Whitney W. The rate of solution of solid substances in their own solutions. JAmerChemSoc1897;19(12):930^934.
9. Brunner L, Tolloczko S. Überdie au£, sungsgeschwindingkeitfester k, rper. Zeitschri¡tf˘rPhysiologischeChemie1900;35(3):283^290.
10. Nernst W. Theorie der reaktionsgeschwindigkeitin heterogenen Systemen. Zeitschri¡tf˘rPhysiologischeChemie1904;47(1):52^55.
11. YuL X, Amidon GL. Analytical solutions to mass transfer In: Amidon GL, Lee PI, Topp EM, eds. Transport Processes in Pharmaceutical Systems, NewYork: Marcel Dekker, Inc.,1999:23^54.
12. Horter D, Dressman JB. In£uence of physicochemical properties on dissolution of drugs in the gastrointestinal tract. Adv Drug Del Rev 2001;46(1^3):75^87.
13. Byrn S, Pfeijer R, Ganey M, Hoiberg C, Poochikian G. Pharmaceutical solids: a strategic approach to regulatory considerations. Pharm Res 1995; 12(7): 945^954.

14. Yu LX, Furness MS, Raw A, Woodland Outlaw KP, Nashed NE, Ramos E, Miller SPF, Adams RC, Fang F, Patel RM, Holcombe FO Jr, Chiu Y, Hussain AS, Scienti¢c considerations of pharmaceutical solid polymorphism in abbreviated new drug applications. PharmRes2003; 20(4):531^536.

15. GrantDJW, Higuchi T. Solubility Behavior of Organic Compounds, NewYork: JohnWiley & Sons,1990.

16. Hancock BC, Parks M. What is the true solubility advantage for amorphous pharmaceuticals? PharmRes2000;17(4):397^404.

17. AguiarAJ, KrcJ, KinkelAW, SamynJC. E¡ect of polymorphism on the absorption of chloramphenicol from chloramphenicol palmitate. JPharmSci1967; 56(7):847^853.

18. Morris KR, Fakes MG, Thakur AB, Newman AW, Singh AK, VenitJJ, SpagnualoCJ, Abu TM. An integrated approach to the selection of optimal salt form for a new drug candidate. IntJ of Pharm1994; 105: 209^217.

19. StavchanskyR, McGinityJ. Bioavailability and tablet technology. In: LiebermanHA, LachmanL, SchwartzJB, eds.Pharmaceutical Dosage Forms: Tablets.Vol.2. NewYork:MarcelDekker1989;2:349^553.

20. Sevelius H, RunkelR, Segre E, Bloom¢eld SS. Bioavailability of naproxen sodium and its relationship to clinical analgesic e¡ects. Br J Clin Pharmacol1980;10(3):259^263.

21. Peck GE, BaleyGJ, McCurdy VE, Banker GS. Tablet formulation and design In: Lieberman HA, Lachman L, Schwartz JB, eds. Pharmaceutical Dosage Forms: TabletsVol.1. NewYork: Marcel Dekker Inc. 1989; 1:73^130.

22. Banaker UV. Pharmaceutical Dissolution Testing. NewYork: MarcelDekker, Inc.,1991:133^187.

23. Solvang S, FinholtP. E¡ect of tablet processing and formulation factors on dissolution rate of the active ingredient in human gastric juice. J Pharm Sci 1970; 59(1):49^52.

24. PinnamaneniS, DasNG, DasSK. Formulation approaches for orally administered poorly soluble drugs. Pharmazie 2002; 54: 291^300.

25. Schwier JB, Cooke GG, Hartauer KJ, YuL. Rayon: A source of fural—are active aldehydecapable of insolubilizing gelatincapsules. PharmTechnol1993:78^80.

26. Lee TWY, Robinson JR. Controlled-Release Drug Delivery Systems. In: Gennaro AR, ed. Remington: The Science and Practice of Pharmacy. Philadelphia. Vol.20. Lippincott Williams & Wilkins 2000;20:903^929.

27. Yi L. Amorphous pharmaceutical solids: preparation characterization and stabilization. AdvDrugDelRev2001;48:27^42.
28. BandelinFJ. Compressed tablets by wet granulation. In: Lieberman HA, Lachman L, Schwartz JB, eds. Pharmaceutical Dosage Forms: Tablets. NewYork:MarcelDekker,Inc.1990;1:199^302.
29. ShangrawRF. Compressed tablets by direct compression. Lieberman HA, Lachman L, Schwartz JB, eds. Pharmaceutical Dosage Forms: Tablets. New York:MarcelDekker,Inc.1990;I:195^246.
30. Carstensen JT. Advanced Pharmaceutical Solids. New York: Marcel Dekker, Inc.,2001:427^438.
31. SeoPR, ShahVP, PolliJP. Novel metrics to compare dissolution Pro¢les. Pharm DevTechnol2002;7(2):257^265.
32. Digenis GA, Gold TB, Shah VP. Crosslinking of gelatin capsules and its rele vance to their invitro = invivo Performance. JPharmSci1994; 83(7):915^921.
33. Code of Federal Regulations—Title 21 Food and Drugs—Parts 300 to 499, O⁄ce of the Federal Register = National Archives and Records Administration: Washington DC2003:181^182.
34. Guidance for Industry: Waiver of Invivo Bioavailability and Bioequivalence Studies for Immediate Release Dosage Forms Based on a Biopharmaceutics Classi¢cation System; Rockville, MD:Food and Drug Administration=Center for Drug Evaluation and Research,2000.
35. Johnson KC, Swindell AC. Guidance in the Setting of Drug Particle Size Speci¢cations to Minimize Variability in Absorption. Pharm Res 1996; 13(12):1795^1798.
36. PolliJE. Dependence of invitro-invivo correlation analysis acceptability model selections. Pharm Dev Technol 1999;4(1):89^96.
37. KukuraJ, Arratia PE, Szalai ES, MuzzioFJ. Engineering tools for understanding the hydrodynamics of dissolutiontests. Drug Dev Industrial Pharm 2003;29(2):231^239.
38. Rainbow Dynamic Dissolution Monitor² System Manual, Northvale, NJ: Delphian Technology Inc., 2002;1^8.
39. Sathe P, Venitz J. Comparison of neural network (NN) and multiple linear regression (MLR) as dissolution predictors. Drug Dev Industrial Pharm 2003; 29(3):349^355.
40. WorkmanJJr, Creasy KE, DohertylS, BondL, Koch M, Ullman A, Veltkamp DJ. Process analytical chemistry. Anal Chem2001;

CHAPTER 1.8

ANDA Regulatory Approval Process

1.8.1 ANDA

An Abbreviated New Drug Application (ANDA) is a document that comprises information that is submitted to the FDA's CDER, Office of Generic Drugs, for examination and approval of a generic drug product.

An application may produce and market the generic drug product once it has been approved, providing the public with a safe, effective, and low-cost alternative.

The FDA's Authorized Drug Medications with Therapeutic Equivalence Evaluations list all approved products, including innovator and generic (Orange Book).

"A drug product that is comparable in dose form, strength, mode of administration, quality and performance attributes, and intended use to a brand/reference listed drug product."

Because they are not needed to provide preclinical (animal) and clinical (human) evidence to show safety and effectiveness, they are referred to as "abbreviated."

1.8.2 Basic Generic Drug Requirements

- Same active ingredient(s)
- Same route of administration
- Same dosage form
- Same strength
- Same conditions of use
- Inactive ingredients already approved in a similar NDA.

1.8.3 Goal of ANDA

- To reduce the price of the drug.
- To reduce the time development.
- Increase the bioavailability of the drug in comparison to references list drug.

PARAMETERS	INNOVATOR DRUG	GENEREIC DRUG
Active ingredients	SAME	SAME
Safety & efficacy	SAME	SAME
Quality & strength	SAME	SAME
Performance and standards	SAME	SAME
Costs/prescription	HIGHLY EXPENSIVE	LESS EXPENSIVE
FDA inspection of manufacturing facilities	YES	YES
FDA reviews reports of adverse reactions	YES	YES
FDA reviews drug labeling	YES	YES
Extensive research and development investments	YES	NO

1.8.4 Generic Drug Approval

- The ANDA was created by the FDA in 1970 as a process for reviewing and approving generic versions.
- Applicants for generic products had to submit complete safety and efficacy data through clinical trials prior to 1978.
- Applicants had to produce published data of such trials showing safety and efficacy after 1978.
- Hatch Waxman Act was enacted in 1984 after neither of these options was deemed sufficient.

1.8.5 Indispensability Ground for Generics

- The active components are the same as in the innovative medicine (inactive ingredients may vary).
- Strength, dose form, and delivery route must all be comparable.
- The use/indications must be the same.

- Bioequivalent is required.
- Identity, safety, and purity must all be met in the same batch.
- FDA GMPs must be followed to the letter.

1.8.6 Hatch-Waxman Act

- The "Drug Price Competition and Patent Term Restoration Act" of 1984 is more often known.
- "The Hatch-Waxman Act regulates the approval of generic medications and the requirements that must be met in order for them to be approved by the FDA, including market exclusivity, rights of exclusivity, patent term extensions, and Orange Book Listing."

Necessitated By:

1. Absence of Generic drug manufacturing.
2. Cumbersome regulatory procedures.
3. Patients were denied the option of cheaper drugs.

1.8.7 General Provisions of the Act

1. Maintaining list of patents which would be infringed.
2. Only Bioavailability studies and not clinical trials needed for approval.
3. Para I, II, III and IV certifications.
4. Data exclusivity period for New Molecular Entities.
5. Extension of the original patent term.
6. The "Bolar" Provision.

1.8.8 Recent additions to the Hatch-Waxman Act

Under the "Medicare Prescription Drug and Modernization Act", 2003:

1. Non-extension of the 30-month period.
2. Time limit for informing patent owner.
3. Provision for allowing declaratory judgment.
4. Benefit of exclusivity for several ANDAs filed on same day allowed.

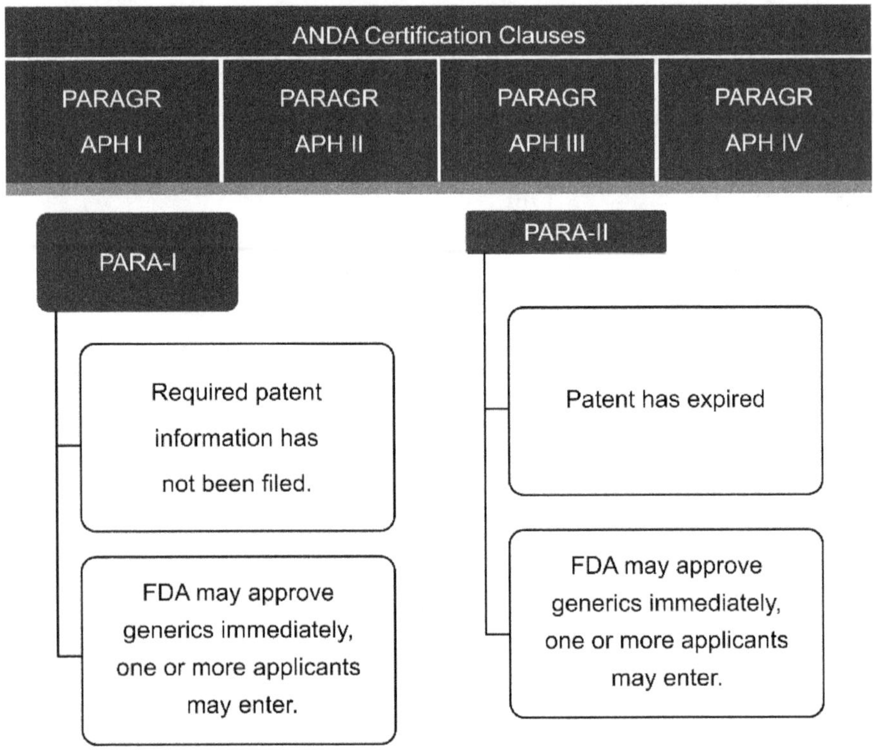

Figure 1

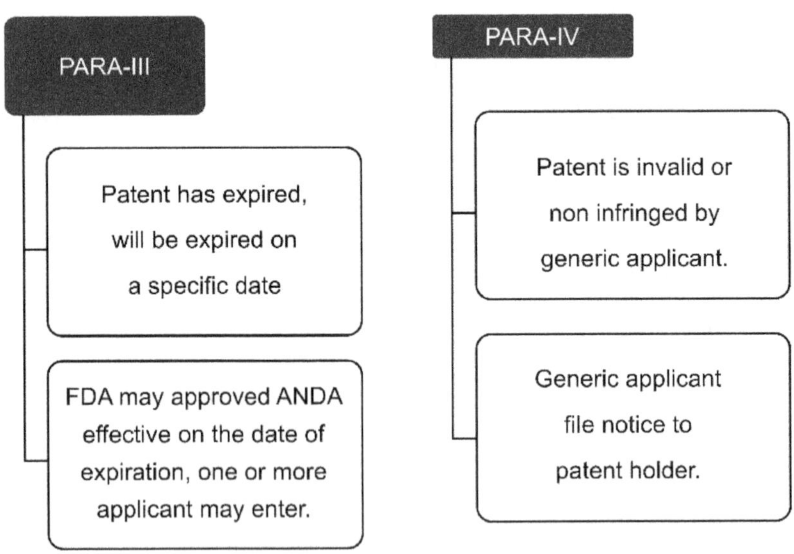

Figure 2

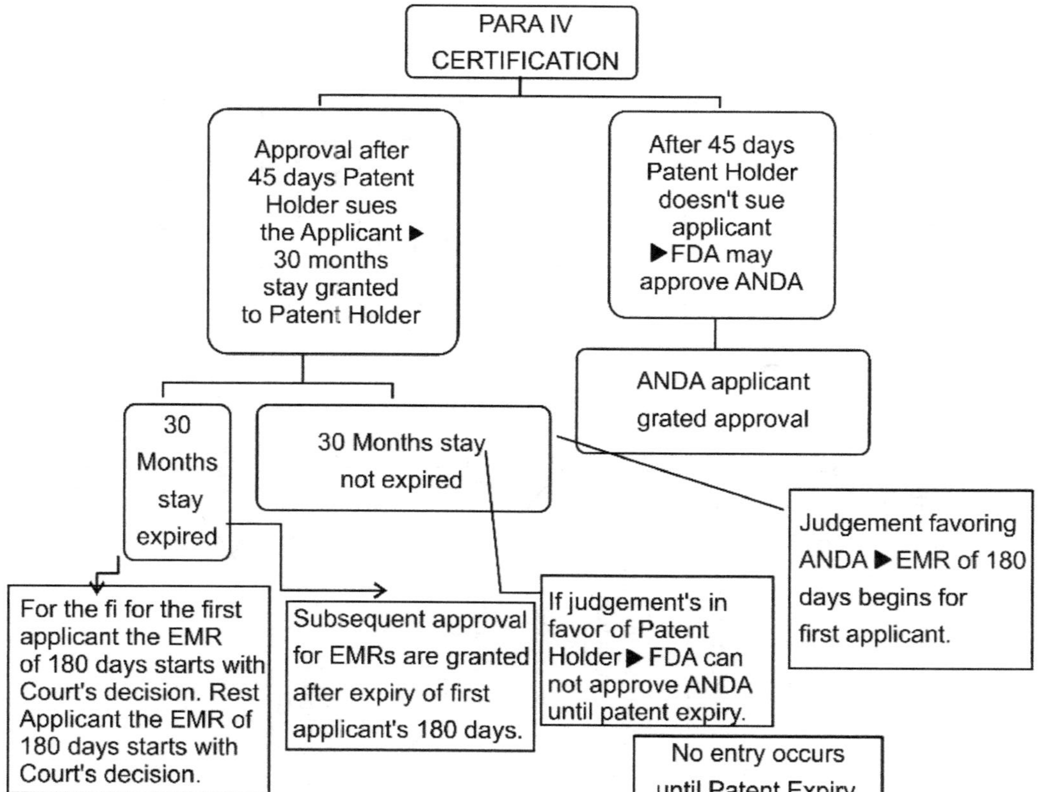
PARA IV CERTIFICATION
Approval after 45 days Patent Holder sues the Applicant ▶ 30 months stay granted to Patent Holder
After 45 days Patent Holder doesn't sue applicant ▶FDA may approve ANDA
ANDA applicant grated approval
30 Months stay expired
30 Months stay not expired
For the fi for the first applicant the EMR of 180 days starts with Court's decision. Rest Applicant the EMR of 180 days starts with Court's decision.
Subsequent approval for EMRs are granted after expiry of first applicant's 180 days.
If judgement's in favor of Patent Holder ▶ FDA can not approve ANDA until patent expiry.
Judgement favoring ANDA ▶ EMR of 180 days begins for first applicant.
No entry occurs until Patent Expiry.

Figure 3

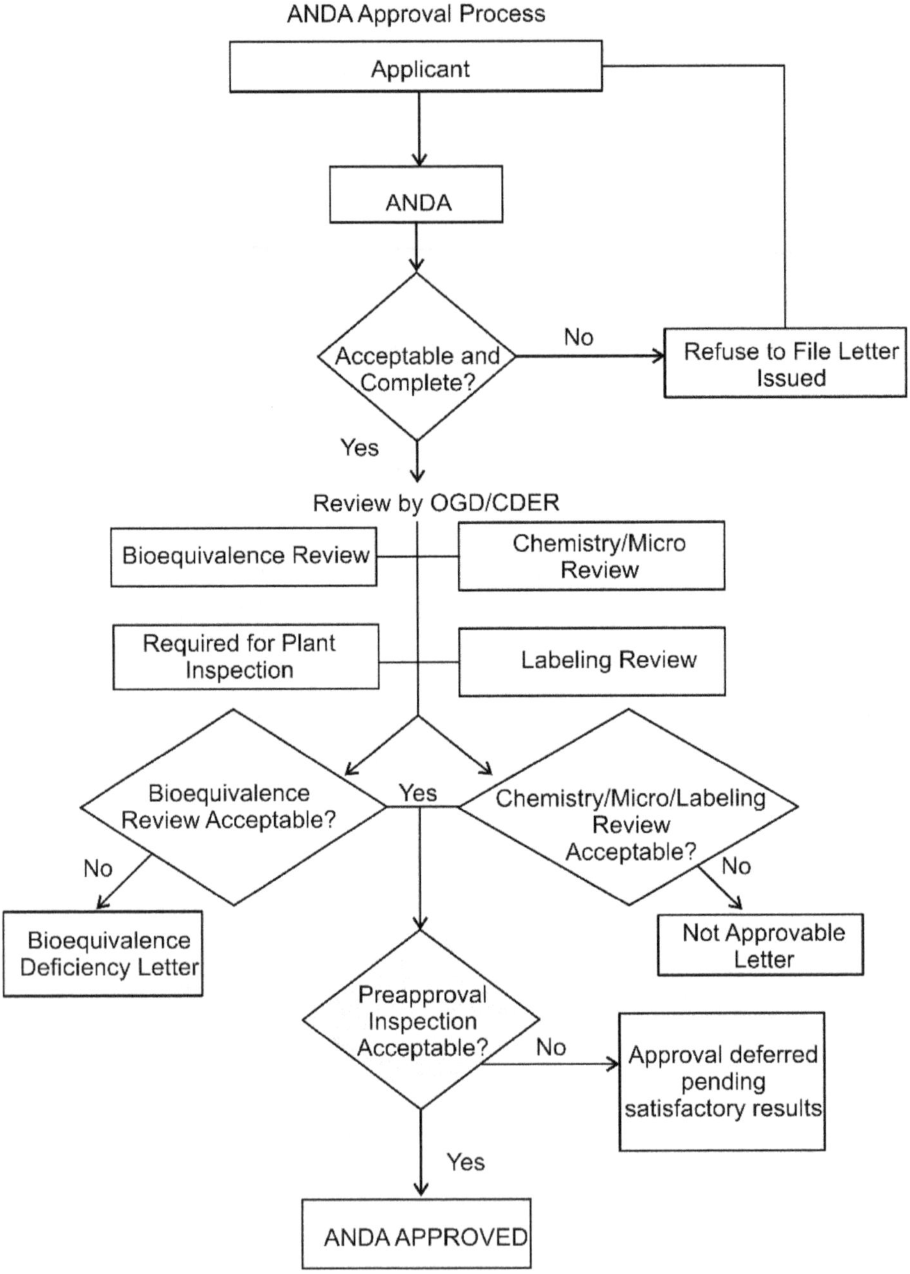
ANDA Approval Process
Applicant
ANDA
Acceptable and Complete?
No
Refuse to File Letter Issued
Yes
Review by OGD/CDER
Bioequivalence Review
Chemistry/Micro Review
Required for Plant Inspection
Labeling Review
Bioequivalence Review Acceptable?
Yes
Chemistry/Micro/Labeling Review Acceptable?
No
Bioequivalence Deficiency Letter
No
Not Approvable Letter
Preapproval Inspection Acceptable?
No
Approval deferred pending satisfactory results
Yes
ANDA APPROVED

Figure 4

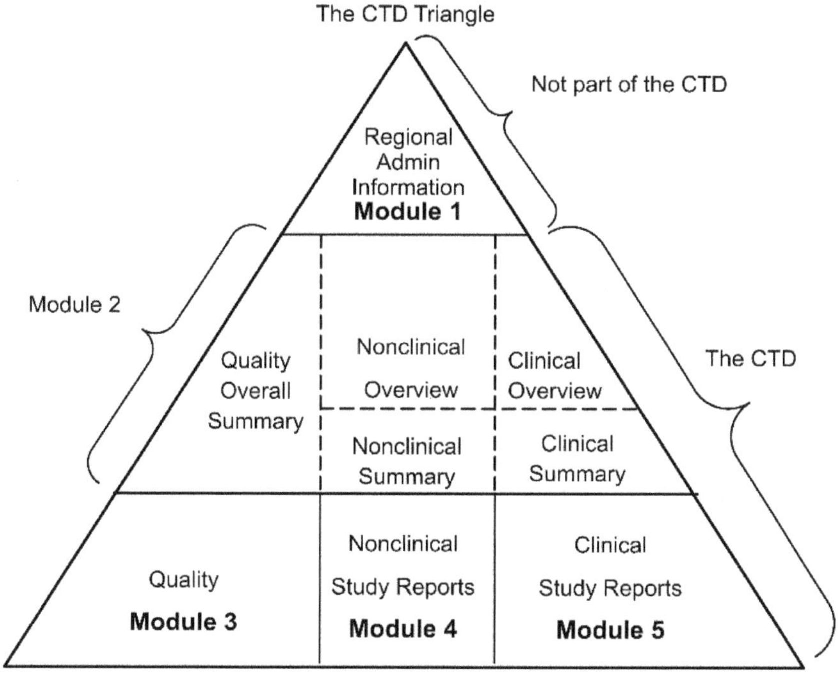

Figure 5

Diagrammatic Representation of the Organization of the ICH CTD Common Technical Document

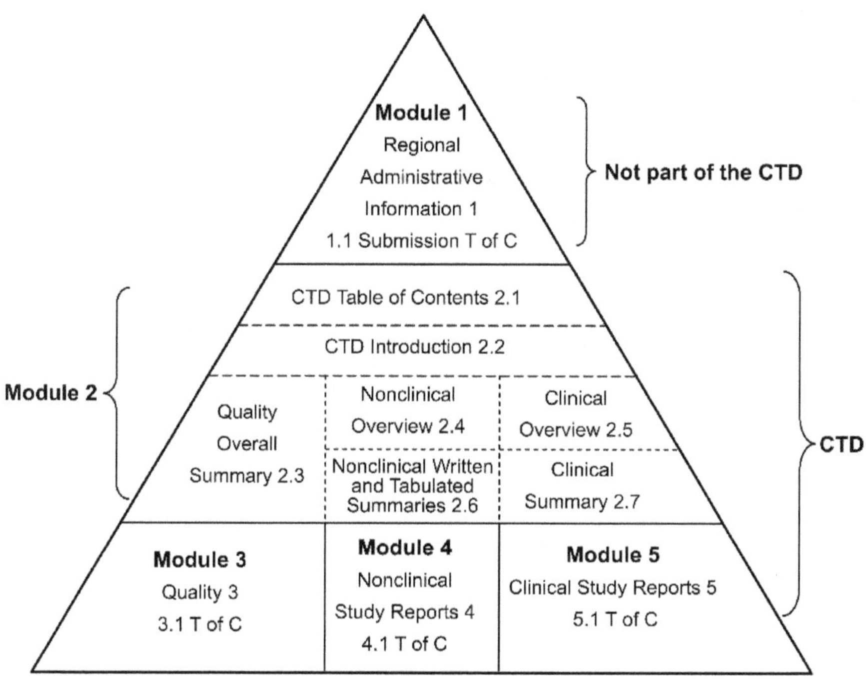

Figure 6

1.8.9 Modules in a CTD

MODULE I: Administrative and Prescribing Information

1. Table of Contents.
2. Includes data of Administrative Documents entailing:
    - Patent Information on patented product.
    - Patent Certifications.
    - Debarment certification.
3. Prescribing information like Package and container labels, packaging inserts, patient leaflets, etc.
4. Labeling Comparison between Innovator and Generic drug.

MODULE II: Summaries and Overviews

1. Table of Contents.
2. Introduction to Summary Documents.
3. Overviews and Summaries: Module II should contain documents like:
    - M4Q: The CTD- quality
    - M4S: The CTD- safety
    - M4E: The CTD- efficacy

MODULE III: information on product quality

1. Table of Content.
2. Body of Data.
3. Literature Reference.

MODULE IV: Non Clinical Study Reports

Not required in ANDA Filing.

MODULE V: Clinical Study Reports

1. Table of Contents.
2. Study Reports including Case Report Forms and Case Report Tabulations.

1.8.10 ANDA CONTENTS [Table 1]

CTD MODULES	ANDA REQUIREMENT
Module 2 **Common Technical Document Summaries**	YES
Module 3 **Quality**	YES

Table *Contd...*

CTD MODULES	ANDA REQUIREMENT
Module 4 **Nonclinical Study Reports (Animal studies)**	NO
Module 5 **Clinical Study Reports (BA/BE studies)**	YES

1.8.11 NDA CONTENTS [Table 2]

CTD MODULES	ANDA REQUIREMENT
Module 2 **Common Technical Document Summaries**	YES
Module 3 **Quality**	YES
Module 4 **Nonclinical Study Reports (Animal studies)**	YES
Module 5 **Clinical Study Reports (BA/BE studies)**	YES

1.8.12 IND CONTENTS [Table 3]

CTD MODULES	ANDA REQUIREMENT
Module 2 **Common Technical Document Summaries**	YES
Module 3 **Quality**	YES
Module 4 **Nonclinical Study Reports (Animal studies)**	YES
Module 5 **Clinical Study Reports (BA/BE studies)**	NO

1.8.13 Broad Outline for ANDA

Product must meet appropriate standards of

- Identity,
- Strength,
- Quality and
- Purity

Efficacy and safety should be equivalent to branded product already established

1.8.14 Information required for Filing ANDA

- Product's formulation
- Manufacturer's procedure
- Control procedure
- Testing,
- Facilities
- Dissolution profile
- Labeling

1.8.15 Recommendations for e CTD

Acrobat Reader 3.0 is required to view PDF files.

In the Portable Document Format, embedded typefaces are used.

The print area is 8.5 inches by 11 inches, with a 1 inch margin on all sides.

Scanned documents should not be used as sources.

Blue-Texts or thin-line rectangles can be used to denote hypertexts.

The numbering on the PDF and the documents should match.

Passwords or security should not be included.

Indexes should be included in their entirety.

Electronic signatures may be added, and procedures for archiving the same are being used.

1.8.16 First-Time Generic Drug Approvals - July 2011 [Table 4]

Generic Drug Name	Generic Manufacturer	Brand Name	Approval Date
FONDAPARINUX SODIUM INJECTION	DR. REDDY'S LABORATORIES LIMITED	ARIXTRA INJECTION	7/11/2011
ALFUZOSIN HYDROCHLORIDE EXTENDEDRELEASE TABLETS	TEVA PHARMACEUTICALS USA	UROXATRAL EXTENDEDRELEASE TABLETS	7/18/2011
ALFUZOSIN HYDROCHLORIDE EXTENDEDRELEASE TABLETS	SUN PHARMA GLOBAL FZE	UROXATRAL EXTENDEDRELEASE TABLETS	7/18/2011
PARICALCITOL INJECTION	SANDOZ CANADA, INC.	ZEMPLAR INJECTION	7/27/2011

1.8.17 Patent Certification condition for ANDA

Described in section 505(j)(2)(A)(vii) of the Act.

I Patent Not Submitted to FDA

Approval effective after OGD scientific determination.

II Patent Expired

Approval effective after OGD scientific determination.

III Patent Expiration Date (honored)

Tentative approval after OGD scientific determination, final approval when patent expires.

IV Patent Challenge

Tentative approval after OGD science determination, final approval when challenge won.

Paragraph IV certification

According to section 505(j) (2) (B) (i), 2157 CFR

- The ANDA applicant must provide appropriate notice of a paragraph IV certification to each owner of the patent that is the subject of the certification and to the holder of the approved NDA to which the ANDA refers.

  And by **Section 505(j) (5) (B) (IV)**

- An incentive for generic manufacturers to file paragraph IV certifications and to challenge listed patents as invalid, or not infringed, by providing for a 180-day period of marketing exclusivity.

1.8.18 Patent Challenge Successful – Award of 180-Day

Exclusivity Period

The first ANDA holder to file a complete application with a patent challenge receives this award.

Protection against generic competition - prevents ANDA approval in the future.

First commercial marketing triggers protection Provisions for forfeiture.

1.8.19 Orphan Drug Exclusivity (ODE)

An orphan medicine is a medication that addresses an illness that affects fewer than 200,000 people in the United States.

7 years of exclusivity

Awarded pending approval of an orphan medication.

The Office of Orphan Products collaborates with OGD.

Table 5

DETAILS	NDA	ANDA	IND
1.Chemistry, manufacturing, and controls	yes	Yes	Yes
2.Nonclinical pharmacology and toxicology (Animal data)	Yes	No	Yes
3. Human pharmacokinetics and bioavailability	Yes	Yes	No
4. Microbiology	Yes	Yes	No
5.Clinical data	Yes	Yes (BABE studies)	No
6.Statistical	Yes	Yes	Yes

ANDA FILING CHECKLIST

(CTD or eCTD FORMAT)

FOR COMPLETENESS AND ACCEPTABILITY of an APPLICATION

ANDA:
APPLICANT:
RELATED APPLICATION(S):

DRUG NAME:
DOSAGE FORM:

LETTER DATE:
RECEIVED DATE:

- ☐ P-IV
- ☐ FIRST GENERIC
- ☐ EXPEDITED REVIEW REQUEST (Approved/Denied)
- ☐ PEPFAR

Electronic or Paper Submission: Type II DMF#

BASIS OF SUBMISSION:
NDA/ANDA:
FIRM:
RLD:

**Document Room Note: for New Strength amendments and supplements, if specific reviewer(s) have already been assigned for the original, please assign to those reviewer(s) instead of the default random team(s).

Review Team:

CHEM Team: ☐ **Activity**	Bio Team: ☐ **Activity**
CHEM Team Leader: ☐ **No Assignment Needed in DARRTS**	Bio PM: ☐ **FYI**
CHEM RPM: ☐ **FYI**	Clinical Endpoint Team: **(No)** ☐ **Activity**
DMF Review Team Leader: ☐ **FYI**	
Labeling Reviewer: ☐ **Activity**	Micro Review: **(No)** ☐ **Activity**

Regulatory Reviewer: Date:	Recommendation: ☐ **FILE** ☐ **REFUSE to RECEIVE**

Comments:
Therapeutic Code:
On Cards:
Archival copy:
Sections:

- **For More Information on Submission of an ANDA in Electronic Common Technical Document (eCTD) Format please go to:** http://www.fda.gov/cder/regulatory/ersr/ectd.htm
- **For a Comprehensive Table of Contents Headings and Hierarchy please go to:** http://www.fda.gov/cder/regulatory/ersr/5640CTOC-v1.2.pdf
- **For more** CTD and eCTD informational links **see the final page of the ANDA Checklist**
- **A model Quality Overall Summary for an immediate release tablet and an extended release capsule can be found on the OGD webpage** http://www.fda.gov/cder/ogd/

1. Edit Application Property Type in DARRTS where applicable for

   a. First Generic Received
   ☐ Yes ☐ No
   b. Market Availability
   ☐ Rx ☐ OTC
   c. Pepfar
   ☐ Yes ☐ No
   d. Product Type
   ☐ Small Molecule Drug
   e. USP Drug Product (at time of filing review)
   ☐ Yes ☐ No

2. Edit Submission Patent Records
   ☐ Yes
3. Edit Contacts Database with Bioequivalence Recordation where applicable
   ☐ Yes
4. EER (in Draft)
   ☐ Yes

ADDITIONAL COMMENTS REGARDING THE ANDA:

MODULE 1: ADMINISTRATIVE

		COMMENT (S)
1.1	1.1.2 **Signed and Completed Application Form (356h)** (Rx/OTC Status) (original signature) **Establishment Information:** 1. Drug Substance Manufacturer 2. Drug Product Manufacturer 3. Outside Testing Facility(ies)	
1.2	**Cover Letter**	
1.2.1	**Form FDA 3674** (PDF)	
*	**Table of Contents** (paper submission only)	
1.3.2	**Field Copy Certification** (N/A for E-Submissions) (original signature)	
1.3.3	**Debarment Certification-GDEA** (Generic Drug Enforcement Act)/Other: (no qualifying statement) 1. Debarment Certification (original signature) 2. List of Convictions statement (original signature)	
1.3.4	**Financial Certifications** Bioavailability/Bioequivalence Financial Certification (Form FDA 3454) Disclosure Statement (Form FDA 3455)	
1.3.5	**Patent Information** Patents listed for the RLD in the Electronic Orange Book Approved Drug Products with Therapeutic Equivalence Evaluations **Patent Certification** 1. Patent number(s) 2. Paragraph: (Check all certifications that apply) MOU ☐ PI ☐ PII ☐ PIII ☐ PIV ☐ (Statement of Notification) ☐ 3. Expiration of Patent(s): a. Pediatric exclusivity submitted? b. Expiration of Pediatric Exclusivity? 4. Exclusivity Statement: State marketing intentions?	
1.4.1	**References** Letters of Authorization 1. DMF letters of authorization a. Type II DMF authorization letter(s) or synthesis for Active Pharmaceutical Ingredient b. Type II DMF# c. Type III DMF authorization letter(s) for container closure 2. US Agent Letter of Authorization (U.S. Agent [if needed, countersignature on 356h])	
1.12.4	**Request for Comments and Advice** - Proprietary name requested If Yes, did the firm provide the request as a separate electronic amendment labeled "Proprietary Name Request" at initial time of filing 1. Yes 2. No - contact the firm to submit the request as a separate electronic amendment.	
1.12.11	**Basis for Submission** NDA#: Ref Listed Drug: Firm: **ANDA suitability petition required?** If Yes, provide petition number and copy of approved petition **ANDA Citizen's Petition Required?** If Yes, provide petition number and copy of petition	

Table *Contd...*

MODULE 1: ADMINISTRATIVE (Continued)

		COMMENT (S)
1.12.12	**Comparison between Generic Drug and RLD-505(j)(2)(A)** 1. Conditions of use 2. Active ingredients 3. Inactive ingredients 4. Route of administration 5. Dosage Form 6. Strength	
1.12.14	**Environmental Impact Analysis Statement** (cite 21CFR 25.31, if applicable)	
1.12.15	**Request for Waiver** Request for Waiver of In-Vivo BA/BE Study(ies)	
1.14.1	**Draft Labeling** (Multi Copies N/A for E-Submissions) **1.14.1.1** 4 copies of draft for paper submission only (each strength and container) **1.14.1.2** 1 side by side labeling comparison of containers and carton with all differences visually highlighted and annotated **1.14.1.3** 1 package insert (content of labeling) and SPL submitted electronically	
1.14.3	**Listed Drug Labeling** **1.14.3.1** 1 side by side labeling (package and patient insert) comparison with all differences visually highlighted and annotated **1.14.3.3** RLD package insert, 1 RLD label and 1 RLD container label	

MODULE 2: SUMMARIES

		COMMENT (S)
2.3	**Quality Overall Summary (QOS)** **E-Submission: PDF** **Word Processed e.g., MS Word** A model Quality Overall Summary for an immediate release tablet and an extended release capsule can be found on the OGD webpage http://www.fda.gov/cder/ogd/ **Question based Review (QbR)** **2.3.S Drug Substance (Active Pharmaceutical Ingredient)** 2.3.S.1 General Information 2.3.S.2 Manufacture 2.3.S.3 Characterization 2.3.S.4 Control of Drug Substance 2.3.S.5 Reference Standards or Materials 2.3.S.6 Container Closure System 2.3.S.7 Stability **2.3.P Drug Product** 2.3.P.1 Description and Composition of the Drug Product 2.3.P.2 Pharmaceutical Development 2.3.P.2.1 Components of the Drug Product 2.3.P.2.1.1 Drug Substance 2.3.P.2.1.2 Excipients 2.3.P.2.2 Drug Product 2.3.P.2.3 Manufacturing Process Development 2.3.P.2.4 Container Closure System 2.3.P.3 Manufacture 2.3.P.4 Control of Excipients 2.3.P.5 Control of Drug Product 2.3.P.6 Reference Standards or Materials 2.3.P.7 Container Closure System 2.3.P.8 Stability	

Table *Contd...*

2.7	**Clinical Summary (Bioequivalence)** Model BE Data Summary Tables **E-Submission: PDF** **Word Processed: e.g., MS Word** **2.7.1 Summary of Biopharmaceutic Studies and Associated Analytical Methods** **2.7.1.1 Background and Overview** Table 1. Submission Summary Table 4. Bioanalytical Method Validation Table 6. Formulation Data **2.7.1.2 Summary of Results of Individual Studies** Table 5. Summary of In Vitro Dissolution **2.7.1.3 Comparison and Analyses of Results Across Studies** Table 2. Summary of Bioavailability (BA) Studies Table 3. Statistical Summary of the Comparative BA Data **2.7.1.4 Appendix** **2.7.4.1.3 Demographic and Other Characteristics of Study Population** Table 7. Demographic Profile of Subjects Completing the Bioequivalence Study **2.7.4.2.1.1 Common Adverse Events** Table 8. Incidence of Adverse Events in Individual Studies	

MODULE 3: 3.2.S DRUG SUBSTANCE

		COMMENT (S)
3.2.S.1	**General Information** (Do not refer to DMF) **3.2.S.1.1 Nomenclature** **3.2.S.1.2 Structure** **3.2.S.1.3 General Properties**	
3.2.S.2	**Manufacturer** **Drug Substance (Active Pharmaceutical Ingredient)** 1. Name and Full Address(es)of the Facility(ies) 2. Contact name, phone and fax numbers, email address 3. Specify Function or Responsibility 4. Type II DMF number for API 5. CFN or FEI numbers	
3.2.S.3	**Characterization** Provide the following in tabular format: 1. Name of Impurity(ies) 2. Structure of Impurity(ies) 3. Origin of Impurity(ies)	
3.2.S.4	**Control of Drug Substance (Active Pharmaceutical Ingredient)** **3.2.S.4.1 Specification** Testing specifications and data from drug substance manufacturer(s) **3.2.S.4.2 Analytical Procedures** **3.2.S.4.3 Validation of Analytical Procedures** (API that is USP or reference made to DMF, must provide verification of USP or DMF procedures) 1. Spectra and chromatograms for reference standards and test samples 2 Samples-Statement of Availability and Identification of: a. Drug Substance b. API lot number(s) **3.2.S.4.4 Batch Analysis** 1. COA(s) specifications and test results from drug substance mfgr(s) 2. Applicant certificate of analysis **3.2.S.4.5 Justification of Specification**	
3.2.S.5	**Reference Standards or Materials** (Do not refer to DMF)	
3.2.S.6	**Container Closure Systems**	
3.2.S.7	**Stability** 1. Retest date or expiration date of API	

Table *Contd...*

MODULE 3: 3.2.P DRUG PRODUCT

		COMMENT (S)
3.2.P.1	**Description and Composition of the Drug Product** 1. Unit composition with indication of the function of the inactive ingredient(s) 2. Inactive ingredients and amounts are appropriate per IIG (per/dose justification) 3. Conversion from % to mg/dose values for inactive ingredients (if applicable) 4. Elemental iron: provide daily elemental iron calculation or statement of adherence to 21CFR73.1200 (calculation of elemental iron intake based on **maximum daily dose (MDD)** of the drug product is preferred if this section is applicable) 5. Injections: If the reference listed drug is packaged with a drug specific diluent then the diluent must be Q1/Q2 and must be provided in the package configuration	
3.2.P.2	**Pharmaceutical Development** Pharmaceutical Development Report	
3.2.P.3	**Manufacture** **3.2.P.3.1 Drug Product** (Finished Dosage Manufacturer and Outside Contract Testing Laboratories) 1. Name and Full Address(es)of the Facility(ies) 2. Contact name, phone and fax numbers, email address 3. Specify Function or Responsibility 4. CGMP Certification (from both applicant and drug product manufacturer if different entities) 5. CFN or FEI numbers **3.2.P.3.2 Batch Formula** **3.2.P.3.3 Description of Manufacturing Process and Process Controls** 1. Description of the Manufacturing Process 2. Master Production Batch Record(s) for largest intended production runs (no more than 10x pilot batch) with equipment specified 3. Master packaging records for intended marketing container(s) 4. If sterile product (Aseptic or Terminally Sterilized) 5. Reprocessing Statement (cite 21CFR 211.115, submitted by the drug product manufacturer and the applicant, if different entities) **3.2.P.3.4 Controls of Critical Steps and Intermediates** **3.2.P.3.5 Process Validation and/or Evaluation** 1. Microbiological sterilization validation 2. Filter validation (if aseptic fill)	
3.2.P.4	**Controls of Excipients** (Inactive Ingredients) Source of inactive ingredients identified **3.2.P.4.1 Specifications** 1. Testing specifications (including identification and characterization) 2. Suppliers' COA (specifications and test results) **3.2.P.4.2 Analytical Procedures** **3.2.P.4.3 Validation of Analytical Procedures** **3.2.P.4.4 Justification of Specifications:** 1. Applicant COA	
	3.2.P.5.4 Batch Analysis Certificate of Analysis for Finished Dosage Form **3.2.P.5.5 Characterization of Impurities** **3.2.P.5.6 Justification of Specifications**	

3.2.P.7	**Container Closure System** 1. Summary of Container/Closure System (if new resin, provide data) 2. Components Specification and Test Data 3. Packaging Configuration and Sizes 4. Container/Closure Testing (recommended additional testing for all plastic) a. Solid Orals: water permeation, light transmission b. Liquids: leachables, extractables, light transmission 5. Source of supply and suppliers address	
3.2.P.8	**3.2.P.8.1 Stability (Finished Dosage Form)** 1. Stability Protocol submitted 2. Expiration Dating Period **3.2.P.8.2 Post-approval Stability and Conclusion** Post Approval Stability Protocol and Commitments **3.2.P.8.3 Stability Data** 1. Accelerated stability data a. four (4) time points 0,1,2,3 **-OR-** b. three (3) time points 0,3,6 (if 3 time points for accelerated stability data are submitted then provide 3 exhibit batches along with 12 months of room temperature stability data –Refer to Guidance for Industry Q1A(R2) Stability Testing of New Drug Substances and Products November 2003, Section B) 2. Batch numbers on stability records the same as the test batch	

MODULE 3: 3.2.R REGIONAL INFORMATION (Drug Substance)

		COMMENT (S)
3.2.R Drug Substance	**3.2.R.1.S Executed Batch Records for drug substance (if available)** **3.2.R.2.S Comparability Protocols** **3.2.R.3.S Methods Validation Package** Methods Validation Package (3 copies for paper and N/A for E-Submissions) (Required for Non-USP drugs)	

MODULE 3: 3.2.R REGIONAL INFORMATION (Drug Product)

		COMMENT (S)
3.2.R Drug Product	**3.2.R.1.P.1** **Executed Batch Records** Copy of Executed Batch Record with Equipment Specified, including Packaging Records (Packaging and Labeling Procedures) Batch Reconciliation and Label Reconciliation a. Theoretical Yield b. Actual Yield c. Packaged Yield Bulk Package Reconciliation required if bulk packaging is used to achieve the minimum package requirement. Provide the following information in their respective sections: a. Bulk Package Label (1.14.1) b. Bulk Package Stability (accelerated stability data [0,1,2,3] **–OR-** room temperature [0,3,6]) (3.2.P.8) c. Bulk Package Container and Closure information (3.2.P.7) **3.2.R.1.P.2 Information on Components** **3.2.R.2.P Comparability Protocols** **3.2.R.3.P Methods Validation Package** Methods Validation Package (3 copies for paper and N/A for E-Submissions) (Required for Non-USP drugs)	

MODULE 5: CLINICAL STUDY REPORTS

		COMMENT (S)
5.2	**Tabular Listing of Clinical Studies**	
5.3.1 (complete study data)	**Bioavailability/Bioequivalence** **1. Formulation data same?** a. Comparison of all Strengths (check proportionality of multiple strengths) b. Parenterals, Ophthalmics, Otics and Topicals (21 CFR 314.94 (a)(9)(iii)-(v) **2. Lot Numbers and strength of Products used in BE Study(ies)** **3. Study Type: IN-VIVO PK STUDY(IES)** (Continue with the appropriate study type box below)	
	5.3.1.2 Comparative BA/BE Study Reports 1. Study(ies) meets BE criteria (90% CI of 80-125, C max, AUC) 2. Summary Bioequivalence tables: Table 10. Study Information Table 12. Dropout Information Table 13. Protocol Deviations **5.3.1.3 In Vitro-In-Vivo Correlation Study Reports** 1. Summary Bioequivalence tables Table 11. Product Information Table 16. Composition of Meal Used in Fed Bioequivalence Study **5.3.1.4 Reports of Bioanalytical and Analytical Methods for Human Studies** 1. Summary Bioequivalence table: Table 9. Reanalysis of Study Samples Table 14. Summary of Standard Curve and QC Data for Bioequivalence Sample Analyses Table 15. SOPs Dealing with Bioanalytical Repeats of Study Samples	
5.4	**Literature References**	
	Possible Study Types:	
Study Type	**IN-VIVO BE STUDY(IES) with PK ENDPOINTS** (i.e., fasting/fed/sprinkle) 1. Study(ies) meets BE criteria (90% CI of 80-125, C max, AUC) 2. EDR Email: Data Files Submitted 3. In-Vitro Dissolution	
Study Type	**IN-VIVO BE STUDY with CLINICAL ENDPOINTS** 1. Properly defined BE endpoints (eval. by Clinical Team) 2. Summary results meet BE criteria: 90% CI of the proportional difference in success rate between test and reference must be within (-0.20, +0.20) for a binary/dichotomous endpoint. For a continuous endpoint, the test/reference ratio of the mean result must be within (0.80,1.25) 3. Summary results indicate superiority of active treatments (test & reference) over vehicle/placebo ($p<0.05$) (eval. by Clinical Team)	
	4. EDR Email: Data Files Submitted	
Study Type	**IN-VITRO BE STUDY(IES)** (i.e., in vitro binding assays) 1. Study(ies) meets BE criteria (90% CI of 80-125) 2. EDR Email: Data Files Submitted 3. In-Vitro Dissolution	

Table *Contd...*

Study Type	**NASALLY ADMINISTERED DRUG PRODUCTS** 1. **Solutions** (Q1/Q2 sameness) a. In-Vitro Studies (Dose/Spray Content Uniformity, Droplet/Drug Particle Size Distrib., Spray Pattern, Plume Geometry, Priming & Repriming) 2. **Suspensions** (Q1/Q2 sameness): a. In-Vivo PK Study 1. Study(ies) meets BE Criteria (90% CI of 80-125, C max, AUC) 2. EDR Email: Data Files Submitted b. In-Vivo BE Study with Clinical End Points 1. Properly defined BE endpoints (eval. by Clinical Team) 2. Summary results meet BE criteria (90% CI within +/- 20% of 80-125) 3. Summary results indicate superiority of active treatments (test & reference) over vehicle/placebo (p<0.05) (eval. by Clinical Team) 4. EDR Email: Data Files Submitted c. In-Vitro Studies (Dose/Spray Content Uniformity, Droplet/Drug Particle Size Distrib., Spray Pattern, Plume Geometry, Priming & Repriming)	
Study Type	**IN-VIVO BE STUDY(IES) with PD ENDPOINTS** (e.g., topical corticosteroid vasoconstrictor studies) 1. Pilot Study (determination of ED50) 2. Pivotal Study (study meets BE criteria 90%CI of 80-125)	
Study Type	**TRANSDERMAL DELIVERY SYSTEMS** 1. In-Vivo PK Study a. Study(ies) meet BE Criteria (90% CI of 80-125, C max, AUC) b. In-Vitro Dissolution c. EDR Email: Data Files Submitted 2. Adhesion Study 3. Skin Irritation/Sensitization Study	

References

1. https://www.fda.gov/drugs/types-applications/abbreviated-new-drug-application-anda .
2. https://www.fda.gov/drugs/electronic-regulatory-submission-and-review/electronic-common-technical-document-ectd .
3. https://en.wikipedia.org/wiki/Common_Technical_Document .

CHAPTER 1.9

Regulatory Requirements for Product Approval

1.9.1 Introduction

An orphan medicine is a medication that addresses an illness that affects fewer than 200,000 people in the United States.

7 years of exclusivity

Awarded pending approval of an orphan medication.

The Office of Orphan Products collaborates with OGD.

Currently, different countries have varying regulatory criteria for the clearance of new medicines. It is nearly hard to create an unified regulatory framework for marketing authorization applications (MAA) that is applicable to several countries. As a result, it is critical to understand the MAA legislation requirements in each country [1]. The essential regulation is depicted in FIGURE 1. A new drug application (NDA) is a request to the appropriate regulatory authority seeking permission to commercialise a new drug. To obtain this permission, a sponsor must provide preclinical and clinical test data, as well as a description of manufacturing practises..

Different Phases of clinical trials:

1. Pre-clinical study - Mice, Rat, Rabbit, Monkeys, Guinea Pigs
2. Phase I - Human pharmacology trial - estimation of safety and tolerability
3. Phase II - Exploratory trial - estimation of effectiveness and short term side effects
4. Phase III - Confirmatory trial - Confirmation of therapeutic benefits
5. Phase IV - Post marketing trial - Studies done after drug approval[2,3,4].

After NDA received by the agency, it undergoes a technical screening. This evaluation ensures that sufficient data and information have been submitted in each area to justify "filing" the application.

At the conclusion of the review of an NDA, there are 3 possible actions that can send to sponsor:

Not acceptable- describe the deficiencies and explain why in this letter.

Approvable - indicates that the drug can be approved with minor flaws that can be addressed, such as labelling revisions and a commitment to do post-approval research.

It states that the medicine has been approved.

If the action taken is either acceptable or unacceptable, the regulatory body allows the applicant to meet with the agency and explain the problems.[5,6].

1.9.2 Drug Approval Process in United States

In 1820, the United States Pharmacopoeia was established, ushering in a new age of drug control in the United States. The first Food and Drug Act was passed in 1906, mandating drugs to fulfil official strength and purity standards [7].

The Federal Food, Drug, and Cosmetic Act (of 1938) was enacted in response to the Sulphanilamide disaster in 1937, which featured new laws requiring new pharmaceuticals to be proved to be safe before being marketed. In addition, the Kefauver-Harris Amendment Act of 1962 mandated that drug manufacturers verify that their product is safe and effective (for the claims made on the label) [8,9].

The United States has some of the world's harshest drug approval regulations. Drug approval criteria in the United States are typically regarded as the strictest in the world. The Food and Drug Administration (FDA) is in responsibility of protecting and promoting public health. Clinical trials (CT) and new drug application (NDA) approval are the two processes in the FDA's new medication approval process, which is comparable to the general drug approval method. The FDA's approval procedure begins only once an investigational new drug (IND) application is submitted.

(a) Investigational New Drug (IND) Application

It's a request to the FDA to commence human clinical trials once the medicine's safety has been established in preclinical studies. To support the drug's human trial, the IND application should include high-quality preclinical data. Around 85 percent of drugs for which IND applications are filed undergo clinical testing. A Sponsor is a firm or organization that submits an IND application.

A pre - IND meeting can be arranged with the FDA to discuss a number of issues:

- The design of animal research, which is required to lend support to the clinical studies
- The intended protocol for conducting the clinical trial
- The chemistry, manufacturing, and control of the investigational drug.

A conference like this will help the Sponsor organise animal studies, collect data, and establish a clinical protocol that follows FDA guidelines. The next step is to undertake phase I clinical studies on 100 human volunteers (1-3 years). This phase focuses on the drug's safety profile and pharmacokinetics. If phase I investigations are successful, the medicine will proceed to phase II research, which will take two years. Phase II is primarily concerned with dosage, broad efficacy, and individual safety (300). If phase II trials show a benefit, phase III trials (3-4 years) will begin. These phase III trials examine the medicine's safety and effectiveness in groups of a few hundred to 3,000 people, using data from a variety of populations, doses, and drug combinations.

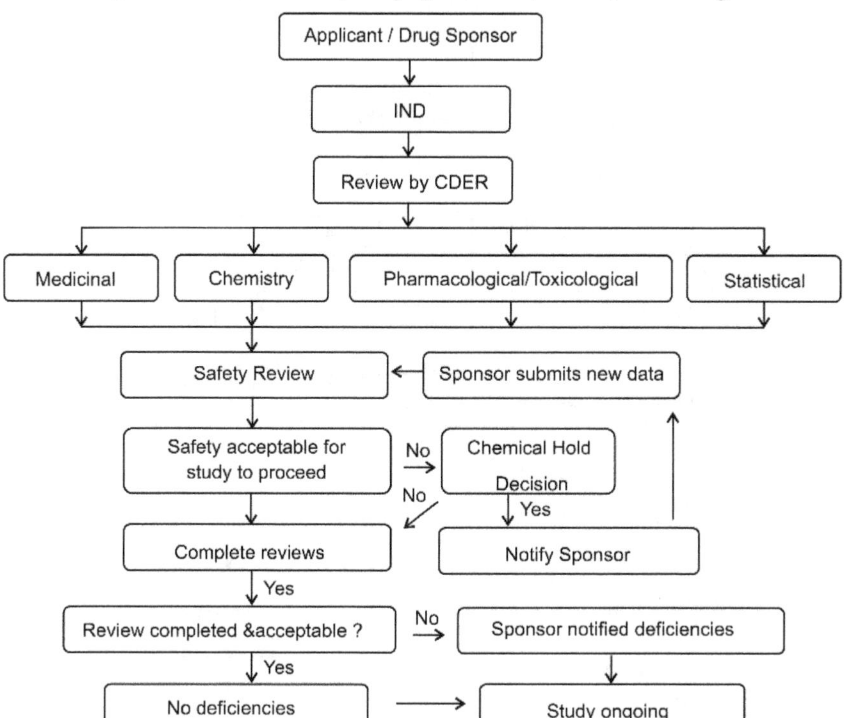

Investigational New Drug Application (IND)

Figure 1 IND Submission.

(b) New Drug Application (NDA) and Abbreviated New Drug Application (ANDA)

(a) New drug application (NDA)

A new drug application (NDA) is only issued if a medication has passed all three rounds of clinical trials and includes all animal and human data, data analysis, drug pharmacokinetics and manufacturing, as well as suggested labelling. A team of scientists at the Centre for Drug Evaluation and Research reviews all preclinical, clinical studies, and risk-benefit analyses (the product's benefits outweigh its potential problems). If clinical trials show that a new treatment is relatively safe and effective, with no notable

NDA Chart

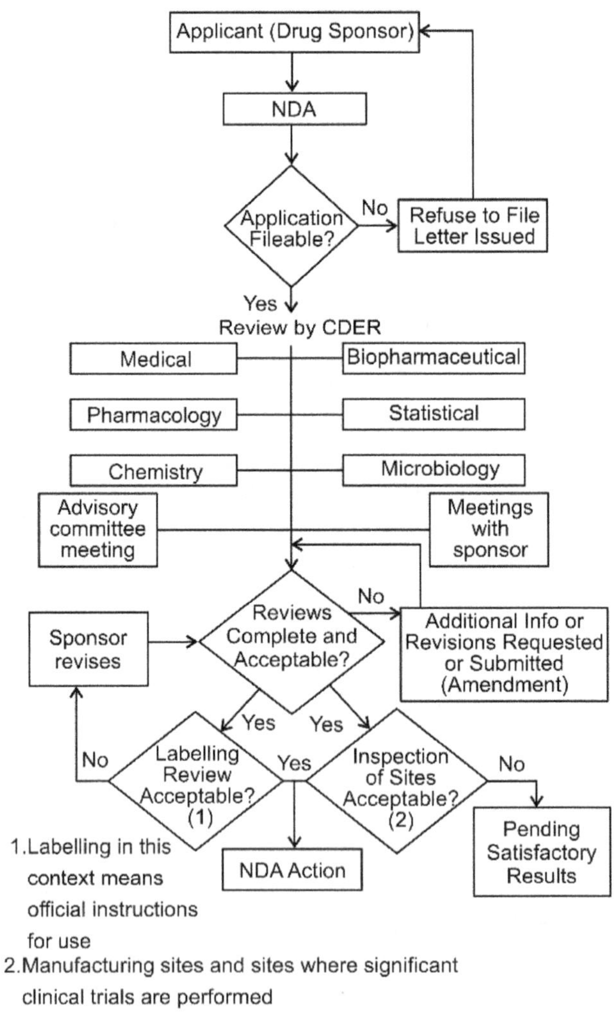

Figure 2 NDA chart.

side effects, the manufacturer submits a New Drug Application (NDA), which is the formal request to manufacture and market the drug in the United States [9,10]. An NDA takes an average of two years to be approved, although it can take anywhere from two months to several years. After receiving NDA approval, the innovative company can commercialise the drug, which is currently in Phase IV testing. This phase investigates new locations, aims, or demographics, as well as long-term effects and how participants react to various dosages. The drug approval procedure in the United States is depicted in FIGURE 2.

(b) Abbreviated New Drug Application (ANDA)

An abbreviated new drug application (ANDA) is a document that comprises information that is submitted to the FDA in order to examine and approve a generic drug product. Once approved, a generic drug product can be manufactured and marketed as a safe, effective, and less expensive alternative to the brand-name drug it replaces. In terms of dose form, strength, method of administration, quality, performance qualities, and intended application, a generic drug product is comparable to an innovator drug product.

The FDA's Authorized Drug Medications with Therapeutic Equivalence Evaluations list all approved pharmaceuticals, including innovator and generics (Orange Book). Because preclinical (animal) and clinical (human) evidence are not required to demonstrate safety and effectiveness, generic medication applications are referred to as "abbreviated." Instead, generic applicants must show that their treatment works in the same way as the original drug through scientific data. The time it takes for a generic drug to reach the bloodstream in healthy volunteers is one way applicants establish that it works in the same way as the innovator drug.

This "bioequivalence" demonstration offers the generic medication's rate of absorption, or bioavailability, which may then be compared to the innovator drug. The generic version must deliver the same amount of active chemicals into a patient's bloodstream in the same period of time as the innovator medicine in order to be approved by the FDA.

The Hatch-Waxman Amendments, sometimes known as the "Drug Price Competition and Patent Term Restoration Act of 1984," established bioequivalence as the cornerstone for authorising generic copies of drug commodities. These modifications enable the FDA to approve generic versions of brand-name pharmaceuticals without the necessity for costly and time-consuming clinical trials to show safety and efficacy. Brand-name firms gained patent term extensions as a result of the Hatch-Waxman Amendments to account for the time the patented product is under FDA evaluation, as well as specific periods of marketing exclusivity. Before selling their products, generic medication businesses now have the ability to challenge patents in court, as well as 180 days of generic drug exclusivity.

Resources for ANDA Submissions

The following resources provide ANDA applicants with the statutory and regulatory requirements of an ANDA application, assistance from CDER to help you meet those requirements, and internal ANDA review principles, policies, and procedures. Summary tables, application forms, and other ANDA submission resources are available in ANDA Forms & Submission Requirements.

Guidance Documents for ANDAs

The Agency's current view on a topic is represented through guidance documents. These publications provide FDA review staff, applicants, and ANDA holders with guidelines for the content, evaluation, and final approval of applications, as well as the design, production, manufacturing, and testing of regulated products.

- Generic Drugs Guidances (Search "Generics" under topics)
- Biopharmaceutics Guidances (Search "Bio-pharmaceutics" under topics)
- Product-Specific Guidances for Generic Drug Development

Laws, Regulations, Policies, and Procedures

The Federal Food, Drug, and Cosmetic Act is the basic food and drug law of the United States. The law is intended to assure consumers that foods are pure and wholesome, safe to eat, and produced under sanitary conditions; that drugs and devices are safe and effective for their intended uses; that cosmetics are safe and made from appropriate ingredients; and that all labeling and packaging is truthful, informative, and not deceptive.

Code of Federal Regulations

The final regulations published in the Federal Register (a daily published record of proposed rules, final rules, meeting notices, etc.) are collected in the Code of Federal Regulations (CFR). Section 21 of the CFR contains most of the regulations pertaining to food and drugs. The regulations document most actions of all drug applicants that are required under Federal law. The following regulations directly apply to the ANDA process:

- 21CFR Part 314: Applications for FDA Approval to Market a New Drug
- 21CFR Part 320: Bioavailability and Bioequivalence Requirements

Manual of Policies and Procedures

CDER's Manual of Policies and Procedures (MAPPs) document internal practices and procedures followed by CDER staff to help standardize the drug review process and other activities, both internal and external. Chapter 5200 covers generic drugs processes and activities.

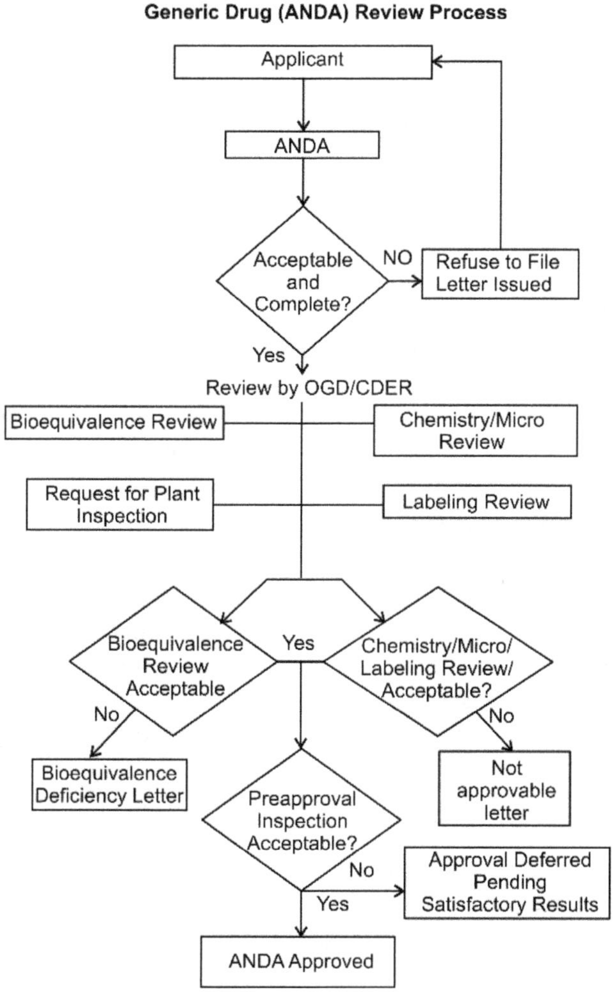

Figure 3 ANDA Review Process

1.9.3 Drug Approval Process in Europe

In the European Union, medical items were originally licenced for marketing at the national level (EU). The mutual restructuring technique was created in 1938 to enable for a single national examination for pharmaceutical and medical items seeking approval for commercialization in EU members. The fundamental purpose of the strategy was to create a uniform standard for product evaluation across all national regulatory authorities.

In 1987, Directive 87/22 established the concentration method for high-tech or biologically derived pharmaceuticals, in which the Committee for Proprietary Medicinal Products (CPMP) assesses the product in addition to the usual national regulatory review. The EU's CPMP examined and granted EU-wide marketing clearance to all high-tech and biologically derived items in 1993, under Council Regulation (EEC) 2309/93.

The two stages of the European medicine approval process are clinical research and marketing authorization. A clinical trial application (CTA) is submitted to the state's relevant authorities to conduct a clinical trial within the EU. The appropriate authorities in that member state assess the application. Clinical research can only commence if authorization has been given. Clinical trials follow the same objectives and phases as the FDA's medication approval process. Figure 2 depicts the European Union's clinical trial authorization process.

When all three phases of a clinical trial are finished, a marketing authorization application (MAA) is submitted, which includes all animal and human data, analysis, pharmacokinetics, manufacturing, and suggested labelling. In EU countries, the company may opt for one of the following regulatory procedures:

(a) Centralized Procedure

EMEA applications are evaluated by the Committee for Human Medicinal Products (CHMP). The CHMP shall offer its opinion to the EU Commission within 210 days of the end of the evaluation [11]. If CHMP gives a favourable ruling, the EU Commission will seek input from other member states. The remaining members have around 28 days to respond. When a licence is approved, a European Public Assessment Report (EPAR) and a marketing authorization are generated. Within the European Union, this authorisation is valid for five years; however, the EMEA can request an extension three months before the time limit expires. The centralised marketing authorisation method is depicted in FIGURE 4.

Centralized process is compulsory for:

Medications derived from biotechnology processes like genetic engineering.

Those drugs that are used to treat cancer, HIV/AIDS, diabetes, neurological illnesses, autoimmune diseases, and other immune disorders [12].

Orphan drugs are medicines that have been formally designated as such (medicines used for rare diseases).

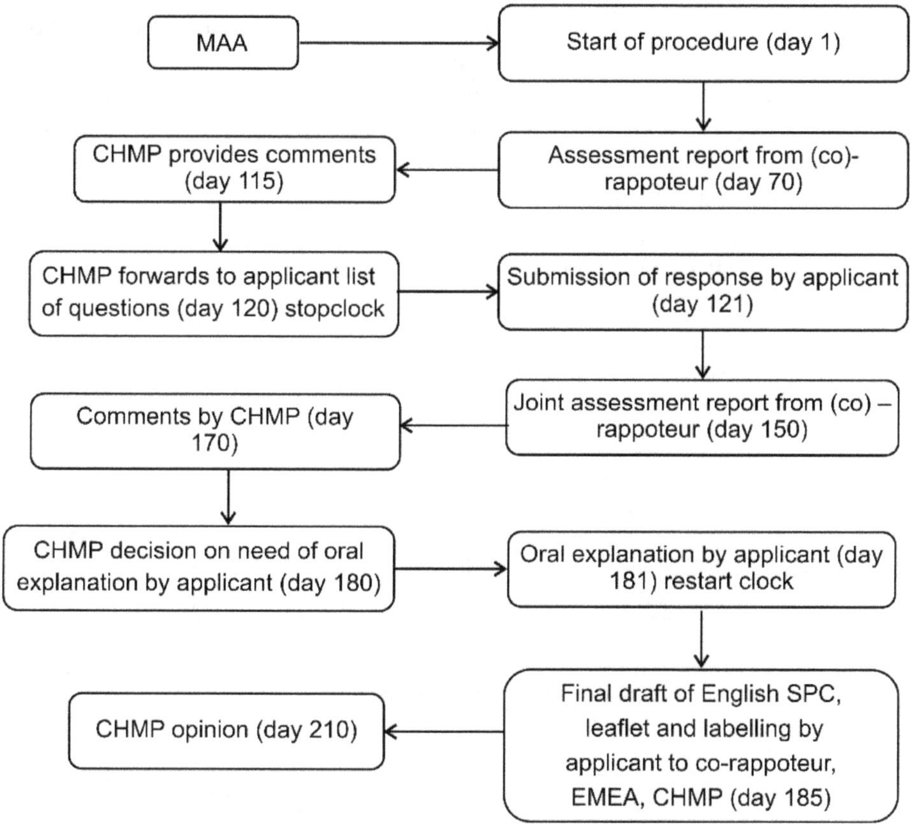

Figure 4 Centralized procedure for marketing authorization in EU

(b) Decentralized Procedure

Many member states do not require marketing authorizations to be obtained in a centralized manner; in this case, the decentralized procedure should be employed. When a marketing authorization is required, an application is sent to each of the member states' competent agencies.

A list of all Concerned Member States (CMSs) and one member state to act as Reference Member State, as well as quality, efficacy, safety, and administrative data, must be submitted (RMS).

A preliminary evaluation report on the medical product is generated in 14 days, and both the CMSs and the RMS accept the application. The

RMS will draught a summary of product features, labelling, and a package brochure within 120 days.

This report can be approved within 90 days. CMS(s) will notify other CMS, RMS, and the applicant if a medicinal product is suspected of posing a major danger to public health, and a decision will be made within 30 days. Within 60 days of being advised of the areas of contention, all member states agree on a course of action [13, 14]. After the involved states reach an agreement, the RMS records it and notifies the applicant. If the member states cannot agree, the CHMP takes over and makes a final decision based on the applicant's written or oral arguments. FIGURE 5 depicts the EU's decentralised marketing authorization mechanism.

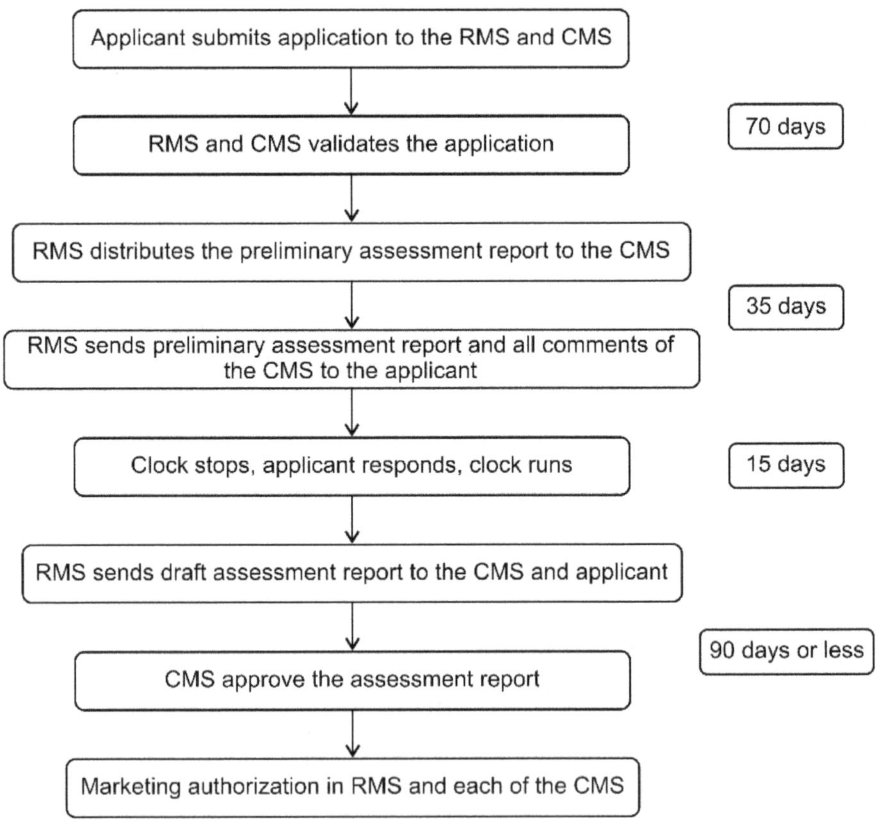

Figure 5 Decentralized procedure for marketing authorization in EU.

(c) Nationalized Procedure

The Nationalized procedure is one which allows applicants to obtain a marketing authorization in one-member state only.

An application must be submitted to the appropriate authority of the Member State in order to receive a national marketing authorisation.

This approach can be used to get marketing permission for new active chemicals that are not required under the Centralized procedure.

This treatment will take 210 days.

(d) Mutual Recognition Procedure

The Mutual Recognition procedure allows applicants to obtain a marketing authorization in the concerned member states (CMS) other than the Reference member state (RMS), where the drug is previously approved [15].

Applicant sends a single dossier with all relevant information to all EU member states where marketing permission is sought.

When one Member State agrees to review a medical product (and thus becomes the "RMS"), it notifies other Member States (and thus becomes the "CMS"), to whom applications have also been submitted.

RMS sends out a report to other states detailing its findings.

This form of medicine approval procedure is most commonly used by the generic industry.

This procedure could take up to 390 days to complete.

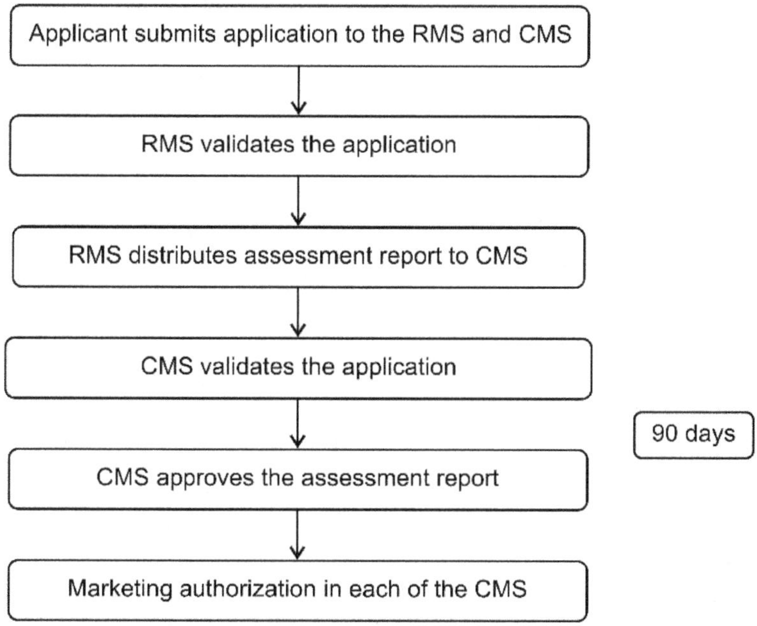

Figure 6 Mutual recognition procedure for drug approval process in EU

1.9.4 Drug Approval Process in India

The Drug and Cosmetic Act 1940 and Rules 1945 were passed by India's parliament to regulate the import, manufacture, distribution, and sale of pharmaceuticals and cosmetics. The Central Drugs Standard Control Organization is overseen by the Drugs Controller General (India) [DCGI] (CDSCO). The Indian government added Schedule Y to the Drug and Cosmetics Rules 1945 in 1988. The criteria and circumstances for clinical investigations are contained in Schedule Y, which was updated in 2005 to align with worldwide norms [16]. Under Schedule Y of the Drugs and Cosmetics Act 1940 and Rules 1945, a company in India that wants to produce or import a new drug must fill out Form 44 and submit the appropriate information to the licencing agency (DCGI). To establish efficacy and safety in the Indian population, it must perform clinical trials in compliance with Schedule Y's standards and submit the results in the format specified.

Under Rule 122A of the Drug and Cosmetics Act, clinical investigations for new medications that have been licenced and used for several years in other countries may be waived.

All phases of clinical trials are required for therapeutic compounds identified in India, according to Schedule Y of the Drugs and Cosmetics Act 1940 and Rules 1945.

For drug substances discovered in countries other than India, according to Section 2.4 (b) of Schedule Y of the Drugs and Cosmetics Act 1940 and Rules 1945, the applicant must submit data from those countries, and the licencing authority may require the applicant to repeat all studies or allow him to proceed to Phase III clinical trials [17].

The Central Drugs Standard Control Organization needs an application to show the drug's safety and efficacy in people before it can be licenced for import or production (CDSCO). The Drugs and Cosmetics Act 1940 and its rules 1945, 122A, 122B, and 122D, as well as Appendix I, IA, and VI of Schedule Y [18], specify the information required for approval of an application to import or develop a novel drug for commercialization.

The Drugs and Cosmetics Act currently covers Phase I-IV trial definitions, as well as investigator and sponsor responsibilities. Clinical studies were further divided into two groups in 2006. Clinical trials can be conducted in other markets with competent and mature regulatory systems (category A), but they are classified separately for the others (type B). Clinical studies in category A are eligible for accelerated clearance in India, with approval expected in eight weeks. Clinical trials in category B are scrutinised more closely and approved in 16 to 18 weeks [19].

DCGI requires an application as well as paperwork on chemistry, production, control, and animal research in order to conduct clinical trials in India. Include the start date of the study protocol, as well as researcher brochures and informed consent forms. Clinical trials are only carried out once DCGI and the ethical committee have given their approval.

Healthy human volunteers are used in Phase I clinical research to determine the maximum permissible dose, as well as adverse effects and other criteria. To investigate therapeutic applications and effective dose ranges, phase II trials with 10-12 patients at each dose level are conducted. Confirmatory studies (Phase III) collect data on the drug's efficacy and safety in around 100 patients (at three to four locations) to verify efficacy and safety claims. Phase III studies should be conducted on a minimum of 500 patients spread across 10-15 centres if the novel medication ingredient is not currently marketed in another country.

A new drug registration (using form # 44 and complete pre-clinical and clinical testing information) is submitted after clinical trials are completed. Aside from safety and efficacy proof, detailed information on the drug's marketing status in other countries is also required. The product monograph, labels, and cartons, as well as the prescription, samples, and testing processes, must all be provided.

The evaluation of the application can take anywhere from 12 to 18 months. India's new drug clearance process is depicted in Figure 5. After gaining an NDA approval, a company is allowed to advertise and sell a product in Phase IV research, which looks into new uses, populations, long-term effects, and other aspects.

The International Conference on Harmonization (ICH) procedure was used to establish the Common Technical Document (CTD) guidance for Japan, the European Union, and the United States.

The great majority of countries have adopted the CTD format. As a result, CDSCO has adopted the CTD format for technical requirements for the registration of pharmaceutical products for human consumption.

(a) Stages of approval [20, 21, 22]:

1. Submission of Clinical Trial application for evaluating safety and efficacy.
2. Requirements for permission of new drugs approval.
3. Post approval changes in biological products: quality, safety and efficacy documents.
4. Preparation of the quality information for drug submission for new drug approval.

Pharmaceutical approval procedures differ from country to country. Only one organisation supervises drugs in some nations, such as the United States, and is responsible for all regulatory operations such as new drug approval, manufacturing licences, and facility inspections. In some nations, these functions are not performed by a single regulatory entity; for example, in India, this responsibility is divided between central and state authorities. Some countries, such as the United States and China, have both traditional and accelerated review processes, whilst others, such as India, only have one. Similarly, there are many formats for delivering a dossier for pharmacological approval. In certain countries, such as the United States, the European Union, and Japan, compiling the dossier in CTD format is obligatory; however, in others, such as India, it is optional.

Table 1 Principe difference between US, EU and INDIA.

REQUIREMENTS	US	EU	INDIA
Agency	One agency USFDA	Multiple agencies • EMEA • CHMP • National health agencies	One agency DCGI
Registration process	One registration process	Multiple registration process • Centralized (European community) • Decentralized (at least 2 member states) • Mutual recognition (at least 2 member states) • National (1 member state)	One registration process
TSE/BSE study data	Not required	Required	Required
Braille code	Braille code is not required on labeling	Braille code is required on labeling	Braille code is not required on labeling
Post approval changes	Post approval changes in the approved drug: • Minor • Moderate • Major	Post variation in the approved drug: • Type IA • Type IB • Type II	Post approval changes: • Major • Moderate

Table *Contd...*

REQUIREMENTS	US	EUROPE	INDIA
Application	ANDA/NDA	MAA	MAA
Debarment classification	Required	Not required	Not required
Number of copies	3	1	1
Approval timeline	18 months	12 months	2 - 18 months
Fees	Under $2 million – NDA application $1,520 – ANDA application	National fee (including hybrid applications): £103,059 Decentralized procedure where UK is CMS: £99,507	50,000 INR
Presentation	e CT D and paper	e CTD	Paper

Table 2 Manufacturing and control

REQUIREMENTS	US	EUROPE	INDIA
Number of batches	1	3	1
Packaging	A minimum of 1,00,0000	Not required	Not addressed
Process validation	Not required at the time of Submission	Required	Required
Batch size	1 pilot scale or minimum of 1 lakh units whichever is higher	2 pilot scale plus 1 lab batch or minimum of 1 lakh units whichever is higher	Pilot scale batch

1.9.5 Discussion

A request for a clinical trial and a request for marketing permission from the regulatory body are the two steps in the drug approval process. Some aspects of the new drug approval process are universal, while others are country-specific. In most counties, the sponsor makes an application to conduct a clinical trial first, and the applicant conducts clinical research only after the regulatory authority authorises the application before submitting an application to the regulatory authority for pharmaceutical marketing authorization.

The quality, safety, and efficacy information presented to regulatory agencies is the same in all countries; however, the time, fee, and review procedure for clinical trials and marketing licence applications differ. By offering suggestions for the consistent interpretation and execution of technical standards and regulations, the International Conference on Harmonization (ICH) has achieved tremendous progress in harmonization. The International Conference on Harmonization (ICH) procedure was used to establish the Common Technical Document (CTD) guidance for Japan, the European Union, and the United States. As a result, India has decided to follow suit. In the long run, this step will remove the need for duplication of effort in novel treatment research and development.

As a result, whether through ICH or WHO, global harmonization of medicine approval processes may be attempted. In the United States and India, the **USFDA** and **CDSCO** are the only regulatory agencies, respectively, but Europe has three regulatory bodies: **EMEA, CHMP**, and the **NATIONAL HEALTH AGENCY**. In comparison to the US and India, Europe has a large number of regulatory procedures. All countries have similar approval times, ranging from 12 to 18 months. The fee for new pharmaceutical approval in the United States is astronomically high when compared to EUROPE and INDIA.

1.9.6 Conclusion

The United States, Europe, and India have some of the most restrictive drug clearance processes in the world. The primary goal of pharmaceutical product regulations in the United States, Europe, and India is to protect public health. Government regulatory organizations require pharmaceutical companies to obey the rules. To ensure patient safety and well-being, drugs must be produced, tested, tracked, and manufactured in accordance with industry standards.

References

1. Rick NG., *Drugs from discovery to approval.* John Wiley & Sons, New Jersey,2015
2. Kuhlmann J., *Int. J. Clin. Pharmacol. Ther,* 1999, 37(12),575-83.
3. *The drug development and approval process.* Available at: www.mhsource.com/resource/process.html. Accessed on SEP 03, 2011.
4. Bhatt A., *Indian J. Pharmacol.* 2004, 36(4), 207-08.
5. *CDER Guidance: A review for OCRA US RAC Study,* www.fda.gov/cder/regulatory/applications/ind_page_1. html. Accessed on AUG 25,2011.
6. Clinical trial registration: a statement from the International Committee of Medical Journal Editors. *Med. J. Aust,* 181, 2004, 293- 94.
7. Significant Dates in U.S. Food and Drug Law History,www.fda.gov/AboutFDA/WhatWeDo/History/Milestones/ucm1 2830 5.html. Assessed on March 09,2010.
8. Lipsky M.S., and Sharp L.K., *J Am Board Fam Pract,* 2001; 14:362-367.

9. Jawahar.N, Prashob Nair, A.Ramachandran ., *Pharma Times,* 2015, vol.47(1),35-39
10. 10Title 21, Food and Drugs: Chapter I--Food and Drug: PART 312--Investigational N Drug Application www.access.gpo.gov/nara/cfr/waisidx_03/21cfr312_03.html, Assessed on March 09,2010.
11. Jawahar. N., Nishit Shrivastava., Ramachandran., Baviya Priyadharshini.R., *J. Pharm. Sci. & Res.* 2015, 7(4),219-225.
12. U. Nitin Kashyap., Vishal Gupta., H. V. Raghunandan., *J. Pharm. Sci. & Res,* 2013, 5(6), 131 -136
13. European Commission: The Notice to Applicants; Volume 2A; Procedures for marketing authorisation, http://ec.europa.eu/health/files/eudralex/vol-2/a/vol2a_chap1_2005- 11_en... Assessed on May 21,2010.
14. Ghalamkarpour A., Marketing Authorization Procedures in the European Union – Making the Right Choice, www.lsnewscr.sgs.com/lsnewscr/lsnewscr-december- issue/marketing-a... Assessed on May 11,2010.
15. Rick NG., Drugs from discovery to approval. Wiley & Sons, New Jersey,2008.
16. www.clinpage.com/article/indias_regulation_timeline/C9. Assessed on February 24,2010).
17. N. Vishal Gupta., C. Mohan Reddy., K. Pradeep Reddy., R. Ajay Kulkarni., H.G. Shivakumar., *International Journal of Pharmaceutical Sciences Review and Research*, 2012;13(2).
18. Honorio S. *Phases of drug development; Good practices in clinical research*. www.hstelearning.mit.edu. Accessed on AUG 26,2011
19. http://infochangeindia.org/200909177947/Health/Analysis/Trial-by-fire.html. Assessed on February 24,2010.
20. Ravinder RB., Suresh N., *Regulatory stages for New Drug approvals*, www.observerindia.com/cms/export/orfonline/modules/occasionalpaper/attachments/Drug_Discovery_Book_1 260179432814.pdf. Accessed on AUG 28,2011.
21. Lachman L, Liberman HA, Kanig JL, *The Theory and Practice of Industrial Pharmacy,* Varghese Publishing House,1987.
22. The drug development and approval process. Available at: www.mhsource.com/resource/process.html. Accessed on SEP 03, 2011.

CHAPTER 1.10

SUPAC

1.10.1 What is SUPAC?

Definition: The scale-up process and the changes made after approval in the composition, manufacturing process, manufacturing equipment, and change of site have become known as Scale-Up and Post-approval Changes, or SUPAC

SUPAC Scale up and post approval changes (changes made after approval) such as drug manufacturing, quantity size, process, equipment, production area.

In the process of developing a new product, the quantity used in early human studies was small.

When the volume sizes are gradually increasing (measurement).

Then the measurements and changes made after approval in the compounding process, equipment production and site modification are known as Scale Up and Post Approval Changes (SUPAC).

1.10.2 SUPAC

FDA has issued various changes to specified guidelines

supac-IR (immediate release solid size format.

Supac-MR (for the modified release solid dosage form).

Supac-SS (for sterile semi-solid dosage forms, including creams, ointments, gels, and lotions)

1.10.3 SUPAC Guidelines [figure 1]

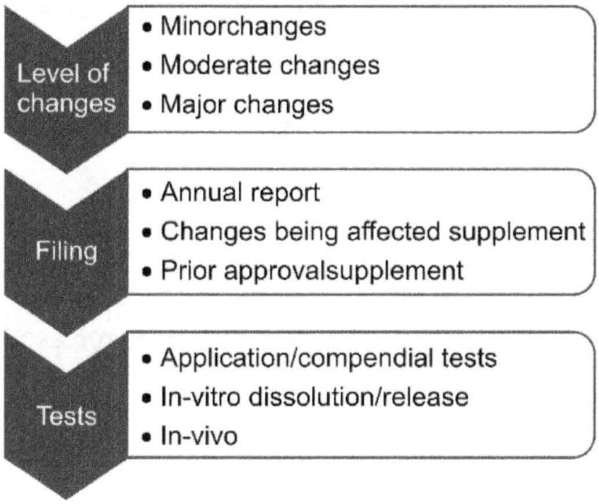

1.10.4 Level of Changes

Potential for impact on build quality and performance

Level 1: Changes that are unlikely to have an impact on product quality and performance. For example, change in color, taste and change in performance is expressed as a percentage (w/w) of total formation less than or equal to the lower limit.

Level 2: Changes can have a significant impact on build quality and performance

Example: Change in expected technical grade (Avicel PH102 vs Avicel PH200) Changes are expressed as a percentage (w/w of total manufacturing) Level 2 change

Level 3: Level 3 changes can have a significant impact on product quality and performance.

Examples of any qualitative or quantitative stimulus change in a short-acting drug after Phase 1 All other drugs that do not meet discontinuation criteria such as Level 2.

1.10.5 SUPAC IR

These guidelines provide a recommendation for post-approval changes.

Part or composition

Workplace

Production volume, and production (process and equipment)

1.10.6 Changes in Components and Composition

Note changes in the number of exhibitors in drug formulation

Do not focus on changing the dosage of the component of the drug.

1.10.7 Changes to Level 1

Test document

Chemical document

Compatibility testing of application/package release requirements (a module is perennial)

Dissolution document

Nothing beyond package requirements

None of vivo bio balance document

Filling out documents

Annual report

1.10.8 Level 2 Changes

Test document.

Chemical document.

Level 1+1 Block 3 Months Accelerated Sustainability Study.

Dissolution document.

Class A - High permeability, high solubility.

Class B - low penetration, high solubility.

Class C - highly permeable, low solubility drug in vivo.

Life balance document - None.

Documentation-Level 1 + Quick Consistency Analysis.

1.10.9 Level 3 Changes

Test document

Chemical Documents - Level 1 + 1 Month Quick Stability 1 vol (SBOIA) or 3 vol (SBOINA)

Documents for Dissolution - Case B

In vivo bio-equilibrium-complete bio-equilibrium study.

Except for verified IVIVC.

Filing of Documents - Supplementary, Annual Report for Annual Approval.

1.10.10 Site Change

This includes changes in the site location of production facilities for both proprietary companies and contract manufacturers.

It does not involve scaling.

(a) level 1 change

Site changes within the same facility with the same equipment, SOPs, environmental conditions and standard staff.

Test documentation, chemistry, dissolution are package based and do not require *in vivo* BE.

Filing of annual report.

(b) level 2 change

Site transitions between facilities within adjacent premises or within adjacent city blocks.

Test Documents - Level 1 + a set of long-term stability in Chemistry Documents

Document-Annual Report Filed

(c) level 3 Transition

Moving the site to another premises

Test document

Chemical document

Volume One Module for Quick Stability (3 Months) + One Module for Long Term Stability for SBOIA

3 Modules for Acceleration and Long-Term Stability (SBOINA)

Disruption Analysis - Case B

BE is not required

Document-Annual Report Filed

1.10.11 Change Package Size

Change from core/pilot size bio-patch material to larger or smaller production after package approval.

Reducing dosage units to less than 100,000 does not fall under this guideline.

The measure of changes should be properly checked and, if necessary, reviewed by appropriate agency staff.

(a) level 1 change

Volume size varies, involving a factor of 10 times the pilot/biopatch size

The principle of uniform design and equipment

both manufacturers. As per cGMP compliance.

Same SOP is followed

Level 2 of the site conversion requirement is both document checking and filing.

(b) level 2 transition

Volume size 10. varies by more than a factor of

test document

As per Level 1 + Three Months Quick Stability Volume + Case B Dissolution Analysis.

1.10.12 Production Changes

A. TOOL

(a) Level 1 Change

Switch parts to move from non-automatic to automatic or vice versa

Switch to replacement equipment with similar or different capabilities with similar design and operating principle

Test document and volume resize according to file-level 1 22 SUPAC /

(b) Level 2 transition

Change the device to a different design

Check Documents Checking and Filing

As per level 3 of the site, except for the dissolution of Case C instead of Case P.

B. PROCESS CHANGE

(a) Level 1 Transformation

Changes This change includes process changes such as mixing time and running speed within the application/verification range.

Testing and filing of documents as per Phase 1 of Site Change.

(b) Level 2 transition

This change includes process changes such as mixing time and running speed.

Purpose of Application / Verification

Level 2 as per level review and document filing changes for site change.

(c) Level 3 transition

Changes in the type of process used in the preparation of products, such as a change from a wet grain to a direct compression of a dry powder.

Documentation - Change of parts and structure according to Level 3.

1.10.13 SUPAC-MR

Components and Compound-Production Non-restrictive Accessory

Focused on changes in non-publication control experiences.

Changes in components or compounds resulting from the addition of a new additive or the removal of an additive are defined in Level 3.

(a) Level 1 change

Test document

Chemical document

Application/package required for product release

Sustainability: Product First Volume-Data Long Term Sustainability Resolution Documentation: none

Life Balance Document: None

Filing of documents

Annual Report - All information including long-term sustainability data.

(b) Level 2 change

Test document

A. Chemical Application Documentation / Compiled Product Release Requirements and Updated Batch Records Implemented. Sustainability: a module with three months of accelerated sustainability data reported in the initial sub-approval and long-term sustainability data. The first production moduleannual report.

B. Dissolution Document

Sustainable production

pH 4.5 and 6.8. Multipoint Resolution Profile on 0.1N HCl and USP Buffered Media

Modified pharmaceutical products and bio-modules or modules sold (unmodified pharmaceutical products).

Survival Balance Documents: None

Filing of documents

Supplement to Initial Approval (Accelerated Sustainability Data) Annual Report (Long Term Sustainability)

(c) Level 3 Change

Test document

Chemical Documentation: Applied Application/Package Product Release Requirements and Update Volume Records.

Stability:

Notable Information Available: A set of three months of accelerated sustainability data with initial sub-approval and long-term sustainability data for the first three production groups reported in the annual report.

Life Balance Documents:

A dose of biological balance study. Bioequilibrium studies may be rejected in the presence of in vitro/in vivo contacts.

Document Filing: Similar to Level 2 changes.

1.10.14 Site Changes

This includes changes to laboratory analysis testing for both the workplace, packaging operations and/or owned companies and contract production facilities.

It does not include any multiplication changes, production changes (including process and/or equipment) or changes to components or composition.

Production New production sites must have satisfactory cGMP inspections.

A separate packaging change may be submitted in addition to changes affecting site work and laboratory changes.

1.10.15 Modifications of Working Tools

Production modifications may include equipment used in the manufacturing process.

(important production variable).

If the manufacturer intends to use a production equipment that is not identical in all aspects to the original production equipment used in the approved application, appropriate verification analysis should be carried out to show that the new equipment is identical to the original equipment.

(a) Level 1 change

1. switch from automatic or non-mechanical equipment to transfer parts to automatic or mechanical equipment
2. Switch to the same design and operating principles for alternative equipment with similar or different capabilities.

The test document and the filing document will be identical under the experience control without rectification.

(b) Level 2 transition

Change the equipment to different designs and different operating principles.

Document Testing and Document Filing

Release is a non-controlling accessory.

1.10.16 Change in Production Process

Changes include the production process.

Verification inspection should be carried out when there is a change in the process.

For classification purposes at the change level, it can be assumed that a change in function will affect the output control component when there are only two types of exhibitors (ie no output and no output control) during transition unit operation.

(a) Level 1 change

Test document

Chemical document.

None other than an application/package product release requirements.

Knowledge implemented information on replacement and submission of updated block records.

Other documents remain under uncontrolled control.

(b) Level 2 transition

This type includes process changes that involve adjustments to the operating conditions of the equipment, such as mixing times and operating speeds outside the originally accepted application limits.

Other documents will remain under control and will not be taken out of the exhibition.

(c) Level 3 transition

This section covers changes in the type of process used in the preparation of products, such as the change from wet granulation to direct compression of dry powder.

Other documents will be under control of non-exhibition.

References

1. https://www.pharmaguideline.com/2021/09/supac.html#:~:text=What%20is%20SUPAC%3F,%2C%20equipment%2C%20site%20of%20manufacturing.
2. https://www.slideshare.net/sonianagvenkar/supac

CHAPTER 1.11

Outsourcing BA & BE to CRO

1.11.1 Introduction

A WORKING DEFINITION OF OUT SOURCING

SERVICES

VENDOR ⟶ COMPANY

Service level and organization level agreement

Service level and organization level agreement

Outsourcing is the business practice of hiring a party outside a company to perform services and create goods that traditionally were performed in-house by the company's own employees and staff

1.11.2 What is Outsourcing?

Outsourcing is the process of hiring a party outside a company and creating products traditionally made at home by the company's own employees and employees.

Outsourcing was first recognized as a business strategy in 1989 and has become an integral part of the international business economy.

Outsourcing is usually done to reduce costs and improve efficient resources within an organization. hall. Outsourcing is the lifeblood of life, balance of life, R&D area.

1.11.3 Reasons to Outsource

The main reasons companies outsource are low mobility and labor costs. Properly covered, it will withstand considerable adverse conditions and can provide significant savings.

Companies prefer to outsource or go offshore so that they can continue to focus on their core business processes while providing contingency processes to outsourced companies.

Allows outsourcing and offshore companies to access world-class capabilities and access a global knowledge base.

Disclosure of internal resources that can be effectively used for other purposes is one of the major benefits that companies accrue when they outsource or live abroad.

Many world-class businesses that often run into internal resource crunch, outsource access to resources that are not available locally.

Outsourcing is often done to save costs and provide companies with internal capital funding, which can be used to maximize company profits.

By delegating responsibilities to outside companies, companies can realize their benefits and delegate tasks that are difficult to manage and control.

Outsourcing and especially offshore companies help in reducing the risk and this is one of the main reasons for launching.

Outsourcing helps the company to realize the benefits of re-engineering, modifying and upgrading the project to suit the needs of the customers.

Some help companies expand and gain access to new market segments by reaching the point of production or providing services to their end users.

1.11.4 Clinical Outsourcing and CRO Market Development

The outsourcing of sponsorships to vendors has increased from 43% to 45% from 2016-2017. According to Pero's analysis, this trend continues and is projected to increase by more than 50% in 2018. In another 2018 study by the Avoca Group of 128 recipients (small and large pharmaceutical/biotech equally distributed), 65% of R&D operations are now outsourced. This trend is projected to remain stable till 2021.

1.11.5 Functional Service Delivery

Functional Service Delivery (FSP) remains a major outsourcing model between sponsors and service providers. This includes vendors who provide full functional support groups to sponsors for specific services. The Avoca Group study in Figure 1 shows that large sponsors split their FSP outsourcing through full-service outsourcing by 48% and 52%, while smaller service providers enter 36% FSP and 64% full-service. Huh. It is expected that smaller providers will adopt the 50/50 model in the future. This opens up many opportunities for CROs, and more and more providers are positioning themselves as FSP specialists.

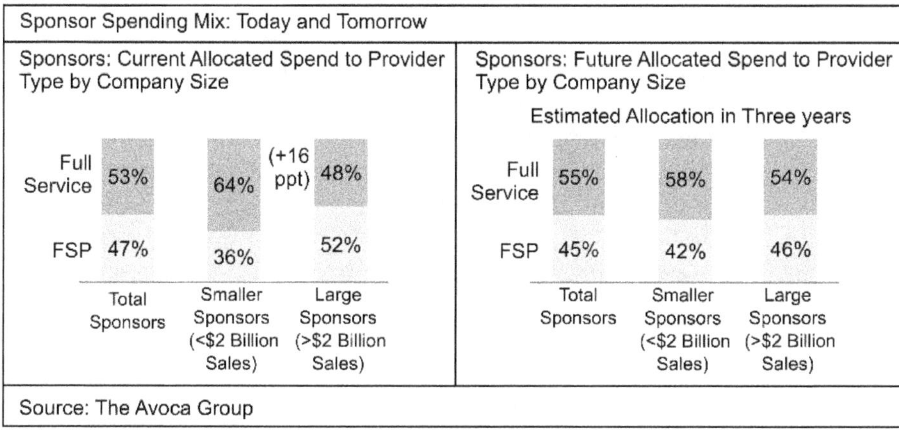

Figure 1

Building a long-term relationship with a CRO is becoming increasingly popular among many services. For CROs, this means a more profitable model and the potential for larger deals and re-businesses. For sponsors, this leads to greater efficiency as CROs focus on a modeling of the business model and medical data and other services.

Providers claim that the bulk of their revenue comes from FSPs compared to full-service provisions (2018: FSP, 57%; full-service, 43%). Furthermore, like sponsors, they expect the future model (2021: FSP, 53%; full service, 47%) to be sustainable in these relevant allocations through 2021.

1.11.6 Real Proof in the World

In 2019, the industry saw the Food and Drug Administration (FDA) approve the first drug (Pfizers Abraham), the trial of which was based largely on real-world data (RWD) [6]. The need for real-world evidence (RWE) is increasing due to the development of rare clinical studies and the emergence of technologies for obtaining data outside of clinical trials and clinical trials - our research Expect more RWD within the protocol in 2020.

RWDs collected through surveillance studies outside the traditional medical system have great potential for rare disease trials, where it is very difficult to enroll small patients and fund a full-scale randomized clinical trial.

1.11.7 e-buy

Appropriate collection of RWD is essential to facilitate its evaluation and to verify the effectiveness of the drug, and should be included in a clinical trial in the design phase. Medical records, electronic health records (EHRs) and post-accreditation reports are some of the sources of RWD. It is important that CROs and Pharmacies monitor the use of this data and be aware of the latest technologies for processing such data. Some examples include the medical tube that connects the EHR to an electronic data capture (EDC) system, and the RWD, e-source and all other EDC systems that are MED-enabled, focused on a single site for analysis.

Some of the most promising advances in e-source technology for future research are:

AI/ML-based sites support inclusion of subjects in clinical trials

Support for AI-based medicine and protocol compliance

Innovations in Electronic Clinical Outcome Assessment (e-CoA) technology to facilitate patient-centered approach to trial design and management

Functionality: Platform for improving performance among various electronic data capture systems such as EDC, EHR, M-Health, RWD sources.

Centralized Database: Intelligent technologies that integrate data from different streams to facilitate data analysis and understanding.

1.11.8 Bioavailability and Life Balance

Bioavailability: Measuring the amount and rate of drug availability from a given dosage form, reaching and acting in an appropriate cycle.

Bioavailability describes the concentration of a drug in the systemic blood relative to a given drug dose.

Bio equilibrium: This is a comparative term used to describe the substance of a drug in two or more homogeneous dosage forms, at the same relative rate and at the same relative level, i.e. in the appropriate cycle. Their plasma concentration timing descriptions are statistically identical without significant differences.

1.11.9 Outsource Standardized Services for BA-BE Courses Biological Analysis Studies

Bioanalysis Selection and Site Qualification

Clinical study design

Development of medical protocols

Medical site selection and eligibility

Medical practice

Medical surveillance

1.11.10 Common Services Outsourced for BA-BE Courses

Data management

Pharmacokinetic testing

Statistical analysis

writing a pharmacokinetic report

writing a joint ICH report

- Project Management

FDA/Regulatory Advice

1.11.11 Advantages [figure 2]

- Improved customer service
- Increase productivity andefficiency
- Better peoplemanagement
- Focus on corecompetencies
- Access to world classsolutions
- Skilledexpertise
- Cost savings

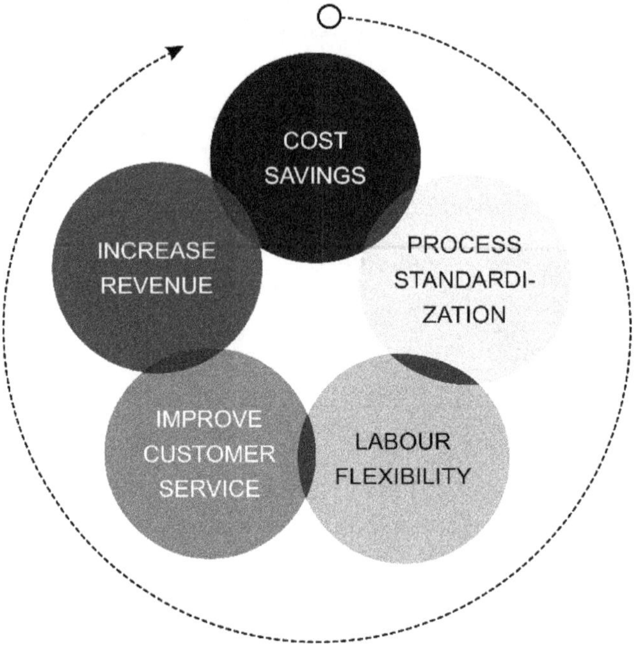

Figure 2

1.11.12 Key Elements for Success

- Liaison between the CRO and the pharmaceutical company at all levels.
- Sensitivity to both project-specific requirements and deadlines.
- Flexibility to detect and correct unforeseen incidents during the project period.

1.11.13 Consider Time/Cost

The two main concepts when a pharmaceutical company decides to outsource are time and cost.

Timing is of the essence when a specific manufacturer wants to file an ANDA with an Article IV patent certificate.

First normal filing (a paragraph IV) 6 months of exclusive rights (ie no ordinary competition).

1.11.14 Medical Site Qualification / Audit- Medical Site Assessment

- Evaluate the volunteer (or patient) population group.
- Review CRO procedures to check for adverse effects

- Review training records for the medical team
- Evaluate the ability of CRO to coordinate plasma/urine exchange in various bioanalytic facilities
- Evaluate ability to integrate operational manuals. For example, timely delivery of protocols to the clinic, samples
- Laboratory and biological analysis data.
- Evaluate medical project management skills.

1.11.15 CRO (Contract Research Organization)

Contract Research Organization (CRO) is an organization that provides support to the pharmaceutical, biotechnology and medical device industries in the form of outsourced research services.

It provides the various drug research needed to conduct clinical trials, including the ICH's technical requirements for registering pharmacists for human use.

(Contract Research Organization): A CRO is an organization that is contracted by another company to manage and guide companies' tests, roles and responsibilities.

This is done by companies and businesses that contract with CROs to obtain specific expertise without hiring permanent employees.

When a pharmaceutical company identifies a promising new molecule, CRO proceeds into an independent system development process.

Examples of CROs: Quintiles, Covance, Icon, Zydus

Cadilla and HMR

1.11.16 The Problem of Outsourcing

- Loss of administrative control
- Hidden costs
- Security and privacy
- Lack of understanding
- Language barrier
- Dependency on service provider
- Quality issues

1.11.17 Summary

The process of effective collaboration with the CRO is essential to defining precisely what the client organization (and CRO) can provide and expect, appointing a competent project team and developing a communication system that will help the company CRO and Works for both clients.

1.11.18 Tips for Safe Outsourcing

Find out what you are outsourcing.

Understand the risks and dependencies.

Access the risk management position of the outsourcer.

Ask about staff level training and background testing.

Make sure the data is properly protected.

References

1. Overby S, 2007 ABC; An introduction of out-sourcing.
2. Babu M,2005 Myth; All outsourcing is off shoring.
3. WWW.CIO.COM
4. Roothman j, 2003; Steps to successful outsourcing.

CHAPTER 1.12

Regulatory Requirements for Registration of API in US and EU

1.12.1 Introduction

Medical supplies, medicines, veterinary drugs, medical equipment and food items - all subject to regulations made by governments to protect public health. In order to produce a high quality, safe and effective pharmaceutical product, there are regulations every industry must follow. The Department of Regulatory Affairs is an integral part of the organizational structure of pharmaceutical companies. In the final stages of product development, regulatory experts will be responsible for submitting documents for registration, e.g. Marketing Authorization Application (MAA) in the European Union or New Drug Application (NDA) in the United States.

(a) Active Pharmaceutical Ingredients (APIs or Pharmaceutical Products)

When a drug is used in combination with a substance or substances used in the preparation of a dosage form, the drug becomes the active ingredient of the dosage form. The purpose of such substances is to provide pharmacological activity or other direct effect on diagnosis, cure, mitigation, treatment or prevention, or to affect the structure and function of the body.

(b) General job description of a regulatory specialist in API (Active Pharmaceuticals) manufacturing company [1-5]

Filing of DMF/ASMF with regulatory agencies in support of NDA/ANDA/INDA/MAA by Formulator (Pharmaceutical Manufacturer using API of specific API manufacturing company).

Filing of API document with EDQM for CEP recovery.

Analyze and submit changes / changes in DMF / ASMF / dossier (may be related to production, control, stability analysis, etc.) of specific APIs to regulatory agencies. Major changes should be reported prior to their implementation, while minor changes may be reported annually.

Obtain API customer approval before implementing major changes to the information specified in the DMF / ASMF / Dossier. The updated

DMF/ASMF may be submitted to the client along with the changes/variations filed with the agency.[6]

1.12.2 Regulatory Authority [7-10]

Regulatory bodies are responsible for identifying whether a drug can undergo clinical trials and whether it should be allowed in the market. The regulatory body must review scientific and medical data to ensure that the drug can be manufactured with consistently high purity, that it has a claimed clinical effect, and that there are no unacceptable side effects. It also has to approve the labeling of the drug and the instructions for its use. In general, once a drug is recognized as an effective drug, the regulatory system is interested in all aspects of it.

(a) USFDA (United States of Food and Drug Administration): The US Food and Drug Administration is a scientific, regulatory, and public health organization that oversees products priced at 25 cents per dollar. In 1862 the U.S. The company grew from a chemist in the agricultural sector to approximately 9,100 employees and in 2001 1. More many. About one-third of the agency's employees live in Washington, DC. There are over 150 regional offices and laboratories outside the region, including five regional offices and 20 district offices.

(b) FDA Organization: The FDA consists of four directorates that oversee the Commissioner's Office and the agency's core functions: Medical and Tobacco Products, Food Products, Global Regulatory Functions, and Policies and Actions.

It has the following centers/offices that review and approve the FDA-regulated products listed below:

1. ORA - Office of Regulatory Affairs CDER - Center for Drug Evaluation and Research
2. CBER- Center for Biological Analysis and Research
3. CDRH-Center for Devices and Radiation Health
4. Center for Tobacco Products
5. CVM- Center for Veterinary Medicine
6. CFSAN- Center for Food Safety and Applied Nutrition
7. NCTR- National Center for Toxicology Research
8. Office of the OFC-Commissioner
9. ORA-Office of Regulatory Affairs [11]

(c) European Pharmaceuticals Agency - EMEA

The European Medicines Evaluation Agency (EMEA) is a London-based decentralized organization of the European Union.

Its primary responsibility is to protect and improve the health of the public and animals through the testing and administration of drugs for human and veterinary use.

EMEA is responsible for the scientific review of applications for European marketing accreditation for medical products (centralized process). Under the centralized process, companies submit a single marketing authorization application to EMEA.

Report If reports of adverse drug reactions suggest a change in the benefit-risk balance of a drug, EMEA will take appropriate action. In 2001, the Orphan Pharmaceuticals Committee (COMP) was established to review referral applications from individuals or organizations seeking to develop drugs for rare diseases (known as 'orphan drugs').

The agency is also involved in setting procedures for pharmaceutical products approved or considered by member states.

(a) EMEA System:

A. Orphan Drug Products Committee (COMP)

B. Pediatric Committee (PDCO)

C. Veterinary Products Committee (CVMP)

E. Advanced Medicine Group (CAT)

I. Committee on Medicinal Products for Human Use (CHMP)

F. Herbal Products Group (HMPC)

Yes. Pharmacovigilance Risk Assessment Group (PRAC) [12]

(d) ICH (International Convention on Compliance): There was a rapid increase in laws, regulations and regulations in the 1960s and 1970s in most countries, whether or not product registration restrictions were first introduced. Guidelines for the reporting and evaluation of data on the safety, quality and effectiveness of new medical products. The integration of regulatory requirements was pioneered by the European Community (EC) in the 1980s. The ICH was born in April 1990 in Brussels at a meeting chaired by the EFPIA. Representatives from regulatory agencies and trade unions from Europe, Japan and the United States met primarily to plan an international conference, but the wider implications of the ICH and the terms of reference were also discussed at the meeting.

The CTD is organized into five modules. Section 1 is region dependent and Sections 2, 3, 4 and 5 are the same for all regions. In July 2003, CTD became a mandatory form of new drug applications in the European Union and Japan, and a strictly recommended selection form for NDA was submitted to the FDA.[13]

1.12.3 Objectives

Purpose of the study

Learn about regulatory agencies and registration procedures for pharmacists in the US and EU.

Review and review US (FDA) and EU (EMEA) API registration requirements

Comparison of API regulatory requirements in the US and EU, based on which registration requirements differ.

Facilitating the registration process for APIs in the United States and the European Union.

1.12.4 Methodology [14-22]

Every study has certain patterns and follows certain paths to achieve the goal. The study was analyzed by dividing the entire study into 4 phases:

1. Type of study
2. Data Source
3. API registration in USA and EU
4. learning process

1. Types of Studies

This study was conducted with the aim of clarifying the regulatory requirements for API registration and regulatory requirements and differences in the registration process in the United States and the European Union.

2. Data Source

The main part of secondary data collection was done by the following sources:

A. Literary Criticism

B. Regulatory agencies of the particular country and respective websites i.e. the United States of America and the European Union.

C. Guidelines given by government officials

A. Literary Criticism:

Educational magazines, online magazines, market research reports, newspaper articles and other sources. and direct liaison with regulatory authorities. Online books have acted as a good source of information.

B. Regulatory agencies of the particular country and respective websites i.e. the United States of America and the European Union.

This usually includes regulatory guidelines officially issued by agencies and websites regarding registration requirements for different countries.

C. Government Officials Guidelines:

The guidelines should provide the most useful information and the information mentioned in the guide is consistent and each endeavor to comply with these guidelines.

3. US and EU API Registration:

Most of the medicines in India are exported to the US and EU countries. The parameters of this study were selected to understand:

Basic requirements for API registration in the United States and the European Union.

Registration process for APIs in the United States and the European Union. In the United States the drug is registered through the Primary File Process (Type-2), while in the European Union the active substance is registered by the Primary File (ASMF) filing.

This will allow us to facilitate API registration in the United States and European Union countries by knowing the requirements.

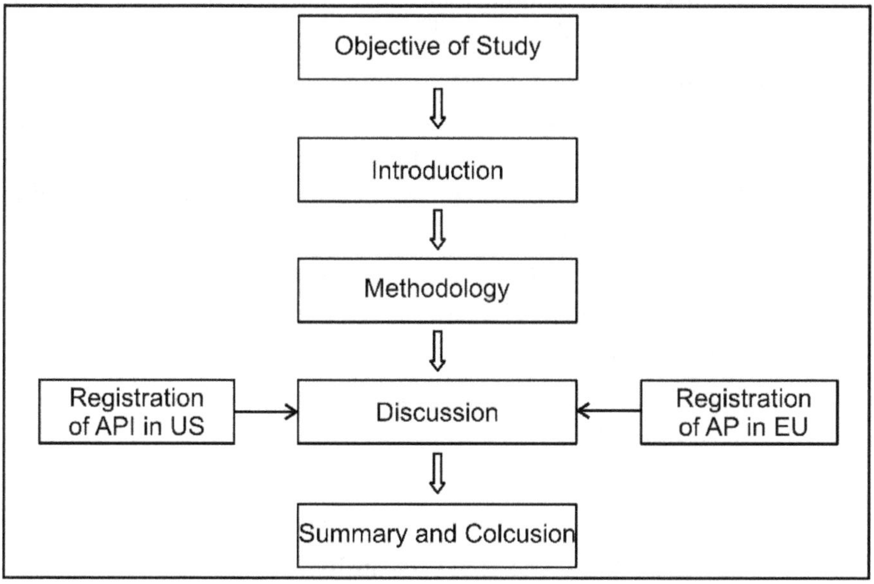

Figure 1 Study process

1.12.5 Discussion

(a) Registration of API in US

Pharmacist Registration: All new drugs are subject to FDA approval before market; It is the responsibility of the new drug manufacturer to demonstrate to the FDA the safety and effectiveness of their specific product. Terms relating to the approval of new drugs include, in the application (eg, new drug application (NDA)) the manufacturing processes and process controls for the new drug product and all its components with full description. About the composition of the drug. In an NDA product, the drug manufacturer must include sufficient data to show that the drug used for a particular drug does not in any way affect the safety or efficacy of the drug.

While serving ANDA we should mention the things related to the substance of the medicine. All information in the DMF

(a) **US-DMF:** A Drug Master File (DMF) is a document containing complete information about an active drug substance (API) or a complete drug dosage form. It is called the Active Substance Master File (ASMF) in the European Union and the US-Drug Master File (US-DMF) in the United States. The DMF contains factual and complete information about a pharmaceutical product's chemistry, formulation, stability, purity, contaminant profile, packaging and cGMP status.[17]

(b) **Drug Master Files**

The Pharmaceutical Drug Master File (DMF) system was created to allow suppliers to provide this information directly to the FDA in their products, to review pharmaceutical company applications, including the use of suppliers' substances.

(c) **DMF can be submitted in support of:**

- Investigational New Drug
- New Drug Application (NDA)
- Abbreviated New Drug Application (ANDA)
- Another DMF
- Export Application
- Supplements or Amendments any of these

A DMF is NOT a substitute for an IND, NDA, ANDA, or Export Application. It is not approved or

Dis-approved. Technical contents of a DMF are reviewed only when referenced in other regulatory filings, such as an IND, NDA or ANDA or Export Application. If requested by FDA headquarters, an FDA inspection may take place at an API manufacturing site after a review of the DMF.

(d) Types of DMF's

Table1: Types of Drug Master Files, Types of Manufacturing Site, Facilities, Operating Procedures, and Personnel (no longer applicable)

Type II: Drug Substance, Drug Substance Intermediate, and Material Used in Their Preparation, or Drug Product

Type III: Packaging Material

Type IV: Excipient, Colorant, Flavor, Essence, or Material Used in Their Preparation

Type V: FDA Accepted Reference Information.

(e) API Registration Requirements

In the United States the active ingredient is known as a pharmaceutical substance. Active Ingredients registration takes the palace with pre-marketing permits like NDA and ANDA. This means that there is no separate registration process for the API. The API manufacturer must submit the information in DMF format. The FDA has reviewed the information and provided the DMF number. Pharmaceutical manufacturers cite a pharmaceutical ingredient's DMF as a supporting document for applications such as NDA and ANDA if they wish to obtain product approval.

(f) Requirements for submission

with the requirements as mentioned above

Section 1 - Contains management information

SECTION 3 - INCLUDING QUALITY INFORMATION

Section 1: Administration

Not all types of DMFs require information forms.

Section 1.2cover letter commitment statement in the General Pharmaceutical User Fee (GDUF) (3794) card sheet,

section 1.3: Administrative information applies

Contact / Sponsor / Applicant Information

Change of address or company name: DMF holder can be used to provide addresses and manufacturing and testing facilities

Contact / Agent Change: Agent can be used to provide the name and address of contact persons and/or agents along with the appointment letter.

Section: 1.4 Reference Section

Authorization letter: submission by the owner of the information, providing authorization for the information used by others.

Note: The recipient submits the authorization letter along with a copy of the LOA and note statement.

(Recommended for DMF submitted to DMF)

List of persons authorized to join by reference: Submitted in the DMF Annual Report.

Environmental analysis[25]

Section 1.2:

(i) Card letter (Transfer letter)

The following should be included

Submission ID:

Original: i.e. DMF submission original or DMF correction for a previously submitted pharmaceutical ingredient.

DMF Types and Its Meaning: Now that we know about API registration, it is Type II DMF. The topic mainly deals with the quality components of pharmaceutical ingredients.

Identifying applications: If the DMF knows which application to endorse, i.e. NDA or ANDA, includes the name and address of each sponsor, applicant or holder and all relevant document holders.

Signature of the holder or authorized representative.

Enter the written name and title of the signatory.

(ii) Pledge

Report statement designed by Holder to certify that DMFs current and DMF Holder comply with the statements set forth herein.

(iii) General Drug User Fee Protection:

The Generic Drug User Payment Act (GDUFA) section of the Food and Drug Administration Safety and Innovation Act (S.3187) covers fees for DMF, initial assessment, and communication. Relationship with DMF holders. GDUFA only applies to active pharmaceutical products (APIs) type II DMFs used to support abbreviated new drug applications (ANDAs).

Section 1.3: Administrative Information

am Original Submission

Name and address of the name holder

Name and address of manufacturing plant

Contact person:

- Name
- Mailing address
- Phone number
- Fax number
- Email address
- Commitment statement
- Name Agent's name and address (if applicable)
- Agent's contact person (if applicable):
- Name
- Mailing address
- Phone number
- Fax number
- Email address
- Commitment statement

(g) Section: 1.4 - Reference Section:

Authorization Letters: If the DMF is in paper form, a copy of all the Authorization Letters (LOA) has to be submitted to the DMF. , A copy of the LOA should be sent by the DMF holder to the authorized party (authorized company or person to add DMF by reference). Failure to submit the LoA to the DMF may delay the review of the DMF. The LOA should specify the name of the specific item to be specified and the date of submission of information about that item. Should not be called **LOA - Access letter.**

LOA is required even if the DMF holder is a company of recognized parties. The LOA should not be submitted along with the original DMF documents (unless the DMF has a pre-determined number) as the LOA must contain the DMF number. Hence the DMF holders have to wait for the acknowledgment letter containing the DMF number before submitting the LoA.

If there is no change in the owner, authorized party, DMF object or specified item, the LOA need not be reissued.

(h) Reference rights statement

Recipient presenting letter of authorization along with copy of LOA and copyright statement. The DMF is submitted only when another DMF is specified. If a DMF holder specifies other DMFs, a list of those DMFs may be provided in this section. And those DMFs are called reference rights. [25]

(i) List of Authorized Persons to be added with reference

This is required when the authorized person updates the DMF annually. Here they must quote all persons approved by the FDA and those persons are cited as referenced

Member. The ADMF must contain a complete list of persons authorized by note [21 CFR 314.420(d)] to engage in DMF formations. I

The language in the CFR is very clear:

The drug master file should contain a complete list of each individual identified by the authorized name, reference number, block and page number, which specifies any information contained in the file.[26]

(j) Environmental Assessment: Since DMFs are not approved or approved, there is no need to file an environmental assessment. For this, we need to specify the commitment statement for the ecosystem surrounding the production area.

The National Environmental Policy Act (NEPA) requires all government agencies to prepare an environmental impact assessment (EIS) or non-impact assessment (FONSI) action when taking action. For example, acceptance of the application of a drug.

The DMF must include a statement that the holder complies with all local environmental regulations

It is the responsibility of the DMF holder to provide sufficient information in deciding whether to allow the Client to register EA.[25.]

(k) Volume 3: API Quality Information: As per ICH CTD format, Volume 3 deals with Pharmaceutical Ingredients and Quality of Pharmaceutical Products. In the current review, I will provide high quality pharmaceutical ingredients information.

1. General Information:
   a. Naming
   b. structure
   c. general characteristics
2. Manufacturers:
   a. manufacturer
   b. Production process details and process control
   c. product control
   d. Controls critical and intermediate stages
   e. Verification and/or Evaluation Process
   f. create work process
3. Properties
   a. Presentation of the Structure and Another Characteristic
   b. dirty
4. Controlling Pharmaceutical Ingredients:
   a. profile
   b. Methods of Analysis
   c. Verification of Analytical Procedures
   d. Volume Analysis
   e. rationalization of specification
5. Standard or reference material
6. Container Closing System
7. Stability
   a. Abstraction and consistency of decisions
   b. After approval of the Sustainability Protocol and Sustainability Commitment
   a. data consistency

(b) DMF Filing Procedure

(a) Filling DMF

- Original and duplicate copy should be submitted for all DMF submissions. Original and duplicate copies must be compiled, fully assembled and individually jacketed.
- Prefer a standard paper size (e.g. 8-1/2 x 11 inches for US DMF). The length of the paper should not be less than 10 inches or more than 12 inches. However, it may sometimes be necessary to use individual pages instead of the standard paper

size to display floor plans, package maps, block formulas or production instructions.

- Those pages must be folded and folded so that the pages can be opened for review without removing the jacket and refolded without being damaged while the module is being stored.
- The agency system for filing M DMF is provided for the meeting on the left side of the page. To ensure that the text in the enclosed area is not obscured, the left margin should be at least three-quarters of an inch.
- The primary drug file will be sent to the FDA's Central Drug Assessment and Research (CDER) signed by a covering letter, along with the original and other required documents.
- Drug Master File staff will review non-technical information for completeness and adequacy for submission. If key components are missing, the staff will contact the proposed holder to obtain the documents required for filing DMF.
- Once the DMF is deemed acceptable for filing, the Document Cell staff will assign a DMF number and a letter will be sent to the contact person listed in the DMF.

(b) M DMF submissions and correspondence should be noted as follows:

- Medicine Drug Primary File Staff Center for Drug Evaluation and Research Central Document Room Food and Drug Administration 5901-B Emmendale Rd. Beltsville, MD 20705-1266
- Delivery charges should be paid in advance for the above address.[24]

(c) Electronic Drug Master File (e-DMF) [25-30]

- Most health officials require a paper copy of the documents. The size of the DMF is easily accessible or may exceed 1000 pages. Each primary file consists of multiple volumes and duplicates.
- All electronic applications must comply with the Electronic Common Technical Document.
- E-CTD is a structured form that allows critical life cycle management for DMFs.
- US marketing applications are submitted electronically in CTD format.

- An application in electronic form is not required to be submitted but it is encouraged to submit it in electronic form. Storing information in an e-CTD backup file can be very efficient.
- The absence of an electronic database in an acceptable format for review and evaluation approval may be considered insufficient and the application may be denied.

The following file formats should be used

PDF for reports and forms

SAS Export (version 5) Transport File (XPT) for the database.

ASCII text files (such as SAS program files, NONMEM control files) that use txt for the file extension.

XML for documents, data, and document information files.

Style sheets for XML Document Information Files (XSL) and Document Type Definition (DTD).

Microsoft Word for draft labeling.

DMF, currently in paper form, has been converted into electronic format, which does not require a pre-determined number. Once an electronic submission is made by the DMF holder, each subsequent submission must be in electronic form. Electronic DMFs can be deposited:

Through Electronic Submission Gateway (ESG) orVia physical media (CD-ROM, DVD, Digital Linear Tape, Linear Tape Open or USB drive) to the same address as DMF papers.

(d) Stages of filing DMF

1. Set the margin of the document to 3/4 inch on the left (minimum) and 1/2 inch on the right.
2. Print transmittal page, management information and DMF information on standard writing size paper. If you need a larger sheet of paper for a map or plan, fold the sheet and enclose it in a letter-sized page to allow the page to be opened and folded again. At most each block of DMF should be no more than 2 inches thick.
3. Calculate the number of blocks to deposit according to the total number of blocks (if more than one). (For example, 3 in 1, 3 in 2, etc.)

4. Sign all required documents (if you are the only DMF holder or authorized representative).
5. Copy and attach the document; You must submit both to the FDA.
6. Punch up documents using a standard hole-punch.
7. Close the original and copy of each volume with the document jacket. Prepare submissions for sending and mailing:

Drug Master File Staff

Food and Drug Administration 5901-B Amendable Road.

Beltsville, MD 20705-1266 271

(e) **Annual Update:** The holder must provide an annual report on the date of original submission. All changes and additional information included in the DMF should be provided from the previous year's report on the subject of DMF. If the purpose of the DMF has not changed, the DMF holder must make a statement that the contents of the DMF are up to date. Type II Active Drug Ingredient (API) 20 Drug Primary Files (DMF) Recommended or Abbreviated New Drug Application[21](ANDA) or ANDA (General Drug[22] Submission) Amendment or Pre-approval Supplement (PAS). ,

1.12.6 API Registration in the European Union

The main responsibility of the European Pharmaceuticals Agency (EMA) is to protect and improve public and animal health through the testing and administration of drugs for human and veterinary use. EU is known as Registered Marketing Accreditation (MA) for Pharmaceutical Products.

(a) **Marketing Accreditation:** The agency is responsible for scientifically reviewing European Union (EU) marketing accreditation applications for human and veterinary medicine. Under a centralized process, pharmaceutical companies submit an application for marketing accreditation to the EMA. Much of the EMA's scientific research work is carried out by its scientific committees, which include representatives from members of the EEA countries, patients, consumers, and the healthcare industry[.31]

Marketing authorization procedures: In the European Union (EU), drugs may be approved through centralized accreditation processes or national accreditation procedures. Introduced in January 1995, the European Organization for the Approval of Medicinal Products for Human and

Animal Use aims to ensure the rapid availability of safe, effective and high quality medicines to citizens throughout the European Union.

According to the European Association of Generic Medicine (EGA), marketing approval for pharmaceutical products in more than one EU country currently has to be enforced through one of two methods:

Centralized Procedure

Mutual Recognition Procedurell(MRP).

Decentralized Procedure, came into force with the newly revised EU pharmaceutical Directive in November 2005[33]

(b) Centralized Procedure [34-39][FIGURE 2]

Notification to EMEA

↓

Appointment of Reporter and Co-Rapporteur

↓

CPMP meeting, validation of dossier by EMEA and delivery to Rapporteursclock starts **Day1**

↓

Preparation of two separate assessment reports by the Rapporteurs in Day**70**

↓

Reports sent to all CPMP members, EMEA and applicant in **Day 100**

↓

Comment of CPMP members

↓

Reports sent to applicant with or without modification by CPMP in **Day 120 clock stop**

↓

Response by the applicant within 180 Days **Preparation of Joint assessment report by the Rapporteurs**

↓

Clock restarts in Day150

↓

Comments of CPMP in **Day 170**

↓

Any outstanding issues communicated to applicant and opinion is deferred by CPMP

↓

CPMP Opinion**With or without further clock stop Day210**

↓

Assessment report to Commission in **Day 240**

↓

If positive opinion by CPMP, then marketing authorization is issuedin Day 300

1.12.7 Decentralized Procedure[40,41][FIGURE 3]

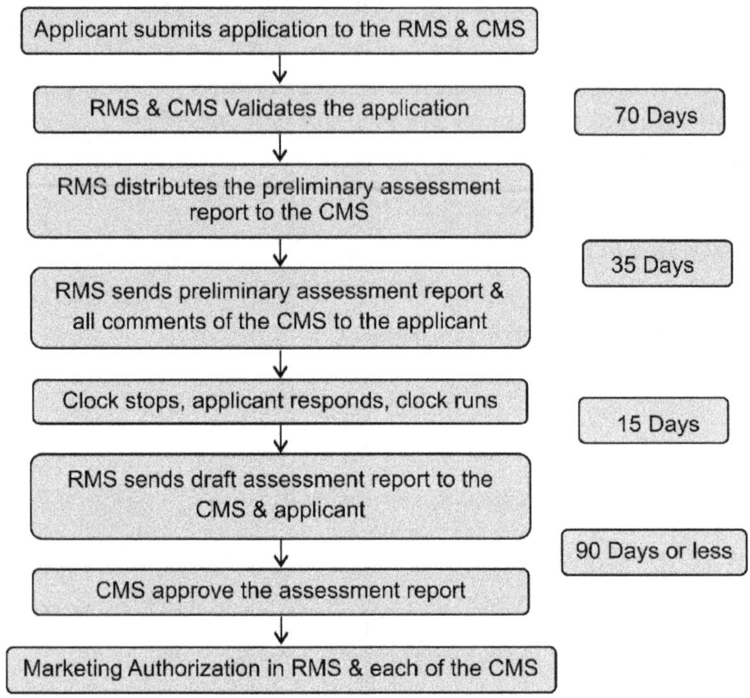

Decentralized Procedure

International Journal of Pharma and Chemical Research I Volume 3 I Issue 2 I Apr – Jun I 2017

1.12.8 Mutual-Recognition Procedure[FIGURE 4]

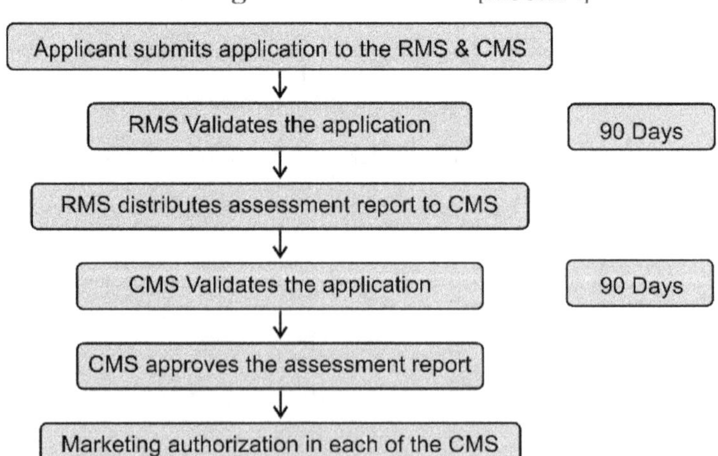

Mutual authorization in each of the CMS

1.12.9 Registration of API in EU

Active Pharmaceutical Ingredient

- **Definition**

  Any component that is intended to furnish pharmacological activity or other direct effect in the diagnosis, cure, mitigation, treatment, or prevention of disease, or to effect the structure or any function of the body of man or other animals.

  (a) Classification of active substances

  - New active substance used for the first time
  - Existing active substances not included in the European Pharmacopoeia (Ph.Eur.) or the pharmacopoeia of an EU Member State
  - Active substances included in the Ph.Eur. or in the pharmacopoeia of an EU Member State.[41]

  (b) Active substance master file [42-44]

  It should be emphasized that the concept of the ASMF shall only apply to a well-defined active substance and cannot be used for excipients, finished products and biological active substances.

  The scientific information in the ASMF should be physically divided into two separate parts, namely

  - The Applicant 's Part (AP) and
  - The Restricted Part (RP).

  The AP contains the information that the ASMF holder regards as non-confidential to the Applicant/MA holder, whereas the RP contains the information that the ASMF holder regards as confidential. It is emphasized that the AP is still a confidential document that cannot be submitted by anyone to third parties without the written consent of the ASMF holder. The RP may contain the remaining information, such as detailed information on the individual steps of the manufacturing method (reaction conditions, temperature, validation and evaluation data of critical steps) and the quality control during the manufacture of the active substance.

  The registration of ASMF requires the quality data of active substance. Nowadays EU also follows CTD format which is referred as EU-CTD. CTD contains five modules. The present work aims to discuss about registration of active substance and it includes Module 1

(c) Administrative, regional or national information

Module 2

(d) Quality information of drug substance

The overall content of the ASMF should contain detailed scientific information as indicated under the various headings of the relevant Notice to Applicants for Marketing Authorizations for Medicinal Products in the Member States of the European Union (NtA).[45]

(e) Submission requirements of ASMF

In the first submission of an ASMF with an allocated EMEA ASMF reference number, the ASMF holder is required to submit:

1. MAA application form stating the correct EMEA ASMF reference number
2. Letter of Access
3. Submission Letter and Administrative Details
4. ASMF dossier (Applicant's part, Restricted part, Quality Overall Summary and Expert's *curriculum vitae*).[46]

1. EMEA/ASMF reference number

- From 1 September 2013, ASMF holders submitting their ASMF dossiers relating to a Centralized and national MAA are asked to send it to the Agency and Committee Members only once.
- According to the new ASMF submission rules the Agency will assign a reference number on request prior to submission of the ASMF that can cover multiple caps.
- The EMEA/ASMF/XXXXX number is an internal reference number sequentially assigned by the EMA to enable an appropriate data lifecycle management of ASMFs used in one or more centralized Marketing Authorization.
- The EMEA ASMF reference number does not replace the responsibility of the ASMF holders to version control their ASMF (in accordance with GMP) nor replaces their own ASMF numbering system.
- Up to two weeks before submitting a complete ASMF, or an update to an already submitted ASMF, the ASMF holder should request the EMEA ASMF reference number.
- It is the responsibility of the ASMF holder to inform the applicant of a MAA or MAV of the allocated EMEA ASMF reference number. Failure to state a valid EMEA ASMF

reference number on the MAA or MAV form will trigger validation questions and may delay the start of procedure.

- For previously submitted ASMFs, in cases where the ASMF is used in more than one MA the ASMF Holder should only request one EMEA ASMF reference number, when applicable.

2. **Letter of Access**

   The Letter of Access is an important document in that it authorizes the NCA/EMA to refer to and review the ASMF in support of a MA application. The letter also notifies the NCA/EMA that the ASMF holder is informed and accepts that assessment reports of the ASMF may be shared amongst the NCA, EMA (including CHMP members and experts) and the Certification of Substances Division of the EDQM. The letter also confirms that the ASMF holder commits to ensure batch to batch consistency and to inform the MA holder of any changes to the ASMF.[32, 50]

3. **Submission Letter and Administrative details**

   Submission Letter:

   The name of the active substance and the EU/ASMF reference number (when available) or national ASMF reference number, as appropriate, should be clearly stated in the subject heading. The Submission Letter should be signed by the authorized contact person for the ASMF holder. Their name, address (if different to the ASMF holder's address stated at the top of the letter) and position should be clearly stated. The EU/ASMF reference number will help identify and track where the same ASMF is submitted in multiple European procedures and/or Member States. Where the EU/ASMF reference number has not been allocated or if an ASMF is used in national applications only, a national ASMF reference number should be provided.

   Administration Details:

   - Recipients of the ASMF submission, the EU/ASMF or national reference number, ASMF version number, active substance name and internal (active pharmaceutical ingredient (API)) code.
   - contact details of ASMF holder and companies responsible for manufacturing and quality control
   - The ASMF holder should confirm, by ticking the appropriate box, whether the submission is a new ASMF in the

NCA/EMA, an update to a previously evaluated ASMF or a response to a deficiency letter.

- format of the ASMF Submission
- List of submitted documents The ASMF holder should confirm they have provided the required documents by ticking the appropriate boxes. A copy of the NCA/EMA deficiency letter(s) should only be provided with any submittedresponse.[47]

1.12.10 ASMF Dossier[48,49]

(a) Quality Requirements for registration of API:

1. General Information:
   a. Nomenclature
   b. Structure
   c. General Properties
2. **Manufacture:**
   a. Manufacturer
   b. Description of Manufacturing Process and Process Controls
   c. Control of Materials
   d. Control of Critical Steps and Intermediates
   e. Process Validation and/or Evaluation
   f. Manufacturing Process Development
3. **Characterization:**
   a. Elucidation of Structure and other Characteristics
   b. Impurities
4. **Control of Drug Substances**
   a. Specification
   b. Analytical Procedures
   c. Validation of Analytical Procedures
5. **Reference standards or Materials**
6. **Container closure System**
7. **Stability**
   a. Stability Summary and Conclusions
   b. Post-approval Stability Protocol and Stability Commitment
   c. Stability Data.

1.12.11 Certification of Suitability

The procedure for Certification of Suitability to the monographs of the European Pharmacopoeia' was established in 1994 and was in the beginning restricted to controlling the chemical purity of pharmaceutical substances. In 1999, the procedure was extended to include products with a risk of transmissible spongiform encephalopathy (TSE), thus enabling their certification on the basis of the European Pharmacopoeia general chapter 5.2.8_Minimising the risk of transmitting animal spongiform encephalopathy agents via medicinal products' and of the new monograph on 'Products with risk of transmitting agents of animal spongiform encephalopathy‘s (1483)'.

(a) Submission Format: Paper or Electronic

Applicants are encouraged to submit electronic versions of their applications. Additionally, there are new requirements for paper submissions. This allows us to manage the applications more efficiently.[50]Requirements for the registration of API in US and EU:

(b) Basic differences between US AND EU: [TABLE 1]

Requirements	US	EU
Agency	Food and Drug Administration (FDA)	European medical agency (EMEA)
Registration process	Single	Multiple 1) Cenralized 2) Decentralized
Braille Code	Not required	Required
Site registration	Required	Not Required
Plant GMP approval	US FDA audits of API manufacturer	Audit by any member state of EU

(c) Administrative Requirements [TABLE 2]

Requirements	US	EU
Submission	Type 2 DMF for API	ASMF
Application	Type 2 DMF is submitted as supporting document for NDA and ANDA	ASMF submission form for administrative information
No. of copies	2	1
Other requirements	1. Cover Letter 2. Statement of Commitment 3. Letter of Authorization 4. Statement of Right of Reference 5. Environmental analysis	1. EMEA/ASMF reference number. 2. Letter Of Access 3. Submission Letter

1.12.12 Quality Requirements

To market the drug substance the regulatory authorities mainly focus on the quality data of drug substance. After ICH harmonization every country follows the guideline framed by ICH member states (US, EU and Japan). For registration of API, US and EU authorities follow the quality guidelines framed by ICH. In US the quality data of drug substance was submitted as type II DMF and the quality requirements are as per ICH CTD module 3. And EU also follows the Module 3 of CTD but the quality part is divided into applicant part (AP) and restricted part(RP).

1.12.13 Conclusion

Active Pharmaceutical Ingredients are not only the heart and brain of drug products, but are also crucial to the regulatory filing success of drug applications. From the current scenario of the regulatory requirements, it is important to keep in mind that FDA is scrutinizing DMFs more closely than ever before. With the considerable increase in the number of DMF submissions and FDA‘s interest in keeping track of such filings electronically and FDA more stringently insists on uniformity in DMF submissions in accordance with its current administrative guidelines. Thus, more than ever before, it is important to consult FDA‘s current DMF guidance when preparing DMF submissions and to adhere to FDA‘s requirements for various types of DMF filings. Moreover, to maintain the active status of a DMF and ensure that it is not retired by FDA making it unavailable for review, it is important to regularly comply with FDA‘s Annual Report requirement. At the end, the Drug Master File is a critical document used to support a drug application. Deficiencies in the Drug Master File can result in the delay of approval of drug applications. It is important that the DMF be filed in a timely manner and that the standards used to compete it are of the same quality as the actual drug application.

References

1. The role and responsibility of the regulatory affairs department [Internet]. [cited on2014 March 17]; Available from: https://www.pharmatching.com/inforena/ the-role-and-responsibility-of-the-regulatory-affairs-department
2. Bulk Drug Substances That May Be Used To Compound Drug Products in Accordance With Section 503A of the Federal Food, Drug and Cosmetic Act; [internet].[cited on 2014 July 24]; Available from: https://www.federalregister.gov/articles/2014/07/02/2014-15367/bulk-drug-substances-that-may-be-used-to-compound-drug-products-in-accordance-with-section-503a-of #h-7

3. Pharmaceutical regulatory affairs - introduction[internet].[cited on 2014 March 12]; Available from: http://www.fermish.com/pharmaceutical_regulatory_affairs/intro.htm
4. Edward lamb. What Are Active Pharmaceutical Ingredients, or APIs[internet].[cited on 2014 January 24];Available from: http://pharmacy.about.com/od/Glossary/g/What-Are-Active-Pharmaceutical-Ingredients-Or-Apis.htm
5. Active pharmaceutical ingredient-API, pharma ingredient [internet]. [cited on 2014 March 5]; Available from: http://www.pharma-ingredients.com/active_pharmaceutical_ ingredients/
6. Akshaybhatt. Introduction to regulatory affairs. Pharma regulatory affairs [internet]. [cited on 2014 March 7]; Available from: http://regulatory12.blogspot.in/2014/06/introduction-to-regulatory-affairs.html
7. Global active pharmaceutical ingredient market forcast 2020.healthcare dive [internet]. September 2014 [cited 15 September 2014]; Available for http://www.healthcaredive.com/press-release/20140909-global-active-pharmaceutical-ingredients-market-forecast-to-2020/
8. Ramesh T, Saravanan D, Praveen Khullar. Regulatory Perspective for Entering Global Pharma Markets. Pharma Times [internet]. September 2011[cited on 2014 March 24]; 43(09): Available from: http://www.altusformulation.com/images/An_Overview_of_505_j_505_b_1_and_b_2_Patways.pdf
9. Geetanjali Sengar, Pranab Tripathy. Pharmaceutical Regulatory Agencies and Organizations around the World: Scope and Challenges in DrugDevelopment [internet].[cited on 2014 March 15]; Available from: http://www.pharmatutor.org/articles/pharmaceutical-regulatory-agencies-and-organizations-around-world-scope-challenges-in-drug-development
10. Andrea Hörner. Comparison of a global submission of new biological entity and a new chemical entity – strategic decisions and criteria for implementation.[internet].august 2005[cited on 2014 March 9] Available from:http://hss.ulb.uni-bonn.de/2011/2546/2546.pdf
11. Strategic Priorities – Introduction Food and Drug Administration [internet] [cited on 2014 January 25]; Available from: http://www.fda.gov/AboutFDA/ReportsManualsForms/Reports/ucm245959.htm
12. European medical agency, Guiding principles, How we work [internet]. [cited on 2014 January26]; Available from: http://www.ema.europa.eu/ema/index.jsp?curl=pages/about_us/general/general_content_000125.jsp&mid=WC0b01ac0580028a46

13. Introduction to ICH [internet].[cited on 2014 march 24]; Available from: http://www.ich.org/fileadmin/Public_Web_Site/ABOUT_ICH/Vision/Introduction_to_ICH.pdf
14. Carlos María Correa. Protection Of Data Submitted For The Registration Of Pharmaceuticals: Implementing The Standards Of The Trips Agreement. SADAG[internet].2012:[cited on 2014 February 6]; Available.from:http://apps.who.int/medicinedocs/pdf/h3009ae/h3009ae.pdf
15. Jitendra Kumar Badjatya. Overview Of Drug Registration Requirements For Pharmaceuticals In Emerging Market. Journal of Drug Delivery & Therapeutics [internet]. 2013;[cited on 2014 February 8]; 3(2): 227-232. Available from: jddtonline.info/index.php/jddt/article
16. Yasuo Ohno.ICH Guidelines—Implementation of the 3Rs (Refinement, Reduction, and Replacement): Incorporating Best Scientific Practices into the Regulatory Process. ILAR Journal [internet].2002;[cited on 2014 february 12];43(1): 95-98. Available from: http://ilarjournal.oxfordjournals.org/content/43/Suppl_1/S95.abstract
17. Pharm Nwoko Valentine Eziokwu. Processing and Submission of Drug Master File, A Review article International Journal of Pharmaceutical Quality Assurance [internet]. July-September 2013; [cited on 2014 February 12]; 4(3): 52-56. Available from: http://ijpqa.com/PDF%20all%20edtions%20IJPQA/Vol4/Issue3/IJPQA,Vol4,Issue3,Article4.pdf
18. Vishal Gupta, Nitin Kashyap U, Raghunandan H V. Comparison of Drug Approval Process in United States &Europe.Journal of pharmaceutical science and research[internet]. 2013; [cited on 2014 February 20];5(6): 131 – 136. Available from: http://jpsr.pharmainfo.in/Documents/Volumes/vol5issue06/jpsr05061302.pdf
19. Sukesh Bhardwaj, VikaasBudhwar, Vipul K. Gupta. Requirements For The Submission Of Generic Drug Application Across US And EU In CTD/eCTD Format. AJPSR [internet]. October 2011 [cited on 2014 March 3]; 1(5): Available from: http://www.ordonearresearchlibrary.com/Data/pdfs/AJPSR22.pdf
20. Rau B S, Appaji P V. Dynamics of Drug Master Filings at United States Food and Drug Administration [internet]. May-June 2012;[cited on 2014 March 6];65-71.Available from: http://pharmexcil.org/uploadfile/ufiles/4DynamicsDrugMasterFilingsUSFDA01may2012.pdf
21. Prajapat Vishal, Goswami Rahulgiri, Makvana Pratik, Badjatya Jitendra Kumar. A review on drug approval process for US, Europe and India. International Journal of Drug Regulatory Affairs [internet].2014;[cited on 2014 May 30]; 2(1): 1-11.Availablefrom: http://oaji.net/articles/756-1397501525.pdf

22. E Gopinath, R S Bhadauria, Jodan Gunjan, zaidiInsha. Pharmaceutical regulatory affairs – Review. IJARPB.[internet]. 2012;[cited on 2014 March 10]; 2 (2): 292-301. Available from: http://www.ijarpb.com/pdf/vol_02/24.pdf.
23. Guideline For The Development Of Type III Drug Master Files (DMFs) [internet]. The Society of the Plastics Industry, Inc. August 2012,[cited on 2014 April 7]; Available from: http://www.plasticsindustry.org/files/FDCPMC/DMF%20Guidance%20Document%20-%20Final.pdf
24. Guideline for Drug Master Files (DMF), Food and Drug Administration [internet]. [cited on 2014 March20]; Available from: http://www.fda.gov/drugs/developmentapprovalprocess/formssubmissionrequirements/drugmasterfilesdmfs/ucm073164.htm
25. Drug master file, Food and drug administration [internet].2013;[Cited on2014march 26]; Available from: http://www.fda.gov/Drugs/DevelopmentApprovalProcess/FormsSubmissionRequirements/DrugMasterFilesDMFs/UCM2007046
26. Shaw B, Drug Master Files. FDA DMF Expert FDA Small Business Office Webinar [internet]. November 14, 2011[cited on 2014 April 12]; Available from: http://www.fda.gov/ downloads/Drugs/Development Approval Process/Small Business Assistance/UCM279666.pdf
27. Guidance for Industry Submitting Marketing Applications According to the ICH-CTD Format — General Considerations [internet].[Cited on 2014april23]; Available from: http://www.fda.gov/downloads/Drugs/Guidance Compliance Regulatory Information/Guidances/UCM073308.pdf
28. Guidance for Industry M4Q: CTD — Quality requirements [internet].[Cited on 2014 April 26]; Available from: http://www.fda.gov/downloads/drugs/guidancecomplianceregulatoryinformation/guidances/ucm073280.pdf.
29. Specifications, international conference organization. Food and Drug Administration. Federal Register[internet]. December, 2000 [cited on 2014 May 4]; 65(251), 83041-83061. Availablefrom: http://www.gpo.gov/fdsys/pkg/FR-2000-12-29/pdf/00-33369.pdf
30. Validation of analytical procedures. Federal Register, food and drug administration [internet].May 19, 1997[cited on 2014 May 4]; 62 (96); 27464-27467.Available from: http://www.gpo.gov/fdsys/pkg/FR-1997-05-19/pdf/97-13063.pdf
31. European medical agency Marketing Authorization [internet].[cited on 2014 May 8]; Available from: http://www.ema.europa.eu/ema/index.jsp?curl=pages/about_us/general/general_content_000091.jsp&mid=WC0b01ac0580028a42

32. European commission public health news and updates on pharmaceuticals EU, Legislation – Eudralex [internet].[cited on 2014 May 16]; Available from: http://ec.europa.eu/health/documents/eudralex/index_en.htm
33. EudraLex - Volume 2 - Pharmaceutical Legislation Notice to applicants and regulatory guidelines medicinal products for human use [internet].[cited on 2014May16]; Available from: http://ec.europa.eu/health/documents/eudralex/vol-2/index_en.htm
34. Notice To Applicants Volume 2A Procedures For Marketing Authorization Chapter 1 Marketing Authorization [internet]. June 2013;[cited on 2014 May 17]; revision 4. Available from: http://ec.europa.eu/health/files/eudralex/vol-2/a/vol2a_chap1_2013-06_en.pdf
35. Authorization Procedures for medicinal products-Procedures for evaluating medicinal products and granting marketing authorization [internet].[cited on 2014 May 18]; Available from: http://ec.europa.eu/health/authorisation-procedures_en.htm
36. Volume 2A Procedures for marketing authorization Chapter 4 Centralized Procedure ofmedicines [internet].2001;[Updated on April 2006,cited on 2014 May 18]; Available from: http://www.ema.europa.eu/ema/index.jsp?curl=pages/about_us/general/general_content_000109.jsp
37. EMA Procedural advice for users of the centralised procedure for generic/hybrid applications [internet] March 2013; [cited on 2014 May 12]; Committee for Human Medicinal Products(CHMP)Available from: http://www.ema.europa.eu/docs/en_GB/document_library/Regulatory_and_procedural_guideline/2009/10/WC500004018.pdf
38. Preetam Nivrutti Chavan. Marketing Authorisation Procedures in Europe: A Regulatory Perspective, Internet International Journal of Pharmacy and Pharmaceutical Science Research [internet]. 2011;[cited on 2014 May 20]; 1(1): 13-19. Available from: http://urpjournals.com/tocjnls/24_3.pdf
39. Marketing Authorization Procedures in the European Union – Making the Right Choice Life science technical bulletin, SGS [internet].december2009; [cited on 2014 June 4];issue 33. Available from: http://www.sgsgroup.in/~/media/Global/Documents/Technical%20Documents/SGS-Clinical-Marketing-Authorization-EN-09.pdf
40. Volume 2A Procedures for marketing authorization Chapter 2 Mutual Recognition [internet]. February 2007[cited on 2014 June 7]; revison 5 Available from: http://ec.europa.eu/health/files/eudralex/vol-2/a/vol2a_chap2_2007-02_en.pdf

41. Guideline on Active Substance Master File Procedure Committee of Human Medicinal Products. CHMP [internet].October 2012;[cited on 2014 June 10];Available from: http://www.ema.europa.eu/docs/en_GB/document_library/Scientific_guideline/2012/07/WC50012 9994.pdf

42. Routes for registration of Active Pharmaceutical Ingredients (API) in EU [internet]. December 2011[cited on 2014 June 12]; Available from: http://budding-regulatory-professionals.blogspot.in/2011/12/do-know-how-many-routes-for.html

43. Guideline on summary requirements for active substance in quality part of the dossier.[internet]. February 2005. [cited on 2014 June 12]; Available from: http://www.ema.europa.eu/ema/index.jsp?curl=pages/regulation/general/general_content_000354.jsp&mid=WC0b01ac05800 28bfd

44. Guideline on active substance master file procedure. [internet]. August 2006 [cite on 2014 June 19]; Available from: http://www.ema.europa.eu/docs/en_GB/document_library/Scientific_guideline/2009/09/WC500002811.pdf

45. Pre submission guidence of active substance master file [internet].[cited on2014June 19]; Available from: http://www.ema.europa.eu/ema/index.jsp? curl=pages/regulation/q_and_a/q_and_a_detail_00002 0.jsp&mid=WC0b01ac0580022713

46. Additional guidance on documents relating to an active substance master file [internet].September 2012[cited on 2014 June20]; Available from:http://www.ema.europa.eu/docs/en_GB/document_library/Scientific_guideline/2012/10/WC50013 3204.pdf

47. Volume 2B Notice to Applicants Medicinal products for human use Presentation and format of the dossier Common Technical Document (CTD) [internet].2008[cited on 2014 June 26]; Available from: http://ec.europa.eu/health/files/eudralex/vol-2/b/update_200805/ctd_05-2008_en.pdf

48. Chemistry of active substances [internet].[cited on 2014 July 13]; Available from: http://www.ema.europa.eu/docs/en_GB/document_library/Scientific_guideline/2009/09/WC500002817.pdf

49. Letter of access, Submission Details [internet].[cited on 2014 July 15]; Available from: http://www.ema.europa.eu/ema/pages/includes/document/open_document.jsp?webContentId=WC500129998)

50. Background and legal framework of certification of suitability [internet]. [cited on 2014 July 18]; Available from: https://www.edqm.eu/en/certification-background-77.html

CHAPTER 1.13

Biologics

1.13.1 Introduction

(a) What is biologics?

Biologics is the production, extraction or semi-synthesis of products from a biological source that are regulated by the FDA and are used to prevent and treat diseases and medical conditions.

They are usually large, complex molecules made by biotechnology, such as microorganisms, plant cells or animal cells.

They can be sugars, proteins, nucleic acids or complex combinations of these substances or organisms.

These are complex compounds that are not easily identifiable and are heat-sensitive and susceptible to microbial contamination, so it is essential to apply aseptic principles from the initial production process.

Examples: Botox, Herceptin, Vaccines, Enprel

(b) History

Vaccines have led to significant advances in the scientific community in the field of vaccination, resulting in vaccines for measles, rabies, typhoid, and diphtheria and tetanus.

These products have found wide use for public health, but there is no pressure to ensure that the products are safe.

In October 1901, 13 children died in St. Louis receiving a diphtheria antidote for tetanus toxin.

In Camden, New Jersey, nine children have died after being vaccinated against smallpox.

This tragedy resulted in the Biological Control Act of 1902.

"Any virus, serum, toxin, antitoxin, treatment serum, vaccine, blood, blood component or derivative, allergy product, or similar products or trivalent arsenic compound suitable for the prevention, treatment or solution of arsenic.

illness or injury to a person. "the biology.

Provisions of the Biological Control Act include licensing requirements, labeling requirements, facility inspection requirements, and penalties for violations, including suspension and revocation of licenses, for companies and products.

The BCA had previously authorized the health laboratory to publish rules governing the provisions of the Act.

In 1934, the health laboratory was renamed the National Institutes of Health (NIH) and in 1948 the Department of Biological Control at the National Institute of Microbiology (NMI).

The Biological Control Act of 1944 was incorporated into Section 351 of the Public Health Services Act (PHSA).

PHSA serves as the current legal basis for FDA regulations covering organic products published in Federal Regulations (CFR) Chapter 21, Sections 600-680.

In 1955, the Salk polio vaccine (injection of the "killed" vaccine) produced by Cutter Laboratories (licensed by NMI) caused 200 strokes of polio.

The above incident led to the creation of an independent body within the NIH, the Division of Biological Standards (DBS).

In 1972 DBS was changed to the Bureau of Biologics (BB) for the FDA.

Established the National Center for Pharmaceuticals and Biology (NCDB) in 1982 in collaboration with B B Pharmaceutical Bureau.

In 1988, NCDB split into two centres; Created by the Center for Biological Assessment and Research (CBER) and the Center for Drug Assessment and Research (CDER).

Biological Control Act-1902

Accredited Health Laboratory

Health In 1934 the name of the health laboratory was changed to NIH

NMI in 1948. biological control units within

The PCA was incorporated into Section 351 of the PHSA in 1944 (CFR Title 21 Part 600-680).

Salk Polio Vaccine -DBS in 1955

In 1972 DBS was converted to an organic field for the FDA.

In 1982, BB merged with NCDB (National Center for Pharmaceuticals and Biology).

(c) Sources and types of Biologics

SOURCES

- Mammalian cell culture

- Bacteria
- Insect cell culture
- Plant cell culture
- Yeast
- Transgenic
- Avian cell culture Humans

Table 1 Types

- Blood derivatives
- Vaccines
- Allergenic extracts
- Whole blood
- Blood components
- Proteins
- Human tissues
- Cellular and gene therapies
- Xenotransplantation products

1.13.2 Comparison between Biologics & Chemical Drug [Table 2]

Properties	Biologics	Chemical drug
Size	Large	Small
Structure	Complex	Simple
Stability	Unstable	Stable
Modification	Complex to ensure identical copy	Identical copy can be made
Manufacturing	Many options	Well defined
Characterization	Difficult	Easy

1.13.3 Regulatory Authority for Biologics

- Center for biologics evolution and research (CBER) is the center within FDA that regulates biological products for human use under applicable Federal laws including the Public Health Services Act (PHS) and the Federal, Food, Drug and Cosmetics Act
- CBER protects and advances the public health by ensuring that biological products are safe and effective.

- FDA's regulatory authority for the approval of biologics resides in (PHS) Act. Biologics are subjected to regulation under Federal, Food, Drug And Cosmetics act (FD&C) Act.
- Some medical devices which are used to produce biologics are regulated by CBER under FD&C Act's medical device amendments of 1976.
- FDA also reviews new biological products and new indications and usage for already approved products on the market for the treatment of known diseases.
- It protects against threats of emerging infectious diseases.
- It provides the public with information to promote safe and appropriate use.

1.13.4 Development and Approval Process

- Advertising and Labeling
- Investigational New Drug Application (IND) or Device exemption process (IDE)
- Expanded Access
- Premarket Approval(PMA)
- Biologics License Application (BLA) New Drug Application Process (NDA).
- Biologics Approvals by Year.

1.13.5 Biologics License Application

(BLA)

- The Biologics License Application (BLA) is quest for permission introduce or deliver for introduction a Biologic product into the market.
- It is mainly regulated by 21 CFR 600-800. It is submitted by any legal person or entity, who engaged in manufacture or an applicant for a license who takes responsibility for compliance with product and establishment of standards.
- A Biologic License application generally applies to vaccines and other Allergenic drug products and cellular and genetic therapies.

DEPARTMENT OF HEALTH AND HUMAN SERVICES
FOOD AND DRUG ADMINISTRATION

Form Approved: OMB No. 0910-0338
Expiration Date: August 31, 2005
See OMB Statement on page 2.

APPLICATION TO MARKET A NEW DRUG, BIOLOGIC, OR AN ANTIBIOTIC DRUG FOR HUMAN USE

(Title 21, Code of Federal Regulations, Parts 314 & 601)

FOR FDA USE ONLY
APPLICATION NUMBER

APPLICANT INFORMATION

NAME OF APPLICANT	DATE OF SUBMISSION
TELEPHONE NO. *(Include Area Code)*	FACSIMILE (FAX) Number *(Include Area Code)*
APPLICANT ADDRESS *(Number, Street, City, State, Country, ZIP Code or Mail Code, and U.S. License number if previously issued)*:	AUTHORIZED U.S. AGENT NAME & ADDRESS *(Number, Street, City, State, ZIP Code, telephone & FAX number)* IF APPLICABLE

PRODUCT DESCRIPTION

NEW DRUG OR ANTIBIOTIC APPLICATION NUMBER, OR BIOLOGICS LICENSE APPLICATION NUMBER *(If previously issued)*

ESTABLISHED NAME *(e.g., Proper name, USP/USAN name)*	PROPRIETARY NAME *(trade name)* IF ANY
CHEMICAL/BIOCHEMICAL/BLOOD PRODUCT NAME *(If any)*	CODE NAME *(If any)*

DOSAGE FORM:	STRENGTHS:	ROUTE OF ADMINISTRATION:

(PROPOSED) INDICATION(S) FOR USE:

APPLICATION INFORMATION

APPLICATION TYPE *(check one)* ☐ NEW DRUG APPLICATION (21 CFR 314.50) ☐ ABBREVIATED NEW DRUG APPLICATION (ANDA, 21 CFR 314.94) ☐ BIOLOGICS LICENSE APPLICATION (21 CFR Part 601)

IF AN NDA, IDENTIFY THE APPROPRIATE TYPE ☐ 505 (b)(1) ☐ 505 (b)(2)

IF AN ANDA, OR 505(b)(2), IDENTIFY THE REFERENCE LISTED DRUG PRODUCT THAT IS THE BASIS FOR THE SUBMISSION
Name of Drug — Holder of Approved Application

TYPE OF SUBMISSION *(check one)* ☐ ORIGINAL APPLICATION ☐ AMENDMENT TO A PENDING APPLICATION ☐ RESUBMISSION ☐ PRESUBMISSION ☐ ANNUAL REPORT ☐ ESTABLISHMENT DESCRIPTION SUPPLEMENT ☐ EFFICACY SUPPLEMENT ☐ LABELING SUPPLEMENT ☐ CHEMISTRY MANUFACTURING AND CONTROLS SUPPLEMENT ☐ OTHER

IF A SUBMISSION OF PARTIAL APPLICATION, PROVIDE LETTER DATE OF AGREEMENT TO PARTIAL SUBMISSION: ____________

IF A SUPPLEMENT, IDENTIFY THE APPROPRIATE CATEGORY ☐ CBE ☐ CBE-30 ☐ Prior Approval (PA)

REASON FOR SUBMISSION

PROPOSED MARKETING STATUS *(check one)* ☐ PRESCRIPTION PRODUCT (Rx) ☐ OVER THE COUNTER PRODUCT (OTC)

NUMBER OF VOLUMES SUBMITTED ____________ THIS APPLICATION IS ☐ PAPER ☐ PAPER AND ELECTRONIC ☐ ELECTRONIC

ESTABLISHMENT INFORMATION (Full establishment information should be provided in the body of the Application.)
Provide locations of all manufacturing, packaging and control sites for drug substance and drug product (continuation sheets may be used if necessary). Include name, address, contact, telephone number, registration number (CFN), DMF number, and manufacturing steps and/or type of testing (e.g. Final dosage form, Stability testing) conducted at the site. Please indicate whether the site is ready for inspection or, if not, when it will be ready.

Cross References (list related License Applications, INDs, NDAs, PMAs, 510(k)s, IDEs, BMFs, and DMFs referenced in the current application)

FORM FDA 356h (9/02)

PSC Media Arts (301) 443-1090 EF

(a) **Application Form FDA 356(h):** First, it is an administrative document providing CBER with information on the **applicant, product, and application.**

Second, it is a legal contract binding the applicant, contractors, suppliers, and physicians to FDA laws and regulations.

Section 1: Index It influences speed and efficiency of the reviewer. Applicants can use this format for indexing the BLA:

Table 3

Item	Description	Volume/page
2	Labeling	1.010

Section 2: Labeling Section: This section encompasses the initial draft labeling submitted with the BLA and the final printed labeling that is submitted just prior to licensure. Labeling includes the immediate container label, carton label, insert, and user instructions.

Section 3: Summary Section: It serves as a guide to the full application.

- It explains the application's intent-to-establish the biologic's safety and effectiveness for a particular indication.
- It can build CBER's confidence in the applicant, the validity of the BLA'sinformation, and the product itself.
- It acts as pivotal in establishing a foundation for product approval.

Summary

1. Description of the drug and formulation
2. Note Draft Entry
3. Pharmacological class of the product
4. Scientific Rationale for Using the Product
5. Medicinal benefits
6. CMC Summary of Foreign Marketing History
    a) drugs
    b) pharmaceutical products
    c) stability
    d) Summary of investigations (list of modules used in clinical studies)

1. Non-medical abstraction
    a) Pharmacology
    b) toxicology

2. Pharmacology and availability of human life
3. Microbiological Summary
4. Medical Summary
5. Benefit/Risk Relationship

A.D. Section 4: Chemistry Section

The Chemistry section of the BLA consists of three parts:

1. Regulates chemistry, manufacturing and information;
2. Samples;
3. 3.Package Verification Methods

AM Section 5: Non-Medical Pharmacology and Toxicology Division

The CBER reviews these studies and evaluates their adequacy and comprehensiveness to ensure that there are no contraindications or toxic effects.

Section 6- Pharmacology and availability of human life.

Section 7- Clinical Microbiology.

Section 8- Medical data section.

Section 9- Security Update Report.

Section 10-Statistics Section.

Section 11-Case Report Tables

Section 12- Case Report Form

Section 13- Patent Information

Section 14- Certificate of Patent

Section 15- Description of Establishment

Section 16- Department Certificate

Section 17- Field copy certificate

Section 18- User Payment Card

Section 19 - Financial information

Section 20-Others

Compliance with established Good Product Practices (GMP) is now primarily assessed during pre-approval reviews conducted by the FDA prior to final BLA approval.

In August 2001, CBER and CDER issued a draft guideline. This document is labeled "Draft----Not for Execution".

This guide is of particular interest in organic produce for two reasons:

i. It is labeled as not for implementation.

ii. This is exclusively for "limited" biotechnology products only.

These specific biotech products, originally called "well-classified biological products", are used for four different types of products.

i. Therapeutic DNA plasmid material.

ii. Synthetic peptide products treated with 40 or fewer amino acids.

Monoclonal antibody product for in vivo use. iv) Material derived from therapeutic remodeling DNA.

1.13.6 BLA Review Process

Subsequently, the current CBER BLA review process was developed to meet the requirements of the Drug User Fee Act (PDUFA) of 1996.

Under this act, the FDA has agreed to set standards and time limits in exchange for user fees paid by BLA sponsors.

The goal is to standardize both the review process and review content.

No. Number issued by CBSE. Guidance documents that provide the types of information to be included in the BLA for each class of organic product.

Some of them are industry guidelines for presenting chemical, production and control information.

ID Guidelines for Chemical Submission, Production and Control Information and Installation Details for Auto-Logo Somatic Cell Therapy Products - January 10, 1997

Industry Guidelines - Changes in Approved Application for Specific Biotechnology and Specific Synthetic Biological Products - July 24, 1997.

The Review Committee will first review the BLA for refusing to file a decision within 60 days (RTF).

If the Review Committee determines that the BLA is complete for filing purposes, it shall file and conduct a thorough review as set forth in SOPP8405.

After a thorough review, CBER will issue a complete response letter stating that there are deficiencies. or an approval letter stating that a marketing license has been issued.

1.13.7 License Application

During the review of the BLA, the FDA's request to address unresolved issues related to the original submission and the response to such request is usually referred to as a revision.

Either Changes that occur in an unauthorized application are called changes (IND, BL and NDA).

Original BLA Supplement:

Changes are submitted to renew or replace unauthorized BLAs, and supplements are submitted to replace approved license applications.

Authorized BLA holders may wish to change this

Expanding production methods, product specifications or making other changes that reflect new technology or make the product or process more competitive.

1.13.8 Collection and Submission of BLA

Submission of BLAs in electronic format will expedite the review process and eliminate bulky paper handling.

Several guidelines have been published providing information on BLA filing in electronic format along with the standard 356H format or the newer CTD format.

Revised Guidelines for Industry: Issue of Regulatory Submissions in electronic form to Center for Biological Assessment and Research (CBER) - Biomarket Application [Bio Licensing Application (BLA), Product Licensing Application (PLA)/ Installation License Application and New Application (NDA)] - 12 November 1999.

Industrial Draft Guidelines: Submission of Marketing Application as per General Ideas of Form ICH-CTD - September 5, 2001

CTD is a five modular format for universal use.

Section 1: Administrative Information (Regional Specified). In the case of the United States, this section includes Form FDA 356(h), draft labeling, and three abbreviations.

Section 2: Summary and Overview.

Section 3: Product quality information.

Section 4: Non-medical Study Reports.

Section 5: Clinical Study Reports.

References

1. The Pharmaceutical Regulatory Process; second edition; edited by Ira R.Berry Robert P.Martin; page number 103.
2. https://www.fda.gov/vaccines-blood-biologics/development-approval-process-cber

CHAPTER 1.14

U.S Registration for Foreign Drugs

The economy of drug development is having a major impact on the strategy for global marketing approval of new drugs. This is especially true when sponsors develop and register a drug in one country and then obtain marketing approval for a new pharmaceutical product from regulatory bodies in another country or territory. Although the drug development process is similar in different regions, differences due to culture, medical practice, population, and other factors can affect how and how quickly new drugs are introduced. Gains access to various markets. For example, the U.S. In sponsors such differences complicate the recording process when asking for recordings. Food and Drug Administration (FDA) pharmaceutical products for the US market. Based on data collected outside the United States. An in-depth understanding of the issues involved and Careful implementation of the regulatory approach. To help manage the process.

1.14.1 Introduction

Development, U.S. There is continued interest in FDA approval. and importing foreign drugs into the US market.

Current FDA regulations present significant challenges for both foreign and US manufacturers.

Foreign companies are subject to the same FDA review as US companies.

Import regulations on foreign drugs must be followed as the FDA has become more enforcement-minded, but with a twist.

Although the drug development process is similar in different regions, differences due to culture, medical practice, population and other factors can influence how and how quickly new drugs are introduced. Gains access to various markets.

The agency is concerned about GMP compliance in the production of APIs used in the United States.

1.14.2 Regulatory Structure

Two regulatory bodies

- US Food and Drug Administration (FDA):

It sets acceptable standards.

- International Conference on Synchronization (ICH):

It refers to the problem using specific guidelines and CTDs.

1.14.3 US Food and Medical Administration

The FDA regulations governing the approval of a new drug on the market will be covered by Federal Regulations (CFR), Chapter 21, Section 314.

If the agency believes it meets the listed criteria, it can approve the product based on foreign research

The FDA has approved about 80 drugs based on clinical data developed outside the United States.

1.14.4 International Conference on Harmonization (ICH)

The ICH reviewed the ways clinical data collected in one region is adopted by regulatory authorities in another.

This ongoing effort resulted in ICH guideline E5, "Ethnic Factors in Obtaining Foreign Medical Data."

For sponsors of foreign drugs, ICH E5 guidelines comply with FDA regulations.

It states that all data from the Department of Medicine must meet standards for research design and conduct and meet regional regulatory requirements.

Once this is done, the sponsor will be able to extend the survey data to the population of the new area, in this case, the United States.

Additional data may be needed if the sponsor or regulatory body is concerned that racial differences may have a significant impact on drug safety or efficacy in a new population.

The core concept of the ICH Guidance E5 is "Bridging Study".

1.14.5 Possible Recession

The issues foreign drug advocates should pay attention to are divided into three broad categories:

CMR (Chemistry, Manufacturing and Regulation) Issues.

Non-medical complications

Medical complications

(a) Chemistry, production and control problems

The FDA requires foreign drugs to have the same CMC information as is used for new non-approved domestic drugs.

All drug manufacturers must comply with the cGMP for ready-made drugs as defined in 21 CFR 211.

Manufacturers must meet USP standards if the drug, its by-product or drug is available.

Sponsors of foreign drugs must comply with ICH quality guidelines regarding stability, testing methods of testing, acceptable levels of contaminants, residual solvents, etc.

Sponsors may submit pharmaceuticals, products, by-products or packaging chemicals and information about the product in the Drug Master File (DMF).

(b) Import procedures and related issues

Foreign manufacturers must register with the FDA Drug Listing Branch and provide them with a pharmaceutical company number.

To import a foreign pharmaceutical product through US Customs, the importer must provide the relevant documents.

Foreign manufacturers must also have US agents. Resident or holds a business place in the United States.

(c) FDA Study of Foreign Manufacturers

FDA can inspect overseas production area.

If the FDA conducts a study and finds problems, the researcher will report their comments on the terms and conditions found on the site in FDA Form 483.

Non-medical complications

Data for patients during clinical trials and when the drug is sold must demonstrate safety for humans.

ICH Guidance M3, "Time for pre-clinical trials related to clinical trials," refers to general considerations when conducting non-clinical trials in a drug development program .

Data on a non-exotic drug must be FDA-compliant and tested for good laboratory practices (as found in the GLP, 21 CFR 58).

The pharmaceutical ingredient and drug product or product tested in non-therapeutic studies must be related to a product that the sponsor intends to sell in the United States.

The final safety database should reflect known safety concerns found in animals or humans during drug development.

It is important to conduct a non-clinical assessment of ADME related species in sponsored humans.

Medical Complications

Sponsoring a foreign drug can be achieved by planning to address ethnic differences, both internal and external, during the drug development process.

Reducing the need for copying studies and creating a stronger position for FDA approval.

1.14.6 Selection of Investigator/Site

Selected investigators should be well-versed in conducting controlled clinical trials in accordance with Good Medical Training (GCP) guidelines.

Selected sites must have sufficient research training and experience to conduct tests, which can eventually be audited by the FDA.

Restrictions on drug production under investigation and control over the conduct of investigations Required for registration.

1.14.7 Drug-Drug Interactions

Drug–drug interaction data from overseas studies in the United States may be of limited use.

A variety of factors can complicate extrapolation

Foreign data supporting labelling for the US population.

The sponsor, and ultimately the FDA, may determine that additional drug-drug interaction tests may be required to support US labelling.

1.14.8 Problems of Patients

Learning or disability can also be a barrier to adherence to therapy.

Receiving foreign data.

Ensuring patient compliance can be difficult in people with a low level of education.

1.14.9 Comparator and Dose Selection

The relevance of foreign medical data may be determined by the choice of comparator and the test dose and the relative dose or dose range for both comparators.

US Careful consideration should also be given to the choice of critical test dosage and dosage to be used to support an application.

1.14.10 Data Interruption

Explanation of Investigator's Qualification

Description of research facilities

Detailed summary of the protocol and inspection results and case records maintained by the examiner

Description of pharmaceutical ingredients and pharmaceutical products used in clinical research

1.14.11 Design

Development of a foreign drug for approval in the US market. Similar to the development of drugs in the United States.

No matter where the drug came from or where the data was collected, sponsors must meet the same requirements.

Companies manufacturing foreign drugs should have a good plan

Contact the FDA "often in advance".

Drug development is difficult for pharmaceutical companies everywhere. The "foreign" element can be a little complicated in the task, but this is not an insurmountable obstacle.

References

1. Ways and Means to U.S. Registration of Foreign Drugs and David Skarinshttps://www.taylorfrancis.com/chapters/edit/10.1201/9780203997048-20/ways-means-registration.
2. https://www.slideshare.net/NivaRaniGogoi/us-registration-for-foreign-drugs

CHAPTER 1.15

Bioequivalence and Drug Product Assessment

1.15.1 Introduction

Bioequivalence studies are pharmacological performance tests that compare the bioavailability of the same active pharmaceutical ingredient from one drug product (test) to another drug product (reference). Bioavailability and bioavailability can be considered as a measure of pharmaceutical product efficacy in vivo.

Io bioavailability and bioavailability studies provide valuable information in the overall data set that ensures the availability of safe and effective drugs.

There has been a concept of availability and equality of life for the last three decades.

Today it is required for worldwide acceptance of brand name and generic drug.

1.15.2 Objectives

The most important goal is to measure and compare the developmental efficacy between two or more drug equivalent drugs.

1.15.3 Subject

By the United States Food and Drug Administration (FDA): There is no significant difference in the ratio and amount of active ingredient or active ingredient in drug equivalents or drug substitutes. Same molar. Dosing under similar conditions in a properly designed study.

World Health Organization (WHO): Although two drug products are equivalent or drug substitutes, their feasibility, rate (Cmax and Tmax) and absorption level (lower part of the curve), and the same molar dose under similar conditions after administration, Their effects are generally similar. Similar to what is expected to be the same.

1.15.4 Requirements

Requirement The demand for bio-equilibrium studies is increasing due to the huge increase in the production and consumption of generic products.

Bio-balance study is done if:

life balance risk

Risk of failure of pharmacological treatment

Medicine There have been no clinical trials on the patient with a generic product to support its efficacy and safety.

1.15.5 Types

1. Chemical Equations

   Two or more drug products containing the same amount of a chemical with the same label.
2. Pharmacological equivalence Two or more drugs are similar in energy, quality, purity, stability of ingredients, dispersion and dissolution.
3. Therapeutic Equation

   Two or more drugs on the same active ingredient in the same treatment have the same pharmacological effect and control the disease to the same extent.
4. Biological Balance

   Indicates that the substance of the drug in two or more equal doses reaches a systemic cycle at the same relative rate and relative amount.

1.15.6 Requirements for *In Vivo* Courses

Appropriate Action Oral Immediate Release Product with Short Healing Margin

Modified release product with proper operation

Non-verbal immediate release products

1.15.7 Statistical Analysis of Bio-equilibrium Data

Statistical evaluation studies are based on blood tests or plasma concentration of the drug.

The lower part of the plasma is concentrated. The v/s time curve (AUC) was used as an indicator of the degree of drug absorption.

In the early 1970s, approval was given based on average data. This means that the AUC and C_{max} values for the generic product must be within 20% of the brand-name product.

1.15.8 Design and Evaluation of Bioequivalence Studies

Fasting study	Food intervention study	Multiple dose study
• Use for immediate release and modified release oral dosage form • Overnight fast and 4 hour after dosing	• Co-administration of food with and oral drug product may affect the bioavialability of drug	• Multiple dose, randomized, crossover srtudy • Three consecutive trough concentration on three consecutive days

1.15.9 Type of Design

1. Complete randomized design All treatment are randomly allocated among all experimental subject

   Example: if there is 20 subjects, number them from 1 to 20. Random select non repeating number

   Advantages

   1. Easy design

   2. Can accommodate any number of treatment and subject

1.15.10 Disadvantages

1. All subjects must be homogenous
2. Randomized block designs

   Subjects are sorted into homogenous group called blocks

   Method

   Subjects having similar background characteristics are formed as blocks

1.15.11 Advantages

- Different treatment not need equal sample size
- Can accommodate any number of treatments
- Statistical analysis is relatively simple Disadvantages
- Degree of freedom is less.

1.15.12 Repeated Measured, Cross Over, Carry Over Design

- Randomized block design
- Administration of two or more treatment one after the other is specified or random order to the same group of patients is called crossover design or change over design

  Advantages

  1. Good precision for comparing treatments
  2. Economic on subjects

  Disadvantages

  1. Order effect which is connected with the position in the treatment order
  2. Carry over effect

1.15.13 Crossover Parallel Design

- A Parallel design is completely randomized design in which each subject receive one and only one formulation of the drug in a random fashion.
- The simplest parallel design is two group Parallel design, which compares two formulation of the drug
- Each group contain equal number of subjects.

1.15.14 Crossover Studies

Randomized complete block design of two subjects receiving four treatments.

SUBJECTS	PERIOD 1	PERIOD 2
1	T	S
2	S	T

1.15.15 Randomized Complete Block Design of Six Subjects Receiving Four Treatments

SUBJECT	PERIOD 1	PERIOD 2	PERIOD 3	PERIOD 4
1	B	C	A	D
2	D	C	A	B
3	B	C	D	A
4	D	C	B	A
5	C	C	A	B
6	D	C	B	A

1.15.16 Replicated Cross Over Design

Use for determination of individual bioequivalence

	PERIOD 1	PERIOD 2	PERIPD 3	PERIOD 4
SEQUENCE 1	T	R	T	R
SEQUENCE 2	R	T	R	T

1.15.17 Latin Square Cross Over Design for a Bioequivalence Study of the Three Drug Products in Six Human Volunteers

DRUG PRODUCT			
SUBJECTS	STUDY PERIOD 1	STUDY PERIOD 2	STUDY PERIOD 3
1	A	B	C
2	B	C	A
3	C	A	B
4	A	C	B
5	C	B	A
6	B	A	C

1.15.18 Types of Evidence

Latin square cross over design for a bioequivalence study of the Four drug products in 16 human volunteers

DRUG PRODUCT				
SUBJECTS	PERIOD 1	PERIOD 2	PERIOD 3	PERIOD 4
1	A	B	C	D
2	B	C	D	A
3	C	D	A	B
4	D	A	B	C
5	A	B	D	C
6	B	D	C	A
7	D	C	A	B
8	C	A	B	D
9	A	C	B	D
10	C	B	D	A
11	B	D	A	C
12	D	A	C	B
13	A	C	D	B
14	C	D	B	A
15	D	B	A	C
16	B	A	C	D

1.15.19 Type of Evidence to Establish Bioequivalence

Bioequivalence in descending order of accuracy sensitivity and reproducibility

In vivo measurement of active moiety or moieties in biologic fluid;

In vivo Pharmacodynamic comparison;

In vivo limited clinical comparison;

In vitro comparison;

Any other approach deemed appropriate by FAD.

1.15.20 Evaluation of Data

Analytical data

Analytical method for measurement of drug must be validated for accuracy, precision, sensitivity and specificity.

More than one method during bioequivalence study may not be valid because different values.

1.15.21 Dosage form Performance

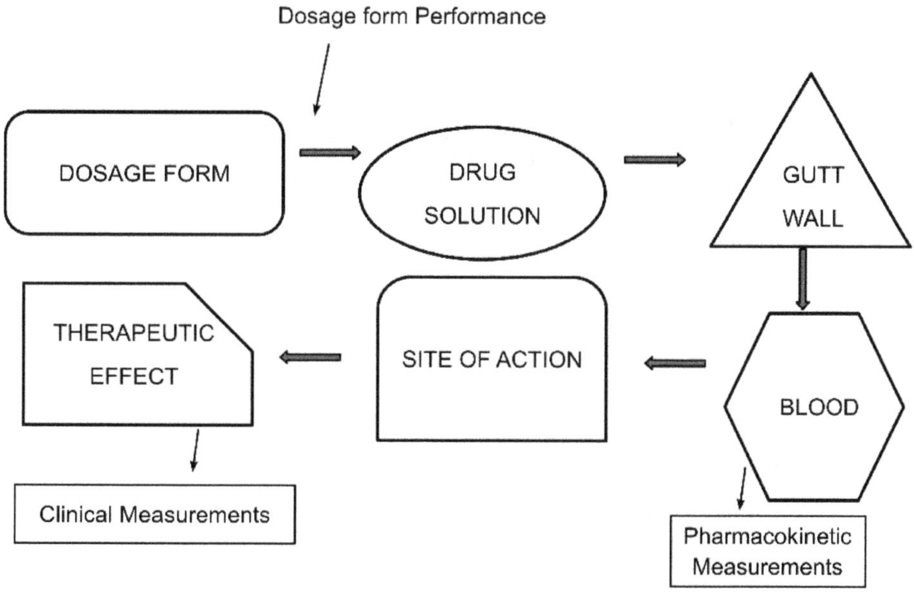

1.15.22 BCS Classifying

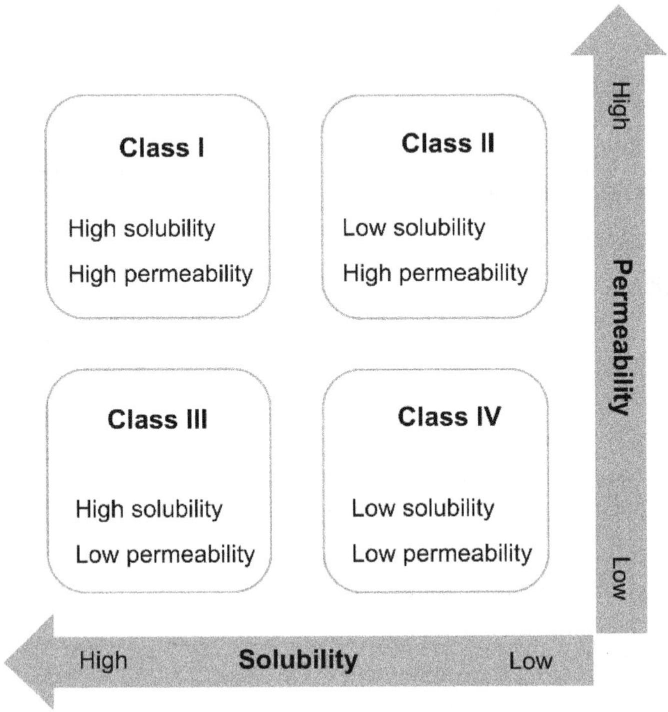

Web Reference

1. https://www.google.com/search?q=bioequalance+and+drug+quality+aSSESMENTS&oq=bioequalance+and+drug+quality+aSSESMENTS&aqs=chrome.69i57j33i10i160l3.23726j0j15&sourceid=chrome&ie=UTF-8
2. https://www.slideshare.net/Gauravchaudhary199/bioequivalence-and-drug-product-assessment

CHAPTER 1.16

Post Marketing Surveillance

1.16.1 Phases of Clinical Trials

Phase I: First in man Safety

Phase II: First in Patient – dose, dosage forms

Phase III: Efficacy, ADRs

Post-marketing Surveillance or Phase –IV: Evaluation of the drug in real clinical setting.

1.16.2 Introduction

For a drug to be sold, the manufacturer must provide evidence of its effectiveness and safety to the US Food and Drug Administration (FDA).

In a primary marketing trial, the number and type of patients used to demonstrate the drug's effectiveness and safety are relatively small compared to the number and type of patients eventually distributed after the drug is sold.

However, post-market surveillance does not provide information about the drug's safety or efficacy when it enters the market.

Post-marketing drug monitoring plays an important role in detecting an adverse side effect that reflects the risk. It provides additional information about the benefits and risks of drugs.

1.16.3 Post-Marketing Surveillance

No fixed duration/patient population

Marketing starts immediately after Report all ADRs

Help with search on rare ADR

Drug interactions

Innovative new applications for drugs [sometimes called Phase V]

1.16.4 History

In the 1960s, at least two serious drug reactions were observed in many patients. Thalidomide causes deformity of the foot (phocomelia).

In Japan, optic nerve damage (subacute myelopathy-neuropathy) is seen.

PMA Senator Edward Kennedy (D-Mass.) suggested that a better system is needed to monitor the use and side effects of prescription drugs after they are sold.

As a result, the Joint Commission on the Use of Prescription Drugs was established in 1976, funded by most pharmaceutical companies, with an mandate to design post-marketing surveillance systems to identify, measure and describe expected and unplanned side effects. was given. over-the-counter medications.

Delay in detecting adverse effects of the protocol improved post-marketing follow-up.

1.16.5 Sources of PMS Information

The following can be considered as sources of information, some sources are proactive and some are reactive.

- Expert User Group ("Focus Panel"))
- Customer review.
- Customer complaints and warranty requests
- After clinical trials in CE-market.
- literary review.
- Device tracking / embedding records.
- User feedback during training with programmers.
- Press.

1.16.6 What are the Benefits of a PMS System?

- Identify production problems;
- improving the quality of medical equipment;
- verification of risk assessment;
- long-term performance intelligence;
- chronic complications;
- performance trends;
- performance across different user populations

1.16.7 Machines that can abuse the Device

- Indications for use, feedback on the instructions for use.
- Necessary training for users; Use on other devices.
- Customer satisfaction.
- Market efficiency and stability.
- Identify incident reports (and area security improvement action reports).

1.16.8 Evaluation

- The intraocular lens manufacturer has collected several complaints from users regarding broken lenses.
- The manufacturer evaluates complaints and considers them to be statistically significant.

1.16.9 Why do we need Post-Marketing Surveillance?

The main purpose of post-marketing surveillance is to generate information about the drug's effects under normal conditions of drug use.

Rare adverse events cannot be found in pre-licensed studies because very large clinical trials are rare.

More patients accessed and data provided

Because of the diversity of data sources, innovative approaches to basic data retrieval may have great potential as compared to an integrated system.

Better background ratio, comparable "control" population.

Increase in "non-medical" data sources – eg. Pharmacy, Supermarket, Boss Vaccine.

1.16.10 Vision for Post-Marketing Tracking

All vaccines and patient health outcomes are immediately and continuously available in an automated database that allows optimal diagnosis and evaluation of potential vaccine safety issues.

Not now - both major limitations and opportunities in current health information systems.

Description Issues and solutions to improve vaccine safety information and evaluation both apply to safety efforts for other medical products.

1.16.11 Post-marketing Monitoring Opportunity

Access to additional health system data.

Access to global data: regulatory, research, health care systems, international surveillance and pharmacological surveillance.

Excellent review tools and methods.

1.16.12 Practical Features of PMS

PMS must be activated.

The manufacturer must document compliance.

The manufacturer's PMS process should discuss the information collected and available as part of the system.

1.16.13 About PMS Process

- It should appoint departments or posts responsible for performing a particular duty.

  Manufacturer can assist in getting one year final report and PMS tracking schedule and registration.
- This information may be user feedback.

1.16.14 PMS Reporting

Information received from the PMS system should be reported to the executive review meeting at least once a year - this is the top management review in the organization's quality management system.

1.16.15 Monitoring System

Therefore, four types of studies are commonly used to determine the effects of drugs:

1. Controlled Clinical Trials,
2. Voluntary or Voluntary Registration
3. Cohabitation, Study and
4. Case Control Study

1. Controlled Clinical Trials:

Reduce dependencies through methods such as randomization and "double-blinding".

Monitor patients directly for the duration of the study.

To evaluate the efficacy and safety of a drug.

They are often expensive

2. **Voluntary or voluntary statement**

   Physicians and other healthcare providers and hospitals may warn the FDA and drug companies about potential side effects of drugs.

3. **Joint Study**

   Studies follow a limited group of patients for a specific period of time.

   The patient is not easily detached, and nothing is blindfolded.

   In case of bad response. Another group of patients with a similar medical condition may receive non-drug and alternative treatments.

4. **Case-Control Study**

   Case control studies identify the patient with an adverse effect analysis and compare it to a sample taken from cases in the same group.

1.16.16 Manufacturer PMS System

These are just some of the knowledge and feedback you can get from the PMS system.

- Identify some production problems
- Improve product quality.
- Compliance with risk assessment (or otherwise).
- Knowledge of long-term performance/reliability and/or chronic issues.
- Knowledge of performance across different user populations.
- Feedback
- Feedback on indications for use.
- Instructional concept for use.
- Feedback on use on other devices.
- Feedback on customer satisfaction.
- Approval of monitoring report.
- Perception of current market credibility.

1.16.17 Summary

Post-marketing monitoring (PMS) is the practice of monitoring the safety of a drug.

Important equipment and pharmacology awareness A significant part of science after its release in the market.

Because drugs are approved in clinical trials involving a relatively small number of individuals selected for this purpose.

Post-market surveillance can further enhance, confirm or disprove the safety of a drug after its use in the general population with a wide range of medical conditions.

Post-marketing surveillance uses a number of methods to monitor the safety of licensed drugs, including automated reporting databases, recommended event tracking, electronic health records, patient records, and interrelationships between health databases.

Medical, product and production data are an important basis for security and performance evaluation before licensing.

However, it is important to monitor post-licensing to ensure product safety.

Lack of complete clinical information.

Vaccines and other medical products are at risk due to unrecognized rare serious adverse events.

References

1. Borden E.K, The upjohn Co., „„POST- MARKETING SURVEILLANCE OF out patient drugs using a pharmacy-based registration system-report of two studies,"" presented at the drug information association Work shop, Williamsburg va, DECEMBER 1981,10-32.
2. CLARREN S.N.et al, "The evaluabdity Assessment of the developing experiment in post marketing surveillance of prescription drugs"", prepared for the experiment technology incentives program, National Bureau of standards, 10-22.
3. FOOD AND DRUGS ADMINISTRATION, „„Supplementary reports to contracts and grants committee on Medicaid", from the division of Drugs Experience, BUREAU OF DRUGS,1982, 10-32
4. KAREN MIDTHUN, „„Deputy Director Centre for biologics Evaluation and Research", FDA, ICDRA Pre-conference Berne, SWITZERLAND September 15.

CHAPTER 2.1

Chemistry, Manufacturing and Controls (CMC)

2.1.1 Chemistry, Manufacturing and Controls (CMC)

Chemistry, Manufacturing and Control (CMC) Regulatory Affairs (RAs) play an important role in the development, licensing, production and marketing of pharmaceutical products. In this role, CMC RA specialists help ensure that pharmaceutical products remain effective, safe and of high quality for consumers. "Simon" Kolek, Jr., PhD, shares his perspective on the most important CMC issues facing companies today. He also gives some great advice for those considering a career in this field.

(a) Definitions

In vitro products are defined as all raw materials and intermediates used in the final test product as defined in 21 CFR 820.3(c).

An *in vitro* product is defined as all integrated components in its final form and the licensed product.

Department of Chemistry, Construction and Control [1-22]

I. *In vitro* Substance

A. Description and Features

1. Description

A clear description of each *in vitro* material should be provided. These descriptions may include, but are not limited to, any of the following: chemical structure, primary and subgroup structure, molecular weight, molecular formula, USAN established name, antibody class/subdivision, etc. if applicable.

2. Properties

Details and results of all analytical tests performed to identify *in vitro* materials should be presented, and information from specific tests relating to the identity, strength, specificity, purity, durability and durability of the material under test should be presented.

A. Physical Chemistry

Examples of reviews include, but should not be limited to, the places where information is submitted.

amino acid analysis

- Amino- and carboxyl-terminal arrays
- Complete Amino Acid Sequence

Peptide mapping/enzymatic mapping

Determination of disulfide link

sodium dodecyl sulfate-polyacrylamide gel electrophoresis (SDS-PAGE) (less and less)

So ISO Electric Focus

Conventional and high pressure fluid chromatography (HPLC) eg, reverse-phase, volume exclusion, ion-exchange, etc.

Mass spectroscopy

Tests for the detection of substance-related proteins, including deaminated, oxidized, clipped, and integrated forms and other variants, eg, amino acid substitutes, additives/derivatives.

Tests to detect remaining unstable host proteins, DNA, reactions

Immunochemical analysis

Tests for the Count of Bioburden and Endotoxin

Antibody neutralization

blood gluten

Prevention of blood gluten

Antibody Nitrogen Levels

All test methods must be fully described, verified and results provided. The application should also contain the actual data such as chromatogram, SDS-PAGE or agarose gel images, spectra.

B. Function of *in vitro* products

Provide details and results of all relevant *in vitro* (and applied *in vivo*) tests performed to demonstrate energy, specificity, functionality, and acceptability criteria for each *in vitro* material. The description and validation of each estimate used should include the methods and criteria used, systematic steps, intermediate and inter-estimate variance, linear and acceptable limits of the estimate.

B. Producer

1. Identity

The name, address, FDA registration number, and other company information of each manufacturer responsible for any part of the manufacturing or testing activities of the *in vitro* product must be submitted. This includes other sites/sites owned and operated by contractors or other subsidiaries or company applicants acting as contractors. A brief description of the activities performed by each party and the responsibilities assigned to each party by the applicant should be submitted.

2. Ground Map

For each production site, a floor map showing the layout of the facility must be submitted. This map should not be a detailed schematic or engineering diagram, but rather a simple diagram describing production areas, rooms or relationships between rooms, and other materials applied by the parts to be made. This map should be clear enough to visualize the tester's *in vitro* product production flow and to identify areas of interest or rooms "near" to the room, e.g.., isolating new and post-virus inactive items and functions. Room numbers or other unique identifiers must be provided, although the location of processing equipment within rooms and premises is not required. Other submission areas may include product flow information and the General Information section of the Installation Details section.

3. Manufacture of other goods

A comprehensive list of all additional components to be developed or operated in the areas used for the product under application must be submitted. The applicant must specify in which rooms the additional components will be inserted and the production steps to be taken. An explanation should be given as to whether additional components will be added depending on the campaign or in conjunction with the production of the element that will be the subject of the application. An indication of additional materials should also be given that may share contact with the equipment used in production (defined in this section or other relevant section of the application as dedicated multi-use equipment for each step of the process). A brief description of the type and stage of development of additional components should be given.

4. Pollution Precautions

The following information regarding precautions to be taken to prevent contamination or cross-contamination should be submitted in all areas where bank cell manufacturing and product preparation activities are carried out:

Classifying the air quality of the room or area where the operation is performed and measured during the operation;

A brief, descriptive description of the processes and/or facility design features of pollution control, cross-pollution and control (such as separation of air pressure layers, functions and products) – this is specifically designed for working with multipurpose areas or organisms is important.,

Provide a general description of the equipment design, for example, whether the design represents an open or closed system or provides sterile or sterile operation.

Description of process controls to prevent or determine contamination or cross-contamination. The handling or processing of more than one substance (eg, cell lines, sera, antigen) by an unrelated device in a field should be described and the measures used to prevent cross-contamination should be discussed.

C. working mode

1. Materials and Materials

A list of all products used with reference to the *in vitro* ingredients and their test and qualification specifications or the official package will be presented. For raw materials purchased, representatives must submit the supplier(s) inspection certificate(s) and the results of in-house acceptance testing. Note that process gases (eg, air, carbon dioxide, etc.) and water are considered raw materials.

A list of eligible tests, test results and acceptance criteria for all special reactions and materials used in the production of all *in vitro* materials, e.g., cultural media, dilutions, dyes, reactions, buffers, sera, antibiotics, Monoclonal antibodies, protection must be presented. In some cases (eg, a peptide or monoclonal antibody used in the manufacture of an *in vitro* substance), a detailed description of the product and character may be required.

Testing and description of items of animal origin that may be contaminated by adventitious agents, e.g., mycoplasma for products derived from bovine, bovine spongiform encephalopathy agents (BSE), and other adventitious agents of human and animal origin, must be submitted.

Must be included in the submission of information (verification data) or certificates supporting the independence of the goods from adventure agents.

In some cases, the applicant may wish to purchase rather than manufacture a licensed part of the final product. There are several regulatory techniques that can be used. It is recommended to discuss these methods in CBER at the planning level.

2. **Flow Chart**

   A complete visual representation of the production process flow must be presented. This flow chart for each production stage should indicate a complete list of equipment and materials used, the operating room or location (other areas of the application may be specified) and the process controls and tests performed on the product. every step. This chart contains information (or should be attached to a descriptive description) of the methods used to move the product between phases, i.e., sterile, steam-in-place (SIP) connections, sanitary connections, of laminar flow units. Under this should include open exchange. , Etcetera. Such transfer should be ascribed to the movement of the product between equipment, areas/rooms, building areas, etc. Other sections of the application may be referred for detailed information on the procedure.

3. **Detailed Description**

A. Animal Resources

Broad guidance in this area can be derived from the draft points to be considered in the production and testing of monoclonal antibody products for human use.

Information used in production, such as mice used to make ascites, rabbits used to make serum-antibodies, or genetically modified animals, should contain detailed information about:

Origin and species of animals used (including genetically modified, method of formation and genetic stability)

Adventurous Agent Screening and Use as Isolated Methods animal care practices

Livestock monitoring for livestock products determines the geographic origin and location of the herd immunogens are used

- Immunity
- particular
- accuracy
- infertility

- Stability
- Vaccine type, dosage and schedule
- sub if any

B. Human resource

The information presented regarding the use of raw materials of the human lineage includes, but not only:

- Donor Fit / Acceptance Criteria
- Collection method, size and container
- Use anticoagulant
- Description of area of interest
- Component Processing and testing
- Infectious disease marker test
- Dieter (Energy)
- Relevance
- Particular sensitivity
- Critical load
- Stability
- Cleaning methods and storage conditions of inactivity
- Ways to deactivate viruses
- Dosage and Vaccination Schedule
- Other properties that are unique to the object, process, or purpose of use.

C. Cellular source

Information presented on the use of cellular material, e.g., monoclonal antibodies or remodeling DNA techniques, may include but is not limited to:

Origin and types of cells

Then the phenotype and genetic type of cells

- Description of parent cell sequence
- Cloning Methods
- Ways of immortality
- Testing and Monitoring Procedures
- Identify genetic makeup
- Vector character

- Establishment, interpretation, maintenance and stabilization of bank cells
- Cell culture methods
- Harvesting methods
- Cleaning and Passive Methods
- Downline Processing Methods
- Other properties unique to the raw material being processed or intended use.

Further information can be found in the August 1996 article "Industrial Guidance on the Presentation of Data on the Chemistry, Production and Control of a DNA-Acquired Therapeutic Reconstruction Product or Monoclonal Antibody Product".

Artificial sources

Information about the use of substances from synthetic sources, such as synthetic peptides, should be presented. Details of the peptide package and purification methods are outlined in the "Carrier Guide for the Presentation of Chemical, Production and Control Information for Synthetic Peptide Products".

D. Process Control

1. Functional Control

Description of the methods used for control in operations, i.e., monitoring, testing, etc., used to ensure that the operational requirements of the final product are met, e.g. The integrity of solid-phase coatings is called enzyme purity. The antibody/antigen conjugate and energy should be deposited.

2. **Verification Process**

Explanation and results of the verification process study should be presented. If the production process is modified or expanded for commercial production and involves changes in production steps, a re-evaluation of the process should be described and data and results provided. To ensure the success of conventional production, studies for the following processes that identify the critical parameters to be used as process controls must be in detail. If applicable, refer to the production flow diagram(s).

Must be submitted for verification study:

- Cell growth and harvesting process
- Cleaning procedures

- Inactivates or eliminates any infectious germs from components used in the manufacturing process
- To demonstrate microbial control over processes that are susceptible to microbial contamination for ingredients labeled as sterile or used as preservatives.
- Solid phase coating process
- Pairing processes
- Possible adjustments
- Other if applicable

E. Standards/Reference Committee

1. Reference Standard

If you use an international reference standard (World Health Organization), CBER reference standard or compilation reference standard (U.S. Pharmacopoeia/National Formulary), you must submit a citation and rating certificate for the standard. If there is no reference standard and the applicant has locally established primary reference standards, an explanation of the nature and specifications of the standards should be provided. Test results such as amino acid analysis and determination of stable biological function should be submitted. The standard operating procedures (SOPs) used to qualify for the new reference standard must be included. Information should be provided on the continuity of any reference criteria.

2. House Reference Standards

Internal employment reference standards must be applied and a description of the product, description, description, test, replacement and results provided. The SOPs used to create and qualify the new internal standards should be included. Results should be presented by comparing the calibration data of employment standards with the primary reference standard.

F. Specifications / Methods of Analysis

1. Description and Analysis of *In vitro* Materials

The specifications and analysis methods used for emission analysis, layer life determination and distribution conditions should be described in detail. The specifications and tests of the *in vitro* material used to ensure the accuracy of the identity, strength and/or quantity of strength, specificity and volume are described in detail. (See applicable guidance document in Appendix A). The analytical methods should be checked and the data provided for the unpacked methods to prove the compatibility of the system.

2. **Corrupted Profile**

Supporting analytical data should provide a discussion of the pollution description. Profiles of protein variants should include *in vitro* products (eg, clipped, aggregated, de-aminated and oxidized forms), as well as non-product contaminants (eg, process reactions and cells. cultural components).

G. **Container / Closing System**

The operation should include a description of the container and sealing system and their compatibility with *in vitro* materials (5). Detailed information about the supplier, address and applicability results, eg, absorption, leakage, biological testing, etc., should be included. Evidence of the container's integrity and closure for the proposed storage period must be provided.

H. **Consistency**

Storage conditions, SOPs, inspection protocols and an explanation of the results supporting the stability of the *in vitro* material should be provided. Data from experiments to monitor biological activity and, if applicable to decomposition products such as bulk, dissolved, oxidized and clipped forms, should be included.

Second. *In vitro* preparation

A. Manufacturer

It contains the names and addresses of all manufacturers involved in the production and testing of an *in vitro* product, including contractors, and a description of the responsibility of each individual. A list of all other products (R&D, medical or approved) manufactured in both rooms must be provided. If the development of an investigative product is different from the finished product that can be marketed, clinical data supporting the equivalence of the two formulas should be provided, if applicable.

B. Structure

According to the "Guidelines for the Submission of Documents for the Production of Pharmaceuticals and for the Control of Pharmaceuticals", a description of all components, including quantities, proportions or formulations, to be used in an *in vitro* product must be included. If a test product being used is different from the finished product, clinical data supporting the similarity of the two formulas should be provided, if applicable.

C. Production and Packaging Method

Must provide a complete description of the production process flow for each generated aggregate. This discussion should include details of sterilization operations, as well as sterilization operations, aseptic processing procedures, wilting/filling, lyophilization, labeling and baking processes. The report should be accompanied by a flow chart indicating the equipment and materials used, the operating room or location (other areas of use may be specified) and a list of inputs depending on the product. -Process control and testing on the product at each stage. This flow chart or description should also include information on connections, health connections and open transfers within laminar flow units. Such transfers must be described for the movement of products between equipment, premises/rooms, buildings and sites. References can be made to other sections of the application for detailed information on the process. Provide analysis of basic environmental conditions, methods of monitoring, description and interpretation of results obtained and description of environmental control methods in all production areas used in product production.

D. Specifications and Test Method

This section should contain a description of all test methods and details used to determine the identity, purity, strength and/or strength, specificity and durability of the final finished product. Product. The information presented should be, but not limited to:

- Sample sampling methods for tracking multiple prepared *in vitro* products.
- System compatibility verification data for all non-penetration tests.
- Results of validation studies to ensure the absence of interference of special inactive ingredients in the compilation methods of the USP.
- In-vitro materials must be provided with test certificates for at least three consecutive qualifications and with analytical results of internal testing.
- Description and results of all *in vitro* (and applied *in vivo*) tests displaying energy, specificity, function(s) and acceptance criteria for each *in vitro* product.
    1. Method and standards used
    2. Practical steps
    3. Transformation of Intermediate and Internal Assessment
    4. Linear
    5. Acceptable rating limits and
    6. Life load analysis.

E. Container / Closure System

Provide a description of the container and closure system and their compatibility with the *in vitro* product. Detailed information about the supplier, address and compatibility and biological test results should be included. This information may refer to a device or a Drug Master File (DMF). Evidence of the container's integrity and closure must be provided within the proposed expiration date.

F. Microbiology

If the product is sterile, the information must be presented as described in "Industry Guidance on Submitting Documents for Contraceptive Procedure Verification in Applications for Human and Veterinary Pharmaceutical Products." For more guidance on other aspects of microbiologically controlled products, see "Guide for the production of *in vitro* diagnostic products".

G. Stability

Details of storage conditions, inspection protocols and findings supporting the stability of the product *in vitro* should be provided. If applicable, it should contain information on the stability of intermediate liquids or the total quantity designed under specific handling or shipping conditions. Stability data supporting the proposed shelf life of 13 reconstituted *in vitro* products and all labeled diluents should be provided. Proven results must be provided for all tests used to monitor the performance characteristics, safety performance and presence of *in vitro* products such as aggregate, de-aminated, oxidized and decomposition products in different forms.

H. Batch Product Records

A complete (executed) volume record of the production/equipment history of the entire production and testing process for an *in vitro* product must be submitted.

III Environmental Assessment

An environmental assessment should be prepared as outlined in section 25 of 21 CFR. Provide a description of the process in question and specify all components involved in product production and disposal. Exemption details may be issued under exempt category, if applicable.

Fourth. proof of law

The information described in "Guidelines for the submission of samples and analytical data for validation methods" should be provided.

2.1.2 Importance

- It plays a vital role in the development, licensing, manufacturing and ongoing marketing of pharmaceutical products.
- The MCCMC team has the same function as the product development team, focusing on production process improvement, registration, production facilities and site inspection.
- It ensures compliance with cGMP, GLP and medical procedures.
- It also audits laboratory research regulations, compliance and readiness for medical and manufacturing facilities and information technologies.
- The essential content and format of the CMC section of the various types of applications are described in the same "International Convention" (ICH) guidelines.

2.1.3 What are the CMC Regulatory Issues?

To conduct clinical studies and market pharmaceutical products, doctors explain. Kolek, pharmaceutical companies must legally obtain and maintain regulatory approval. Regulatory issues is a regulatory and strategic role within the overall organizational structure of a pharmaceutical company, relating directly to government regulatory agencies with respect to regulatory approvals. For example, the Food and Drug Administration (FDA), the European Pharmaceuticals Association (EMA), and the Japan Pharmaceuticals and Medicines Agency (PMDA) are government regulatory agencies that are usually involved in the approval process.

Chemical, Manufacturing and Regulatory (CMC) Regulatory Affairs (RA) is a specialized area within the RA with the ultimate responsibility of providing CMC regulatory leadership and the strategy needed to obtain regulatory approval. As a strategic role, CMC RA works in a wide range of scientific, technical, quality and business areas within an organization or in collaboration with external contract manufacturing companies (CMOs). "To help companies obtain regulatory approvals effectively and efficiently," explains Dr. Kolek, "provides knowledge, understanding, interpretation and application of CMC regulatory issues and regulatory guidelines and regulations as well as best practices and trends across industry and government agencies."

For example, CMC regulatory submissions may contain active related information – but they are not the only ones.

Key role in converting "molecules" with potential medicinal properties into "commercial medical products"

Understand and explain the rules and guidelines of health authorities

local vs global

Identify requirements from rules

Liaison between Biopharma and Health Authority

Responsible for writing regulatory documents

other contacts

meeting

Various areas of regulation include Clinical, CMC, Labelling, Advertising and Promotion, Pharmacovigilance.

2.1.4 CMC Regulatory Affairs (CMC-RA)

- **CMC RA group provides**
    - CMC regulatory leadership
    - Strategy
- **Ensures the medicinal product is**
    - Supreme Quality
    - Safe for the use in treatment of individuals
    - Manufactured per regulations • Interactions inside the company is with
- **Technical operations or Manufacturing team**
    - Quality Assurance
    - Analytical
    - Contract Manufacturing organizations
    - Supply chain
    - Labelling
- **Interactions with health authorities**
    - Authoring of regulatory dossiers
    - Briefing books
    - Any communication regarding quality of the product (e.g.: field alert reports, CPPs etc.)
- **Maintenance of regulatory dossiers**

2.1.5 Regulatory Dossiers and its Contents

- Some light on Pharma development:
  - Timeline for development of a product takes 10-15years
  - For a chemical/ biological entity to become a medicinal product includes various phases
  - Regulatory approvals are required to conduct clinical studies and marketing the product.
- **Regulatory dossiers: Provide comprehensive information on**
  - Indication for use
  - Nonclinical data
  - Clinical data to support indication
  - Data to support the quality of the product
  - Label and storage conditions

Regulatory Dossiers and its contents

Types of Regulatory dossiers:

- Pharmaceutical Regulatory dossiers are of 2 types
  - Clinical applications:
  - IND- Investigational New Drug Applications (in USA) or
  - CTA- Clinical trial application (Ex USA)
- Market applications:
  - NDA- New Drug applications (FDA- for small molecules)
  - BLA- Biologic license Application (FDA- for Large molecules)
  - MAA- Market authorization application (Ex USA for both small and large molecules)

Format of Regulatory dossier

CTD- Common Technical document

- ICH M4Q (R1) proposes the CTD format for all the regulatory dossiers.
- The CTD format has 5modules
  - Module 1- Regional Information includes forms and country specific requirements
  - Module 2: provides summary for quality (CMC- 2.3), Efficacy (clinical)and
  - Safety (non-clinical)
  - Module 3, 4,5: Detailed information on quality, safety and efficacy respectively

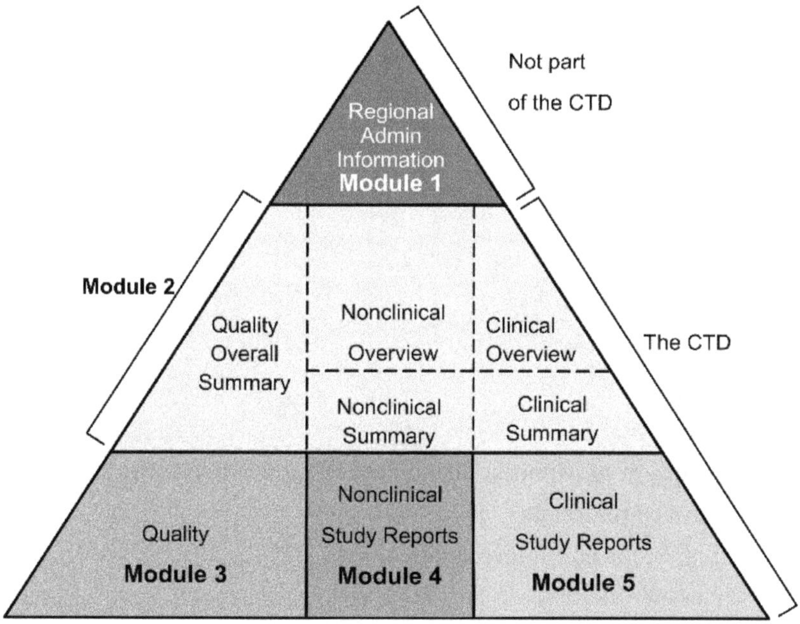

2.1.6 CMC Modules of Regulatory Dossier

Quality information is presented in Module 3 and Module2.3

Chemistry:

Structure, synthesis the drug substance, the composition of drug product, the materials involved in it

Manufacturing:

Description of manufacture of the product, equipment used, Facility information

Controls:

Ensure the quality of the product

In-process controls

Specifications for testing drug substance and drug product

Stability of the product

The detailed quality information presented in Module 3

Summary of information in Module 3 is presented in Module 2.3 and is called as Quality Overall Summary(QOS)

Module 3 is classified into 4parts

3.2.S- Drug Substance

3.2.P- Drug Product

3.2.A-Appendices

3.2.R- Regional Information

Drug Substance- 3.2-S

S.1 General Information

- S.1.1-Nomenclature
- S.1.2-Structure
- S.1.3-GeneralProperties

S.2- Manufacture

- S.2.1-Manufacture
- S.2.2- Description of Manufacturing process and Process controls
- S.2.3- Control of materials
- S.2.4-Critical Steps and Intermediates
- S.2.5- Process Validation
- S.2.6- Manufacturing Process Development

S.3- Characterization

- S.3.1- Elucidation of Structure
- S.3.2-impurities

S.4- Control of Drug Substance

- S.4.1-Specifications
- S.4.2- Analytical Methods
- S.4.3- validation of Analytical procedures
- S.4.4- Batch Analyses
- S.4.5- Justification of Specifications

S.5- Reference Standards

S.6- Container Closure System

S.7- Stability

- S.7.1- Stability Summary and Conclusion
- S.7.2- Stability Protocol
- S.7.3-StabilityData

Chemistry of the drug substance is described in S.1 and S.3sections

- Nomenclature: Internal names, IUPAC, USAN, INN etc.-S.1.1
- Structure, stereochemistry, etc.-S.1.2
- Physical properties-S.1.3

- Elucidation of Structure –S.3.1
- Impurities of the drug substance-S.3.2

Synthesis of the drug substance is provided inS.2

- Manufacturers and their responsibilities are provided inS.2.1
- Detailed Steps of DS synthesis, process flow is described inS.2.2
- Materials that are used in the synthesis are discussed in S.2.3; Including
  - Starting materials,
  - Raw materials,
  - Reagents,
  - Residual solvents
- Critical Steps in the process is discussed in S.2.4 which includes
  - Process design,
  - Process parameters
- Validation of the process and supporting data is provided in S.2.5
- The "story" behind how did we come up with the manufacturing process S. 2.6

DS container closure inS.6:

- Dimensions and materials used
- Any quality testing requirements for packaging

Drug Product-3.2-P

P.1- Description and composition of drug product

P.2- Pharmaceutical Development

- P.2.1- Components of Drug product
- P.2.1-1-DrugSubstance
- P.2.1-2-Excipients
- P.2.2- Drug product
- P.2.2.1-FormulationDevelopment
- P.2.2.2-Overages
- P.2.2.3-Physiochemical and Biological properties
- P.2.3-Manufacture and Process development
- P.2.4-Container closure system
- P.2.5-MicrobialAttributes
- P.2.6-Compatibility

P.3-Manufacture

- P.3.1-Manufacturer
- P.3.2-Batch formula
- P.3.3.-Description of manufacturing process and process controls
- P.3.4-Control of Critical Steps and Intermediates
- P.3.5-Process Validation

Drug Product-3.2-P

P.4-Control of Excipients

- P.4.1-Specifications
- P.4.2-AnalyticalMethods
- P.4.3-Validation of analytical methods
- P.4.4-Justification of Specifications
- P.4.5-Excipients of Human or Animal Origin
- P.4.6-NovelExcipients

P.5-Control of Drug Product

- P.5.1-Specifications
- P.5.2-AnalyticalMethods
- P.5.3-Validation of analytical methods
- P.5.4-BatchAnalyses
- P.5.5-Characterization of Impurities
- P.5.6-Justification of Specification

P.6-Reference Standards or Materials

P.7-Container closure System

P.8-Stability

- P.8.1- Stability Summary and Conclusion
- P.8.2-StabilityProtocol
- P.8.3-StabilityData

Chemistry of the drug product is described in sectionP.1

- The description of the drug product: solid or liquid;
- Dosage form: capsules or tablets; solution or suspension
- The composition of the drug product is described in P.1 and P.2.1
    - Drug Substance
    - Excipients: Additive agents which bulk up and have certain function

The Pharmaceutical Development of the drug product is described in section P.2'

- Section P.2.2 includes
  - Information on development of formulation
  - Formulation studies to come up with the formulation including any overages allowed
  - Properties of the drug product is presented in the section
- Section P.2.3includes
  - Detailed steps of Manufacturing,
  - Flowcharts
  - Process development
  - Process parameters including equipment
- Section P.2.4 details the container closure system and DP compatibility it
- The testing strategy for microbial attributes is presented in P.2.5
- The compatibility of drug product is presented in P.2.6

The manufacturing information for the drug product is described inP.3

- Similar to S.2.1, manufacturer including responsibilities of analytical testing, packaging, release and labelling of the product is outlined in P.3.1
- Batch formula and scale of the batch is presented in P.3.2
- The detailed in P.3.2 are about
  - Steps of manufacturing,
  - Manufacturing flowcharts,
  - Process parameters
- Critical Steps in the process are discussed in P.3.4
- Process design,
- Process parameters
- Validation of the manufacturing process and supporting data is provided in section P.3.5

DP container closure in P.7:

- Dimensions
- Materials used
- Any quality testing requirements for packaging

Control of Drug Substance and Drug Product

- **Certain sections like 3.2.S.4 and 3.2.P.5 outlines how does the sponsor makes sure that the quality of the product is intact- S.4 and P.5**
  - Specifications: Information on tests and acceptance criterion for quality testing for release and stability is presented in S.4.1 for DS and P.5.1 for DP
  - Analytical methods **descriptions** for the tests are presented in S.4.2 for DS and P.5.2 for DP
  - Validation procedure and data for the methods is presented in S.4.3 for DS and P.5.3 for DP
  - The batch release results based on the release specifications are presented in S.4.4and P.5.4
  - The characterization of impurities of DP is presented inP.4.5
  - The justification for the specification is presented in S.4.5and P.5.6

The control of excipients section P.4outlines

- Specifications of the excipients inP.4.1
- Analytical procedures for the tests for excipients inP.4.2
- The validation data of the analytical procedures inP.4.3
- Justification of Specifications inP.4.4
- For excipients which are human and animal origin, information including the information on manufacturing and analytical information inP.4.5
- Goes the same for new excipients in novel excipients section inP.4.6

Control of Drug Substance and Drug Product Contd.

- **Reference standard in Sections S.5 andP.6**
  - Is highly purified compound used as base for the measurement for batches
  - Information on reference standard presented in sections S. 5 and P.6 respectively includes
    - The lots for reference standard,
    - Specifications for reference standards
- **The stability of DS and DP is presented in S.7 andP.8**
  - The outlines the types of studies conducted and the summary of results in S.7.1 and P.8.1
  - The protocols for the stability studies including temperature conditions and studies that will be performed is outlined in S.7.2 and

P.8.2. These also include any commitments like post approval studies are also provided in these sections

- The detailed data results for the lots that have been tested per specifications and stability protocols is presented in S. 7.3 andP.8.3

3.2.A, 3.2.R and QOS

- **The information on flow diagrams of the manufacturing areas if required will be presented in 3.2.A**
- **Any information specific to particular region is presented in 3.2.R**
  - E.g.: Comparability protocol or change management protocol
- **Quality Overall summary:**
  - The QOS is presented in Module 2 in section 2.3 also consists of 4 parts like Module 3
    - 2.3.S- Drug Substance
    - 2.3.P- Drug Product
    - 2.3.A-Appendices
    - 2.3.R- Regional Information
  - It is the concise version of Module 3 sections and provides good summary of the same

2.1.7 Guidance used to Build Quality Section

- ICH M4Q provides guidance on the format which is accepted in all the countries
- For the content of the Module3
- Country specific regulations
- For e.g.: 21 CFR 314.50- Content and format of an application
- Health Authority Guidance
- Other ICH guidance like ICHQ1A-C, ICHQ3A-B, ICHQ6A-B, ICH8, ICH Q9, ICH Q10, ICH Q11, ICHM7

2.1.8 Drug Ingredient (API) and Complete Dosage Form

Product and Test Site Names and Locations API Identification and Dosage Form Structure API and raw material used in preparation of finished drug Product Description and Development Process Description of Production Processes Raw Materials, Process Control, Container and Closure Systems, API and Dosage Form Release and Stability Test Data

Analysis methods and specifications are used for testing and release of API and form dosages.

2.1.9 Most Important CMC Problem

New Molecular Company Approval - "For the regulatory approval of the New Molecular Body (NME)," said Dr. Kolek, "the management of all functions and requirements of CMC regulatory affairs is a product of a robust, disciplinary submission process." he points out. Regulatory document change through product approval – to achieve a successful outcome (i.e., approval of a product), an adaptive, disciplinary approach is followed and the initial clinical examination leads to pre-registration, A progressive statement is expected after approval and life cycle management.

Even after post-marketing approval, multiple CMC RA actions are required to support CMC modifications made to maintain the shelf life of the approved drug. In addition, an efficient and effective conversion control process is essential to maintain product consistency and compliance.

"It is very common for pharmaceutical companies to use CMC regulatory affairs advisors," Dr. Koleck. He said that CMC RA consultants can provide knowledge, experience, guidance and advice to pharmacists.

2.1.10 CMC Regulatory Issues

"CMC regulatory issues would be a great career option for individuals working in the pharmaceutical industry or a closely related industry," said Dr. Kolek, "with a scientific or technical background, analytical mindset, problem-solving skills, and strong communication and communication skills." They also believe that it is important to understand the diversity of issues associated with the invention, development, commercialization and maintenance of a pharmaceutical product.

CMC RA is a highly value-added function within an organization that is critical to the successful development, registration, approval and life cycle management of pharmaceutical products. Keeping in mind the importance of regulatory approvals for pharmaceutical products, Dr. Kolek, CMC RA individuals in departments have greater visibility at all levels of the organization and the regulatory bodies they interact with. So they should be comfortable and able to work in such an environment.

"There is no right or wrong way to start a business in CMC regulatory matters," said Dr. Kolek explains. While the majority of those starting a business at CMC RAs have some skill to work in the pharmaceutical industry, many employees come from a variety of backgrounds such as biological or chemical scientists, engineers, lawyers, quality control and quality assurance workers, as well as in the stages of drug production and development.

In some cases, the CMC RA staff has had a personal leader, Dr. Kolek, or CMC, was interested in the diversity of jobs and the challenges and opportunities offered within the RA. In other cases, people are more proactive - completing a certificate or degree in RA or working in another area of the company will increase the chances of transferring quality assurance to a position in RA.

In addition, doctors encourage. To learn more about the Kolec business and network, CMC RA offers active members:

- Drug Information Association (DIA) Parenteral Drug Association (PDA)
- American Association of Pharmacologists (AAPS) Association of Regulatory Experts (RAPS)
- The Organization for Professionals in Regulatory Affairs (TOPRA)

2.1.11 CMC Future

"The history of CMC regulatory issues in the pharmaceutical industry is a story of continuous change," said Dr. Kolek said collaboration between industry and regulators, and global collaboration with regulatory agencies - is one of the most positive trends.

For example, in the United States in the late 1980s, the FDA was involved in efforts to rewrite the Investigative New Drug (IND) and New Drug Use (NDA) regulations. "Indeed, this is one of the earliest transparency efforts requested by the industry," Dr.Kolk explained. However, at the time, the RA environment was more complex as each country had its own unique requirements for conducting clinical trials, obtaining regulatory approval, and making changes after approval. Approved pharmaceutical products.

The first paradigm shift in the regulatory environment, Dr. Kolek, A Collaborative Effort - Quality, Safety, Performance and Miscellaneous Guidelines – 20. This is still under the direction of the International Convention on the Synchronization of Technical Requirements for the Registration of Pharmaceuticals for Human Use (ICH) several years ago.

This includes joint ventures with regulatory agencies from the United States, the European Union, and Japan, as well as trade organizations from the pharmaceutical industry in these countries. However, the ICH initiative would not have been possible without the establishment of the European Medicines Agency (EMA) in 1995. Dr. Kolek points out that a document was eventually used to allow a product to be regulated in several European countries. Similar joint ventures are underway with various regulatory agencies around the world, he said, in the areas of information sharing on pharmaceutical products, research and pharmaceutical monitoring. In this way, regulatory agencies can make better use of their limited resources and collectively ensure patient safety and product quality.

"Continuing socio-economic and political changes will put pressure on both industry and regulatory agencies to increase cooperation in the current development of regulatory requirements," he said. Koleck. Innovation, advances in science, technology, regulatory science, and especially information technology and chemistry, its results will continue to be the driving force for future development.

Dr. Ashton tweeted for this interview. I would like to thank Kolek. If your organization needs assistance from CMC RA Area or any other member of the Ashton Tweed Life Sciences Executive Talent Bank, we can provide that support on a temporary or permanent basis. Alternatively, we would like to ask CMC RA professionals who are looking for temporary or permanent opportunities. In any case, please email us or call 610-725-0290. Ashton is pleased to continue to provide insightful articles of interest to the Tweet industry.

2.1.12 CVM CMC Guidelines

- Administrative and general guidance
- CVM GFI # 156 Comparison Protocol - Chemistry, Production and Control Information for New Veterinary Medicines
- CVM GFI Technical Section # 227 Two-Step Chemistry, Manufacturing and Regulation (CMC)
- CVM GFI # 234 Question - Analysis Based for the Technical Section on Chemistry, Manufacturing and Control of Veterinary Applications

Master File and Drug Substance Guidances

- CVM GFI #57 Preparation and Submission of Veterinary Master Files

- CVM GFI #92 (VICH GL10(R)) Impurities In New Veterinary Drug Substances
- CVM GFI #126 BACPAC I: Intermediates in Drug Substance Synthesis Bulk Actives Post approval Changes: Chemistry, Manufacturing, and Controls Documentation
- CVM GFI #169 Drug Substance Chemistry, Manufacturing, and Controls Information
- CVM GFI #216 Fermentation-Derived Intermediates, Drug Substances, and Related Drug Products for Veterinary Medicinal Use

Manufacturing Guidance

- CVM GFI #23 Medicated Free Choice Feeds - Manufacturing Control
- CVM GFI #50 Target Animal and Human Food Safety, Drug Efficacy, Environmental and Manufacturing Studies for Teat Antiseptic Products

Analytical Controls Guidance

- CVM GFI #63 (VICH GL1) Validation of Analytical Procedures: Definition and Terminology
- CVM GFI #64 (VICH GL2) Validation of Analytical Procedures: Methodology
- CVM GFI #135 Validation of Analytical Procedures for Type C Medicated Feeds
- CVM GFI #136 Protocols for the Conduct of Method Transfer Studies for Type C Medicated Feed Assay Methods
- CVM GFI #137 Analytical Methods Description for Type C Medicated Feeds
- CVM GFI #176 (VICH GL39) Specifications: Test Procedures and Acceptance Criteria for New Veterinary Drug Substances and New Medicinal Products: Chemical Substances
- CVM GFI #177 (VICH GL40) Specifications: Test Procedures and Acceptance Criteria for New Biotechnological/Biological Veterinary Medicinal Products
- CVM GFI #238 Modified Release Veterinary Parenteral Dosage Forms: Development, Evaluation, and Establishment of Specifications
- CVM GFI #264 Standardized Medicated Feed Assay Limits

Impurities Guidance

- CVM GFI #92 (VICH GL10(R)) Impurities in New Veterinary Drug Substances
- CVM GFI #93 (VICH GL11(R)) Impurities in New Veterinary Medicinal Products

- CVM GFI #100 (VICH GL18(R)) Impurities: Residual Solvents in New Veterinary Medicinal Products, Active Substances and Excipients (Revision)
- CVM GFI #211 Residual Solvents in Animal Drug Products Questions and Answers
- CVM GFI #255 Elemental Impurities in Animal Drug Products Questions and Answers

Stability Guidance

- CVM GFI #5 Drug Stability Guidelines
- CVM GFI #73 (VICH GL3(R)) Stability Testing of New Veterinary Drug Substances and Medicinal Products
- CVM GFI #74 (VICH GL4) Stability Testing of New Veterinary Dosage Forms
- CVM GFI #75 (VICH GL5) Stability Testing: Photostability Testing of New Veterinary Drug Substances and Medicinal Products
- CVM GFI #91 (VICH GL8) Stability Testing for Medicated Premixes
- CVM GFI #99 (VICH GL17) Stability Testing of New Biotechnological/Biological Veterinary Medicinal Products
- CVM GFI #198 (VICH GL45) Bracketing and Matrixing Designs for Stability Testing of New Veterinary Drug Substances and Medicinal Products
- CVM GFI #219 (VICH GL51) Statistical Evaluation of Stability Data
- CVM GFI #242 In-Use Stability Studies and Associated Labeling Statements for Multiple-Dose Inject able Animal Drug Products
- CVM GFI #259 (VICH GL58) Stability Testing of New Veterinary Drug Substances and Medicinal Products in Climatic Zones III and IV

Post-approval Changes Guidance

- CVM GFI #83 Chemistry, Manufacturing, and Controls Changes to an Approved NADA or ANADA
- CVM GFI #126 BACPAC I: Intermediates in Drug Substance Synthesis Bulk Actives Post approval Changes: Chemistry, Manufacturing, and Controls Documentation
- CVM GFI #271 Reporting and Mitigating Animal Drug Shortages during the COVID-19 Public Health Emergency

(a) Other CMC Guidance

Other FDA guidance may also provide useful information for the submission of CMC information for animal drugs, including Cross-Center guidance, Center for Drug Evaluation and Research (CDER) guidance, and International Conference on Harmonization of Technical Requirements for Registration of Pharmaceuticals for Human Use (ICH) guidance. Any other Cross-Centre, CDER, or ICH guidance pertaining to CMC information may also be considered applicable to animal drugs. Drug sponsors should contact CVM's Division of Manufacturing Technologies if they have any questions regarding the applicability of a guidance to animal drugs.

Administrative and General Guidance

- CDER/CBER/CVM GFI: Providing Regulatory Submissions in Electronic Format – Drug Establishment Registration and Drug Listing
- CDER/CVM/ORA GFI: PAT — A Framework for Innovative Pharmaceutical Development, Manufacturing, and Quality Assurance
- OC GFI: Considering Whether an FDA-Regulated Product Involves the Application of Nanotechnology
- CDER/CBER/CVM GFI: Contract Manufacturing Arrangements for Drugs: Quality Agreements
- CDER/CBER/CVM/ORA GFI: Quality Systems Approach to Pharmaceutical Current Good Manufacturing Practice Regulations
- CDER/CVM GFI: Pharmaceutical Components at Risk for Melamine Contamination
- CDRH/CDER/CBER/CVM GFI: Recommendations for Labeling Medical Products to Inform Users that the Product or Product Container is not Made with Natural Rubber Latex
- CDER GFI: Tablet Scoring: Nomenclature, Labeling, and Data for Evaluation
- CDER/CVM GFI: Harmonizing Compendia Standards With Drug Application Approval Using the USP Pending Monograph Process Guidance for Industry

Master File and Drug Substance Guidance

- CDER GFI Drug Master Files: Guidelines
- CDER GFI Drug Master Files for Bulk Antibiotic Drug Substances
- CDER GFI: Regulatory Classification of Pharmaceutical Co-Crystals
- CDER GFI: Development of New Stereo isomeric Drugs
- ICH GFI Q7: Good Manufacturing Practice Guidance for Active Pharmaceutical Ingredients
- ICH GFI Q7: Good Manufacturing Practice Guidance for Active Pharmaceutical Ingredients Questions and Answers
- ICH GFI Q11: Development and Manufacture of Drug Substances

- ICH GFI Q11: Development and Manufacture of Drug Substances (Chemical Entities and Biotechnological/Biological Entities) Questions and Answers

Manufacturing Guidance

- CDER/CVM GFI: Submission Documentation for Sterilization Process Validation in Applications for Human and Veterinary Drug Products
- CDER/CBER/CVM GFI: Process Validation: General Principles and Practices
- CDER/CBER/CVM GFI: Submission of Documentation in Applications for Parametric Release of Human and Veterinary Drug Products Terminally Sterilized by Moist Heat Processes
- CDER/CBER/ORA GFI: Sterile Drug Products Produced by Aseptic Processing – Current Good Manufacturing Practice
- CDER GFI: Quality Attribute Considerations for Chewable Tablets
- CDER GFI: Nasal Spray and Inhalation Solution, Suspension, and Spray Drug Products – Chemistry, Manufacturing, and Controls Documentation
- CDER GFI: Metered Dose Inhaler (MDI) and Dry Powder Inhaler (DPI) Products – Quality Considerations
- CDER GFI: Botanical Drug Development
- CDER GFI: Non-Penicillin Beta-Lactam Drugs: A cGMP Framework for Preventing Cross-Contamination
- ICH GFI Q8(R2): Pharmaceutical Development
- ICH GFI Q9: Quality Risk Management
- ICH GFI Q10: Pharmaceutical Quality System
- ICH GFI: Q8, Q9, and Q10 Questions and Answers (R4)

Analytical Control Guidance

- CDER/CVM GFI: Bioanalytical Method Validation
- CBER/CDER/CDRH/CVM GFI: Container and Closure System Integrity Testing in Lieu of Sterility Testing as a Component of the Stability Protocol for Sterile Products
- CDER/CBER/CVM/CDRH/ORA GFI: Pyrogen and Endotoxins Testing: Questions and Answers
- CDER GFI: Dissolution Testing of Immediate Release Solid Oral Dosage Forms
- CDER GFI: Investigating Out-of-Specification (OOS) Test Results for Pharmaceutical Production

Container Closure Guidance

- CDER/CBER GFI: Container Closure Systems for Packaging Human Drugs and Biologics

Impurities Guidance

- CDER/CBER/CVM GFI: Possible Dioxin/PCB Contamination of Drug and Biological Products

Post-approval Changes Guidance

- CDER GFI: PAC-ATLS: Post approval Changes – Analytical Testing Laboratory Sites
- CDER GFI: SUPAC-MR: Modified Release Solid Oral Dosage Forms: Scale-Up and Post approval Changes: Chemistry, Manufacturing, and Controls; *In vitro* Dissolution Testing and *In vivo* Bioequivalence Documentation
- CDER GFI: SUPAC-IR: Immediate Release Solid Oral Dosage Forms: Scale-Up and Post approval Changes: Chemistry, Manufacturing, and Controls, *In vitro* Dissolution Testing and *In vivo* Bioequivalence Documentation
- CDER GFI: SUPAC-IR: Questions and Answers about SUPAC-IR Guidance
- CDER GFI: SUPAC-SS: Non-sterile Semisolid Dosage Forms: Scale-up and Post approval Changes: Chemistry, Manufacturing, and Controls; *In vitro* Release Testing and *In vivo* Bioequivalence Documentation
- CDER GFI: CMC Post approval Manufacturing Changes to be Documented in Annual Reports
- ICH GFI Q12: Technical and Regulatory Considerations for Pharmaceutical Product Lifecycle Management

2.1.13 CMC Guidance Documents Applicable to Minor Use or Minor Species (MUMS)

Guidance are available that may also provide useful information for the submission of CMC information for Minor Use or Minor Species (MUMS) animal drugs, biotech animal drugs, and bio therapeutics. This other guidance includes Cross-Cutting guidance, CBER guidance, and ICH guidance. Any other guidance pertaining to CMC information in addition to those listed below may also be applicable to such animal drugs. Drug sponsors considering an approach outlined in this CMC guidance should contact CVM's Division of Manufacturing Technologies if they have any questions regarding the applicability of a guidance to MUMS.

Administrative/General/Manufacturing Guidance

- CBER/CDRH GFI: Regulatory Considerations for Human Cells, Tissues, and Cellular and Tissue-Based Products: Minimal Manipulation and Homologous Use
- CDER/CBER GFI: For the Submission of Chemistry, Manufacturing, and Controls Information for a Therapeutic Recombinant DNA-Derived Product or a Monoclonal Antibody Product for *In vivo* Use
- CBER GFI: Guidance for Human Somatic Cell Therapy and Gene Therapy
- ICH GFI Q5D: Derivation and Characterization of Cell Substrates Used for Production of Biotechnological/Biological Products
- CBER GFI: Points to Consider in the Manufacture and Testing of Monoclonal Antibody Products for Human Use
- CBER GFI: Current Good Tissue Practice (CGTP) and Additional Requirements for Manufacturers of Human Cells, Tissues, and Cellular and Tissue-Based Products (HCT/Ps)

Analytical Controls Guidance

- ICH GFI Q5B: Quality of Biotechnological Products: Analysis of the Expression Construct in Cells Used for Production of r-DNA Derived Protein Products
- CBER GFI: Potency Tests for Cellular and Gene Therapy Products
- ICH GFI Q5A(R1): Viral Safety Evaluation of Biotechnology Products Derived from Cell Lines of Human or Animal Origin

Stability Guidance

- ICH GFI Q5C: Quality of Biotechnological Products: Stability Testing of Biotechnological/Biological Products

Post-approval Changes Guidance

- CDER/CBER GFI: Demonstration of Comparability of Human Biological Products, Including Therapeutic Biotechnology-derived Products
- ICH GFI Q5E: Comparability of Biotechnological/Biological Products Subject to Changes in Their Manufacturing Process
- CDER/CBER GFI: Chemistry, Manufacturing, and Controls Changes to an Approved Application: Certain Biological Products
- CDER/CBER GFI: Established Conditions: Reportable CMC Changes for Approved Drug and Biologic Products
- CDER/CBER GFI: Changes to an Approved Application for Specified Biotechnology and Specified Synthetic Biological Products

References

1. Guidance for Industry for the Submission of Documentation for Sterilization Process Validation in Applications for Human and Veterinary Drug Products (1994)
2. Guideline on Sterile Drug Products Produced by Aseptic Processing (1987)
3. Guideline for Submitting Documentation for the Stability of Human Drugs and Biologics (1987)
4. Guideline for Submitting Samples and Analytical Data for Methods Validation (1987)
5. Guideline for Submitting Documentation for Packaging for Human Drugs and Biologics (1987)
6. Guideline on General Principles of Process Validation (1987)
7. Guideline for Collection of Blood and Blood Products from Donors with Positive Tests for Infectious Disease Markers ("High Risk" Donors) (1989)
8. Guideline for Determination of Residual Moisture in Dried Biological Products (1990)
9. Draft Guideline for Reporting-ABR's-Adverse Reactions to Licensed Biological Products (1990)
10. Draft Guideline for Quality Assurance in Blood Establishments (1993)
11. Draft Recommended Methods for Evaluating Potency, Specificity, and Reactivity of AntiHuman Globulin (1992)
12. Draft Recommended Methods for Blood Grouping Reagents Evaluation (1992)
13. FDA's Policy Statement Concerning Cooperative Manufacturing Arrangements for Licensed Biologicals (1992)
14. Guideline for the Manufacture of *In vitro* Diagnostic Products (1994)
15. Guidance for Industry for the Submission of Chemistry, Manufacturing, and Controls Information for Synthetic Peptide Substances (1994).
16. Draft Points to Consider in the Manufacture and Clinical Evaluation of *In vitro* Tests to Detect Antibodies to the Human Immunodeficiency Virus, Type 1 (1989)
17. Points to Consider in the Manufacture and Testing of Monoclonal Antibody Products for Human Use (1997)
18. Points to Consider in the Manufacture and Testing of Therapeutic Products for Human Use Derived From Transgenic Animals (1995)
19. Points to Consider-Characterization of Cell Line Used to Produce Biological Products (1993)

20. Points to Consider in the Design and Implementation of Field Trials for Blood Grouping Reagents and Anti-Human Globulins (1992)
21. Points to Consider in the Manufacture of *In vitro* Monoclonal Antibody Products for Further Manufacture into Blood Grouping Reagents and Anti-Human Globulins (1992)
22. https://www.ispeboston.org/download/educational_presentations/2016/2016-11-10-Regulatory-Symposium-BMamidipudi.pdf

CHAPTER 2.2

CTD and E CTD

2.2.1 CTD and its Organisations

Common Technical Document [CTD]: It is a format set by ICH that was agreed upon by Regulatory Agencies of Europe, Japan & the U.S.

The FDA described CTD as "A package of clinical, non-medical, productive, technical data for the same content that will be sent to register new drugs in all 3 ICH regions namely the U.S., European Union and Japan.

The purpose of the CTD was simple - it would provide a standard format of technical documents that would significantly reduce the time and resources required to process applications for registration of human medicines and would make it easier to prepare for electronic submissions.

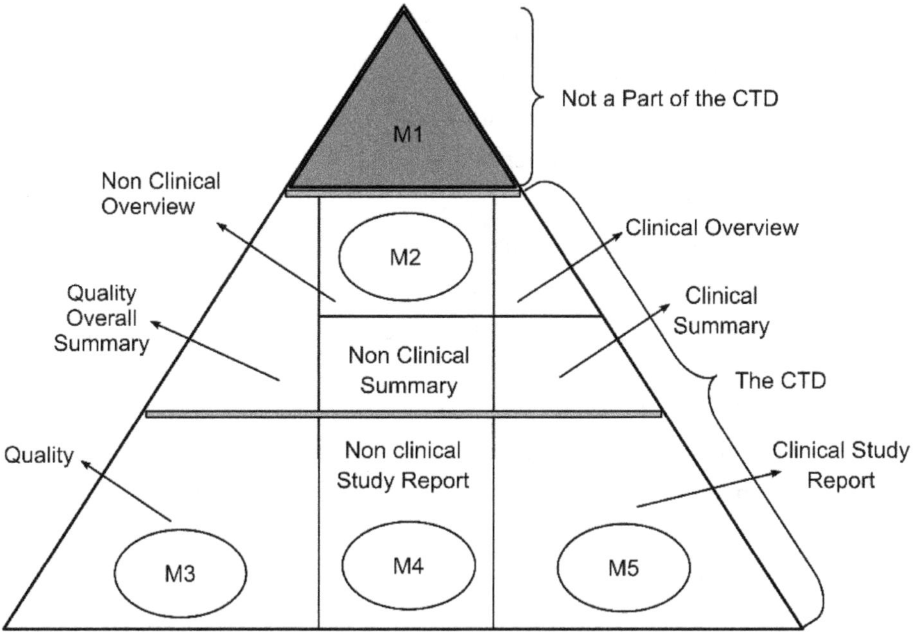

Figure 1 The CTD Structure.

System of CTD

It should be arranged in 5 blocks

Section 1- Administrative Information [Region Specific]

Section 2- CTD Summary [QoS]

Section 3- Grade [CMC]

Section 4 - Reports on Non-Medical Studies

Section 5 - Clinical study reports

(a) Section 1- Administrative Information [Region Specific]

This module should contain specific documents for each area.

EX: Prescription information, application on the prescribing label.

This module is not part of the CTD.

The content and format of this module may be prescribed by the relevant regulatory authorities.

(b) Section 2 CTD Summary [QoS]

It should begin with a pharmacist's general introduction, including its drug type, mode of action, and recommended medical use. That is, the information should not exceed one page

It has 7 sections in the following order:

- 2.1 CTD TOC [Volumes 2 - 5] [Table of Contents]
- 2.2 Introduction to CTD
- 2.3 Composite Score Summary
- 2.4 Non-medical observation
- 2.5 Clinical Overview
- 2.6 Non-medical abstracts
- 2.7 Medical Summary

The structure of these summaries is described in 3 separate documents:

a] M4Q - CTD quality

b] M4S - Protection of CTD

c] m4e - CTD performance

(c) Section 3 Grade [CMC]

Volume 3. 3.1 TOC

3.2 Data body

- 3.2S -Pharmaceutical substance
- 3.2.P - Pharmaceutical Products

- 3.2.a - Appendix
- 3.2.R - Regional Information

3.3 References in the literature

(d) Section 4 Non-Medical Study Report

4. 4.1 Volume 4. TOC of

4.2 Study Report

- 4.2.1 Pharmacology
- 4.2.2 Pharmacology
- 4.2.3 Toxicity

4.3 Literary Reference

(e) Section 5 Clinical Study Report

5.1 TOC 5 of Volume

5.2 Schedule of Clinical Trials

5.3 Clinical Study Report

- 5.3.1 Engaged Biomedical Studies [BA-BE]
- 5.3.2 PK [Biomaterial] Study Report
- 5.3.3 Report of PK Study
- 5.3.4 PD Study Report
- 5.3.5 Performance Reports and Safety Inspection
- 5.3.6 Marketing Experience Report
- 5.3.7 Case Report Form and Individual Patient List

5.4 Literary Notes Section 5 Clinical Study Report

ASEAN Common Technical Document for the Registration of Pharmaceutical Products for Human Use (ACTD)

Document system

Introduction

The ASEAN Common Technical Dossier (ACTD) is an accepted standard design guide for the production of well-structured Common Technical Documents (CTDs). of man. This guide describes the CTD format, which will significantly reduce the time and resources required to compile registration applications and make it easier to prepare documents to be submitted electronically in the future. Regulatory review and communication with the applicant will be done through a standard document of common elements.

This guide only shows the appropriate write formats for the recovered data. However, applicants may, if necessary, be adapted to provide a better interpretation of technical information to facilitate the understanding and evaluation of pharmacy registration results.

Throughout the ACTD, the presentation of information should be clear and concise, to facilitate the analysis of sensitive data and to enable the selector to focus immediately on the content of the application. Text and tables should be drawn using margins that allow the document to be printed on A4 or 8.5 x 11 paper.

The left margin should be large enough that the information is not obscured by the binding method. The font and size, (Times New Roman, 12-point font), must be large enough for the text and size to be easy to read, even after copying text and tables.

Each page should be numbered and the first page of each section should be marked as Page 1. For a sheet of paper, common technical acronyms and abbreviations should be defined for the first time in each section. Reference should be made to the 1979 Vancouver Declaration on Uniform Requirements for Manuscripts Submitted to Biomedical Journals.

The standard technical document is organized into four parts:

Part I. Materials, Management Data and Product Information.

Part I initially contains a general table of contents for the entire ACTD, which provides systematic viewing information. Second, the next material is the administrative data that compiles the required specific documents such as application forms, labels and package inserts. The last part of this section is product information, which includes recommended information, procedures, and side effects.

A general introduction to pharmacist, pharmacology class and its mechanism of action should be included.

Part II. quality document

Part II will provide a general summary after the study report. Quality control documentation should be as detailed as possible.

Part III. Non-Medical Document

Part III provides a non-medical perspective, followed by a non-medical written summary and a non-medical tabular summary. Documentation in this section is not required for general products, minor variants, and certain major variants. For ASEAN member countries, NCE, biotechnology products and other major diversity products do not require an inspection report if the original products are already registered and approved for market recognition in the reference countries. Therefore, the authority required for the specific inspection report should search for the required documents.

PART IV Medical Documents

Part IV provides a clinical overview and clinical summary. Documentation in this section is not required for general products, minor variants, and certain major variants. For ASEAN member countries, NCE, biotechnology products and other major diversity products do not require an inspection report if the original products are already registered and approved for market recognition in the reference countries. Therefore, the authority required for the specific inspection report should search for the required documents.

The general structure of the normative technical document is presented in the following parts:

Part I: Content Management Information and Recommendation Information

Section A: Introduction

Section B: GENERAL ASEAN GENERAL TECHNICAL DOCUMENTS Table of Contents

Section C: Documents required for registration (eg, application form, labeling, product data sheets, referral information)

Part II: Quality Documents

Section A: Content Section B: Overall Quality Summary Section C: Data Body

Part III: Non-Medical Documents

Section A: Content Section

Section B: Non-Medical Overview

Section C: Clinically Unwritten and Scheduled Abbreviations

1. Content
2. Pharmacology
3. Pharmacokinetics
4. Toxicology

Section D: NON-MEDICAL STUDY REPORTS

1. Content
2. Pharmacology
3. Pharmacokinetics
4. Toxicology

Part IV: Medical Documents

Section A: Content Section

Section B: Clinical Overview

Section C: Medical Summary

1. Summary of Biopharmaceuticals and Related Analysis Methods
2. Summary of Clinical Pharmacological Studies
3. Summary of Clinical Performance
4. Summary of Medicare
5. Individual Studies Section D: Schedule of All Medical Studies Section E: Clinical Study Reports

   Volume F: List of Important Literary References

2.2.2 e CTD

Electronic This is the electronic version of the CTD, Electronic General Technical Document [e CTD]

The Electronic General Technical Document (eCTD) is the standard format for submitting applications, corrections, supplements, and reports to the FDA's Center for Biological Assessment and Research (CBER) and the Center for Drug Evaluation and Research (CDER).

e CTD (Electronic Common Technical Document) is a standard format for submitting regulatory information (such as applications, supplements and reports) to the relevant health authorities (HAs). It provides a coherent solution for the electronic processing of Common Technical Documents (CTDs). An ECTD consists of separate documents in PDF format which are arranged in a hierarchical format according to the structure of the CTD. It also has an XML backbone that provides information on cross-linking and submission of required documents. The objective of introducing eCTD is to reduce the burden on the selectors of HAs. It simplifies the submission process as all regulatory authorities use it as a standard form.

(a) eCTD. has a total of five modules

1. **Region - Specific Information**
2. **Summary Document**
3. **Quality Information**
4. **Non-Medical Study Report**
5. **Medical Research Report (CSR)**

ECTD submissions are accepted for the following applications:

- Trial New Drug (INDs)
- New Drug Application (NDA)
- Summary New Drug Applications (ANDAs)
- Bio Licensing Application (BLA)

- All applications after submission of above application
- All primary files (MFs) that are part of the specified application.

Major countries such as the United States, Europe, Australia, Canada, South Africa, Thailand and Japan use eCTD as the standard format for document submission, as it offers several advantages over the traditional method. submit. Some of these are:

Allows agencies to upload queues automatically with the help of XML backbone

Reviewers can easily cite information with the help of hyperlinks

No need to scan, copy or save paper documents

Easily identifiable changes and updates to documents

Easy Product Life Cycle Monitoring

It is possible to access documents simultaneously

(b) ICH eCTD Details

Introduction

The ICH M4 Expert Working Group (EWG) defined the Common Technical Document (CTD). The ICH M2 EWG defines the specification for the electronic general technical document (eCTD) in the current document. ECTD is defined as the interface for the regulatory enterprise communications industry to facilitate the creation, evaluation, life cycle management and collection of electronic submissions.

The ECTD specification lists the technically valid criteria for electronic submission. The focus of the specification is to provide the ability to electronically transfer the registration application from the industry to the regulatory authority. Industry-to-industry and agency-to-agency transitions were not observed.

The specification is divided into a series of key sections, followed by detailed technical descriptions. It provides a mechanism by which parts of a specification are updated or modified on an independent basis without updating all accepted new technologies or standards. This feature will be discussed in the Change Control chapter.

Background

The specification for the eCTD is based on the content defined within the CTD provided by the ICH M4 EWG. CTD describes the structure of blocks, sections, and documents. The structure and position of the description defined in the CTD were used as the basis for determining the structure and content of the ECTD, but where appropriate, additional details were developed within the ECTD specification. The philosophy of ECTD is to use open standards. Open standards, including proprietary standards, which may be considered practical standards due to their wide application, are generally considered relevant.

Opportunity

The CTD defined by the M4 EWG does not cover the entire submission made in a field. It describes 2 to 5 sections common to all areas. This Section 1 does not describe the content of the Regional Administration Information and Recommended Information or the documents that may be submitted as changes or alterations to the initial application.

The cost of preparing the specification for generating the electronic submission will be lower only on the basis of modules mentioned in the CTD. Therefore, M2 EWG has developed a specification for eCTD that applies to all modules of the initial registration application and to other information submissions, such as changes and changes throughout the product's lifetime.

This document describes certain life cycle requirements for components and products of the Common Registration Application for all regions. The areas of registration application specific to a region will be under regional guidance. However, the backbone was constructed to handle both the regional and static elements of submission.

Requirements

The specification is designed to support high-level performance requirements:

- Copy and paste
- View and print documents
- Document note
- Manage the export of information to the database
- Search within apps
- Guide the entire eCTD and subsequent changes/modifications

(c) General architecture

Business model

The supported business process can be described as follows:

Business <------> News <------> Agency

The business process sets specific requirements for the message. The main focus of eCTD is to provide data transfer messaging between industry and agencies. Starts the industrial process by making initial submissions based on electronic CDT. Throughout the life of this process, additional information will be submitted to update or replace the information in the initial submission. Sub, Improve, Variation, etc. The company may submit acknowledgments, queries and requests to the industry. These are considered simple messages that use e-mail or other means of transportation. The overall eCTD architecture is designed to provide a generally accepted submission and submission framework, with minimal restrictions on industry and agencies.

Modular Structure of eCTD

The structure of the electronic submission in terms of structure and navigation should be consistent with the modular structure of the general technical document. The purpose of this design principle is to standardize the electronic format of common Ectd components.

Based on XML ECTD

XML eCTD defines the overall structure of the DTD (Document Type Definition) submission. The purpose of the XML Backbone is twofold: (1) to manage the meta-data for the entire submission and each document within the submission, and (2) to provide contextual support for creating a comprehensive table of contents and navigation.

Submission-level meta-data includes information about the company's submission and acceptance, manufacturer, publisher, submission ID and type, and related data items. Examples of document-level metadata include descriptive information such as version information, language, document name, and checks.

XML ECTD The XML occurrence of any submission must be executed and verified in accordance with the DTD. The XML eCTD DTD describes a step-by-step structure of a CTD as defined by the ICH M4 Expert Task Force. It involves a number of steps depending on the specific quantity defined in the CTD. Actual submissions may have more hierarchical levels than those specified in the CTD. XML eCTD events include complete submissions at all hierarchical levels and notes for each individual file.

Submissions should include the presentation of XML events, navigation according to the table of contents, and a style sheet that provides access to all documents within the submission.

A standard style sheet is defined and provided by the ICH M2 EWG. Presentation and navigation through other style sheets should be possible on the welcome page.

The XML eCTD DTD contains a reference to each document in the physics file in the folder system. The XML eCTD includes attributes for the descriptive names of DTD folders and documents.

Support for multiple regions

The scope of each submission according to the standard technical document is universal, i.e., sections 2 to 5 of the submission are intended for all regions (such as the volume standard) except for selected documents with regional coverage. Section 1 of the submission is of a regional nature.

The DTD, as defined by the ICH M2 Expert Task Force, defines the structure of the common components of the eCTD. It mainly focuses on Blocks 2 to 5. This allows you to connect the regional DTD for Volume 1.

Life cycle management

Applicative creates submissions stored in the local repository. The applicant will submit the initial submission to the agency, which will then import the submission into another local repository.

The nature and type of local repositories are not within the scope of eCTD. Initial submissions must be self-contained, meaning that all documents are included and there is no reference to other submissions. Reference to other submissions may be required, as may regional guidelines.

After the initial submission, the applicant can submit incremental updates such as changes and variations. Updates to documents may indicate past submissions. Updates must be designed so that they can be loaded into the repository through version control, completely preserving the initial or previous submissions.

The XML backbone should contain meta-data indicating updates and provide navigation support for filtering for different submission types.

When submitting a standard technical document electronically, it is desirable that the entire submission be in electronic form, with the exception of some field forms that currently require a written signature.

ECTD Element/Attribute Algorithm

ECTD consists of 5 main subsets:

M1-Administrative-Information-and-Recommendation-Information

M2-general-technical-documents-summary

M3 Quality

M4-Nonclinical-Study-Report

M5-Clinical-Study-Report

The first 5 sub-modules are decomposed into sub-components, each with an individual representation of the location of the CTD table of contents. The steps should be performed as shown in the following example, where all files from blocks 1 to 5 are submitted:

1. To submit a document or file, you must select a tag element that matches the CTD table of contents. For example, select the tag to submit a non-medical observation document.
2. You have to create child element under tag.

3. In the "xlink:href" attribute for the element you must provide the corresponding location and filename of the actual file containing the non-medical observation.
4. You must provide a descriptive title for the file containing the non-medical observation in the <TITTLE> element of <LEAF>.
5. You have to provide information for the appropriate element properties as described in Table 6-2.

(d) Form submission specification

Introduction

The description of submission formats describes how files are created for inclusion in ECTD. The file formats covered in this section are the most commonly used formats for electronic submissions. Other forms may be used in accordance with the guidelines published in each region.

PDF

Adobe Portable Document Format (PDF) is a published format developed by Adobe Systems Incorporated (http://www.adobe.com). You don't need to use Adobe or any particular company's product to create PDF documents. PDF is accepted as the standard for the documents specified in this specification.

The following recommendations support the creation of PDF files that can be effectively reviewed by agencies. For details on the Japanese version of Adobe Acrobat or the Japanese character file, see the regional guide.

To ensure efficient access to PDF files, PDF files should not exceed 50 megabytes. The files should be stored "better" as shown in the image below.

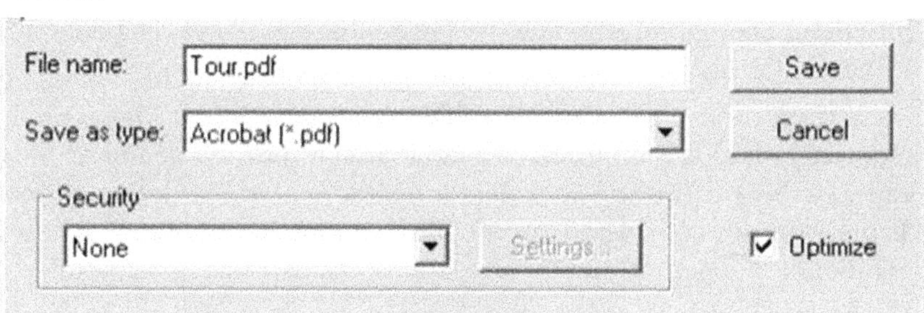

Figure 2

version

Agencies also have the ability to read all PDF files in Acrobat Reader version 4.0 or higher. Agencies do not require additional software to read and navigate PDF files. However, testing with Adobe Acrobat may be easier because this product has more functionality than Acrobat Reader.

Fonts

If the font chooser used to create the text is not on the computer, PDF viewing software automatically converts the text to be displayed. Changing the font can affect the look and structure of the document, and in some cases the information that the document sends. Agencies cannot guarantee the availability of fonts other than the fonts supported in Times New Roman, Arial and Courier and Acrobat product packages. Therefore, all additional fonts used in PDF files must be embedded.

When embedding a font, not only a subset of the font used in the document, but all fonts for the font must be embedded. One problem with embedding fonts is that embedding them requires additional computer storage.

Here are three strategies to help you reduce storage by embedding fonts:

Controls the number of fonts used in each document

Uses only TrueType or Adobe Type 1 fonts

Avoid customized fonts

Resizing the document is useless because the content is too small to read. Times New Roman, 12-point font, The font used for this document is large enough to read story text and should be used as closely as possible.

It is sometimes tempting to use fonts that are less than 12 points in tables and charts, but it should be avoided as much as possible. When selecting a point size for tables, a balance must be struck between providing enough information on a page that facilitates data comparison for the reviewer to be readable at the same time.

As a result, the point size may increase and additional tables may be required, which complicates data comparison for the selector as the data can now be integrated into separate tables. Generally, the point sizes in Table 9-10 are considered acceptable, but smaller point sizes should be avoided.

Using color fonts

It is recommended to use black font color. Blue font can be used for hypertext links. If you use a font color other than black, avoid bright colors that don't print properly on a grayscale printer. Color reproduction can be tested prior to submission by printing sample pages from the document using a gray scale printer. Avoid using background shadow.

Side orientation

Pages must be viewed correctly so that all portrait pages are displayed in portrait and all landscape pages are displayed in landscape. To achieve this, the page orientation of landscape pages must be set to landscape before the PDF document can be saved in its final form.

Page size and margins

The printing area for the pages should fit on an A4 or sheet of paper. If the reviewer prints and binds pages for temporary use, the left side of each page should be large enough (at least 2.5 cm) to avoid covering up the information.

Small margins (at least 2.0 cm above and 0.8 cm left and right) are allowed for landscape orientation pages (standard tables and publications) to clearly display additional information on the page (see section 3, Fonts). It is acceptable for header and footer information to be visible within these margins, but not too close to the edge of the page dangerous to get lost in the axis.

Electronic document proof

PDF documents created by scanning paper documents are often smaller than documents created from an electronic document source. Scanned documents are very difficult to read and do not allow reviewers to find, edit, copy or paste. Avoid them as much as possible.

How to Create PDF Documents and Images ?

The method used to create PDF documents is to create the best copy of a paper document. To ensure that the paper and PDF versions of the document are identical, the document must be printed from the PDF version.

Documents that are available only on paper should be scanned at resolutions that ensure that the pages are readable even when printed on a computer screen. At the same time, the file size should be minimal. To balance readability and file size, scanning at a resolution of 300 points per inch (dpi) is recommended.

The use of grayscale or color is not encouraged due to file size. After scanning, avoid resampling at a lower resolution.

When creating a PDF file with images, the images should not be minified. Down sampling does not protect all the original pixels. For PDF images, use one of the following lossless compression techniques:

For seamless compression of color and grayscale images, use Zip/Flat (a technology with two names). It is defined in Internet RFC 1950 and RFC 1951 (http://info.internet.isi.edu/in-notes/rfc/files/rfc1950.txt).

For smooth compression of black and white images, use the CCITT Panel 4 fax compression technology. It is defined as the recommendations of CCITT T.6 (1988) – Fax Coding Schemes and Code Control Functions for Group 4 Fax Tools.

Paper documents containing handwritten notes should be scanned at 300 dpi. Handwritten notes should be done in black ink for clarity. For photographs, the image should be taken with a resolution of 600 dpi.

If black and white images are submitted, 8-bit grayscale images should be considered. If color images are submitted, 24-bit RGB images should be considered. The captured image should not be subjected to random scaling (ie, resizing).

Gel and karyotype should be scanned directly instead of photograph. Scanning should be done at 600 dpi and 8-bit grayscale depth. Plotter output graphics must be scanned at 300 dpi or taken digitally.

High pressure fluid chromatography or similar images should be scanned at 300 dpi.

Applicants must check the quality of the supply.

Hypertext links and bookmarks

Hypertext links and bookmarks are techniques used to improve navigation through PDF documents. Hypertext links can be separated by thin lines or rectangles with blue text. Generally, for documents containing a table of contents, bookmarks must be provided for each item listed in the table of contents, along with all tables, figures, publications, other references, and appendices.

These bookmarks are essential for efficient navigation through documents. In general, it is helpful to add a bookmark to the main table of contents to block or block submissions.

The bookmark hierarchy should be the same as the table of contents, with no additional bookmark levels beyond what is in the table of contents.

Each additional level increases the space requirement for reading bookmarks. It is recommended to use no more than 4 levels per stage. Hypertext links throughout the document improve navigation performance in favor of annotations, related sections, notes, appendices, tables, or figures that are not on the same page. Relative paths should be used when creating hypertext links to reduce the loss of hyperlink functionality when moving folders between disk drives.

After submissions are loaded on the agency's network servers, absolute links pointing to specific drives and root directories will not work.

When creating bookmarks and hyperlinks, the Inherit Zoom magnification system should be used so that the target page displays the same magnification as the reviewer uses for any other document.

Page counting

If the submission contains more than one document, no additional blocks or page numbers are required. Only page number is required for individual documents.

The electronic document is easier to navigate if the page number of the document and the PDF file are the same. To accomplish this, page 1 must be numbered without using Roman numerals or numbered pages on the first page of the document. Otherwise, Acrobat Reader will add such a number to its page number, thus placing the Acrobat number with the document's internal page numbers.

There are two exceptions to this rule, details of which can be found in the Guide to the CTD module.

First, if a document is split because of its size (eg> 50MB), the second or subsequent file must be the same number as the first or previous file number.

Second, when multiple small documents with their own internal page numbers are compiled into a single file, the event is not considered necessary to provide additional page numbers, but must be bookmarked at the beginning of each subdocument. .

SVG FILES

SVG is a language that describes two-dimensional graphics in XML. SVG allows three types of graphic objects: vector graphic formats (eg, paths with straight lines and curves), images, and text. Graphic objects can be compiled, formatted, modified and mixed with already rendered objects.

Application-matched text can be in any XML namespace, which increases the searchability and accessibility of SVG graphics. The Feature Package includes built-in transitions, clipping paths, alpha masks, filter effects, template objects, and extensions.

SVG maps are dynamic and interactive. The Document Model (DOM) for SVG, which includes the full XML DOM, allows direct and efficient vector graphics animation through scripting. You can assign a rich set of event handlers, such as mouse over and on-click, to any SVG graphical object.

Because of its compatibility and application to other web standards, features such as simultaneous scripting can be performed on different SVG elements and other XML elements. on the same webpage. 8 The specific use of SVG in submission should be discussed with the regulatory authority.

Indexing PDF Documents

Full text codes are used to help locate text in specific documents and/or documents. When a document or group of documents is indexed, all the words and numbers in the file and all the information stored in the document information fields are stored in special code files that can be accessed using the search tools available in Acrobat.

The parts of the document with the image are not tabular. Even if the document contains only images, the text in the document information field of the file will be indexed.

These full text codes should not be confused with the Table of Contents. Adobe Acrobat Catalog is an example tool for indexing PDF documents. Indexes do not require extensions or additions to off-the-shelf Acrobat programs.

Additional recommendations for full text codes will be provided in the regional guide.

(e) Comparing Paper CTD and E CTD Paper CTD E CTD [table 1]

CTD	eCTD
MODULE 1	m1
MODULE 2	m2
MODULE 3	m3
MODULE 4	m4
MODULE 5	m5

eCTD is highly recommended by USFDA for all NDAs, BLAs, DMFs and INDs filling.

References

1. https://www.hsa.gov.sg/docs/default-source/hprg/therapeutic-products/guidance-documents/actd_organizationofdossier.pdf
2. http://xml.coverpages.org/eCTD-SpecificationV201.pdf

CHAPTER 2.3

ICH Guidelines

2.3.1 Introduction

- ICH is the "International Conference on Harmonization of Technical Requirements for Registration of Pharmaceuticals for Human Use".
- ICH is a joint venture between regulators and industry representatives based on research in the European Union, Japan and the US in scientific and technical discussions on testing practices needed to evaluate and ensure the safety, quality and efficacy of drugs.

2.3.2 ICH Objectives

Enhancing international compliance with technical requirements to ensure the development of safe, effective and high-quality drugs.

Matching technical requirements for registration or marketing approval.

- Creating and registering pharmacists in the most efficient and cost effective manner.
- Improving public health.
- Avoid unnecessary copies of medical tests for humans.
- Minimize the use of animal testing without compromising the safety and efficacy of the drug.

2.3.3 ICH Location

- The ICH Secretariat is located in Geneva. The biennial meetings and conferences of the ICH Steering Committee revolve around the European Union, Japan and the United States.

2.3.4 Purpose of ICH

Coordinating representatives of the three ICH regions (EU, Japan and the United States) to promote international integration

- Discuss and establish general guidelines.

  To provide ICH information, ICH activities and ICH guidelines to any country or organization requesting the information
- Improve mutual understanding of regional efforts to facilitate reconciliation processes related to ICH guidelines in the region and around the world
- Strengthening the capacity of pharmaceutical and industry regulatory authorities.

2.3.5 ICH Members

The ICH consists of representatives from six parties representing regulatory bodies and research-based industries in the European Union, Japan and the United States.

In Japan, the Ministry of Health, Labor and Welfare (MHLW), and the Japan Pharmaceutical Manufacturers Association (JPMA) are members.

In Europe, the members are the European Union (EU), and the European Union of Pharmaceutical Industries and Associations (EFPIA).

Member of the Food and Drug Administration (FDA) in the United States, and of Pharmaceutical Research and Manufacturers (PHRMA) in the United States.

Member Additional members include observers from the World Health Organization (WHO), the European Free Trade Association (EFTA) and Canada. Observers represent non-ICH countries and territories.

2.3.6 ICH System

The ICH organization consists of the ICH Steering Committee, the ICH Coordinator, the ICH Secretariat and the ICH Working Group.

Or the ICH Steering Committee, the Steering Committee that oversees the ICH, sets policies and procedures for the ICH, selects topics for synchronization, and monitors the progress of synchronization efforts. Each of the six ICH parties has two seats on the ICH Steering Committee.

2.3.7 ICH Coordinator

Coordinators are essential for the smooth functioning of the ICH and are appointed by six parties. An ICH Coordinator serves as the primary point of contact in the ICH Secretariat.

2.3.8 ICH Secretariat

The General Secretariat is primarily concerned with the preparation of coordination for Steering Committee meetings and documentation and preparation of Working Group and Discussion Group meetings. Information on ICH guidelines and the overall ICH process can be obtained from the ICH Secretariat.

2.3.9 ICH Working Group

Depending on the type of synchronization process required, the Steering Committee may approve the establishment of one of three types of task forces, namely the Expert Task Force (EWG), the Implementation Task Force (IWG) or the Informal Task Force.

2.3.10 ICH Operation

The ICH operates through the ICH Steering Committee with the administrative support of the ICH Secretariat and the ICH Coordinators.

The Steering Committee meets twice a year. In these meetings, new topics for adoption will be considered, progress reports on current topics will be received, and maintenance and implementation of the guidelines will be discussed.

Topics identified for compliance by the management team were selected from safety, quality, performance and diversity.

2.3.11 Stages of the ICH Process

Phase-1: Draft will be prepared and published in multiple revisions till the "Final Consolidated Draft" is completed

Phase-2: The draft has been signed in a draft approved by the EWG and sent to the Steering Committee for signature, which means each of the six co-sponsors will be accepted for consultation.

Phase-3: The three regulatory sponsors begin their natural consultation process to receive feedback.

Phase-4 is achieved when the Steering Committee agrees that there is sufficient scientific consensus on technical issues. This approval is based on the signatures of three regulatory parties to ICH, confirming that the guidance has been recommended for adoption by regulatory bodies in the three regions.

Phase-5: The process is completed when the guidelines are integrated into national or regional internal practices (applicable in 3 ICH regions).

2.3.12 Guidelines [Figure 1]

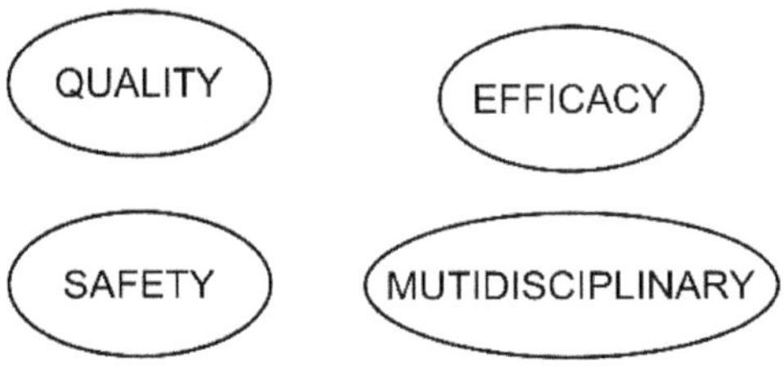

- Related to "quality" topics, such as chemical and pharmaceutical quality assurance (stability testing, contamination testing, etc.)

  or "performance" subject, i.e., relating to clinical studies in the human case (dose response studies, good clinical practice, etc.).
- Safety issues, ie related to in vitro and in vivo pre-clinical trials (carcinogenicity testing, xenotoxicity testing, etc.)

  Or "multidisciplinary" titles, i.e. cross-cutting titles that do not fit into any of the above categories individually.

  or 2.3.12a. Quality guidelines pertain to "quality" topics, i.e., chemical and pharmaceutical quality assurance (consistency testing, impurity testing, etc.).

Q1A-Q1F---Stability:

Q1A (R2): Sustainability analysis of new products and pharmaceutical products

The purpose of stability testing is to provide evidence of how the quality of a drug or drug changes over time under the influence of various environmental factors such as temperature, humidity and light. , Pharmaceutical product or shelf life of pharmaceutical product.

Q1B: Photo fastness test of new products and pharmaceutical products

Provide guidance on basic testing protocols needed to assess photosensitivity and stability of new drugs and products.

Q1C: Stability analysis for new dosage forms

Provides guidelines for new formulations of already approved drugs and identifies situations where low stability data is acceptable.

Q1D: Sealing and matrixing design for stability testing of new products and pharmaceutical products

Q1E: Data Consistency Analysis

This guideline refers to the analysis of stability data to be submitted in registration applications for new molecular weight companies and related pharmaceutical products. The guidelines provide recommendations for establishing shelf lives for pharmaceutical components and pharmaceuticals intended to be stored at "room temperature" or lower.

Q1F: Sustainability data set for registration applications in climate zones III and IV

Describes integrated global sustainability testing requirements that facilitate access to drugs by reducing the number of different storage conditions. WHO conducted a survey of its member countries to find consensus on long-term storage conditions for hot-dry and hot-humid regions of 30 °C / 65% RH.

Q2-Analysis Verification

Q2 (R1): Validation of Analysis Procedures: Lesson and Method

- The purpose of verifying an analysis method is to show that it is suitable for its purpose
- Provides necessary validation parameters for various analysis methods.
- It also discusses the features to be considered during validation of analysis methods.

Types of Analysis Process for Verification:

- Detection test;

  Quantity testing for contaminants in o;

  limited testing for sewage control;

  Quantitative analysis of active ingredients in samples of pharmaceutical substances or pharmaceutical products or other components selected in drug formulations.

  General Features of Validation Analysis Methods

  Accuracy, Accuracy (Repeatability, Intermediate Accuracy), Specificity, Detection Range, Quantity Range, Linear, Range.

Q3A- Q3D----Contaminants

Q3A (R2): Contaminants in new medical products

The guide specifies the chemical and safety characteristics of sewage, including sewage inventory, entry limits, identification and quantity.

Types of waste classification: there are 3 types

Organic waste (process and pharmaceutical)

mineral waste

residual solvents.

Q3B(R2): Impurities in New Drug Products

Q3C(R4): Impurities: Guideline for Residual Solvents 21

Benzene	2ppm
Carbon tetrachloride	4ppm
Dichloromethane	5ppm
Dichloroethane	8ppm
Acetonitrile	410ppm
Chloroform	60ppm
Chlorobenzene	360ppm
Formamide, Hexane	290ppm
Toluene	890ppm
Pyridine	200pm
Nitromethane	50ppm
Methanol	3000ppm.

- Q4: Pharmacopoeias
- Q4A: Pharmacopeial Harmonization
- Q4B: Evaluation and Recommendation of Pharmacopeial Texts for Use in the ICH Regions
    - This document describes a process for the evaluation and recommendation given by the Q4B Expert Working Group (EWG) for selecting pharmacopeial texts to facilitate their recognition by regulatory authorities for use, interchangeable in the ICH regions.

- Q4B Annex 1: Evaluation and Recommendation of Pharmacopeial Texts for Use in the ICH Regions on Residue on Ignition/Sulphated Ash
    - Annex 2: Test for Extractable Volume of Parenteral Preparations
    - Annex 3: Test for Particulate Contamination: Sub-Visible Particles
    - Annex 4A: Microbiological Examination of Non-Sterile Products: Microbial Enumeration Tests
    - Annex 4B: Microbiological Examination of Non-Sterile Products: Tests for Specified Micro-organisms

  - Annex 4C: Microbiological Examination of Non-Sterile Products: Acceptance Criteria for Pharmaceutical Preparations and Substances for Pharmaceutical Use
  - Annex 5: Disintegration Test
  - Annex 6: Uniformity of Dosage Units
  - Annex 7: Dissolution Test
  - Annex 8: Sterility Test
  - Annex 9: Tablet Friability
  - Annex 10: Polyacrylamide Gel Electrophoresis
  - Annex 11: Capillary Electrophoresis
  - Annex 12: Analytical Sieving
  - Annex 13: Bulk Density and Tapped Density of Powders
  - Annex14: Bacterial Endotoxins Test.

- Q5A-Q5E---Quality of biotechnological products:
- Q5A(R1): Viral Safety Evaluation of Biotechnology Products Derived from Cell Lines of Human or Animal Origin
  - This document is concerned with testing and evaluation of the viral safety of biotechnology products derived from cell lines of human or animal origin (i.e., mammalian, avian, insect)
  - The objective is to provide a general framework for virus testing experiments for the evaluation of virus clearance and the design of viral tests and clearance evaluation studies.
    - Three principal, complementary approaches have evolved to control the potential viral contamination of biotechnology products:
      (a) selecting and testing cell lines and other raw materials, including media components, for the absence of undesirable viruses which may be infectious and/or pathogenic for humans;
      (b) Testing the capacity of the processes to clear infectious viruses;
      (c) testing the product at appropriate steps for absence of contaminating infectious viruses.

Q5B: Quality of Biotechnological Products: Analysis of the Expression Construct in Cells Used for Production of r-DNA Derived Protein Products

- This document presents guidance regarding the characterization of the expression construct for the production of recombinant DNA protein products in eukaryotic and prokaryotic cells.
- expression construct should be analyzed using nucleic acid techniques.

Q5C: Quality of Biotechnological Products: Stability Testing of Biotechnological/Biological Products

Q5D: Derivation and Characterization of Cell Substrates Used for Production of Biotechnological/Biological Products

- The objective of this guideline is to provide broad guidance on appropriate standards for cell substrates.

Q5E: Comparability of Biotechnological/ Biological Products Subject to Changes in Their Manufacturing Process

- The objective of this document is to provide principles for assessing the comparability of biotechnological/ biological products before and after changes are made in the manufacturing process for the drug substance or drug product.
- Therefore, this guideline is intended to assist in the collection of relevant technical information which serves as evidence that the manufacturing process changes will not have an adverse impact on the quality, safety and efficacy of the drug product.

Q6: Specifications for New Drug Substances and Products

- Bulk drug substance and final product specifications are key parts of the core documentation for world-wide product license applications.
- This leads to conflicting standards for the same product, increased expenses and opportunities for error as well as a potential cause for interruption of product supply.

Q6A: Specifications: Test Procedures and Acceptance Criteria for New Drug Substances and New Drug Products: Chemical Substances

- The main objective of this guideline is to establish a single set of
- global specifications for new drug substances and new drug products.
- A specification is defined as a list of tests, references to analytical procedures, and appropriate acceptance criteria, which are numerical limits, ranges
- This guideline addresses specifications, i.e., those tests, procedures, and acceptance criteria which play a major role in assuring the quality of the new drug substance and new drug product during shelf life.
  - Universal Tests:
  - The following tests are considered generally applicable to all new drug substances and drug products.
- Description

- Identification
- Assay
- Impurities
- Specific Tests for drug substances:
- Physicochemical properties
- Particle size
- Polymorphic forms
- Tests for Chiral new drug substances
- Water content
- Inorganic impurities
- Microbial limits.

Specific Tests for drug products (oral dosage form):

- Particle size distribution:
- Dissolution
- Disintegration
- Hardness/friability
- Uniformity of dosage units:
- Microbial limits
- Antioxidant preservative content:
- Alcohol content:
- Rheological properties:
- Re-dispersibility.

Specific Tests for drug products (Parenteral Drug Products):

- Uniformity of dosage units
- Particle size distribution
- pH (Osmolarity)
- Sterility
- Endotoxins/Pyrogens
- Particulate matter
- Water content
- Antimicrobial preservative
- Antioxidant preservative content
- Functionality testing of delivery systems.

Q6B: Specifications: Test Procedures and Acceptance Criteria for Biotechnological/Biological Products

- This document provides guidance on justifying and setting specifications for proteins and polypeptides which are derived from recombinant or non-recombinant cell cultures.
- A valid biological assay to measure the biological activity should be provided by the manufacturer.
- Examples of procedures used to measure biological activity include:
  - Animal-based biological assays, which measure an organism's biological response to the product;
  - Cell culture-based biological assays, which measure biochemical or physiological response at the cellular level;
  - Biochemical assays, which measure biological activities such as enzymatic reaction rates or biological responses induced by immunological interactions.

Q7: Good Manufacturing Practice Guide for Active Pharmaceutical Ingredients

- The main objective of this guideline is that to maintain the quality of the active pharmaceutical ingredients
- Personnel:
- Buildings and Facilities:
- Process equipment:
- Documentation and Records:

Q8(R2): Pharmaceutical Development

- This guideline is intended to provide guidance on the contents of Pharmaceutical Development of drug products
- The aim of pharmaceutical development is to design a quality product and its manufacturing process to consistently deliver the intended performance of the product.
- The Pharmaceutical Development section also describe the type of dosage form and the formulation that are suitable for the intended use.
- Q8 gives information about Drug Substance, Excipients, Container Closure System.

Q9: Quality Risk Management

- The purpose of this document is to offer a systematic approach to quality risk management.
- This guideline provides principles and tools for quality risk management that can be applied to all aspects of pharmaceutical quality

including development, manufacturing, distribution; and the inspection and submission/review processes throughout the lifecycle of drug substances and drug (medicinal) products, biological and biotechnological products, including the use of raw materials, solvents, excipients, packaging and labeling materials.

Principles of Quality Risk Management

- Two primary principles of quality risk management are:
- The evaluation of the risk to quality should be based on scientific knowledge and ultimately link to the protection of the patient; and
- The level of effort and documentation of the quality risk management process should be commensurate with the level of risk.

General Quality Risk Management Process[figure 2]:

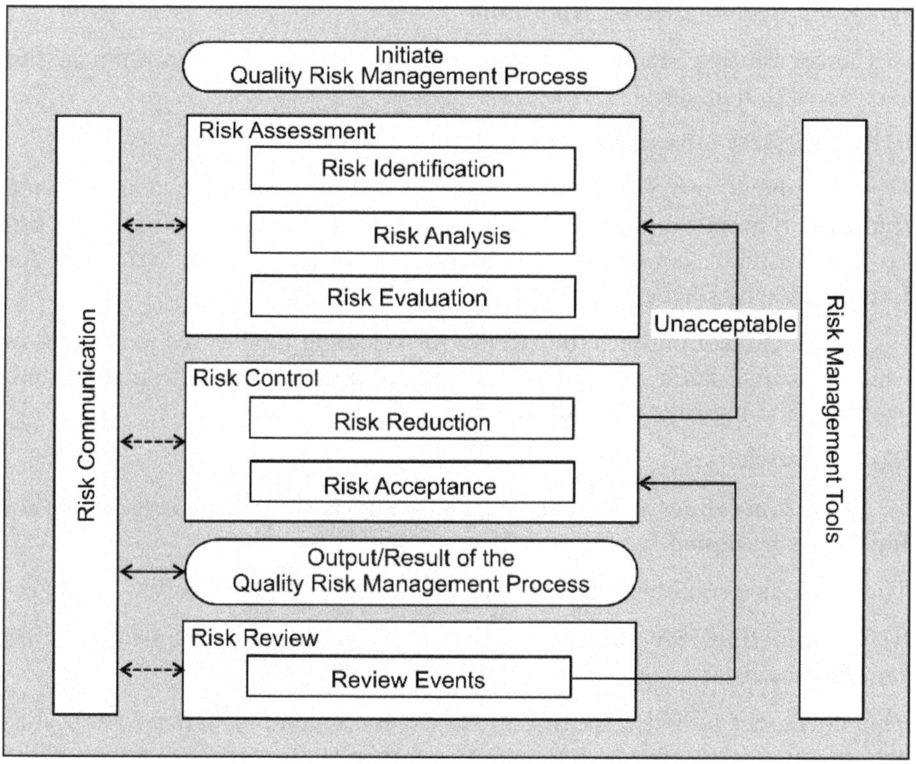

Q10: Pharmaceutical Quality System

This document establishes a new ICH tripartite guideline that outlines the model for an effective quality management system for the pharmaceutical industry, called the Drug Quality System.

The comprehensive model for effective pharmaceutical quality systems is based on International Standards Organization (ISO) standards including applicable Good Product Practices (GMP) regulations.

Status of safety topics Safety topics related to pre-clinical studies (eg carcinogenicity analysis, genotoxicity analysis, etc.)

S1A-S1C ---- Carcinogenicity Studies:

S1A: Request guidelines for pharmaceuticals for carcinogenicity studies

Any pharmacist who continues to use the drug for at least 6 months should be screened for cancer.

This document provides a coherent definition of the conditions under which cancer research on new drugs should be conducted. These recommendations take into account known risk factors and intended symptoms and duration of exposure.

Cancer-causing studies aim to identify potential tumors in animals and assess risk to humans.

S1B: Drug test for cancer

This document provides guidance on the need to conduct carcinogenic studies in both rats and mice, as well as alternative testing methods that can be used without compromising safety. orS1C (R2): Dose Selection for Carcinogenicity Studies

This document outlines the criteria for selecting high doses to be used in cancer-causing studies with new therapeutic agents to synchronize current practices and improve study design.

S2- Genotoxicity:

S2 (R1): Guidelines for Genotoxicity Analysis and Data Interpretation for Drugs Designed for Human Use

This guide is a combination of the ICH S2A and S2B guidelines:

S2A: Guidelines for specific aspects of regulatory genotoxicity testing for pharmacists;

This document provides specific guidance and recommendations on in vitro and in vivo tests and evaluation of test results. In order to improve the stability of applications, it includes regulations relating to genetic toxicity testing.

S2B: Genotoxicity: Generic Battery for Pharmaceutical Genotoxicity Testing:

This document identifies two major components of genetic toxicity testing: the identification of standard tests performed for recording and the amount of testing confirmed with any specific genetic toxicity test on the standard battery.

Pharmacists' records require a comprehensive assessment of their genetic toxicity. It is clear that no single test can detect all the genotoxic agents associated with it. Therefore, in vitro and in vivo tests for genotoxicity should be the standard approach for performing batteries.

The aim of this guide is to develop a sustainable genetic toxicology battery that can predict potential human exposures and interpret results, with the ultimate goal of improving risk identification for cancer-causing effects based on genetic mutations. To do.

S3A -S3B --- Genotoxicity and Pharmacokinetics:

S3A: Reference to toxicogenomic guidelines: systematic risk analysis in toxicology studies

In accordance with ICH guidelines, no toxic genetic testing is required to be performed on pregnant or lactating animals prior to initiation of fertility studies.

In this context, toxicogenic studies is defined as the production of pharmacokinetic data as an integral part of conducting non-pharmacological toxicology studies or in adjunctive studies specifically designed to systematically evaluate expression of Is. ,

This document provides information on the development of toxico-genetic testing techniques and the need to incorporate this pharmacokinetics into toxicity testing, explaining toxic findings in medicine and their relevance to safety issues.

Toxic genetics Primary Objective: Describes the systemic exposure and dose regimens obtained in animals and the time course of toxicity studies.

S3B: Pharmacokinetics: Guidelines for Repeated Studies on Dose Tissue Distribution

Tissue distribution studies are important in providing information on the distribution and accumulation of compounds and/or metabolites, especially with respect to potential areas of activity; This information will be useful in designing toxicological and pharmacological studies and in interpreting the results of these experiments.

This document provides guidance on the need for recurrent analysis of dose tissue distribution (ie, when appropriate data cannot be obtained from other sources). It also makes recommendations for conducting such studies.

S4: Duration of Acute Toxicity Testing in Animals (rodent and rodent non-toxicity testing) The purpose of this guideline is to formulate applicable considerations for severe toxicity testing as part of the evaluation of drug safety in rats and non-rodents. Product

or rodents (6 months study)

or non-rodents (nine-month study).

S5: Reproductive toxicity to medical products and detection of toxicity to male fertility

This document provides guidance on tests for reproductive toxicity.

It specifies the treatment duration to be used in animals to better reflect human exposure to medical substances and to more accurately identify endangered conditions.

This should promote a full assessment of the safety of chemicals in the development of offspring.

S6: Pre-clinical safety evaluation of drugs derived from biotechnology

This document covers pre-clinical safety testing requirements for biotechnology products. It refers to the use of animal disease samples, the assessment of genetic toxicity and determining when studies for cancer should be performed and the effect of antibody formation during toxicology studies. The main objectives of advance security assessment are:

1. To determine an initial safe dose and subsequent dose in humans;
2. To determine potential target organs for poisoning and to study whether such poisoning is reversible;
3. Determining safety standards for clinical monitoring.

S7A: Safety Pharmacological Studies for Human Medicines

- This guideline was developed to protect clinical trial participants and patients receiving commercial products from potential side effects of drugs.
- This document outlines the definition, scope and scope of defense pharmacology studies.
- Step 1 Specifies what research is needed before starting a medical course and the information needed for marketing.

S7B: Clinical Evaluation of the Efficacy of Delayed Ventricular Resection (QT Interval Prolongation) of Human Drugs

This guideline describes a noninvasive clinical approach to evaluate the potential of a test substance to delay ventricular remodeling.

This guide contains information about nonmedical assessment and integrated risk assessment.

S8: Immunotoxicity studies for human drugs

This guideline refers to non-therapeutic testing recommendations for vaccination.

Guideline also applies to drugs that show clinical signs of immunosuppression during clinical trials and after market approval.

In this guideline the term immunotoxicity mainly refers to immunity, i.e. susceptibility to infection or the development of a tumor.

S9: Non-clinical evaluation of anticancer drugs

This guide provides information for pharmacists who wish to treat cancer only in patients with end-stage or advanced disease, regardless of the route of administration, including drugs derived from small molecules and biotechnology.

Describes the type and timing of non-medical studies related to the development of anticancer drugs and refers to other relevant guidelines.

The purpose of this guidance is to facilitate and accelerate the development of anti-cancer drugs and to avoid unnecessary use of animals and other resources, as well as to protect patients from unwanted side effects.

- Performance guidelines related to "performance" subjects, ie, clinical studies for human subjects (dose response studies, good clinical practice, etc.).

Medical Care:

E1-E2F---Medical Care:

E1: Threshold of population exposure to assess clinical safety for drugs targeted for long-term treatment of life-threatening conditions

This document provides recommendations on the duration of exposure to the number of patients and the safety evaluation of long-term treatment drugs for life-threatening conditions.

These guidelines provide information on the relationship between drug exposure and the duration and extent of adverse events.

E2A: Medical Care Data Management: Definitions and Standards

This document provides general definitions and terms for the key features of the Medicare Report.

It also provides guidance on how to deal with adverse drug reactions during the investigational phase of drug development.

E2B (R3): Medicare Data Management data component for individual case safety report submission

The objectives of the task force are to define, define and standardize the data components for the issuance of individual case safety reports (adverse reaction, adverse event reports).

After submission to ISO for development as an international standard. Key elements of this updated guide will be covered in a practical guide to the electronic submission of personal safety reports.

E2C (R1): Medical Safety Data Management: Periodic Safety Update Reports for Marketed Drugs

This document provides guidance on the form and content of safety updates, which should be provided to regulatory authorities at regular intervals to ensure maximum effectiveness and prevent duplication of drugs being sold.

E2D: Post-approval Security Data Management: Definitions and Standards

This document provides a standardized process for post-approval security data management.

Definitions of specific terms for the level of approval are also provided.

Quality data management practices received from consumers are standardized, and the literature and the Internet are all specific to post-approval data management.

E2E: Pharmacovigilance Scheduling

This guideline is designed to assist in planning pharmacological surveillance activities, particularly in preparation for the initial marketing of a new drug (in this guideline, the term "drug" refers to products derived from chemical companies, biotechnology and vaccines). Refers).

The primary focus of this guidance is on the safety profile and pharmacy monitoring plan, which can be submitted at the time of license application.

The guideline describes a method of summarizing important identified risks, significant potential risks, and important missing drug information.

E2F: Development Security Update Report

DSUR's primary focus is on data collection from clinical trials of trial drugs, including biologic drugs, with or without marketing permission.

DSUR must provide safety information from all clinical trials conducted or completed by Sponsor during the evaluation:

Clinical trials using a drug that has been tested with or without market approval, i.e. Human Pharmacology, Clinical Trials and Treatment Confirmation Trials (Phase I-III)

or clinical trials conducted using antidepressants on approved symptoms, ie, clinical utility trials (Phase IV);

or other medical use of the drug under investigation;

or comparative tests conducted to support changes in the manufacturing process of medical products.

E3: Organization and Content of the Clinical Study Report

This document describes the format and content of a study report that is acceptable in all three ICH regions. This includes a basic statement appropriate to all submissions and addendums.

The clinical study report described in this guide is a complete report of an individual study of any treatment, prophylactic or diagnostic agent (herein referred to as a drug or therapy) given to patients.

Guidance is to help sponsors create a complete, clear, systematic and easily reviewable report.

Organization and content of medical research reports

- Title page

Table of Contents for Individual Medical Study Report

List of abbreviations and definitions of words

Ethics (protocol study behavior, patient information and approval).

Investigators and studies of administrative structures

Introduction

Learning Objectives

General Research Design and Planning - Interpretation

Study population selection

study size selection

performance and security variables

Tables of performance results and individual patient data

- Security Testing.

E4: Dose response information to support drug records

This document provides recommendations on study design and practice to evaluate the relationship between dosage, blood levels and clinical response during clinical development of a new drug.

This information will help you determine the correct starting dose, adjust the dosage to suit the needs of a particular patient, and identify any levels that may not be acceptable.

E5 (R1): Ethnic factors in acceptance of foreign medical data

The objective of this guidance is to facilitate drug registration in ICH areas.

This document refers to the intrinsic characteristics of the drug recipient and the external characteristics associated with the environment and culture, which may affect the results of clinical trials conducted in the fields.

Describes the concept of a "bridging study" sought by a new region to determine whether data from another region is relevant to its population.

E6 (R1): Good Medical Practice: Integrated Guidelines

Medical Good Medical Training (GCP) is an international protocol and scientific standard for the design, conduct, recording and reporting of experiments involving the participation of human subjects.

This Good Medical Practice document describes the responsibilities and expectations of all participants in the conduct of clinical trials, including investigators, supervisors and sponsors.

GCPs include features for monitoring, reporting and accessing clinical trials and incorporating them into required documentation and investigator brochures.

E7-E11----Diagnostic Trial:

E7: Special Population Support Study: Geriatrics

This document provides recommendations for special consideration in the design and conduct of clinical trials of drugs that may be of importance to the elderly.

Example: new molecular substances that could be of significant use in the elderly because the disease being treated is characteristic of geriatric disease (such as Alzheimer's disease).

E8: General considerations for clinical trials

- This document sets out general scientific principles for the conduct, performance and control of clinical trials.

- Guidance refers to a wide range of topics in the design and conduct of clinical trials.
- The purpose of the ICH document is "General considerations for clinical trials" to: (a) establish globally accepted policies and practices in the conduct of both individualized clinical trials and general approaches in the development of new medical products. Creates an outline.

  or (b) facilitating the review and acceptance of foreign medical examination data by promoting a common understanding of public policy

  or (c) provide an overview of the ICH safety and diagnostic performance documentation and facilitate user access to the guide

  or (d) provide a different glossary of terms used in performance documents relating to ICH's medical safety and clinical trials.

E9: Statistical Principles for Clinical Trials

This biostatistical guideline describes important considerations in the design and evaluation of clinical trials, in particular the basis on which "confirmed" (hypothesis-testing) tests reveal performance.

E10: Problems associated with control panel selection and diagnostic tests

This document specifies the selection of control groups in clinical trials.

Control groups in clinical trials can be classified based on two main characteristics: (1) the type of treatment and (2) the method of determining who will be in the control group.

Types of control therapy may include any of the following four: (1) placebo, (2) no treatment, (3) a different dosing or treatment regimen in the study, or (4) other active treatment.

E11: Clinical Study of Medical Products in the Pediatric Population

This document conducts clinical trials of drugs in the pediatric population.

This document will facilitate the development of safe and effective use of the drug in pediatrics.

Typical clinical studies include:-

1. what time during drug development does the child's studies begin;
2. type of study (pharmacokinetic, pharmacokinetic/pharmacodynamic (PK/PD), efficacy, safety);
3. age group;
4. Ethics of pediatric investigation.

E12—Guidelines for Clinical Evaluation by Treatment Type

- O ICH performance guidelines apply to all treatment classes of drugs, but there are some treatment classes that require individual drug evaluation guidelines in all three areas.

E13: Principles for the clinical evaluation of new antihypertensive drugs

- This document provides general principles for the clinical evaluation of new antihypertensive drugs.
- It describes the basic principles for the assessment of hypertension resistance adopted in the three sections of the ICH, but some differences remain regional, so this document should be considered an "ICH policy document" rather than an "ICH guideline". ,

E14: QT/QTc interval prolongation and clinical evaluation of pro-arrhythmic potential for antiarrhythmic drugs

This document provides sponsors with recommendations on the design, conduct, evaluation and interpretation of clinical trials that evaluate the drug's potential to delay cardiac resuscitation.

This analysis includes the QT/QTc between effects of the new agents and a collection of adverse cardiovascular events.

The investigative approach applied to a particular drug should be individualized based on the pharmacological, pharmacological and safety properties of the drug and its proposed clinical application.

E15: Definitions of genomic biomarkers, pharmacogenomics, pharmacogenetics, genomic data and sample coding types

In order to develop a coherent approach to drug regulation, it is important to ensure that the same definitions are applied across all jurisdictions of the International Coordinating Council for Syndication (ICH).

The Agreement on Definitions facilitates compliance in the pharmaceutical and pharmacological sectors for global drug development and approval processes.

E16: Drug Response-Related Genomic Biomarks: Reference, Structure, and Forms of Submission

The guideline outlines recommendations regarding the context, structure and format of regulatory submissions for the qualification of genetic biomarkers (E15).

Clinical and non-clinical genetic markers associated with drug response, including pharmacology, pharmacology, efficacy, and safety features.

Versatile Guide

"Multidisciplinary" titles, i.e. titles not unique to any of the above categories (MedDRA, ESTRI, M3, CTD, M5).

M1 medical conditions

New the New Medical Dictionary for Regulatory Activities (MedDRA) was developed by the ICH Task Force and is owned by the International Federation of Pharmaceutical Manufacturers and Associations (IFPMA), which serves as a trustee of the ICH Steering Committee.

It provides an international medical dictionary applicable to all stages of product development.

It aims to provide comprehensive and specific terms that will help standardize, simplify and streamline regulatory processes.

Electronic Standard for M2 Regulatory Communication (ESTRI)

- Manage international electronic communications by reviewing and recommending details

  The first detail generated by the M2 EWG was the Individual Case Protection Report (ICSR) prepared as an electronic message to the ICH E2B (R2).

  The second specification created by O M2 EWG is the Electronic Generic Technical Document (eCTD) prepared as an electronic message for the generic technical document developed by ICH M4.
- ICH M2 begins to improve the durability, flexibility and long-term messaging stability of the next major version of eCTD (eCTD NMV).

M3 (R2): Guidelines for Non-medical Safety Studies and Marketing Approval for Drugs to Perform Human Clinical Trials

Current guidance reflects consensus on the type and duration of non-medical safety studies and the timing of support for pharmacists to conduct human clinical trials and marketing accreditation.

Medical non-clinical safety evaluations for marketing approval of a drug typically include pharmacological studies, general toxicity studies, toxicogenetic and non-pharmacological pharmacokinetic studies, and reproductive toxicity studies. Studies, genotoxicity studies and, are intended for drugs with a specific cause of concern or for long-term use.

Objectives of non-therapeutic safety assessment generally include description of toxic effects including target organs, dose dependence, relationship to risk, and, if appropriate, possible relapse.

This information is used to evaluate the initial safe starting dose and dosage range for human trials and to define parameters for clinical monitoring for potential adverse effects.

M4: Standard Technical Document

Standard technical documentation provides a consistent structure and design for new product applications. The General Technical Document was adopted in November 2000 in San Diego, USA.

The general technical document is divided into four different sections. The four sections refer to the Application System (M4 Regulation), the Standards Section (M4Q), the Security Section (M4S) and the Compatible Application Performance Section (M4E).

An electronic version of the Common Technical Document (eCTD) developed by the eCTD Enforcement Task Force. The Electronic General Technical Document (ECTD) allows the applicant to submit the Common Technical Document (CTD) electronically to the regulator.

M5: Data Components and Standards for Pharmaceutical Dictionaries

This document provides medical product information and guidance on consistent standards regarding basic packages of medical product terms.

Facilitating the transfer and practical use of medical product data by regulators and the pharmaceutical industry.

References

1. https://www.fda.gov/media/104916/download
2. https://www.pharmaguideline.com/2010/10/ich.html
3. https://www.dcvmn.org/IMG/pdf/b1_02_general_introduction_international_laws.pdf

CHAPTER 2.4

Regulatory Requirement of EU, MHRA and TGA

2.4.1 European Union

- Intergovernmental political and economic union of 28 European countries having internal single market through the standardized systems of laws.
- Established under the name in 1992 by the Treaty on European Union (the Maastricht Treaty)
- **European Medicines Agency (EMA)** is a decentralized agency of the European union.
- EMA protects public and animal health by ensuring that all medicines available on the EU market are safe, effective and of high quality.
    - The Agency is responsible for the scientific evaluation, supervision and safety monitoring of the medicines developed by pharmaceutical companies for the use in EU.
    - EMA and the Member States cooperate and share expertise in the assessment of new medicines and of new safety information.
    - By working closely together, Member States reduce duplication, share the workload and ensure the efficient and effective regulation of medicines across the EU.

(a) Market Authorization

- To protect public health and ensure the availability of high quality, safe and effective medicines for European citizens, all medicines must be authorized before they can be placed on the market in the EU.
- The Agency's Committee for Medicinal Products for Human Use (CHMP) or Committee for Medicinal Products for Veterinary Use (CVMP) *carries out a scientific assessment of the application and gives a recommendation to the European Commission on whether or not to grant a marketing authorization.*

- EMA enables one application, one assessment, one market authorisation for the whole of the EU.
- A European Public Assessment Report, or EPAR, is published for every human or veterinary medicine that has been granted or refused a marketing authorization following an assessment by EMA.

(b) The Role of EMA

EMA plays an important role in the regulation of medicines in the EU. On the basis of scientific assessments carried out, it grants or refuses, changes or suspends marketing authorizations for medicines that have been submitted via the centralized procedure.

The European Commission can also take action concerning other aspects of medicine regulation:

- Right of initiative – it can propose new or amended legislation for the pharmaceutical sector;
- Implementation – it can adopt implementing measures as well as oversee the correct application of EU law on pharmaceuticals;
- Global outreach – it ensures appropriate collaboration with relevant international partners and promotes the EU regulatory system globally.

(c) Guidelines and Scientific Advice

- EMA prepares scientific guidelines in cooperation with experts from its scientific committees and working groups.
- These guidelines reflect the latest thinking on developments in biomedical science.
- They are available to guide the development programs of all medicine developers who wish to submit an application for a marketing authorization in the EU, and to ensure that medicines are developed consistently and to the highest quality.
- EMA also gives product-specific scientific advice to companies for the development of medicines.

(d) Authorization and Supervision of Manufacturers

- Manufacturers, importers and distributors of medicines in the EU must be licensed before they can carry out those activities.
- The regulatory authorities of each Member State are responsible for granting licenses for such activities taking place within their respective territories.
- All manufacturing and importing licenses are entered into Eudra GMDP, the publicly-available European database operated by EMA.

- Manufacturers listed in the application of a medicine to be marketed in the EU are inspected by an EU competent authority.
- *Inspection outcomes can be accessed by all Member States and are made publicly available across the EU through Eudra GMDP.*
- In order to be imported into the EU, an active pharmaceutical ingredient needs to be accompanied by a Written Confirmation issued by the competent authority of the country where it is produced, confirming that the good manufacturing practice (GMP) applied is at least equivalent to the recognized EU GMP standards.
- Every batch of medicines must be certified as having been manufactured and tested in accordance with GMP and in conformance with the marketing authorization before it can be released onto the market in the EU.
- If the product is manufactured outside the EU and has been imported, it needs to undergo full analytical testing in the EU.

(e) Safety Monitoring of Medicines

- The European regulatory system for medicines monitors the safety of all medicines that are available on the European market throughout their life span.
- All suspected side effects that are reported by patients and healthcare professionals must be entered into Eudra Vigilance, the EU web-based information system operated by EMA that collects, manages and analyses reports of suspected side effects of medicines.
- These data are continuously monitored by EMA and the Member States in order to identify any new safety information.
- The committee provides advice and recommendations to the European medicines regulatory network on risk management planning and benefit-risk assessment for medicines after marketing.

(f) Clinical Trials

- The authorization and oversight of a clinical trial is the responsibility of the Member State in which the trial is taking place.
- The European Clinical Trials Database (EudraCT) tracks which clinical trials have been authorized in the EU. It is used by NCAs and clinical-trial sponsors to enter information protocols and results of clinical trials.
- *A subset of this information is made publicly available by EMA via the EU clinical trials register.*

2.4.2 MHRA

- **Medicines and Healthcare products Regulatory Agency** is an executive agency of the Department of Health of United Kingdom.
- **MHRA** was set up in April, 2003 bringing together the function of **medicines Control Agency** (MCA) and the **Medical Devices Agency (MDA).**
- **MHRA** is responsible for ensuring that medicines and medical devices work, and are acceptably safe.
- **MHRA** *functions when the company wants to start clinical trials in patients.*

(a) Roles

- Licensing
  - o Manufacturer and dealer licenses
  - o Clinical trial licenses
  - o Parallel import licenses
  - o Safety and efficacy monitoring
  - o Enforcements of laws
  - o Regulation of clinical trials
  - o Providing information to public and health professionals

➢ MHRA does not regulate dietary supplements, veterinary products and cosmetics.

(b) Licensing Process [figure 1]

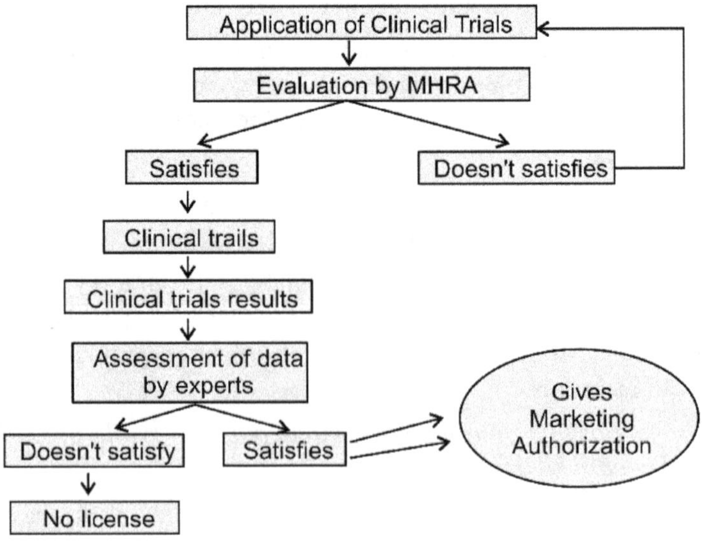

(c) Marketing Authorization

Majorly by 4 processes:

1. Centralized procedures
   - In EU, a company may submit a single application to the EMA for a marketing authorization that is valid simultaneously in all EU Member States.
2. National procedures
   - Each EU member states has its own procedures for the authorization of medicines that fall outside the scope of the centralized procedure.
   - Applicants must submit an application to the competent authority of the Member State
3. Decentralized Procedure
   - Using the decentralized procedure, *companies may apply for simultaneous authorization on more than one EU country of products that have not yet been authorized in any EU country and do not fall within the mandatory scope of the centralized procedure.*
4. Mutual recognition procedure
   - Here, a medicine is first authorized in one EU member state, in accordance with the national procedures of that country. Following this, further marketing authorizations can be sought from other EU countries in a procedure whereby the countries concerned agree to recognize the validity of the original, national marketing authorization.

(d) Renewal of License [figure 2]

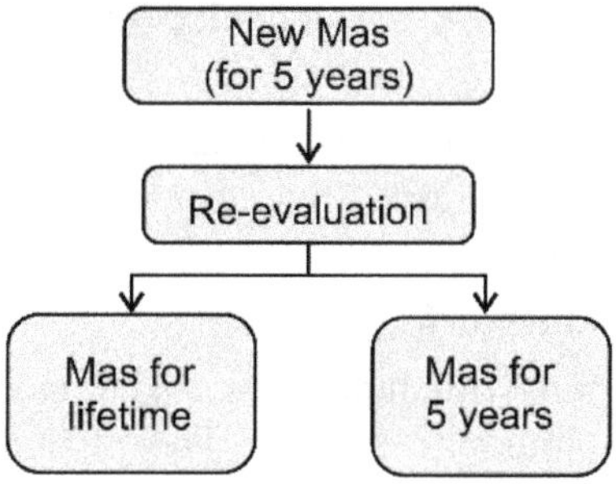

- New Marketing Authorization (MA) are valid for 5 years and then may be renewed on the basic of a re-evaluation of the risk-benefit balance.
- Applications for renewal should be submitted at least six months before expiry.

2.4.3 TGA

- Therapeutics Goods Administration is the regulatory body for therapeutic goods in Australia.
- TGA is responsible for conducting assessment and monitoring activities to ensure that therapeutic goods available in Australia are of an acceptable standard.
- The objectives of Therapeutic Goods Act 1989, which came into effect on 15 Feb, 1991 is **to provide a national framework for the regulation of therapeutic goods in Australia to ensure quality, safety and efficacy of the medicines and ensure quality, safety and performance of medical devices.**
  - Essentially therapeutic goods must be entered on the Australian Register of Therapeutics goods (ARTG) before they can be supplied in Australia.
  - ARTG is a *computer database of information about therapeutic goods for human use approved for supply in, or export from, Australia.*
  - Australian manufacturers of all **medicines must be licensed under part 4 of the Therapeutic Goods Act 1989** and their manufacturing process must comply with the principles of GMP.
  - Once approved for marketing in Australia, medicines are included in the ARTG and can be identified by the **AUST R** number (for registered medicines) or an **AUST L** number (listed medicines) that appears on the packaging of the medicines.
  - Medicines that are assessed to be higher risk are individually evaluated for quality, safety and efficacy. Higher risk products approved by the TGA are included on the ARTG as registered medicines.
  - Listed medicines are low risk medicines and are included on the ARTG via low-cost and streamlined electronic application and validation process.

(a) Regulatory Framework

- In consultation with industries, TGA has developed Australian Regulatory Guidelines for The Complementary Medicine (ARGCM) to assist sponsors of complementary medicines to meet their legislative obligations.
- Products are evaluated by the TGA for quality, safety and efficacy under the provision of section 25 of the Therapeutic Goods Act 1989.
- Products in category include:

- Products included in Schedule of Pharmaceutical Benefits
- Products containing sunscreen active ingredient that is not included in the list of sun-screening agent permitted as active ingredient in listed products
- Products that make therapeutic claims other than sun screening.

(b) Elements to Regulate

- Licensing and Audit of Manufactures

  Act requires each Australian manufacturer of medicinal products for human use to hold a manufacturing license. License holders are required to comply with the manufacturing principles of the Act, including compliance with GMP.

- Pre-Market Assessment

  This includes study of toxicity and dosage form of medicines. The product risk is determine by side effects, inappropriate self-medication, adverse effect for prolonged use.

(c) Post-Market Regulatory Authority

The essential elements of this systematic rick-based approach include:

1. Monitoring of adverse reactions to medicines.
2. Targeted and random surveillance in the market place.
3. An effective, responsive and timely recalls procedure.
4. Audit of GMP.
5. Effective controls for the advertising of therapeutic goods.

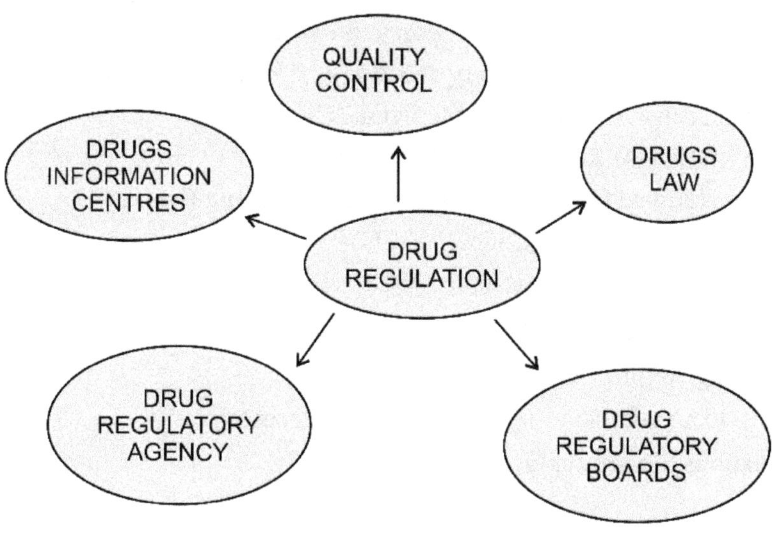

2.4.4 Regulatory Requirements in Row Countries

Key function of RA:

1. Product registration
2. Regulation of drug manufacturing, importation and distribution
3. Adverse drug reaction monitoring
4. Licensing of premises, person and practices.
5. Main goal of the agency is to guarantee the safety, efficacy and quality of the available drug product.

(a) India: Regulatory Bodies

- **Central Drug Standard Control Organization (CDSCO)**
- Ministry of Health and Family Welfare (MHFW) ˜ Indian council of Medical Research (ICMR)
- Indian Pharmaceutical Association (IPA)
- Drug Technical Advisory Board (DTAB)
- Central Drug Testing Laboratory (CDTL)
- Indian Pharmacopoeia Commission (IPC)
- National Pharmaceutical Pricing Authority (NPPA).

Points to know

Important organizations

- World health organization(WHO)
    - Centre for Biologics Evaluation and Research (CBER)
    - Centre for Devices and Radiological Health (CDRH)
    - Centre for Drug Evaluation and Research (CDER)
    - Centre for Food Safety and Applied Nutrition (CFSAN)
    - Centre for veterinary Medicine (CVM)
    - Office of Regulatory Affairs (ORA)
    - National Centre for Toxicological Research (NCTR)
    - Office of Chief Council (OCC)
    - Office of Commissioner (OC)

What USFDA regulates?

- Biological products
- Product manufacturing establishment Licensing
- Nations blood supply

- Research to establish product standards and to develop improved testing methods
- Cosmetics
- Labeling
- Drugs
- Product approvals

References

1. http://www.mhra.gov.uk
2. http://www.Europa.eu/European-union/index
3. http://www.mespharmacy.org/wp-content/uploads/2020/07/Introduction-to-Regulatory-agency.pdf
4. https://www.slideshare.net/HimalBarakoti/regulatory-requirement-of-eu-mhra-and-tga

CHAPTER 3.1

Investigational Medicinal Product Dossier (IMPD)

3.1.1 European Medicines Agency (EMA)

- It is an organization divided into European regions.
- The Management Board is the most important management body of the European Medicines Agency.
- The Agency is responsible for conducting clinical testing, surveillance and protection of improved drug tracking with the help of pharmaceutical companies for use in the EU.
- The EMA protects the resilience of human and animal health in the 27 EU member states, in addition to the European Economic Area nations, with the help of implementing to ensure that every drug in the EU market is safe, effective and of the highest quality.
- EMA operates a market place for more than 500 million people living in the EU.

3.1.2 History

- Founded in 1995, it has worked across the EU and around the world to monitor the resilience of people and animals through drug testing to strict medical needs and to provide independent, scientifically based science-based therapies.
- The EMA has a 20-year platform to ensure the effectiveness and safety of human and veterinary medicine throughout Europe, as well as to market new courses and methods within the development of medicines.
- In the first decades, the company promoted the approval of all 975 human therapies and 188 veterinary medicine.

3.1.3 Drug Approval Process

- There are precautionary measures that must be taken before a drug can be approved for marketing within the EU.

  These steps are: -

  1. Application for clinical examination
  2. Applying for marketing authorization

- Clinical evaluation programs are accredited at the national member level. Marketing authorization programs are accredited in each member state or at intermediate levels.
- A qualified person must ensure that the product of Investigative medicinal (IMP) complies with GMP.
- The armed officer has the right to inspect the GMP compliance production center, GLP compliance clinic and GCP compliance medical testing centers.

3.1.4 Application for Clinical Screening

- EU Directive 2001/20 / EC (April 2001) incorporates new policies and policies for the accreditation and management of scientific experiments in Europe.
- The sponsor sends a request for a medical examination to the Competent Managers in all Member States where difficulties will arise.
- The Competent Authority has 60 days to study and approve or reject the application.
- The application is in the prescribed form and includes the proposed clinical trial protocol, production and quality controls in the drug and assisted data, such as: - chemical, pharmaceutical and organic data - non-medical medical and toxicological data - pre-human and medical data (medical data) if available)

3.1.5 Investigational Medical Product Dossier

- The IMPD is the basis for the authorization of clinical trials in the form of armed government within the EU.
- The Clinical Trial Directive came into force, aligning the laws, policies and administrative provisions of Member States with regard to the use of the GCP within the conduct of clinical evaluation of medical equipment used by individuals.

- The directive provided a coordinated strategy for authorization to conduct medical examinations in any of the EU Member States.
- In addition, it describes the documents that must be submitted to the Ethics Committee in addition to the Investigational Medicinal Product Dossier (IMPD) for submission to the authorities for approval.

3.1.6 Introduction

- Document

  "Data collection is about someone, an event or title "

  Eg. Patient medical record
- Dosage of medical product

  "A file containing detailed information about a particular drug product "

3.1.7 IMPD: Content

- IMPDs are submitted as part of the application form for clinical examination, as the basis for the authorization of clinical trials by competent authorities within the European Union.

  IND application equals U.S.

  Contents: texts for the next trial

  1. Goals
  2. Informed consent forms
  3. Investigator's notebook
  4. Research reports
  5. Discussion topics
  6. Risk management systems
  7. Periodic safety review reports

3.1.8 Requirement of IMPD

- Risk factors
- Product type of product
- State of development
- Number of sick people
- The nature and severity of the disease
- The nature and duration of the clinical trial itself

3.1.9 What is an IMPD?

The Investigational Medicinal Product Dossier (IMPD) is one of the few pieces of Investigational Medicinal Product (IMP) related data needed whenever the clinical trial performance is targeted at one or more European Union countries.

The IMPD includes summaries of information related to the quality, production and control of any IMP (including reference product and placebo), as well as data from non-clinical and clinical studies.

(a) Purposes

Since clinical trials will often be designed as multi-institutional courses, which may involve Many Member States, it is the purpose of this guide to outline the agreed documentation requirements that will be sent to the entire European Community.

(b) Width

- The guide considers the chemical and pharmaceutical documentation of IMPs containing chemical active ingredients, synthetic peptides, herbs, herbs and radio-labeled / radio-labeled substances that must be submitted to competent authorities for approval before commencement. a competent clinical authority to authorize prior to initiating clinical trials in humans.
- Includes requirements for IMPs to be tested in phase I, phase II and phase III as well as requirements for adjusted and unadjusted comparisons of modified and unmodified compound products and IMPs to be tested in standard bioequivalence studies [and placebo products].

(c) Common points about all IMPs

IMPs should be produced in accordance with the principles and guidelines with detailed guidelines for the development of medical products (Regulations governing medical products in the European Community, Volume IV)

(d) Discussion

The investigational Medical product document (IMPD) should be provided in a clearly structured format that follows the CTD format of Part 3 and includes the most recent available information related to clinical trials at the time of submission of the clinical trial application. If the active ingredient is already approved for a finished product within the EU / EEA or one of the ICH regions the reference may be made to a valid marketing authorization. However, depending on the type of product, additional information may be required. The statement must be made that the active ingredient is the same quality as the authorized product.

The name of the completed product, marketing authorization number or similar, the owner of the marketing authorization and the country that issued the marketing permit must be provided.

Data's on bio-logical, chemical parameters and pharmaceutical information related to biological research products in clinical trials

(e) Operations

Professional File Reference or Certification of Compliance (CEP) of the European Director of Medicinal Quality is not acceptable and does not apply to functional biological / biotechnological applications.

(f) General information

Nomenclature

Information relating to the names of the active ingredient (e.g. International Non-Proprietary Name (INN), Pharmacopoeia name, ID name, company code, Other names or codes, if any) should be provided.

Structure

A brief description of the predicted structure should be provided. A high-order structure, amino acid sequence sequencing showing glycosylation sites or other post-translation modification and associated molecular weight should be included, accordingly.

(g) General properties

A list of physic-chemical components and other relevant active ingredients should be provided that include biological activity (i.e., specific ability or product capacity to achieve a defined biological effect). The proposed approach should be discussed.

Production

Manufacturer (s) The names and addresses (s) and responsibilities of each manufacturer, including contractors, and each proposed production facility or area involved in the production, testing and bulk production must be provided.

(h) Investigation on production process and process controls

Production process and in-process control should be adequately defined. The production process usually begins with one or more cell bank container and includes cell culture, harvesting, cleaning, reaction preparation and filling. Shipping and shipping conditions should be specified.

A blueprint or flow diagrams of all sequential steps including the appropriate processing parameters and pending test should be provided. The control strategy should focus on safety control compliance (IPCs) and the adoption of key actions (e.g. the scope of procedures involved in virus removal) should be established in phase I / II activities. These internal process controls (process parameters and process analysis as defined in ICH Q11) should be provided for initial action or initial acceptance conditions. For some IPCs, management may be appropriate and acceptance criteria or action limits do not need to be provided. Since pre-development control limits were usually depends on a less No of development clusters, they are not an evolutional start. During the development stage, as more process information may be available, additional IPC information should be provided and the review process updated.

Collection / collection and scale should be defined, which includes information on any yield or medium collection.

Any reconsideration during the operation of the active object (e.g. failure of filtering integrity) should be explained and justified. Reconsideration can be considered in different contexts. In biological products, these conditions are usually limited to specific re-screening steps and re-focus on the technical failure of the device or the impairment of the function of the chromatography column.

(i) Control

Mature and starting items

Materials in the manufacturing of active ingredient (e.g. raw materials, raw materials, cell culture media, growth factors, column frames, solvents, stimulants) should be pointed out where each item is used in the manufacturing process parameters. References to quality range (e.g. compensation monograph or internal manufacturer details) should be done. Quality data and control over free items should be provided. data's indicating that materials (including biological resources, e.g. media components, monoclonal antibodies, enzymes) meet the prescribed standards in their intended use should be given, appropriately.

For all materials of human or animal origin (including those used in cell banking), the source and the appropriate state of the production process in which the item is used should be pointed out. Summaries of the safety data of incoming agents for these items should be given with Appendix A.2.

Source, history and production of the cell substrate

A detailed description of the source and generation (flow sequence) of the cell substrate, oral vector analysis for genetic modification and incorporation into the parent cell / host used to develop Master Cell Bank (MCB), and a strategy by which genetic expression should be developed and controlled in production should be provided, in accordance with ICH Q5D standards.

Mobile banking system, character classification and testing

The MCB should be established before the start of the phase I assessment. Admittedly, the Working Cell Bank (WCB) may not be established on a regular basis.

Information about the production parameters, qualifications and maintenance of cell banks is needed. MCB and / or WCB when used should be noted and the results of the tests performed should be provided. Cell banking interactions should be directed at the mammalian cell lines. Production and segregation of mobile banking components must be done in accordance with ICH Q5D standards.

Cell banks should be marked with appropriate phenotypic and genotypic markers so that the identity, function, and purity of the cells used for production are guaranteed.

The nucleic acid sequence of the speech cassette including the code sequence should be verified before the start of the clinical examination.

In the case of any process change, the introduction of the WCB may have an impact on the quality profile of the material and should be comparable in comparison (see paragraph S.2.6. Development of a production process).

The safety assessment of adventitious agents and the suitability of bank cells used for the production of active substances should be provided in A.2, if applicable.

Stabilization of cell substrate

Any data available on cell substrate stability should be provided.

(j) Critical and central step management

The evaluation and acceptance process for controlling key steps in the production process should be provided. A reference to section S 2.2 may be accepted in terms of acceptance or limitation of action. Admittedly, due to limited data at the beginning of development (phase I / II) complete information may not be available. Capture times and intermediate process conditions should be justified and supported by data, if appropriate.

(k) Confirmation process

Proof of process verification should be collected during development, although it does not need to be submitted to the IMPD.

For production measures aimed at removing or eliminating the virus, relevant information should be provided in section A2, the safety assessment of Adventitious agents.

(l) Development of production process

Process development

The production processes and their control strategies are continuously developed especially during the development phase and the first stages of clinical evaluation. Changes in production process and controls should be summarized. This definition should allow for a clear identification of the variables used to produce each set used in non-clinical and clinical studies, in order to obtain positive correlations between pre- and post-transition groups. Flow comparison charts and / or a list of process changes can be used to present the emergence of a process. When systemic changes are made to the steps involved in removing the virus from the blood, reasons should be given as to whether a new viral clearance study is needed, or whether previous research is still valid.

Comparing work

Depending on the results of the proposed change and the development phase, a comparative task may be required to show that the modification will not adversely affect the quality of the material. In the first few months the main purpose of this work is to provide assurance that the postoperative product is ready for future clinical trials and that it will not raise concerns about the safety of patients included in the clinical trial. In addition, in recent stages, it should be noted that post-transformation factors may influence the effectiveness of the IMP.

This comparative work should generally follow a sequential process, which involves comparing the titles of the active material with the appropriate materials, using appropriate analytical methods. Analysis methods usually include standard tests, and may be supplemented with additional character tests (including orthogonal methods), as appropriate. Where manufacturers' information and other relevant information are not sufficient to assess the risk of change, or if potential risks to patients are expected, comparative work based solely on quality assumptions may be invalid. During the early stages of non-medical and clinical studies, comparative testing is often not as enjoyable as an approved product. In the first case in a human clinical study, the IMP representative of the substance used in non-clinical studies should be used.

3.1.10 Characterisation

(a) Structural specifications and other features

The identification of biotechnological or biological materials (including the determination of physico-chemical structures, biological activity, antimicrobial properties, purity and pollution) with appropriate techniques is required to allow certain resources to be established. Reference to textbooks alone is not acceptable, unless previously supplied with previous information from the same molecules for correction in the absence of safety concerns (e.g. C-terminal lysine for monoclonal antibodies). Adequate procedures should be performed in the development phase prior to phase I and, where necessary, following important process changes.

All important information contained in the basic, advanced and advanced structures including translation (eg Glyco forms) and other operational changes should be provided. Information should be provided on a biological function (i.e., a specific skill or product volume to achieve a defined biological effect). Generally, before the start of phase I studies, biological work should be determined using an appropriate, reliable and appropriate approach. The lack of such tests should be excused. It is noted that the size of the character's data will increase during development.

The reason for the selection of methods used for the inclusion of characters should be given and their suitability should be justified.

(b) Pollution process

Process-related impurities (e.g. host cell proteins, cell DNA, media residues, leak column) and product-related impurities (e.g. precursors, various forms, decomposition products, measurements) should be addressed. Dosage information about the infection should be provided which includes the maximum dose for a large dose. For certain process-related contaminants (e.g. antifoam agents), the permitted limit may be waived.

In the unlikely event that quality data is provided with certain impurities, this should be excused.

3.1.11 Active Control

If process verification data is incomplete, the quality indicators used to control the active ingredient are important to show product quality, product consistency and comparisons after process changes. Therefore, quality attributes controlled throughout the development process should not be limited to systematic evaluation when setting initial acceptance criteria.

(a) Clarification

The specification of the materials to be used in clinical research should describe the acceptance and evaluation method used to adequately control the quality of the materials. The inspection and defined terms of acceptance are binding on quantity, ownership and purity and the limit of 'record' or 'report results' will not be acceptable to these quality standards. Biological performance tests should be included unless there is a reason. Higher limits, in consideration of safety, should be placed on the wall. Microbiological quality of the active ingredient should be specified.

Since the acquisition method is usually based on a limited number of development groups and clusters used in non-medical and clinical studies, they are naturally a natural start and may need to be reviewed and adjusted during further development.

Product characteristics that are not fully explained in a particular developmental stage (e.g. Glycosylation, charge heterogeneity) or where available data are too limited to obtain appropriate acceptance criteria, should also be recorded. As a result, such product features can be integrated into the system, without predicting acceptance parameters. In such cases, the limit of 'record' or 'report results' is acceptable. Results should be reported in the Analysis section (S.4.4).

Additional information for phase III clinical trials

As knowledge and knowledge increase, more may be needed or the removal of boundaries and modification of analysis methods. The specifications and methods of previous tests should be reviewed and, where appropriate, adjusted to include the current stage of development.

(b) Analysis processes

Analysis methods used for all tests included in the instrument data (e.g. chromatographic methods, biological assay, etc.) should be included in the list that includes those reported tests without acceptance limits. A brief description of all the compulsory analysis processes, i.e. the analysis method, should be provided, highlighting the controls used in the analysis.

On routes compliant with European Pharmacopoeia (Ph. Eur.), EU region pharmacopoeia, United States Pharmacopoeia (USP) or Japanese Pharmacopoeia (JP), the appropriate monograph guide will be accepted.

(c) Validation of Analysis Processes

Validation of analytical procedures during clinical development is seen as a dynamic process.

Analysis procedures, which may be described in Ph. Eur., Pharmacopoeia of Member States, USP or JP, or linked to a monograph of a particular product, are generally considered certified. Proposed changes or alternatives must be guaranteed

In phase I and II clinical trials, the validity of the analytical methods used must be verified. Receipt limits (e.g., content restrictions for content, where applicable) and parameters (specified, compliance, width, accuracy, accuracy, quantity and acquisition limit, as appropriate) to ensure appropriate analytical methods. Introduced in a wonderful way. If validation studies are performed in a first phase test, a summary table of the results of the validation study can be provided for further confirmation.

Additional information for phase III clinical trials

As knowledge and knowledge increase, more may be needed or the removal of boundaries and modification of analysis methods. The specifications and methods of previous tests should be reviewed and, where appropriate, adjusted to include the current stage of development.

(d) Analysis Processes

Analysis methods used for all tests included in the instrument data (e.g. chromatographic methods, biological assay, etc.) should be included in the list that includes those reported tests without acceptance limits. A brief description of all the compulsory analysis processes, i.e. the analysis method, should be provided, highlighting the controls used in the analysis.

On routes compliant with European Pharmacopoeia (Ph. Eur.), EU region pharmacopoeia, United States Pharmacopoeia (USP) or Japanese Pharmacopoeia (JP), the appropriate monograph guide will be accepted.

(e) Validation of Analysis Processes

Validation of analytical procedures during clinical development is seen as a dynamic process.

Analysis procedures, which may be described in Ph. Eur., Pharmacopoeia of Member States, USP or JP, or linked to a monograph of a particular product, is generally considered certified. Proposed changes or alternatives must be guaranteed

In phase I and II clinical trials, the validity of the analytical methods used must be verified. Receipt limits (e.g. acceptance limits for contaminated content, where applicable) and parameters (specified, compliance, width, accuracy, accuracy, quantity and acquisition limit, as appropriate) to ensure appropriate analytical methods. Introduced in a wonderful way. If verification studies are performed on phase one tests, a summary table of validation study results can be provided for further verification.

Information for phase III clinical trial

Verification of analytical methods used for release and stability testing should be provided. A summary included in the verification results table should be submitted (e.g. results or values obtained for specification, line, width, accuracy, accuracy, quantity and acquisition limit, as appropriate). At the end of phase III verification of the full method should be completed, which includes confirmation of durability. It is not necessary to provide a full verification report.

(f) The collection is analytical

As the specification may be broad at first, actual data collection is essential to ensure quality. In quantity parameters, the actual numerical values must be presented.

The focus of this section is to indicate the quality of the collections (in line with the original definition) that will be used in clinical research. In pre-clinical phase clinical trials in which only a limited number of functional groups were performed, test results from appropriate and non-clinical clinical groups should be provided, including those to be used in IMPD-supported clinical research. For functional items with a long production history, it may be acceptable to provide results in a number of representative groups, if appropriate.

Group number, batch size, production location, production date, control methods, acceptance method and test results should be listed and the use of batches. The production process used for each collection and any differences in these processes should be noticeable.

A statement should be made as to whether the bulk of the data generated from the collection will be used in clinical research, or whether additional data has not yet been developed during the IMPD submission process.

(g) Description Correction

The reason for the quality requirements included in the specification and how to accept the purity, contamination, biological function and any other quality attributes that may be associated with the performance of a pharmaceutical product should be provided. Adjustments should be based on relevant development data, collections used in non-clinical and / or clinical studies as well as data from stabilization studies, taking into account the methods used for self-regulation. Admittedly, during clinical development, acceptance may be extensive and may not reflect the competence of the procedure. However, for those quality factors that may contribute to patient safety, limitations should be carefully considered taking into account the available information (e.g. process strength, product type, volume, dosage length etc.). Compliance with the selected power test and the proposed acceptance limits should be waived.

Changes to previously used definitions (e.g., adding or deleting parameters, extensions of acceptance terms) should be indicated and amended.

3.1.12 Reference Levels or Building Materials

Due to the biological / biotechnology nature of the materials, a good indicator is important to ensure consistency between different groups but also to ensure comparisons of products to be sold with those used in clinical studies and to provide inter-system communication. trade and manufacturing development. Indication of indicators should be done with reliable high-quality analytical methods, which should be adequately defined. Information about the production process used to create reference materials should be provided.

If more than one reference level is used during the development of the clinic, a qualification record must be provided explaining how the relationship between the different levels is maintained.

If available, international or Ph. Eur. the standard should be used as the primary reference. Each level of internal performance should be appropriate in comparison to this reference reference information. However, it should be noted that international use or Ph. Eur. the level may be limited to certain defined test methods, e.g. biological work. If international or Ph. Eur. quality is not available, internal level should be established during development as a key indicator. The stability of the reference material should be noted. This can be handled within the company's quality system

3.1.13 Container Closure Plan

Fast packaging used for a functional item should be mentioned. The possible interaction between the active object and the current packaging should be considered.

3.1.14 Stability

Summary of stability and conclusions (protocol / material and method)

A stability protocol that includes the proposed storage time of an active object should be provided, which includes specifications, analysis methods and test intervals. The test time should follow the instructions given in ICH Q5C.

The level of functional groups placed in the stabilization program should represent the quality of materials to be used in the planned clinical trial.

The active ingredient included in the stabilization program should be kept in the same container and made of the same materials as those used to store active ingredients for use in clinical trials. Reduced size containers are generally acceptable for testing the durability of a functional object.

Studies should assess performance stability under the proposed maintenance conditions. Accelerated studies and stress conditions are recommended as they can help understand product degradation profile and support shelf life.

The methods used to analyze performance indicators should be discussed, or discussed in S.4.3, in order to provide assurance of change / hygiene.

Pollution profile and active power will be obtained. The power test should be included in the protocol, unless there is a reason.

The re-examination period (as described in ICH Q1A guidelines) does not apply to the active components of biology / biotechnology.

Data Compatibility /Results

Consolidation data should be presented at least one amount made by the process representative of the one used to produce the materials to be used in clinical research. In addition, the stability data of appropriate development groups or collections produced using previous production processes should be provided, if available. Such collection data can be used on an active shelf item if it provides a valid quality reason representing the clinical trial equipment.

Appropriate stabilization data should be summarized in table format, specifying tested batches, production date, process version, composition, storage conditions, times, test methods, reception method and results.

In quantity parameters, the actual numerical values must be presented. Any considered data trends should be discussed.

Ongoing requirements will need to be used to reflect the amount of data available and the emerging information about the stability of the functional object during the various stages of clinical development. In Phase III the applicant must have a complete understanding of the operational sustainability profile.

Shelf Life Determination

The required shelf life of the active item under the proposed storage conditions should be stated and accompanied by an assessment of the available data. Any considered tendencies should be discussed.

The requested storage time should be based on long-term, real-time research and real-time temperature stability, as described in ICH Q5C. However, extending the shelf life beyond the time covered by real-time robust data may be acceptable, if supported by relevant data, which includes accelerated stability studies and / or appropriate stability data generated by independent materials.

The shelf life of the shelf after the extension should not be more than double, or more than twelve months during the period covered by real-time durability data obtained by groups representing others. However, extending the shelf life beyond the intended duration of long-term stability studies is not acceptable.

When planning to extend the shelf life, the applicant should take the initiative to develop a proposed stability plan in line with the proposed protocol, and, in the event of unforeseen problems, notify the competent Authority of the situation, and recommend remedial action.

Previous information incorporating field technology can be considered when developing a stability protocol. However, in itself this data is not considered sufficient to justify the shelf life of an active object.

For an extension of the shelf life of an extended shelf, see section 6.

3.1.15 Investigative Drug Product Testing

(a) Description and composition of the research drug product

The quality structure and value of the IMP should be specified. The information provided should include:

- A brief statement or presentation of volume
- composition, i.e. a list of all parts of the volume form and their value per unit (including over-age, if any), functional part, and reference of their quality levels (eg compendia monographs or manufacturer details)
- Definition of corresponding diluents
- Type of container and closure used in volume form and any associated reconstruction of filters and equipment, if applicable. A full explanation should be given in paragraph P.7.

(b) Drug development

For early development there may be only limited information to be included in this category.

A brief description of the construction process, which includes the release of any new pharmacy or supplement form, should be provided.

For products that require additional repairs (e.g. reconstruction, cleaning, mixing), compliance with used materials (e.g. solvents, diluents, matrix) should be indicated and the preparation method should be minimized (reference may be provided by full clinical description. Protocol).

It should be noted that the combination of targeted products and packaging does not interfere with the correct volume mixing, ensuring for example that the product is not advertised on the wall of the container or supply system. This is especially important for low volume and highly refined presentations. Where appropriate, reliable management of the smallest doses in the first population study should be considered as set out in the Strategic Guide for the Identification and Risk of Preliminary Clinical Trials of People with Research Therapeutic Products (EMEA / CHMP / SWP / 28367/07).

Development of production process

Changes in the production process that include changes in production and volume form compared to previous clinical trials should be explained. Appropriate comparison work should support important changes, e.g. structural changes. In this regard, the expectations are the same as those described in S.2.6. This data should be detailed enough to allow for a proper understanding of the changes and evaluation of potential patient safety outcomes.

Any changes in clinical practice should be documented and adjusted in relation to their impact on quality, safety, clinical facilities, capacity and product stability.

(c) Production

1. Producer (s)

The names, addresses and obligations of all manufacturers and each proposed production facility involved in construction, testing and production must be provided. In a situation where many producers contribute to the drafting of an IMP, their relevant obligations should be clearly stated.

2. Bulk formula

The bulk formula for collections to be used in clinical trials should be presented. This should include a list of all the components. Collection size or collection size should be provided.

3. Description of production process and process controls

A flow chart showing all the steps of the production process, including the relevant IPCs (process parameters and process testing), should be given a brief description of the process. IPCs may be labeled as performance restrictions or reported as conditions of initial admission and focus on appropriate safety features. For some IPCs, monitoring may be the same and the terms and conditions of admission do not need to be reported. During development, as more process information becomes available, additional IPC information should be provided and the review process updated.

Many products containing synthetic proteins and monoclonal antibodies are produced by an aseptic process, which is considered rare. Unusual production processes or new technologies and new packaging processes should be explained in more detail (see Product Process Guidelines Guidelines - information and data to be provided in a controlled post, EMA / CHMP / CVMP / QWP / BWP / 70278/2012).

Re-processing may be acceptable for certain production steps (e.g. re-filtering) only if the steps are adequately defined and appropriately justified.

4. **Critical and central step management**

The evaluation and acceptance process for controlling key steps in the production process should be provided. Admittedly, due to limited data at the beginning of development (phase I / II) complete information may not be available.

If photographic timing is predicted by intermediate processes, duration and storage conditions should be provided and data validated in accordance with the physicochemical, biological and microbiological structures.

Sterilization by filtering the acceptable number of organisms prior to filtration should be specified in the application. In most cases NMT 10 CFU / 100 ml will be acceptable. Test doses of less than 100 ml can be used if necessary.

5. **Proving the evidence**

The condition for confirming aseptic processing and lyophilisation should be briefly described, if any. Processing EudraLex Vol. 4, Appendix 13, validation of disinfection procedures should be at the same level as the approved product. Capacity should primarily include information directly related to product safety, i.e., biological load and media filling.

(d) Control of excipients

1. **Clarification**

Ph. Eur., Pharmacopoeia of EU member states, USP or JP can be made. For services not covered by any of the above standards, internal information must be provided.

2. **Analysis processes**

   In cases where reference to the pharmacopoeia monograph listed under P.4.1 is not possible, the analytical methods used should be indicated.

3. **Validation of analysis processes**

   Validation of an analytical procedure is the process by which it is established, by laboratory studies, that the performance characteristics of the procedure meet the requirements for the intended analytical applications.

   1. Accuracy. ...
   2. Precision. ...
   3. Specificity. ...
   4. Linearity. ...
   5. Limit of detection and Limit of Quantitation (Intra day and Inter day)
   6. Range. ...
   7. Robustness.

4. **Description correction**

   For non-compendia assistants as listed above in P.4.1, in-house details should be released.

5. **Excipients on Natural origin**

   For practitioners of human or animal origin, Data's should be given about agent safety assessments (e.g. sources, details, description of the tests performed) and viral safety data in accordance with the Biotechnological Medical Product Testing Guidelines (EMEA / CHMP / BWP / 398498/05)) in Appendix A.2. In addition, compliance with the guidelines for reducing the risk of transmitting animal spongiform encephalopathy agent through human and animal medicine products (EMA / 410/01) should be noted in paragraph A.2.

   If human albumin or any other plasma-based drug product is used as a receptor, information relating to the safety of incoming agents should follow the relevant chapters of the Plasma Drug Products Guide (CPMP / BWP / 706271/2010). If the plasma-based component is already used in an Authorized Product then an indication of this can be made.

6. **Novel excipients**

   With first aid in a new medical product or management path, full construction details, character segments and controls, as well as various clues to make a backup copy of security data.

(e) Product control

1. **Clarification**

The same principles applied to the active ingredient should be applied to the medical product. In the specification, the tests used and the terms of your acceptance should be specified in the product (s) to be used in the clinical trial to enable adequate control of the product quality. Content testing, ownership and hygiene are mandatory. Infertility testing and endotoxins are mandatory for sterile products. Biological function tests should be included unless there is a specific reason. Higher limits, taking into account safety considerations, should be placed on the dirt. They may need to be updated and adjusted during further development.

The IMP quality qualification approach should consider safety considerations and the development phase. Since the method of admission is usually based on a limited number of development groups and groups used in non-clinical and clinical studies, their nature for the first time. They may need to be updated and adjusted during further development.

Analysis methods and content limits and bioactivity performance should ensure high volume.

With uncovered impurities the specific ingredient specification, high limits should be set, taking into account safety considerations.

More information on Phase III clinical trials

As information and knowledge increase the addition or removal of parameters and the modification of analytical methods may be necessary. The decision-making process set by previous tests should be reviewed in phase III clinical trials and, where appropriate, adjusted to achieve the current stage of development.

2. **Analysis processes**

Analysis methods for all the tests included in the specification should be described. For some proteins and drug forms that are complex or new, a high level of detail may be required.

For more requirements see S.4.2.

3. **Validation of analysis processes**

For requirements see S.4.3.

4. **Collection analysis**

As the specification may be broad at first, actual data collection is essential to ensure quality. In quantity parameters, the actual numerical values must be presented.

The focus of this section is to indicate the quality of the collections (in line with the original definition) that will be used in clinical research. In pre-clinical phase clinical trials where only a limited number of clusters have been performed, test results from appropriate and non-clinical clinical groups should be provided, including those to be used in IMPD-supported clinical research. For products with a long production history, it may be acceptable to provide results in a number of representative groups, if appropriate.

Group number, batch size, production location, production date, control methods, acceptance method and test results should be listed and the use of batches. The production process used for each collection must be identified.

A statement should be made as to whether the bulk of the data generated from the collection will be used in clinical research, or whether additional data has not yet been developed during the IMPD submission process.

5. **Manifestations of pollution**

   Additional impurities and perishable products noted in the IMP, but not included in paragraph S.3.2, should be identified and calculated as required.

6. **Description correction**

   Adjustment of the quality attributes included in the product specification should be provided primarily based on the specification of the functional object. Stability that reflects quality qualities should be considered. The proposed reception conditions should be waived.

(f) Reference levels or building materials

References to the reference level should be provided, where appropriate.

Section S.5 may be referred to, where appropriate.

(g) Container Closure System

The primary packaging intended for use by the IMP in clinical research should be described. Where appropriate, refer to the appropriate pharmacopoeia monograph. If the product is packaged in an unusual holding device, or if a highly economical device is used, a description and description must be provided.

If a medical device is to be used for administration it must be stated whether the device is marked with CE for its intended purpose. If there is no CE mark for the intended purpose, a statement of compliance with the essential requirements of medical equipment in respect of device features related to safety and performance is required. An important component of a composite product, as defined in the Medical Device Directive, is exempt from CE marking.

For products intended for parental use where there is an opportunity for interaction between the product and the container closure system, additional details may be required (e.g., removable / openable in phase III courses).

(h) Stability

The same requirements as the active component apply to a medical product, including stability protocol, stability effects, shelf life determination, which includes extended shelf life over a period covered by real-time firm data, commitment and post-authorization extension. Stability studies should provide sufficient assurance that the IMP will be stable at the end of the target period. The data presented should support the shelf life of the proposed product from its release to patient management. The IMP stability profile should take into account the information obtained from the validity profile of the active profile.

Brackets and matrixing methods may be acceptable, where appropriate.

Internal use data should be presented for use after reassembling, cleaning, mixing or multidose presentations. These courses are not required if repairs will begin immediately after opening or rebuilding.

3.1.16 Appendices (A)

1. **Goods and equipment**
2. **Security testing of adventitious agents**

   All human or animal materials used in your production process for both the active ingredient and the pharmaceutical product, or similar substances that interact with the active drug or drug product during the production process, must be identified. Information on risk assessment of potential contamination by emerging individuals or animal agents should be provided in this section.

   TSE agents

   Detailed information should be provided on preventing and controlling agents of infectious spongiform encephalopathy. This information may include, for example, certification and production process management, local suitability, process and agent.

   Guideline note to reduce the risk of transmitting the animal spongiform encephalopathy agent through human and animal medicine products (EMEA / 410/01) in its current version will be used.

Viral protection

Where appropriate, a risk assessment for potential infection should be provided at this stage. The documents must comply with the requirements set out in the safety guidelines for biotechnological research products (EMEA / CHMP / BWP / 398498/05).

Other adventitious agents

Detailed information about other adventitious agents, such as viruses, mycoplasma, and fungi should be given in appropriate categories within the main dose.

3. **Excipients**

   The information as indicated in section S should be provided in accordance with the relevant clinical category.

4. **Recombinant solvents and solvents**

   Reconstructions and refineries, relevant information as shown in section P should be provided.

5. **Quality information for authorized, unmodified biological tests and comparative products in clinical trials**

   Information on the approved, unadulterated product / comparative product provided in the IMPD must meet the requirements set out in section 3 of the Guide regarding the requirements for chemical and medical quality documentation relating to clinical trial products (EMA / CHMP / QWP / 834816/2015).

   In the event that only re-packaging is done without modifying the original packaging, the following information should be included in the simplified IMPD in addition to the requirements listed in section 3 of EMA / CHMP / QWP / 834816/2015:

   - Information that will satisfy the requirement to ensure that the medical product under investigation will have the appropriate identity, power, quality and hygiene (eg a brief indication of the Product Symbols of the EU market product).
   - Details on the site of re-packaging / re-labeling tasks.

6. **Quality information for approved products for the biological component in clinical trials**

   Information on the authorized test / comparison product provided by the IMPD should meet the requirements set out in this guide.

   Categories that can be affected by modification may refer differently to an authorized product.

7. **Chemical knowledge and quality of medicines related to placebo products in clinical trials**

   Information about the placebo product to be provided to the IMPD must meet the requirements set out in section 6 of the Guide regarding the requirements for the literature of chemical and pharmaceutical products related to medical research products (EMA / CHMP / QWP / 834816/2015).

8. **Changes in the medical product under investigation and the medical assistant required to request major IMPD changes.**

   In accordance with Product Practice, the Product Description File should be kept in each IMP in the appropriate place and updated regularly as product development progresses, ensuring proper compliance with previous versions. The following is an incomplete list of changes that are generally 'major' and need to be informed by competent authorities.

   - Changes to the manufacturer / producer of an active drug or pharmaceutical product
   - Major changes in the production process (such as a new speech cell line, the addition or omission of the cleaning step, changes in steps affecting the removal of the virus, and any refinements not specified in the IMPD)
   - Changes that lead to the emergence of new pollutants and product related products
   - A change in schedule, if the terms of acceptance are extended or the evaluation procedures are removed or changed
   - Structural changes that include changes in the focus of the active object and the structure of the receiver
   - Changes in packaged goods immediately, if the condition of the goods changes
   - Changes in approved performance standards
   - Any extension of the shelf life without the agreed stability protocol or without prior commitment (see paragraphs S.7 and P.8)

   However, the extended shelf life based on agreed protocol is generally not considered a significant change if:

   - Each extension of the additional shelf life does not exceed twice, and does not exceed twelve months than the available real-time data and does not exceed the length of time as stated in the agreed firmness protocol.
   - The extension is covered and compliant with an approved stability protocol

- No significant trends or outdated outcomes (OoS) were obtained from ongoing studies of sustainability at constant storage temperatures.
- The applicant undertakes to inform the competent Authority of unforeseen stability issues in the ongoing research (including trends and OoS) and to recommend remedial measures as appropriate.

3.1.17 Guidance and Legal Basis

- Guidance is based on Regulation (EU) No 536/2014 on Clinical Trials on Medicinal Products for Human Use (Repealing Directive 2001/20 / EC) regarding the limitations of the laws, regulations and administrative provisions of Member States related to use. effective clinical practice in conducting clinical trials on human-based products (often referred to as 'Clinical Trials Directive').
- The Regulation comes into force, aligning the laws, principles and administrative provisions of Member States related to the implementation of Good Clinical Practice (GCP) in conducting clinical trials in medical products for individual use.
- The Member States of Europe provide the requirements set out in the Code for national legislation.

The IMPD includes summaries of quality-related information, the production and management of a Medical Investigative Product, data from non-medical studies and its clinical use.

Overall risk assessment, critical analysis of non-clinical and clinical data in relation to potential risks and benefits of the proposed study should be part of the IMPD.

In some cases, e.g. when a Medical Product Investigation has already been approved as a medical product in one of the EU Member States or where clinical studies and IMPs have been accredited by Member States, a simplified IMPD will be sufficient.

References

1. EMA/CHMP/BWP/534898/2008 rev. 1 corrigendum Committee for Medicinal Products for Human Use (CHMP) September 2018
2. https://www.slideshare.net/HimalBarakoti/investigation-of-medicinal-product-dossier-impd

CHAPTER 3.2

Investigator's Brochure

3.2.1 Introduction

- Investigator's Brochure (IB) is a combination of clinical and non-clinical data on research products that are related to product research in human studies. IB is a document of critical importance throughout the drug development process and is updated with new information as it becomes available.

  The purpose of the IB is to compile data relevant to studies of the investigational product in human subjects gathered during preclinical and other clinical trials to provide the investigator with information necessary for the management of study conduct and study subjects throughout a clinical trial.

3.2.2 Purpose

- Its purpose is to provide information to investigators and others involved in research such as volume, frequency / interval, management methods: and the security monitoring process.
- IB also provides insights to support clinical management of research topics during clinical trials.
- Information should be presented in a concise and simple way.
- IB empowers the clinic or potential investigator, to understand and self-assess a neutral risk benefit in terms of the validity of the proposed study. For this reason, a medical professional should regularly participate in IB planning.

3.2.3 Investigator's Brochure

- Title Page
  1. Client name

2. Ownership of each research product (i.e., research number, chemical or generic name and brand name where applicable) and required by the sponsor).
3. Release Date.
4. Confidential statement
   - Privacy Statement
   - The sponsor may wish to submit a statement instructing the investigator (s) to treat IB as a confidential information document and the use of the investigative team and the IRB / IEC.

3.2.4 Contents IB

- The investigator's manual should include:
  1. **Table of Contents**
  2. **Summary**

     A brief summary (preferably not more than two pages) should be provided, highlighting important physical, chemical, pharmaceutical, pharmaceutical, toxicological, pharmacokinetic, metabolic, and clinical information relevant to the clinical product development phase of research (IP).
  3. **Introduction**

     Contains the chemical (and commercial) name (and names) if approved) of IP, all active ingredients, IP pharmacy category and its expected status within this category (e.g., benefits), reason for research. by IPs, as well as expected prophylactic, therapeutic, or diagnostic indicators.

     The most common procedure to follow in IP testing.
  4. **Description of IP**
     - It should be briefly summarized on appropriate physical properties, chemicals, and medications.
     - A description of the formulation to be used, including the assistant, should be provided and justified if appropriate clinically.
     - Instructions for the maintenance and administration of the form (s) should also be provided.
  5. **Non-Clinical Studies**

     The results of all nonclinical pharmacology, toxicology, pharmacokinetic, and research studies of product metabolism should be presented in a concise manner.

The information provided may include

- Tested types;
- Number and sex of animals in each group;
- Unit capacity (eg, milligram / kilogram (mg / kg));
- Volume interval;
- Management system;
- Duration of treatment;
- Information on formal distribution;
    - Duration of follow-up period after exposure;
    - Results, which include the following features:
        - The nature and frequency of drug or toxic effects;
        - The magnitude or severity of pharmacological or toxic effects;
        - Start time for results;
        - Modification of results;
        - Length of results;
        - Volume 1 response.

1. **Nonclinical Pharmacology**
    - A summary of the medicinal properties of the research product and, where appropriate, its important metabolites studied in animals should be included.
2. **Pharmacokinetics and Product Metabolism in Animals**
    - A summary of the pharmacokinetics and biological changes (finding the drug in its proper place in the body and in the proper concentration) of the research product in all species of animals studied should be provided.
3. **Toxicology**
    - A summary of the toxic effects found in relevant studies on different species of animals should be described under the following headings where appropriate:
        - Single dose;
        - Double dose;
        - Carcinogenicity;
        - Special subjects (e.g., irritability and sensitivity);
        - Reproductive toxicity;
        - Genotoxicity (mutagenicity).

6. **Effects on People**
   - A comprehensive discussion of the known product results (s) of human research should be provided, including drug knowledge, metabolism, pharmacodynamics, dose response, safety, efficacy, and other medical activities. Where possible, a summary of each completed clinical trial should be provided.
   1. **Pharmacokinetics and Product Metabolism in Humans**
      - o A summary of the pharmacokinetics of the research product (s) should be presented, including the following, if available:
      - o Pharmacokinetics (including metabolism, fitness, and absorption, binding to plasma proteins, distribution, and elimination).
      - o Availability of the bioavailability of the research product (complete, where possible, and / or relative) using the reference measurement form.
        - A small group of people (eg, gender, age, and function of a disabled organ).
        - Interaction (e.g., product interaction with food effects).
        - Other pharmacokinetic data (e.g., results of human studies conducted during a clinical trial).
   2. **Safety and effectiveness**
      - Summary information should be provided about the safety of the research product (including metabolites, where appropriate), pharmacodynamics, efficacy, and dose responses obtained from previous human trials (healthy volunteers and / or patients.).
   3. **Marketing Information**
      - o The IB should identify the countries in which the research product market is marketed or approved.
      - o The IB should also identify all countries where the product of the investigation did not receive approval / registration for marketing or withdrew from advertising / registration.
7. **Summary of data and direction of investigator**
   - This section should provide an overview of non-clinical and clinical IP data.
   - IB gives the investigator a clear understanding
   - Possible danger
   - Adverse reactions
   - Observation and monitoring required in clinical research.

References

1. Guidance for Industry E6 Good Clinical Practice: Consolidated Guidance by ICH.

CHAPTER 4.1

Development of Clinical Trial Protocol

4.1.1 What is Protocol?

The protocol provides documentary evidence of the need and feasibility of research. It provides a complete and detailed description of the objectives, design, methodology, statistical considerations and research structure, including specific details of how the research will be conducted and evaluated. The protocol will be strictly followed by researchers throughout the study period, so the final protocol should be clear and provide sufficient information for all study participants to use it.

Why is Protocol Needed?

Writing a detailed research protocol will require you to decide on the research objectives what measurements should be made, the group of patients to be researched and how the data will be analyzed. The time spent writing a detailed protocol will avoid problems during research, and will make publishing results even easier.

A well-written and complete protocol is essential for high-quality research.

(a) Who Learns Processes?

- Language / content to be understood
- Some doctors
- Nurses / CRAs
- IRB members
- Science reviewers
- IC for just one person

(b) Objectives

Objectives should be clearly identified as factors of consideration to be considered.

Each objective should have the same discussion in the mathematical category

(c) Background and reason

All protocols require a detailed section on the scientific reasons for the protocol and the release of medical and scientific documents on the proposed concept.

Part of the presentation should be logically organized, with consistent flow.

(d) Scheduling Clinical Examinations

- Create a Research Questionnaire
- Create a Reading Design
- Describe the population survey.
- Select Balance Tools / End Points
- Determine Sample Size and Statistical Analysis
- Data Collection and Storage

(e) How to Choose a Reading Design?

Selection of the study design is based on: study question, ethical considerations and resources

(f) Study Subject Selection

- Subjects who may benefit
- Subjects who may be at greater risk
- Subject's ability to comply
- Subject's concurrent conditions
- Inclusion criteria
- Exclusion criteria

For example

- The eligibility method provided by the National Institute of Neurological Disorder and Stroke for recruiting participants in a clinical study entitled Study of Brain Activity during Speech Production and Speech Perception.
- The inclusion criteria specified by the assessment team were (a) right-handed children and adolescents, (b) native American English speakers, and (c) stuttering or sound disorders.
- The comparison (control) group usually included right-handed children and adolescents who spoke American English.

- The conditions of exclusion were (a) the use of language at home other than American English, (b) speech restriction limits of more than 25d B, and (c) crosses on magnetic resonance scanning.

Security

- Side effects and side effects these terms are closely related to the drug.
- Used by doctors and nurses.
- Safety or adverse events include the following principles:
    - Detailed information on reporting adverse events, including reporting to the FDA and / or sponsor
    - Eye-opening procedures (if available)
    - List of expected adverse events

(g) Determine Mathematical Analysis

- Get a mathematician to get involved early
- Proper analysis plan for objectives and design
- Mathematical methods to be used
- How to solve common problems
- Security data management

(h) Determine Sample Size

- How can you deal with dropping out of school / withdrawal?
- Interventions:

1. How important is the difference between treatment groups 2. Include sufficient participants to obtain statistically significant value
    - Estimate the appropriate number of lessons for a particular learning project
    - Examine the hypothesis

(i) Protection of Human Studies

- This section includes discussions:
    - Choice and release of topic
    - Suggested ways to hire a patient
    - Percent representation of minorities
    - The hiring (or outsourcing) of specialized courses, including those at risk

Topics

- History of potential risks and benefits, including risk mitigation

(j) Data Collection and Storage

- Identify important data features to collect
- Create case report forms (which may be required to submit to the IRB or FDA)
- A secure and secure way to store data
- Expect clinical data testing
- Duration of end time
  - Know the FDA rules
  - Know the appropriate institutional policies

(k) Informed Concent

- Disclosure of relevant information to those seeking research
- Understanding information provided by the topic
- Voluntary title agreement

Approved protocol permission must be:

- Complete
- Written in simple, non-technical language.
- Carefully written to avoid complexity.

A protocol-informed consent should be granted

- Statement that involves research
- Purpose of the study and the duration of the study
- Description of risks and benefits
- Discuss alternative therapies
- Privacy policy
- Injury compensation
- Contact for more questions / information
- Statement of voluntary participation

4.1.2 Phase II, A Randomized, Duplicate Study, Controlled by Placebo Tests for TJ301 (FE 999301) Injections for Patients with Active Ulcerative Colitis

- Protocol number: CTJ301UC201
- Investigational Medicinal Product: TJ301 (injectable solution), also referred to such as FE 999301 and Olamkicept
- Investigators: Many institutions, internationally, throughout Mainland China, Taiwan, Republic of Korea and Australia

- Index: Active Ulcerative Colitis
- Category: 2
- Integrated Investigator Prof. Drs. Minhu Chen

Chair, Vice President of the Department of Gastroenterology and Hepatology

First Integrated Hospital, Sun Yat-sen University 58 Zhongshan Road, Guangzhou, China.

Expert Committee Prof. Drs. Stefan Schreiber

Schleswig-Holstein Schittenhelmstrasse 12, 24105 Kiel, Germany

Sponsor Name and Address: Leading Biopharm Limited

Yin Liu, Suite 802, OmniVision Park West Tower 88 Shangke Road, Pudong, Shanghai, 201210,

GCP Statement: This test will be performed accordingly

GCP

(a) Backgroung

Ulcerative colitis-Interleukin 6 is increased in patients of Ulcerative colities
Response in infection and tissue damage

↓

Complex of two extracellular domain of gp 130, fc region
Human immunoglobin G1

↓

Drug-neutralizes the complex

(b) Scientific Justication Of Clinical Trail Protocol

- Safety, efficacy and pharmacokinetics
- Healthy volunteers - 4 weeks
- Dose -0.75 mg to 750 mg
- Half life - 5 days
- management route-Iv to give him

4.1.3 Objectives of Test and Conclusion

(a) Objectives

Main Purpose

- To evaluate the safety and efficacy of TJ301 in patients with active ulcerative colitis.

Second Objectives

- Investigate the pharmacokinetics of TJ301 in patients with active ulcerative colitis.
- Investigate the pharmacodynamics of TJ301 in patients with active ulcerative colitis.
- Investigate the immunogenicity of TJ301 in patients with active ulcerative colitis.

Objectives of Testing

- To evaluate the relationship between the pharmacokinetics and pharmacodynamics of TJ301 in patients with active ulcerative colitis.

(b) Test Points

Main End Points

- Clinical and endoscopic discharge Week 12, defined as the full outcome of Mayo ≤2, no lower score per person> 1, rectal bleeding subscore = 0.
- Adverse events, significant symptoms, 12-lead Electrocardiography (ECG), and abnormalities in the clinical safety laboratory

Second Test Points

- Clinical and endoscopic reactions (decrease from Baseline to full Mayo ≥3 result and ≥30%, including decrease from Baseline in lower extremity bleeding ≥1 or lower rectal bleeding points ≤1) Weekly 12th.
- Clinical release Weeks 4, 6, 8, 10, and 12 are defined as stool frequency sub score = 0, rectal bleeding sub score = 0, and Mayo component with 9 ≤1 points.
- Clinical reaction (decrease from Baseline to 9 points for Mayo ≥2 fraction and ≥30%, including decrease from Baseline to lower rectal ≥1 points or rectal bleeding sub score ≤1) Weeks 4, 6, 8, 10, and 12.
- Mucosal treatment is defined as Mayo endoscopic sub score = 0 or 1 Week 12.

- Switch from base to weeks 4, 6, 8, 10, and 12 for 9 points that are part of Mayo.
- Switch from Baseline to Week 12 with full Mayo effects.
- Switch from Baseline to Week 12 on a modified Mayo result (= full Mayo result outside of Physician's Global Assessment (PGA) sub-school.
- Switch from base to weeks 4, 6, 8, 10, and 12 at PGA result.

Final Test Points

- This is a multidisciplinary, randomized, double-blind, placebo-controlled study.

  Tests include Running Period (if regular treatment is required), 4-Week Test Period, 12-Week Treatment Period, and a 3-week Safety Tracking Period of 105 days.
- 90 patients will be given a central, alternate, randomly assigned group of 3 (1: 1: 1) to receive 600mg TJ301 biweekly (Q2W), 300mg TJ301 Q2W or placebo Q2W. TJ301 or placebo administration will occur on days 0, 14, 28, 42, 56, and 70 days. Randomization will be separated by previous treatment of corticosteroids (yes / no) and permission to participate in a small PK study (yes / no).
- During the treatment period and the follow-up period, patients should be on standard stabilized UC treatment for double vision except those who cannot tolerate standard stable treatment. Typical UC treatment can be a combination of UC treatment or a previously diagnosed UC treatment, which includes corticosteroids no more than 20 mg prednisone (or equivalent), and / or medications containing 5- amino salicylates (5- ASA), and / or azathioprine (AZA) / mercaptopurine (6-MP)

(c) Study flow chart

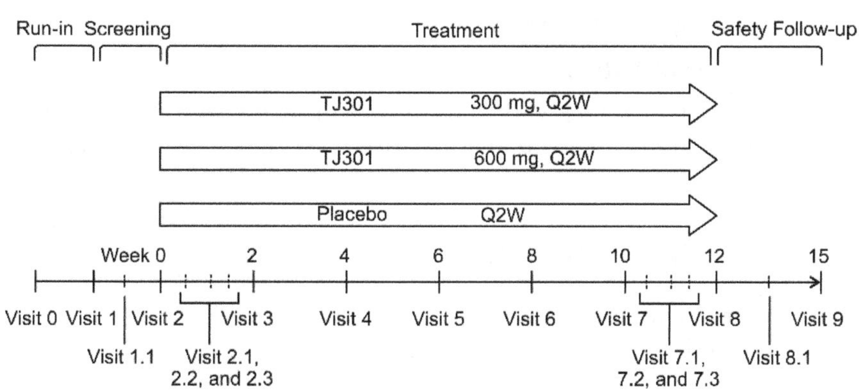

4.1.4 Overall Design

Visit 1: Exploration Tour, beginning of the Exploration Period (-28 to -1 days before Visit 2)

Visit 2: Random Visit (Basic), beginning of the 12-Week Treatment Period

Visit 3-7: 5 visits during 12 weeks of Treatment

Visit 8: End of Treatment (EoT) Visit, Completion of a 12-Week Treatment Period

Visit 9: Security Tracking Visit, scheduled 35 days after final IMP dose (Day 105).

(a) Test Facts

- First patient for the first quarter of 2017
- Patient-last quarter of 2020
- Duration - 2.5 years

4.1.5 Security Review Committee

- Includes medical monitoring, physician and pharmacist.
- Reviews blind data and provides recommendations to the Sponsor based on that their estimation.
- The SRC operating procedure will be prepared and signed prior to the first patient registration.
- The charter will set out the specific purpose and functions of the SRC related to monitoring patient safety in the study.

4.1.6 Discussion of Trail Design Blinding

- Selection and Duration of Individual Patient dose
- Process Withdrawal of Tracking Procedures

(a) Number of Patients

In total, 90 patients with active UC will be registered competitively, and randomly assigned to three arms with TJ301 (two dose levels) or placebo.

4.1.7 How to Include?

(a) Terms of Installation

- Male and female patients aged 18-70 (inclusive) aged.

- Active UC is confirmed by colonoscopy by biopsy or flexible sigmoidoscopy with biopsy Examination, by extension> 15-cm beyond the anterior margin from endoscopy.
- Active UC with full Mayo≥5 effect and rectal bleeding amaphuzu1 points on test.
- During Day 35 to Day 6 before Randomization, endoscopy sub score ≥2.
- A woman who is infertile or has a menstrual period, or who is pregnant does not have a pregnancy plan during the study and voluntarily takes effective contraceptive measures.
- The patient is able and willing to comply with the requirements of this study

(b) Release Terms

The title will not be eligible for inclusion in this study if any of the following methods apply:

- Women who are pregnant or breastfeeding.
- Contraindication to colonoscopy or sigmoidoscopy.
- Allergies to any component of TJ301.
- History of colostomy, colectomy or partial colostomy.
- Current diagnosis of randomized bowel disease, Crohn's disease, ischemic colitis, fulminant colitis and / or mega colon toxicity, patients with ulcerative colitis limited to rectum (ulcerative proctitis), infective enteritis, amebic bowel disease and intestinal schistosomiasis.
- History of a fatal disease other than non-metastatic cutaneous squamous cell successfully treated or basal cell carcinoma and / or local carcinoma in the cervical area. If Screening colonoscopy shows evidence of dysplasia or malignancy, the patient is not eligible.
- Primary or secondary immunodeficiency that includes neutron-penia (total neutrophil count <1500 / μL); or lymphopenia (total lymphocyte count below 500 / μL).
- Serious acute illness outside of UC in the opinion of the investigator.
- A history of drug addiction during the last 1 year or drug addiction or illicit drug use.

4.1.8 How to Assign Patients to Treatment Groups?

- Employment
  Random performance
- Limitations
- Prior Treatment and Compliance
- Prohibited Treatment
- Other Limits
- Withdrawal Terms
- Treatment
- Symbols and Source of Provision
- Packing and labeling
- Terms of Reference and Use of Compliance with Treatment on Physical Exercises
- Key Signs
- Parameters for Clinical Safety Laboratory
- Electrocardiogram
- Blood and Sewage Testing Urine Sampling Drug Testing for abuse
- Medical and Surgical History Urine Testing for Abuse Drugs
- Drug Concentration Measures
- Handling biological samples

4.1.9 Data Handling

- Source Data – International Conference on Harmonization (ICH)
- Trial-specific Source Data Requirements
- Electronic Case Record Form
- Use of Patient Reported Outcome Instruments
- Data Management
- Monitoring procedures
- Audit and Inspection
- Confidentiality of Patient Data

4.1.10 Changes in the Conduct of the Trial

- Protocol Amendments
- Deviations from the Protocol
- Premature Trial Termination

Publications and Public Disclosure

- PublicationPolicy
- Public DisclosurePolicy

4.1.11 Moral Responsibilities and Administrative Organizations

Ethics can be linked to legal obligations in two ways, one common and one practical. Generally, we can judge credit law as "fair" if you place a liability on a group that feels it should bear responsibility in a particular case. Legal obligation is about sharing responsibility.

There are seven ethics that form the basis of the content of our teaching framework:

1. Do not do wrong. ...
2. Profit. ...
3. To prolong life. ...
4. Efficiency. ...
5. Respect for independence. ...
6. Justice. ...
7. Measurement.

(a) Data Analysis

- Volume voltages will be defined by the default value, definition, standard deviation (SD), media, and small / high values. Quality variables will be defined by the number and percentage of patients with each quality feature. Missing values will not be included in the percentage calculation. All data will be listed for each patient along with the study visit.
- The main outcome of efficacy is clinical and endoscopic remission Week 12 This binary effect (release status = yes / no) will be analyzed by the entry regression model. A patient who has lost data about the exemption status will be deemed unforgiven.
- All second dichotomized points will be analyzed using a recurring regression model and the last continuous points will be analyzed using repeated Covariance Model (ANCOVA) analysis steps.
- In addition, patients in both the placebo and treatment groups will be divided into smaller groups based on baseline IL-6 / sIL-

6R complexes. Comparisons in the latter areas will be made in different subgroups.

(b) Adverse events

Adverse event is any adverse medical incident in a patient who participated in a clinical study. Includes:

- Any negative or unintentional symptom, symptom or disease temporarily associated with IMP use, whether considered to be caused by the IMP or not.
- Common adverse events and expected adverse events based on the impact of the IMP medical science.
- Any laboratory abnormalities, significant symptoms or findings of physical examination that were evaluated as clinically significant by the investigator (pre-existing conditions detected by examination and examination visit or during testing are not adverse events, but recorded as medical history).
- Accidental injuries, reasons for any medication changes (drugs and / or dosage), reasons for any medical consultation, nursing or pharmacy, or reasons for hospitalization or surgical procedures.
- Overdoses and side effects of clinical and non-clinical effects.

References

1. **Clinical Trial Protocol Development,** *Developed by Center for Cancer Research, National Cancer Institute Endorsed by the CTN SIG Leadership Group.*
2. TJ301 Date: 16 May 2017 Ver.1.1 Supersedes: Ver.1.0, Page 1of97 Protocol No: CTJ301UC201, Solution for Injection Clinical Trial Protocol.
3. Allen Cato, Lynda Sutton, clinical drug trails and development, second Edition, revised and expansion, Dekker publication, pg no-152-165

CHAPTER 4.2

Institutional Review Board (IRB)

Institutional Review Boards (IRBs) and Independent Ethics Committees (IECs) have been charged with protecting the rights and safety of clinical research participants. The regulations governing review, accreditation, and conduct of human research refer to these independent bodies such as IRBs or IECs. In 2001 the Association for the Accreditation of Human Research Protection Programs (AAHRPP) was established.

Since then many institutions have redesigned various support and review resources related to human rights research including the IRB as part of their Human Research Protection Program (HRPP). Similarly, in the IRB, these programs have their primary objective in protecting human research topics. Other IRB obligations such as clinical trial monitoring, investigator education and participant research, and evaluation of research records may be transferred to specialized units within the HRPP.

These programs may also facilitate the investigator's relationship with sponsors in order to promote safe and ethical research processes.

In many institutions in the USA the committee also serves as the privacy board of the Health Insurance Portability and Accountability Act of 1996 (HIPAA) for research-related activities.

There are at least three programs that institutions use to reach people requirements for reviewing research principles.1 It is important to determine the IRB that will be responsible for reviewing and approving research. Some institutions require their IRB to review all research, while others rely solely on the use of a central IRB, or allow for a review of the central IRB for certain types of studies.

Medium IRBs are particularly useful in multidisciplinary research because only one IRB is responsible for authorizing the legal process and the informed consent form. This can make meeting this regulatory requirement more efficient. The advantages and disadvantages of a mid-site IRB review compared to the area are well defined by Fitzgerald and Phillips[1]. Potential concerns over the use of an intermediate IRB surround that committee's ability to understand relevant local issues. Local issues are often related to the Chief Investigator's (PI) ability to conduct research, the adequacy of institutional resources to conduct research safely, and any considerations that should be given to potential research participants such as cultural or economic factors.

In a European community where the national health agency can verify the skills of physicians and institutional resources, some argue that there are no local issues related to whether the study has ethical standards[2]. The premise is, in theory, true; however it is based on the assumption that all good doctors will be good researchers. Considering the current regulatory guidelines, it is unlikely that the requirement for review and approval of research by local IRBs will be abandoned in the near future. Given this, sponsors and investigators should verify what IRB review process applies to their research.

4.2.1 Composition, Processes, and Function

(a) Composition

The IRB must have at least five members reflecting diversity of scientific and non-scientific backgrounds as well as professional and cultural interests, including bisexuality, and at least one member who is not directly or indirectly associated with the institution. member (commonly referred to as a member of the public). Although a minimum number of members is limited to five, most IRBs will contain more to meet additional technologies and to ensure that a quorum can be convened to conduct the meeting.

The driving force behind the formation of the committee is the type of research that is being reviewed. By regulations, the International Conference on Harmonization (ICH), the Department of Health and Human Services (DHHS), and the Food and Drug Administration (FDA) require IRBs to bring together members with sufficient expertise to assess scientific quality., the medical aspects of the proposed study, and the ethical principles of conducting research.

The net effect of this rule is to require at least one committee member to be a physician, as there is no other way to obtain the necessary expertise to evaluate the medical aspects of research. IRBs are allowed to use another member program, where another member may visit if the first member is absent. Also, the IRB may invite external consultants if necessary, to provide insight into scientific or ethical issues beyond the technical expertise of the convened committee. Although consultants may assist in protocol review, they may not be able to participate in voting to authorize research.

IRB membership is also influenced by people who are eligible to participate in the protocol. The risk figures referred to in DHHS, FDA, or ICH laws include children, prisoners, pregnant women, pregnant women, the disabled and the mentally handicapped. In order to review the research that includes these groups of participants, the rules require that people who are knowledgeable about those nations and who understand how they can be at risk be included in the committee. However, these are by no means the only risk groups for study participants. Students may be at risk if they participate in research conducted by a member of the faculty. Similarly, employees and employees may be considered vulnerable if requested to participate in research conducted by the head of department.

The IRB needs to be aware that there are a number of social, economic, and cultural factors that can put a person at risk. In addition, the nature of the underlying disease and clinical prognosis can affect the patient's perception of planned interventions and may lead to increased risk.

Unlike the ICH and DHHS, the FDA requires committee members who can evaluate the proposed study 'in accordance ... with institutional obligations.' The effect of this section of the rules is to allow the institution to limit research that falls outside. of its own standards or places an unnecessary burden on the institution's resources. Although the institution may prevent IRB-approved research from being conducted, the institution may not allow research that has not yet been approved by the IRB.

(b) Procedures and functions

The operational requirements and procedures of the IRB are set out in 21 CFR Section 56, Subsection C, and ICH E6 Sections 3.2 and 3.3. These sections outline what needs to be done to comply with the regulations, and do not recommend specific procedures to be used. Thus, each institution develops its own policies and procedures to achieve the goal of protecting the rights and safety of human research participants. For this reason, it is best for the sponsor to work with investigators who are knowledgeable about the IRB delivery requirements of the institution.

Both FDA and ICH regulations require IRBs to follow written procedures for initial and ongoing reviews, frequency of continuous updates, immediate reporting of changes in research, immediate reporting of unexpected events, adverse reactions, and deviations or non-compliance. Under FDA and ICH regulations, IRBs may approve research protocols, require modification of protocols in order to obtain approval, not approve research, or suspend or discontinue research that has already received approval. The IRB's determination should be documented within the 'appropriate time' and should provide specific recommendations for changes required to ensure accreditation, or if approved, the conditions of accreditation.

The ICH E6 Guideline for Good Clinical Practice was written specifically for research that required a full review of the board at a convened meeting. Accelerated reviews (i.e., reviews by IRB chair or nominee) are mentioned only as they relate to the 'minor changes' to the protocol which has received full board approval. In contrast, FDA regulations identify research categories that may be released or follow a quick review process and do not go to the full committee. Of the four research categories eligible for review release, the most relevant to IRBs reviewing biomedical research is related to the urgent use of a research drug or device.

The first use of an investigative drug or emergency device is exempt from IRB reviews; However, such use must be reported to the IRB within 5 business days. Any subsequent use of a drug or device at that facility requires protocol approval at a meeting of the full IRB. Research eligible for immediate review and approval is no more than a small risk or minor modification of research that has already received full board approval. Examples of research exempt from review or that may be expedited under DHSS rules are available

4.2.2 Categories of Released Research

1. Research conducted on formal or accredited educational programs, involving general educational processes, such as (i) research of general and special teaching strategies, or (ii) performance appraisal or comparisons between teaching strategies, curriculum, or classroom. - room management methods.
2. Research involving the use of academic tests (comprehension, diagnostics, competence, achievement), research procedures, interview procedures, or public ethics observations, unless: and (ii) any disclosure of answers to human subjects without research may place the subject at risk of criminal or legal liability or damage the financial position, employment, or dignity of the individual.
3. Research involving the use of academic tests (comprehension, diagnostics, competence, achievement), survey procedures, interview procedures, or observance of public conduct that may be exempt from paragraph (b) (2) of this section, if: (i) persons are nominated or appointed by government officials or candidates for public office; or (ii) the rules of the organization require (s) decisions without prescribing that the confidentiality of the identified personal information will be maintained throughout the study and thereafter.

4. Research, which includes the collection or research of available data, documents, records, pathological examples, or diagnostic examples, if these sources are publicly available or if the information is recorded by an investigator in such a way that the subjects cannot be identified, directly or by subjects linked to subjects.
5. Research and exhibition projects are conducted or subject to the approval of departmental or agency heads, and are designed to study, evaluate, or otherwise evaluate: (i) public benefits or service plans; (ii) procedures for obtaining benefits or services under those programs; (iii) potential changes or any of those systems or processes; or (iv) potential changes in the methods or levels of payment for benefits or services under those plans.
6. Taste and quality food testing and consumer acceptance courses, (i) when using healthy foods without additives or (ii) when food is eaten containing a nutrient at or below the level and consumption found safe, or agricultural chemicals or environmental pollution at or below the level found safe, by the Food and Drug Administration or accredited by the Environmental Protection Agency or the Food Safety and Inspection Service of the US Department of Agriculture.

4.2.3 Research Categories that can be Reviewed with Quick Procedures

Research activities that present low risk and fall into one of the following categories are eligible for immediate review by the IRB through a rapid review process.

1. Clinical study of drugs and medical devices only when condition (a) or (b) is met.

   drug research where new drug application is not required (21 CFR Section 312). (Note: Research into marketable drugs that significantly increase risk or reduce the acceptance of risks associated with the use of the product should not be reviewed immediately.)

   b Medical equipment surveillance where (i) no application for release of investigative equipment is required (21 CFR Section 812); or (ii) the medical device has been deleted / authorized for marketing and the medical device is used in accordance with the deleted / authorized label.
2. **Collection of blood samples from a finger stick, heel, ear, or venipuncture as follows:**

   from healthy, non-pregnant adults weighing 110 pounds. In these studies, doses should not exceed 550 mL over a 8-week period and collection may not occur more than 2 times a week;

b or for other adults and children, taking into account the age, weight, and health of the subjects, the collection process, the amount of blood to be collected, and the frequency with which they will be collected. In these studies, the dose may not exceed 50 mL or 3 mL per kilogram for 8 weeks and collection may not occur more often than 2 times per week.

3. Expected collection of biological samples for research purposes in non-invasive ways.
4. Data collection through non-invasive procedures (excluding general anesthesia or silencing) that are routinely used in clinical practice, other than procedures involving X-rays or microwaves. Where medical devices are used, they must be erased / approved for marketing. (Studies aimed at testing the safety and efficacy of a medical device are generally not eligible for immediate review, which includes research of deleted medical devices for new indications.)
5. Research that includes materials (data, documents, records, or templates) collected, or will only be collected for non-research purposes (such as treatment or diagnosis).
6. Collection of data from voice, video, digital, or image recording for research purposes.
7. Research on individual or group characteristics or behaviors (including, but not limited to, research on theory, understanding, inspiration, identity, language, communication, cultural beliefs or practices, and social behavior) or research using survey, interview, interview history, focus group in it, system testing, human resource testing, or quality assurance methods.
8. Further review of research previously approved by the IRB named as follows:
   A. when (i) the study is permanently closed the registration of new courses; (ii) all studies have completed all research-related interventions; and (iii) research remains valid only in the pursuit of long-term studies; or
   B. Where no studies have been registered and no additional risks have been identified; or c where the remaining research activities are limited to data analysis.

   Continuing the review of the study, which was not done under the new drug application under investigation or the release of the investigative device where sections two (2) to eight (8) were not applicable but the IRB decided and wrote at a meeting convened that the study did not involve more than small. risk and no additional risks were identified.

4.2.4 Protection of Human Subjects

The process of protecting human research topics is varied. Basic principles for protecting research topics are found in the Nuremberg Code, the Helsinki Declaration, and the Belmont Report.

Payment to IRBs to apply these principles in the evaluation of every aspect of the proposed research work to protect the rights, safety, and well-being of study participants. In line with this, IRB staff assist investigators in maintaining adherence to the principles of corporate governance and policies. Therefore, it is not surprising that when a research protocol is submitted to multiple IRBs the final decisions of committees, their queries, and requests for more information can vary greatly.[1, 2, 3, 4]

Stress is placed on the IRB 'mission creep': a real or perceived need to consider all potential risks, not only to study participants but to potential risks to researchers and the institution itself.[5] As part of the process of authorizing research, IRBs also consider issues that may not seem relevant. directly with research hazards such as investigator and / or conflict of interest of the institution, legitimacy of research science, and safe custody and appropriate access to research records.

Many sponsored trials are increasingly requesting (or requiring) the collection and preservation of biological templates for future research, which presents another series of IRB challenges. This may be particularly troubling when studies using DNA are reviewed because of the discriminatory power of certain ethnic or cultural groups.[6] It has been suggested that IRBs consider the risk to third parties (people not directly involved in the study) depending on the level of risk to them.[7, 8]

In most cases the IRB encounters, there is little direction. As a result, IRBs may establish very different delivery requirements and review procedures to meet the prescribed guidelines. The major impact of these additional commitments and the variability of the review options are the probability of starting a research delay. The necessary effort to ensure compliance with regulatory and institutional policies also diverts the IRB's efforts in its primary function of protecting the rights and well-being of study participants[5].

The requirements for the IRB to obtain and review in order to make a decision on accreditation are set out in Table 8.3. It should be noted that FDA regulations do not explicitly require a committee to obtain an Investigator Manual (IB). The need to review IB is derived from CFR 21.56.111, where the IRB is required to assess the risk and determine whether the risk is reasonable in relation to the expected benefits. Sponsors and investigators have done a commendable job of making these publications available to investigative teams and the IRB.

The process can be very difficult in some institutions where 'paper copies' (as opposed to electronic copies) have to be distributed. Despite providing all this information, sponsors and investigators still face difficulties in obtaining IRB approval. This suggests that the main problem is not a lack of information, but a failure to provide information on the format and details the IRB needs to review.

4.2.5 Documents for IRB/IEC

Materials submitted	IRB considerations	Potential problems
Trial protocol(s) and amendment(s)	The protocol is current and all amendments have been incorporated or appended.	All protocol features are not fully detailed. This often happens when biological samples are collected.
Investigator's brochure	Currently approved IB	See Table 6.3.
Written informed consent form(s) and consent form updates	Reading level. Adherence tolocalI RB requirements for the format and any standard language.	IB does not have the required information. The research mentioned in the protocol is not specified in the brochure. Is the most recent brochure distributed?
Subject recruitment materials	Provides sufficient detail to inform the potential participant of study requirements, duration, and compensation.	Failure to follow local IRB permit form template. The use of language of consent form differs greatly from institutional standards. Incorporate the HIPAA language into the permit where the institution is using an independent HIPAA accreditation.
Written information to be provided to subjects	Reading level. Not coercive. Indicate that the materials are related to a research activity.	The hiring process does not protect patient privacy, and / or privacy. Do patients receive unsolicited phone calls or letters?
Available safety information	All of the available information regarding preclinical studies and sufficient safety data to support the use of the test article for the expected duration of participant enrollment.	The level of learning is appropriate, but problems exist with type of size and ease of use.
Information about payments and compensation to subjects	Compensation should not create an unfair inducement for study participation. Timing and method of payment should be clear. Pro-rating for partial study completion should be explained.	Although it is usually provided in IB, additional medical and clinical data, or safety reports may be available prior to submission to IB.

Table *Contd...*

Materials submitted	IRB considerations	Potential problems
Investigator's current curriculum vitae and/ or other evidence of qualifications	Licensure and training necessary to safely perform all study-related activities. Inclusion of other study team members where special expertise is required.	The process should be clear to the IRB and the study participant. Some institutions require W-9 to be completed before processing the check. This should be reflected in the protocol and consent form.
Any other documents required by the IRB/IEC	Completion of an IRB-approved course in human subjects' research.	There are many laboratory tests and clinical procedures used for testing and monitoring. It should be clear that qualified people are being used to translate this information.

Complicating matters is the lack of research and guidance on how IRBs should deal with research reviews and approvals.9 The following sections are not intended to provide details of the various texts reviewed by the IRB. Instead, they highlight the type of information that is generally expected to be available to IRB members when negotiating agreements.

4.2.6 Protocol Review, Investigator Handbook, and Informed Consent

The IRB supports its decisions primarily in the review of sponsored documents and PI. Although the sponsor provides a number of requirements for submission to the IRB, it is up to the investigator to ensure that the request is made in accordance with local IRB policies and procedures. Failure to 'follow the delivery guidelines' occurs frequently and may result in initial research delays.10 Some IRBs may invite a PI to an IRB meeting to present a research plan and clarify research issues, but even with these additional inputs, written documents will be required to support the basis of the IRB decision.

In the industry-sponsored protocol and IB-funded experiments specialists are developed in their field of research. Consequently, the need for research, composition, and procedures required by law often has a sound scientific basis. Roadblocks may be encountered when these documents are sent to the IRB for 'local review.' investigators and the institution to provide the care and services required by law in view of existing obligations and resources. The problems encountered as a result of the review of the study area are well documented.[2,11–13] However, in the foreseeable future it is unlikely that the requirement for a site review will change. In view of this, there are steps that can be taken by research sponsors and researchers to alleviate this difficulty as discussed below.

4.2.7 Protocol Review

The research protocol is the main text used by the IRB to determine whether research should be approved at all. Depending on the needs of the institution, one or more copies of the full sponsor protocol will need to be submitted. The protocol should be the most current version and should already include any existing amendments. Many IRBs use an initial review process in which one member receives a copy of all the initial reading papers. When this process is implemented, the IRB often requires the submission of a summary of the protocol, which highlights important aspects of the case and disseminates it to all committee members. The protocol summary is not as detailed as the full protocol but provides sufficient information for the committee to understand the key components of the study.

These components include a brief overview of the condition, the appropriateness of the current treatment intervention, the reason for the study, the purpose of the study, the parameter identification of the primary outcome, eligibility requirements, treatment plan, risk and treatment modality. this has been reduced, benefits, alternative therapies, sample size estimates, primary and secondary outcome parameters, and statistical analysis systems.[14] Because IRBs include members with scientific and non-scientific backgrounds, as well as community representatives, protocol summaries need to be written in simple language and avoid technical jargon. Sponsors and investigators should not assume that what is clear to them will automatically become clear to all IRB members.

4.2.8 Background

A short section providing background of the condition being treated should be included. Most groups do not require extensive education about common diseases such as high blood pressure, heart failure, or diabetes. But even in these situations the proposed intervention can be passed on to a component of the disease such as peripheral neuropathy, edema management or maintenance of renal function. In these situations, the background material should provide a basis for the team to conclude that the intervention has the potential to improve or positively alter the course of the disease.

The FDA or the European Pharmaceuticals Agency (EMA) may have issued a guideline document affecting the study design. Guidance may suggest the need for a placebo arm or specific performance or safety standards. IRB members, and sometimes local investigators, may not always be aware that the protocol is designed to conform to a specific guideline. A simple background report to the Steering Committee will help in their review.

The lack of details within the protocol can generate questions from the IRB and slow down the process. Although the purpose of the study is clear (compare new drug A with established drug B), the reason for conducting the study is not easily observed. Not all patients respond to established medications, so is the need for a new drug justified? Or does the new drug have a better side effect profile or offer the possibility of a more convenient dosage form or less frequent dosing? This information helps IRB members understand why research is important and should be conducted. It also introduces potential profit opportunities for research topics and other basic positions. The committee wanted to see the rationale put forth in the study of the subjects in the approval document.

4.2.9 Main Impact Parameters

In conducting research it is important to identify the main outcome and define it clearly. The protocol should provide the basis for the selection of the primary decision variable and how it will be measured accurately. Some studies may use the primary effect parameter as an alternative to the expected benefit from the intervention. For example, research on antihypertensive agents may use lower blood pressure, although the actual goal is to reduce heart disease and mortality. Sponsor must provide reasons as to how the result relates to the disease process being investigated. For comparative studies, the protocol should address not only differences in outcome measures that are shown to be statistically significant, but also whether those differences have any clinical significance.

4.2.10 Eligibility Limit

IRBs closely monitor the eligibility criteria for research. Addition and exclusion criteria are the first step in securing sponsored and investigative research topics. Again, sufficient detail must be provided to define the study population. While specific criteria are easily identifiable, eligibility criteria should not be expressed in general terms (normal renal function). Some protocols may define normal renal function as <1.5 mg/dL of serum creatine; Other creatine clearance >80 ml/min.

If the latter definition is used, how can it be determined? Is this a 24-hour urine collection or an estimate of creatine clearance? If an estimate is made, which formula is used? The protocol should clearly state when the eligibility assessment will be conducted with respect to obtaining informed approval from the course. The panel will determine whether an individual is eligible as part of standard treatment received based on existing clinical and demographic information, or on the basis of information created solely for research purposes. These and other issues may affect the course and cause you to withdraw from the course for which you are no longer eligible.

4.2.11 Intervention Studies and Methods

While the background, scope and eligibility criteria for research generally raise some questions from the IRB, the methods and interventions defined in the research represent potential sources of risk, thus attracting the most attention of the IRB. The IRB should consider all possible sources of risk. Some of these can be easily identified by an intelligence tool or methods related to medicine and research. Discomfort, emotional damage and loss of privacy caused by travel may be difficult to diagnose or may be the result of local conditions, so the sponsor is not fully mentioned in the protocol. It would be of great help to the team if the protocol specified the standards of care interventions and standards carried out for the purpose of the study only. Input from the PIs at each site is important in decision making because the representation of quality of maintenance in one company will not be the same in another.

IRB members seek specific information in the protocol as it relates to the source of the risk. In biomedical research, IRBs often consider the risks of drugs, equipment, and research-related methods. The sponsor should play a primary role in notifying the team when drugs and equipment are being tested. Individual investigators usually attend a meeting of investigators but are not familiar enough with the drug or equipment to answer specific questions. The IB may have some information that the IRB would like to review, but as noted above, not all members will receive a copy of the IB prior to the meeting. In addition, some practical elements may be the result of decisions made by the sponsor during protocol development or may require regulatory guidance and it may not be easy to determine why they were included.

In the case of a drug whose drug-related risk is not yet marketable, the amount of information available may vary greatly. Conclusions may be limited to the results of animal trials (primarily to studies in humans) or to the results of large, studies showing the tolerability and efficacy of the drug based on the expression of thousands of participants. study. To facilitate protocol review, the sponsoring protocol should include key pre-clinical and clinical review findings reported to the IB.

The panel will seek justification for the amount and duration of treatment. For example, how have clinical studies influenced the choice of doses to be tested in humans? How does the tolerance demonstrated in the two-week human safety study support the transition to the six-month performance study? Most IRBs do not have the expertise to determine whether animal test results are safe for first trials in humans and dosages to be tested. To facilitate the review process, the sponsor is useful in addressing these protocol issues, teaching IRB regulatory guidelines, and teaching the scientific basis for drug dosage and duration. If sponsors continue to intensify micro-dose studies or other FDA drug development efforts, the issues surrounding dose selection for initial clinical trials will become more complicated.

Although there is no deceptive method for predicting adverse events (AEs),

Identifying similarities in drug composition or function gives the team important insight into examining products sold with established side effect profiles. The question that Cohen raised is, 'Should we have tolerance in early drug development as a goal?' The IRB is directly related to drug safety concerns. Most groups review early-stage clinical trials, although rare, but serious, AEs are unlikely to be identified even after studying a large number of subjects. [15,16,17] Although it is not possible to sell a completely safe drug, members are aware that some of the IRB's rare, but serious side effects cause the drugs to be approved and sold.

If the drug is not taken off the market, regulatory authorities may include warning statements or restrict the types of patients who may need to receive the drug. In the absence of any information to the contrary, these warnings can spread to a whole class of drugs. This may affect the IRP's assessment of the risks of the drug being tested, such as a drug or a systemically withdrawn drug. For these types of drugs, the sponsor should not only highlight the components of the protocol that define and reduce the potential for this AE.

4.2.12 Device Risks

In the United States and Japan and the European Union it is recommended that regulatory approval is required before the start of device testing, which can affect development costs and the speed at which new devices are brought to market. Mainly based on the potential for risk. Some of the factors considered in making this decision include the characteristics of the device (invasive and non-invasive), duration of use (short-term and long-term) and the need for specialized training for safe and effective use of the device.

The FDA defines devices as having a 'significant risk or insignificant risk'. However, this determination applies only to the device, and not to the manner in which the device is used in the study. Therefore, a non-critical risk instrument may be determined by the IRB as a critical risk instrument based on its scope, patient demographic analysis, or the results of equipment failure. In the United States, IRBs are also responsible for the recognition of humanitarian utility equipment (HDE) within their organizations. These are devices that must be used in situations that affect fewer than 4000 patients per year, making clinical trials nearly impossible. Many IRBs have little or no experience in this type of equipment, so be prepared to educate team members by providing sponsor regulatory guidance information and defining sponsor responsibilities.

4.2.13 Risks Associated with the Procedure

Research-related methods contribute to the overall risks associated with the protocol, even if they have not been tested within themselves. It would be very important to the team if the sponsor and PI could clearly describe the practices that are considered to be quality maintenance carried out for research purposes only. This decision-making is not always easy and can vary across research areas depending on local skills and available expertise. For example, chest radiographs may be taken at regular intervals for quality care for certain conditions. According to protocol, the study participant must have had a chest radiograph within the past six months. If a patient's last radiograph was obtained nine months earlier, a radiograph is required to qualify for the examination.

It is not part of the maintenance standard, so the weight of the radiation, at least, may still be a reason for further research. Depending on the company, the PI must submit protocols to a separate panel from the IRB to assess radiation risks. The number and frequency of study visits may exceed the considered standard of care; Thus contributing to the discomfort that occurs within the study. It is necessary to work closely with the PI of the sponsor site to identify local issues related to research methods.

Another type of procedure is the risk associated with requiring a patient to withdraw other treatments to qualify for a diagnosis. Today, most diseases require at least one drug, sometimes dozens, to treat the condition. Therefore, it is not uncommon for potential participants to discontinue drugs for meeting eligibility criteria. Although it is possible to restrict eligibility to newly diagnosed patients, this approach poses a major obstacle to enrollment. Most IRBs are empirical studies that require a patient to remove the most effective treatment in order to participate in a clinical trial. If effective treatment is withdrawn, the underlying condition is expected to worsen, leading to a return of minor bothersome symptoms or an exacerbation of clinically significant diseases.

The protocol should be explained in detail how to monitor participants for withdrawal of other treatments, to detect improvement in the underlying condition, and to reduce the duration of poor disease control. In addition, some form of recovery therapy or recovery drugs may be included in the protocol as an additional precautionary measure for patients.

The use of the placebo control group will be closely monitored by the IRB. A detailed discussion of the protocol application of placebo in medical research is beyond the scope of this chapter; However, it is important to recognize that the inclusion of a placebo control arm in clinical trials may conflict with scientific, ethical and regulatory principles. As a result, why use a placebo control group? Amdur and Fiddle proposed a mechanism for the ethical use of placebos. [18-21]They suggest a number of factors that IRPs should consider in evaluating the ethical application of placebo controls in clinical research. These include the effectiveness and tolerability of current treatments, the long-term and short-term harm from using placebo, and the potential value of future treatments for patients with such conditions. Considering the ethical use of placebos is not limited to clinical drug trials. There is a similar concern for studies that require incorrect operating modes or inactive device plugging. Justifying the use of placebo in the experiment.

4.2.14 Process

The method of study is different from the methods of study. In addition to the overall trial design (superior, equivalent, non-inferior), other aspects of the trial important for IRB include randomization method, stacking based on one or more patient characteristics, blinded procedures, comparator selection, and placebo application. Sample size assessment and planned data analysis. Many aspects of research methods may seem outside the scope of the IRB because they are not directly related to individual participant risks. However, they are often related to the combined risks of study participants. For example, a lower limit should be set for non-inferior tests to estimate sample size[22-24]. Give the reason for choosing this range.

If the comparison is associated with significant toxicity and the consequences of treatment failure are not life-threatening, setting the lower limit to 30% may be acceptable to the committee. On the other hand, if the comparator is very effective and causes minimal toxicity, this margin would be unacceptable. In both cases, Sponsor must provide a reason for choosing this lower limit. Individual clinical researchers were generally unable to provide satisfactory feedback to the team, resulting in delays in study initiation.

Sample size estimates are important to the team. Often, sample size calculations are based on the performance endpoint because it is clearly identifiable and the variance of participant response to the intervention can be estimated from responses found in similar studies. Same disease stage. Although possible, it is not practical to base sample size estimates on safety outcomes because of their unpredictability and low incidence, which would require a large research population. Although the sample size is easily ascertainable for most studies, experiments commissioned by many investigators and supported by NIH funds lack the ability to detect significant therapeutic effects. [25, 26]

This problem is rarely encountered in studies conducted by the pharmaceutical industry, but it appears to have registered a large number of participants. Such studies can be 'crossed' to the main conclusion; That is, fewer participants can register and answer the diagnostic question. More powerful studies can cause problems during the research process because each participant of the study must complete all study-related procedures (including blood sampling and radiation exposure) or be randomly converted to low-performance treatments. The syllabus may be prescribed on the basis of limited number of subjects. However, enrollment may exceed the number of participants needed to better identify rare AEs and improve performance to ensure exposure.

The regulatory landscape is changing with regard to the high cost of conducting human research, and the difficulty of recruiting and retaining study participants, driven by the design of clinical trials. Alternative strategies such as micro-dosing are recommended by regulatory agencies. 15 In addition, adaptive trial designs have been proposed to allow modification of the randomization method, dose evaluation, and modification of the primary outcome parameter. [27-30] Many IRBs do not have access to statisticians or others trained in these types of clinical testing practices. It is in the best interest of the sponsor to assist team members by providing the basics behind the design of these experiments.

4.2.15 Special Concerns with Life Banks

Any experienced physician will know that patients vary in their response to medication. A clinically effective dose for one patient may cause severe toxicity to another patient. In developing sensitivity analysis methods, demographic and clinical characteristics such as age, weight, and renal and liver function have been identified to influence the pharmacokinetic profiles of various drugs. Although the dynamics of a drug is still important in understanding the factors that contribute to a drug's effectiveness and safety, there are differences between individuals that cannot be explained by kinetics alone. Increasingly, industry-recommended protocols require study participants to provide blood or tissue samples to identify genetic polymorphisms that elicit a different response in drug recipients. Other applications of banking products include proteomic and biomarker studies, which may be useful in identifying new treatment targets.

Although the sponsorship protocol provides detailed information on eligibility criteria, randomization procedures, safety monitoring and potential adverse effects, procedures for the collection and use of biological samples sometimes accept less than one paragraph within the protocol. Lack of this information may delay the approval of this part of the research. Because genetic research methods and risks differ from other risks associated with research, some IRBs require a separate approval form for genetic research. Listed in Table 8.4 are IRB frequently asked questions related to research on blood or tissue that should be specified in the protocol. Sponsors will be responsible for providing this information to the team as local investigators are usually unaware of how the biobank operates and what steps need to be taken to protect donor confidentiality.

4.2.16 Protocol Elements and Tissue Banks [table 2]

1.1 Title * Should state that it is a tissue bank
1.2 Objectives Purpose of the bank, why is it important? Who is it for? What kind of testing will be performed?
1.3 Background
1.4 Eligibility criteria How are participants identified? Will normals be used? Samples from outside sources?
1.5 Treatment plan How will samples be collected? Departures from standard of care? Consider how clinical and demographic information will be handled. What types of testing will be performed? Only for the disease the patient has or unrelated? Alzheimer's? Genetic testing? Other disease states? Hep. B, Hep. C,HIV? What happens to future test results? Procedures for releasing samples to other investigators. Plans to compensate for new product development.
1.6 Risks Major concern –confidentiality. Inaccurate pathological diagnosis. Duetoalterations in procedures to accommodates pecimen collection.
1.7 Benefits Generally none for the participant. Itisfairtoincludepotentialtobenefitpatientswithsimilarconditions;societalbenefits.
1.8 Alternative treatments * Don't participate.
1.9 Data collection and statistics * Generally, not an issue.
1.10 Other issues that should be addressed Coded samples – possibility to identity participant. Certificate of confidentiality.

4.2.17 Investigator Brochure

The ICH E6 guideline for good clinical practice describes the recommended content of IB. Although the protocol describes what needs to be done and how to do it during the study, the IB provides insight into why certain monitoring methods and parameters have been included in the protocol. The IB serves as a source for the IRB and investigator, who determines everything known (and unknown) about the drug or device being investigated. For drugs and devices in early development, the published literature on product efficacy or safety may be limited or unpublished. As a result, the IRB relies heavily on the information provided in this document to provide a decision approving a protocol.

As with the protocol, questions will be raised based on specified but not provided or unclear information. For example, participants' earnings continue to be slower than expected, which could lead to research sites opening after the original start date. or the IB version submitted by the investigator, dated two years before the due date for the protocol for IRB review. How will this group find out about the current version? The IB may suggest that extended studies in humans have been initiated and long-term toxicity studies in rats are pending. Is this done? The updated IP may also not contain sensitive information. The IB claims that the chemical structure of the drug is well classified and that no structure is provided, which is a poor service to the group. Most IRB committees may not have the expertise of a clinical chemist, but the ability of a physician to compare a sold agent with a known side effect profile can provide the environment for expected performance and toxicity. Sponsors can help themselves by keeping the IB up-to-date and by providing information for local investigators to share with the IRP regarding surveys conducted.

4.2.18 Informed Consent

Despite the greater focus on the approval document, the IRB is equally concerned about the process and timing of obtaining approvals. Informed consent is discussed in Chapter 3. The material presented here primarily deals with potential obstacles that sponsors and investigators may face in approving the approval form.

Some problems are easy to predict, so they can be prevented. One of the most common problems is the inclusion of HIPAA language in an approval document. Some companies require HIPAA accreditation in a separate review-specific document. Study approval informs participants about the rationale, methods, risks and options of the study, and their rights and responsibilities. HIPAA certification informs participants that their participation in the study will result in the sharing of personal health information with the sponsor, IRB and regulatory authorities. Another principled reason for separating HIPAA accreditation from research accreditation is to reduce the company's liability if any of these documents are found to be in short supply. The local investigator can provide the sponsor with some guidance as to which method the company uses.

Another common problem with approval forms is within the injury report. This is undoubtedly the result of increasing cases around medical research, highlighting sponsors, researchers, organizations and even IRB members. The contract may contain specific procedures for assigning the obligation to the sponsor or the organization conducting the research. While it is important to describe the process prior to initiating an investigation, it should be of little concern to the research participant and should not be included in the approval form.

Trials offered by the pharmaceutical industry are more likely to provide coverage for medical expenses caused by research-related injuries than locally or government funding. Some meet medical guidelines for providing compensation for research-related injuries. Sometimes, in the parlance of placing a certain level of responsibility on the research participant, 'if you follow your doctor's instructions' or 'if you follow all procedures related to the study'. Sometimes the PI and company are also linked by additional changes such as 'formally executed procedures ....' It is not clear why these explicit restrictions on consent forms, other than preventing participants from reporting problems appear, because the study participants did not relinquish their right to seek legal redress in the event of an injury. Because the language is so vague, study participants may feel that they have no way of getting treatment as a result of unsuccessful placement or failure to complete the study process. Although everyone involved in the research organization is concerned about potential liability, the risks considered by the research participants are real and are generally accepted without guarantees of profit.

4.2.19 Qualifications of Investigator and Inquiry Committee

Patients expect that the medical care they receive will be provided by physicians, nurses, and other health professionals who are qualified to provide these services. Medical researchers must meet this standard and meet other obligations to sponsors, regulatory authorities and IRBs. The importance of these additional responsibilities pertains to the safety of study participants and the reliable use of new drugs or devices for future patients. In other words, the research team should focus on patient care and scientific integrity.

The process by which the IRB determines whether an investigator is eligible to conduct a clinical study relates to the ability of the IRB to meet standards established by the research organization, sponsors, and regulatory authorities. Investigator responsibilities are outlined in the ICH E6 Guidelines for Good Medical Training and the FDA Guidelines for Industry. IRBs require proof that a PI (usually a physician, pediatrician or dentist) can provide the medical care necessary for diagnosis. event (SAE). This is usually evidenced by the investigator's curriculum. If the investigator is expected to perform a procedure as part of the study, the IRB may ask for proof that the investigator has been authorized to perform the procedure. Most IRBs require the investigator to submit Form FDA 1572 or a Medical Examination Agreement to show that the investigator intends to fulfill the promises made to the sponsor. To verify the data collected during the protocol and the study. We need to establish that investigators are trained to conduct human research and that it is up to date. The IRB will usually ask the investigator to indicate the total number of tests performed, the number of registered participants, and the staff to be provided at the hearing.

4.2.20 Risk-Benefit Analysis

One of the first decisions made by the IRB president or designer is to determine the level of risk associated with the proposed research. Occasionally, industry sponsors are interested in unspecified data derived from medical records, which may be eligible for exemption from IRB review. Examples of these types of studies include retrospective analysis of methods that suggest certain conditions or meta-analysis of current data. FDA rules are silent on exclusion studies related to drug or device testing, except in special cases where emergency use of the drug or device is required. In the United States, compliance with HIPAA regulations may be necessary and may affect the way data is collected.

Future studies that have been proven to be low-risk may deserve rapid review and approval. Minimal risk is defined in these terms: 'the likelihood and extent of injury or discomfort expected in the research not to exceed the risk in daily life or during a routine physical or psychological examination or test. Differences in the definition of 'minimum risk' can lead to very different solutions in the IRB. This is especially true in the use of FDA standards for research involving children. This type of comprehensive team review for all expected studies.

Most drug or device research is beyond minimal risk and requires full team review. The criteria for IRB approval of FDA-regulated research are found in Table 8.5. Although the standards are clear and concise, approval problems can arise as each protocol group, intentionally or accidentally, creates a functional definition for terms such as 'minimum' and 'benefit'. , "risk," "equal," "reasonable," "reasonable," and "adequate." ,

In addition, the drug or device to be tested may vary from protocol to protocol, even within group definitions, depending on the research team, research location, level of study, and population. It analyzes. If the above terms do not include comparative value, better consistency can be achieved within and across the IRB. The ability to measure benefits and risks provides an opportunity to manipulate these 'values'. It determines whether the benefits outweigh the risks. It is not clear how this can be consistently used to measure social benefit – risk, risk – benefit to individual research subjects. The myriad benefits and risks do not mean that Sponsor and Investigators are helpless and subject to the preferences of the individual IRB. To help IRBs better understand what benefits may be to participants and whether risks are reasonable and minimized, there are methods, even if they are not always used. The following paragraphs describe what sponsors and investigators can do to educate IRB members and facilitate the review process, based on the FDA's criteria for research approval.

4.2.21 Requirements for Approval of Research

- Risks to subjects are minimized
- Risks to subjects are reasonable inrelation to anticipated benefits
- Selection of subjects is equitable
- Informed consent will be sought
- Informed consent will be documented
- Where appropriate, adequate provisions for data monitoring to ensure subject safety
- Where appropriate, adequate provisions to protect subject privacy and confidentiality
- Adequate safeguards to protect the rights and welfare of vulnerable subjects

(a) The risk to the subjects will be reduced

The first step that Sponsor and Investigators can take is to identify all risks and difficulties associated with participating in the Protocol. Often, the risks are identified only by those associated with the drug or device being tested. IRB, sponsor and investigator intervention may be considered the most significant risk, which, as discussed above, is one of the risks and difficulties associated with the protocol. Once all risks have been identified, the sponsor and investigator can facilitate the IRB review process by conducting an honest assessment of the risks that the participant is experiencing as part of routine care, and those relevant only to the research. Some of the risks are undoubtedly the result of research such as placebo use, studies and additional blood sampling; Others may be less clear. If two radiographs are the standard of care, then three? Some studies do not allow the use of drugs that are considered standard care, and researchers may implement a rinse period to qualify patients for the study. Were the risks of withdrawing effective treatment seen? Equal consideration should be given to each aspect of the protocol, including the amount of blood taken and the number of office visits during a study.

Once all risks have been identified, the sponsor and investigator can Begin to find out how these risks are mitigated. The details of how the risks are mitigated vary by research, but they are divided into three broad areas: selection and qualification of study participants, study methods and techniques, and monitoring and monitoring. Ultimately, Sponsor may facilitate the review process by demonstrating how well the protocol selects participants and avoids the inclusion of high-risk individuals who have experienced AE; how study visits and procedures are planned to be as consistent as possible with standardized medical care practices; And for those risks that cannot be completely eliminated, appropriate monitoring procedures have been added to reduce AEs. Since local investigators generally do not have the intelligence to answer questions about how the protocol was developed, the sponsor must provide this information.

(b) Risks were justified for subjects in relation to expected benefits

This is the only requirement for approval, citing potential benefits for research participants. Most drug and device protocols are relatively transparent about potential risks; However, the potential benefits are not often discussed. The ICH E6 guideline for good medical practice states that IBs should publish information that will help a clinician or potential investigator to understand and make their own unbiased risk-benefit assessment. Suitable for the proposed test. 'Often the background provided in study protocols does not provide any benefit that could be expected to the individual or community through drug or device development.

The sponsor has a better understanding of the potential benefits and should incorporate their thinking into them. Regulations require that the information available allows for an 'unbiased risk-benefit assessment'. Removal of any Sponsor's assessment of benefits and risks that may allow for an unbiased assessment may result in a completely anonymous assessment. The IRB makes the final decision about which risks are justified in relation to the potential benefits and is free to ignore the Sponsor's assessment.

(c) The choice of subjects is fair

The purpose of appropriate material selection is to ensure the dissemination of research risks to the groups of individuals who are expected to benefit from the findings – the policy of justice described in the Belmond Report. The sponsor and the local investigator should be involved in achieving this goal. As part of meeting this requirement the local IRB will review eligibility criteria and recruitment practices, but may only affect recruitment at the organizational level. Sponsors can help demonstrate their risk-sharing efforts by providing information about other sites involved in several major trials.

(d) Informed approval to be sought

Merely allowing information is not sufficient for the template. As recently published articles point out, informed consent is a process; There is excessive reliance on the approval form; And procedures are often inadequate to assess participants' understanding of the risks, benefits and their responsibilities. [37,38] Despite all the details provided in the sponsor's protocol for study-related procedures, the research team was not generally provided with the expectations. For the timing and process of obtaining informed approvals. Ultimately, the local IRB is responsible for ensuring that appropriate procedures are used to obtain consent. However, sponsors can help research participants fulfill this important duty.

(e) Informed approval will be documented

Again, more credibility is often found on the approval document. As evidenced by the signed consent form, investigators must document not only the approval obtained, but also the procedure, timing and circumstances surrounding the consent recorded in the medical record. The record should reflect any questions the participant asked, how they were answered and the methods the investigator used to determine each participant's understanding of informed consent. Sponsors can play an active role in achieving this goal by training the investigator and providing forms or checklists to assist investigators in documenting the approval process.

Adequate provision for data monitoring, if applicable, to ensure material security

Like the other sections of the Sponsored Research Protocol, excellent information is provided on AEs and how they should be communicated to the sponsor. Care should be taken to clearly differentiate between the underlying causes of the underlying disease and those that may be considered side effects of the drug. Reporting requirements are outlined for the local investigator, and inspectors often visit the site to ensure that the report is accurate and timely. How to handle these reports as soon as they are received by the sponsor is often left discussed, but is very important to the IRB. This is especially true for multicenter trials, where AEs can find their way to the site analyst and eventually weeks or months after the IRB is due. IRB members understand that immediate access or unforeseen issues are unrealistic for AEs; But they want some guarantee that a process will be followed to help protect the registered research participant in their organization. This process usually culminates in a clinical trial protocol. In the absence of any information, the IRB is of the view that there are no plans to look into adverse and unforeseen circumstances in a timely manner. This raises questions for the sponsor to answer, resulting in delays in starting the course. The process of handling these events needs to be described in some detail. It would be helpful for the sponsor to include rules that site analysts can use to determine whether a study participant should be excluded from investigation. Similarly, a program to analyze all reported cases and disseminate this information to investigators and the IRB would address some of the concerns.

As discussed, not all tests require a Data Security Monitoring Board (DSMB). It is important that sponsors provide a timeline for the DSMB constitution and share a team-designed plan for interim review, termination rules and other patient care issues. Timely submission of DSMB reports to IRBs provides evidence that Sponsors and DSMB members take participant safety seriously. Unfortunately, the IRP received some reports that the DSMP collected and decided that the action should continue.

This information is of no use to the IRP. The DSMB must provide acknowledgment of the AE in addition to the total number of study participants, the enrollment rate of the study, the frequency of violations and deviations from the study, and the study's conclusion.

Adequate arrangements to protect the confidentiality and confidentiality of the Content, if applicable. To achieve this goal, health information from hundreds or thousands of individuals is combined and filtered to provide innovative treatments. It is the responsibility of researchers and advocates to protect an individual's health information. Negligent disclosure of health information may affect an individual's ability to obtain employment or health insurance, or may induce individuals in the community. In the United States, HIPAA regulations require individuals to specify how their health information will be used, how long it will be available, and who will have access to it. Since its implementation, investigators have identified HIPAA exposure as another barrier to research recruitment for all types of research. Rule Compliance Research.[42]

The other two issues that the IRB continues to discuss relate to HIV testing and drug abuse testing. Laws regarding HIV testing vary by jurisdiction. Some states require counseling before and after the exam and may require them to use a separate approval form. Sponsors have an interest in ensuring that registered participants in the trial do not use abusive drugs. Not only can illicit drug use confound research results, but these participants may, at least in theory, express support for additional research costs and liabilities. Since recreational drug use is illegal in most countries, collecting and documenting this illegal activity can lead to individual prosecution and legal penalties. To protect study participants, the IRB must obtain a Certificate of Confidentiality from the sponsor.

Adequate protections to protect the rights and interests of children, prisoners and pregnant women, the disabled and the mentally ill are widely considered vulnerable to research exploitation. These people are granted special protection for children in FDA-regulated research by 45 CFR Section 46 Subsections B, C and D and 21 CFR Section 50 Subsection C. The ICH E6 Guidelines for Good Medical Training expand the definition of vulnerable groups to include those with lower-level roles in the hierarchical system, such as students, personnel or members of the armed forces. Many possible problems related to weak subjects can be solved by changing the eligibility criteria. When this is not possible, the informed approval process is scrutinized closely. The admission process for the weaker sections is thoroughly discussed in Chapter 3.

4.2.22 Continuing Studies

The DHHS, FDA and ICH guidelines should require an ongoing review of each ongoing trial of IRBs in human subjects at appropriate risk levels, but at least once a year. During initial approval, the IRB must determine how often the research should be reviewed for re-accreditation. A one-year interval is typically used for most research; However, the initial phase of drug or device testing should be resubmitted within three or six months.

In any case the IRB should be informed of any research initiated by the investigator or of research using innovative therapies where the risks are unknown. The current review addresses a variety of issues, including the number of registered participants and their statistics, the need for changes to AE reporting, the informed consent document, and a review of the literature to further address the research question addressed. Available to sponsor. Typically, their assessment will be based on participants recruited on their site, which may or may not reflect the experience of the entire trial. Some sponsors facilitate the review process by providing regular updates on recordings and summaries of AEs to local investigators. Despite the importance of the ongoing review process, the IRB is often cited for not providing adequate continuous research review.[44]

4.2.23 Final Thoughts

Investigators and sponsors often experience frustration in dealing with local IRBs. Although some IRBs are tasked with blocking medical research, this rarely happens. Sponsors, investigators and IRB members each work to fulfill regulatory orders and 'comply with the rules'. Unfortunately, the rules are not always very specific and sometimes come from others. other games. The chances of success for sponsors are increased by selecting investigators who have relationships with local IRBs and understand the information needed to ensure a timely and thorough review.

References

1. Fitzgerald MH, Phillips PA. Centralized and non-centralized ethics review: a five nation study. *Account Res* 2006; 13(1):47–74.
2. Wainwright P, Saunders J. What are local issues? The problem of the local review of research. *J Med Ethics* 2004; 30(3):313–317.
3. Angell E *etal.* Consistency in decision making by research ethics committees: a controlled comparison. *J Med Ethics* 2006; 32(11): 662–664.
4. Dyrbye LN *etal.* Medical education research and IRB review: ananalys is and comparison of the IRB review process at six institutions. *AcadMed*2007;82(7):654–660.
5. Gunsalus CK *et al.* The Illinois White Paper: improving the system for protecting human subjects: counteracting IRB 'mission creep'. *Qual Inq* 2007; 13(5):617–649.
6. Meslin EM, Quaid KA. Ethical issues in the collection, storage, and research use of human biological materials. *J Lab Clin Med* 2004; 144(5):229–234.
7. Jonathan K. Missing the forest: further thoughts on the ethics of by stander risk in medical research. *Camb Q Healthc Ethics* 2007; 16(4):483–490.
8. Resnick DB, Sharp RR. Protecting third parties in human subjects research.[Coverstory].
9. *IRB: Ethics & Human Research* 2006; 28(4): 1–7.
10. Candilis PJ *et al.* The need to understand IRB deliberations. *IRB: Ethics & Human Research* 2006; 28(1):1–5.

11. StairTO *etal.* Variation in institutional review board responses to a standard protocol for amulticenter clinical trial. *Acad Emerg Med* 2001; 8(6): 636–641.
12. Burman W *et al.* The effects of local review on informed consent documents from amulticenter clinical trials consortium. *Control Clin Trials* 2003; 24(3):245–255.
13. Dilts DM, Sandler AB. Invisible barriers to clinical trials: the impact of structural, infra- structural, and procedural barriers to opening on cology clinical trials. *J Clin Oncol* 2006; 24(28):4545–4552.
14. NowakKS *etal.* Reforming the oversight of multi-site clinical research: are view of two possible solutions. *Accountability in Research: Policies & Quality Assurance* 2006;13(1):11–24.
15. ColtHG, Mulnard RA. Writing an application for a human subjects institutional review board. *Chest* 2006; 130(5):1605–1607.
16. Kimmelman J. Ethics at Phase 0: clarifying the issues. *J Law Med Ethics* 2007; 35(4): 727–733.
17. Cohen A. Should we tolerate tolerability as an objective in early drug development? *Br J Clin Pharmacol*2007; 64(3):249–252.
18. Borer JS *etal.* Cardio vascular safety of drugs not intended for cardiovascular use: need for a new conceptual basis for assessment and approval. *Eur Heart J* 2007; 28(15): 1904–1909.
19. Nose Y. Institutional review board approval for clinical application of new medical device sratherthan government agency. *ArtifOrgans* 2004;28(12):1057–1058.
20. Miller FG, Silverman HJ. The ethical relevance of the standard of care in the design of clinical trials. *Am J Respir Crit Care Med* 2004; 169(5): 562–564.
21. Freedman B, Glass KC. Placebo orthodoxy in clinical research II: ethical, legal, and regulatory myths. *J Law Med Ethics* 1996; 24(3):252.
22. Amdur RJ, BiddleCJ. Analgorithm fore valuating the ethics of a placebo-controlled trial. *Int J Cancer* 2001; 96(5): 261–269.
23. Miller FG. Ethical issues in surgical research. *Thorac Surg Clin* 2005; 15(4):543–554.
24. Connolly SJMD *et al.* Pacemaker therapy for prevention of syncope in patients with recurrent severe vasovagal syncope: Second Vasovagal Pacemaker Study (VPS II): a randomized trial. *JAMA* 20037; 289(17):2224–2229.
25. Christensen E. Methodology of superiority vs. equivalence trial sandnon-inferiority trials. *J Hepatol*2007; 46(5): 947–954.

26. Halpern S D*etal.* The continuing unethical conduct of under powered clinical trials. *JAMA* 2002; 288(3): 358–62.
27. Rosoff PM. Can under powered clinical trials be justified? *IRB: Ethics & Human Research* 2004; 26(3):16–19.
28. Koch A. Biostatistical methods for demonstrating efficacy in the regulatory setting. *BundesgesundheitsblattGesundheits for schungGesundheitsschutz* 2005; 48(5): 572–579.
29. Freidlin B, Simon R. Adaptive signature design: an adaptive clinical trial design for generating and prospectively testing a gene expression signature for sensitive patients. *Clin Cancer Res* 2005; 11(21):7872–7878.
30. Kelly PJ *etal.* Anadaptive group sequential design for phaseII / IIIclinical trials that select a single treatment from several. *J Biopharm Stat* 2005; 15(4):641–658.
31. Zhang L, Rosenberger WF. Response-adaptive randomization for clinical trials with continuous outcomes. *Biometrics* 2006; 62(2): 562–569.
32. Mello MM *et al.* The rise of litigation in human subjects research. *Ann Intern Med* 2003; 139(1):40–45.
33. Paasche-Ortow MK, Brancati FL. Assessment of medical school institutional review board policies regarding compensation of subjects for research-related injury. *Am J Med* 2005; 118(2): 175–180.
34. Shah S *etal.* Health law and ethics. How do institutional review boards apply the federal risk and benefit standards for pediatric research? *JAMA*2004;291(4):476–482.
35. Sharp HM, Orr RD. When 'minimal risk' research yields clinically-significant data, maybe the risks aren't so minimal. *Am J Bioethics* 2004; 4(2):W32–W6.
36. Chuang-SteinCER, Pritchett Y. Measures for conducting comparative benefit: risk assessment. *Drug Inf J* 2008; 42(3):223–233.
37. Garrison LP J r*etal.* Assessing a structured, quantitative health out comes approach to drug risk–benefit analysis. *Health Aff (Millwood)*2007;26(3):684–695.
38. May T *et al.* Viewpoint: IRBs, hospital ethics committees, and the need for 'translational informed consent'. *Acad Med* 2007; 82(7):670–674.
39. Sabik L *etal.* Informed consent: practices and views of investigators in a multinational clinical trial. *IRB: Ethics & Human Research* 2005; 27(5):13–18.
40. Silverman H. Ethical issues during the conduct of clinical trials. *Proc Am Thorac Soc* 2007; 4(2): 180–184; discussion 4.

41. NessRB. Influence of the HIPAA Privacy Rule on health research. *JAMA* 2007; 298(18): 2164–2170.

42. Dunlop AL *et al.* The impact of HIPAA authorization on willingness to participate in clinical research. *Ann Epidemiol* 2007; 17(11):899–905.

43. De Wolf VA *et al.* Part II: HIPAA and disclosure risk issues. *IRB: Ethics & Human Research* 2006; 28(1):6–11.

44. Gordon B, Prentice E. Continuing review of research involving human subjects: approach to the problem and remaining areas of concern. *IRB* 1997;19(2):8–11.

45. Bramstedt KA, Kassimatis K. A study of warning letters issued to institutional review boards by the United States Food and Drug Administration. *Clin Invest Med* 2004; 27(6): 316–323.

CHAPTER 4.3

Regulatory Requirements in Clinical Trails

4.3.1 Introduction

Medical examination is mandatory for drug approval to ensure the safety and efficacy of the drug. In order to protect patient safety and ethical conduct of medical examination, India has laid down CT rules. It is mandatory to follow the ICH-GCP guidelines which describe the quality assurance and safety of the subjects. Medical examination is regulated under the Drugs and Cosmetics Act 1940 and Rules 1945, which provide rules for conducting medical examination. On March 19, 2019, The Federal Ministry of Health and Family Welfare announced the 2019 new drugs and clinical trial guidelines for the advancement of medical research in the country. The Central Government has declared the final provisions in the Gazette of India as per G.S.R.227(E). The objective of this study is to provide an overview of the regulatory requirements for conducting clinical trials in India and the challenges involved.

The development of new drugs will improve patient quality and longevity. As clinical trials play an important role in new drug development, the government seeks to protect the safety and rights of human citizens and ensure that the quality of trials completed in India is up to international standards. The Indian regulatory body has established guidelines for informed consent, compensation in case of injury or death and reporting of Serious Adverse Events (SAEs). The clinical trials conducted in India must comply with the Y Schedule of Medical Tests and Drugs and Cosmetics Act guidelines and the International Committee for Synchronization-Good Medical Practice (ICH-GCP).

Table 1 Phases of clinical trials.

Phase	No. of subjects	Description
Phase 1	10-30	Detection of highest dose of treatment can be given safely without side effects.
Phase 2	200-300	Detection of safety, efficacy and unexpected side effects.
Phase 3	1000-3000	Safety and efficacy of drug for specified indication
Phase 4	PMS	Detection of unforeseen side effects.

Objective of this study is to provide regulations as well as approval process involved in clinical conducting clinical trials in India and to study challenges involved in it.

4.3.2 Discussion

(a) Regulations in India

Regulations has been set to ensure integrity of the data collected from clinical trials which assure the safety, right and welfare of the subject. [1][2]

Regulations involved:

- Law: Drugs and Cosmetics Act 1940 and Rules 1945.
- Regulation: Schedule Y for clinical research by CDSCO.
- Guidelines:

ICMR guidelines.

GCP guidelines.

1. The Drugs and Cosmetics Act 1940 and Rules 1945

Table 2 Drug and Cosmetic Act1940 and rules 1945.

Rules	Description
Rule 122DA	Approval to perform clinical trial
Rule 122 DAA	Clinical trial definition
Rule 122 DAB	Compensation in case of trial-related injury or death
Rule 122 DAC	Conditions of Clinical Trial approval and audit
Rule 122 DD	Ethics Committee registration
Rule 122 E	Definitions of New Drugs

Table 3 Amendments to Drug and Cosmetic Rules (DCR), 2013[3].

122DAB	First Amendment	-Providing free medical services to subject in case of injury. -In case death or injuries provide compensation - Report requirements for serious adverse events has been provided.
122-DAC	Second Amendment	- Approval for clinical trial - Permission of ECs before trial initiation. - Annual reports of clinical trial status. - Audit at trial site and personnel by CDSCO to check GCP and schedule Y compliance.
122-DD	Third Amendment	- Ethics committee's registration. - Requirements and guidelines for Ethics committee registration with application, record maintenance.

2. **Schedule Y**

   Guidelines and requirements for approval to import or manufacture new drugs for sale or to start clinical trials. [4] Table 4: Appendices of Schedule Y provide guideline to conduct clinical trials

Table 4 Appendices of Schedule Y provide guideline to conduct clinical trials.

Appendices	Description
Appendix V	Informed consent
Appendix VII	Undertaking by the Investigator
Appendix VIII	Ethics Committee
Appendix X	Protocol content
Appendix XI	Data elements for reporting serious adverse events.

3. **Guidelines**

   India follows ICH-GCP guidelines to conduct clinical trials which describes responsibilities of ethics committee, sponsor and investigator and the requirements of a protocol, the investigator's brochure (IB) and documents to pass audits and inspection. [5][6]

   GCP Requirements:

   - Safety assessment
   - Finance and insurance
   - Quality assurance

   ICMR requirements

   - Study timeline.
   - Explanation for placebo, plan to withdraw from trial, risk-benefit assessment. Explanation for the standard therapies to be withheld.

- Policy to continue the secrecy and maintain confidentiality of the human subject.
- Adverse event reaction
- Plan for management of minimum risk
- Proposed reward, compensation of incidental expenses for injury or death
- Facility to take care for distinct illness during research
- Maintaining data obtained during clinical trial.

(b) Fundamentals of conducting a clinical trial in India

Step 1: Approval from the Drugs Controller General, India.

Step 2: Permission from particular Ethics Committee where the clinical study is designed.

Step 3: Compulsory registration on the ICMR website www.ctri.in.

1. **Approval procedure for clinical trials in India**

To reduce the time lag for permitting clinical trials in India, a "three-tier" review process has been implemented on Feb 2013. Application is first reviewed by Technical committee and then Apex Committee after an initial approval from Subject Expert committee. After obtaining approval from all three stages DCGI will grant approval for conduct of clinical trials.[7]

Timeline for approval of clinical trial

Initially 6 months was the approval timeline for clinical trials from DCGI, but now Ministry of Health and Family Welfare notified New Drugs and Clinical Trial Rules, 2019 according to which clinical trial approval timeline reduced to 30 days for the clinical trials conducting inside the India. For the clinical trials to be conducted abroad, approval timeline for clinical trial is 90 days.[7]

Documents required[8]

- Clinical trial application form
- Treasury Challan
- Source of bulk drugs
- Information in chemicals and pharmaceutical drugs
- Pharmacology data of Animals
- Toxicology data of animals
- Clinical pharmacology information
- Regulatory conditions in other countries
- Information given/ prescribed
- Protocol for quality control

- Protocol for clinical study
- Investigator's Brochure
- Case Report Form
- Patient data sheet and informed consent form
- Investigator list in India and site address

Clinical Trial agreements

Before starting the clinical trials sponsor has to sign clinical trial agreement with Investigator. Agreement specifies the financial support, fees, payment and honorium.

It also includes duties of sponsor towards:

1. GCP compliance
2. Data reporting and recording
3. Retaining trial related essential documents.

2. **Ethics committee approval for review and approval for clinical trials**

   It is mandatory for sponsor to obtain confirmation of EC analysis and approval for clinical trial. Sponsor should obtain following before starting clinical trial:

   - Profile of ethics committee members which includes name, address, qualification and experience of each member
   - GCP compliance confirmation from ethics committee
   - Documented approval from ethics committee
   - Copy of Ethics Committee approvals in case its approval is based on changes if any.
   - Copy of Ethics committee documents involving re-evaluations/ re-approvals with favourable suggestions, and of any removals or suspensions of favourable opinion.

3. **Registration for clinical trial**

   It is compulsory for the sponsor to register for clinical trial before initiating clinical trial. Clinical trial has been registered with Indian Council of Medical Research's Clinical Trials Registry, India. Once the sponsor registered at the CTRI, the designated REF number indicates successful registration of clinical trial.

(c) Progress reporting of clinical trial

Investigators, sponsors, or visiting ethics committees can submit study progress reports periodically to the Ethics committee. Periodic report of study can submitted by the investigator.

Types of report

- Annual report: It is mandatory for sponsors to submit an annual status report of clinical trial to the Drugs Controller General of India. If trial have been stopped early for any cause, sponsor need to submit a summary report within three months. The summary report includes study details, total participants exposed to the drug, period and exposure dose, information of adverse drug reactions occurred in any situation and the purpose for discontinuation of study.
- Final report: It is submitted by investigator with his sign and date on the final report with declaration of terminating the study to the institution, and have verification of ethics committee and the sponsor for the data's validity. All the data along with signature can be forwarded to the sponsor and the ethics committee. In case of multicentre study, sign of coordinating investigator is also taken into consideration for some case or if agreed in the protocol.

(d) New drugs and clinical trials rule 2019

Union Ministry for Health and Family Welfare notified New Drugs and Clinical Trials Rules on March 9, 2019 for promoting clinical research in India. The aim is speedy approval process and transparency in clinical trials. The novel rule is related to new drugs, ethics Committee and investigational new drugs proposed for clinical trial, bioequivalence study and for human use against disease condition.

By considering suggestions and objections from stakeholders, Central Government notified final rules in Gazette of India vide G.S.R.227(E). Schedule Y and Part XA are no longer applicable for new drugs and investigational new drugs except for the drugs approved prior to initiation to the new rules. G.S.R.227(E) contains 13 chapters, 107 rules and 8 schedules. According to new rules, The Drug Controller, India is referred as Central Licensing Authority (CLA).[9]

Table 5 Revised application fees for clinical trials and BA-BE studies (covered under 6th schedule) [9]

Application	Fees(Rs)
Approval to initiate Phase I Clinical Trial • For reconsideration of application	3,00,000 50,000
Approval to initiate Phase II / III Clinical Trial • For reconsideration of application	2,00,000 50,000
Approval to initiate Phase IV Clinical Trial • For reconsideration of application	2,00,000 50,000
Approval to initiate BA/BE study with new drug • For reconsideration of application	2,00,000 50,000

*No fee is required to pay for manufacturing permission of new drugs depend on fruitful completion of Phase I to Phase III of clinical trials.

Table 6 Forms for application and issuance of permission:[9]

Application towards	Apply in	Permission in	Valid for
Ethics Committee registration for performing CT or BA/ BE study.	CT-01	CT-02	5 Years
For conducting Phase I / II / III / IV clinical trials with new drug or investigational new drug.	CT-04	CT-06	2 Years
To perform BA/BE study with new drug/ investigational new drug.	CT-05	CT-07	1 Year

1. **Biomedical and health Research**

   GSR 227(E) has included "Biomedical and health research" (under chapter IV) and laid out the requirements for carrying out such studies. Rules applicable to biomedical and health research have been given an extension, in the sense that they shall come into force after six months of publication of GSR 227(E).

Table 7 Timeline for review of application: [9].

Application	Timeline for review	If, no communication within timeline:
CT application for new drug/ investigational new drug	Within 30 working days	• Approval to conduct clinical trial have been granted. • Prior to initiate of clinical trial applicant has to submit Form CT-04
New drugs already available in market in countries given by central licencing authority.	Within 90 working days	-
BA-BE studies of new drug/ investigational new drug	Within 90 working days	-

2. **Academic Medical Test**

   Academic clinical trials are required to comply with ICMR guidelines.

   Comments from academic clinical trials are not used for any advertising purposes.

   Academic clinical trials are not required to submit a CLA for review and approval.

3. **Record of Clinical Trials**

   Before enrolling patients for clinical trials, it should be registered under CTRI portal. As per GSR 227(E), BA/BE testing of new clinical drugs under CTRI is mandatory before enrolling patients for clinical trials.

4. **Retention Records and Collection of Samples**

   As per GSR 227(e) it is mandatory to keep data and records for at least 5 years after BA/BE examination or study or termination. The package date of the new pharmaceutical product, which is the latter. Table Y does not specify sample retention, but in accordance with GSR 227(e) regulations, it is mandatory for all test specimens and reference drug products to be used in BA/BE studies. Within 5 years after the study was conducted or 1 year after the end of the drug, whichever is later.

5. **Marketing Studies**

   According to G.S.R.227(E), the requirements for Phase IV clinical trials/post-marketing trials and post-marketing surveillance differ:

   Post-Marketing Tests: These tests will be conducted as per approved protocols with limited test scope, additional criteria, exclusion criteria, safety and performance standards.

   Then after marketing surveillance studies: In these studies, the study of drugs from the perspective of the protocol involved is part of the patient's treatment. The regulatory guidelines for CT of a new drug are not valid in these cases as the drugs are already in the market.

6. **Pharmacy Monitoring System**

   The applicant is required to have a pharmacy monitoring system and the same is reported to the licensing authority.

7. **Clinical Trial of Indigenous Medicine**

   Any drug manufactured in India shall be subject to clinical trial and shall be approved for clinical trial within 30 working days by the Central Licensing Authority for its manufacture in India . If the applicant does not get any response from the CLA, the CT will be approved. [10]

   Made outside India. The validity period of clinical trial approval is defined as two years for pharmaceutical companies to initiate a study, which may be extended by one year. [10]

8. **Availability after trial of a new drug**

   If there is no alternative treatment for the specific context and the new drug under investigation is useful to the researcher, then the new drug will be available for that symptom. Policies were set in place to provide post-medication access to patients in need for the first time. Under the new rules, the sponsor will have to provide the drug for the course test at no cost.

9. Import of a drug for sale or distribution

For drugs sold abroad, local medical tests are not covered under the new rules for importing drugs for sale and distribution. In view of this rule of DCGI, availability of medicine is possible soon.

If there are no more or less serious adverse events for the drug

Whether the applicant is prepared to undergo post-marketing monitoring for the drug's safety and efficacy.

Whether the drug is prescribed for fatal diseases or whether the treatment for rare diseases is made available at high cost to the Indian population where medicines are not available in the market. [10]

10. Compensation and Monitoring

Patient safety is the primary goal of this rule, and in the event of any adverse event, compensation should be provided and strictly monitored against similar requirements. Informed consent should have a monitoring and compensation process in the event of an adverse event.

If an injury occurs during medical examination and medical examination confirms the injury, medical management of the subject is imperative. Compensation for cases such as permanent disability or death during medical examination is subject to the discretion of the Comptroller and Auditor General of India. [10]

11. Orphaned Drugs

Orphan drugs were earlier defined as a drug used to treat a condition that has not reached a population of more than 5 lakh in India. Under the new rules, medical tests conducted for rare diseases in India will not be charged. The guidelines exclude local medical tests for orphan drugs already approved for import into India for the purpose of sale and distribution. [10]

(e) Challenges of Conducting Clinical Trials in India

1. Moral Concerns

(a) Although India's history of medical examinations and unethical practices have led to the establishment of manpower and restrictions for medical examinations in India, international organizations are losing faith in Indian companies.

(b) Ethics committees are not required to register under DCGI, which would lead to independent employment and manipulation of clinical trial results, leading to emergence of adverse events in future, which is a challenging situation for India.

(c) It is very difficult to protect human material and maintain confidential data during clinical trials.

(d) Failed to maintain transparent procedures in informed approval process.

   (i) Attending medical examinations of vulnerable people like villagers, pregnant women, illiterate people misbehaves and results are manipulated.

2. **In terms of quality**

   (a) Data security, improper documentation, data quality and GCP issues.

   (b) Various quality standards for local clinical trials and global clinical trials.

   (c) Common approaches to some notable protocols in clinical trials involving inappropriate documentation.

3. **Regulatory Considerations**

   (a) Delay in approval of medical examinations: Shortage of technical staff or trained staff.

   (b) Lack of transparency in approval, standardization and improper audit during medical examination.

4. **Cultural Concepts**

   In India, the physician has a strong influence on the patient's decision, which can lead to ethical issues in patient admission if the procedure is unclear. Known permits must be in the local language. There should be translation in all the local languages of the region.

5. **Media and Advertising**

   There are a lot of harmful advertisements of medical tests in India due to misleading safety data provided by the media related to medical tests, resulting in misconceptions about human, industrial and government subjects, leading to laws rather than supporting development. rigorous development.

6. **Training or Instruction**

   The main concern is the lack of GCPs and the continuous improvement and certification of clinician clinical practice training.

4.3.3 Conclusion

New Rules for Drug Development, 2019 Comprehensive, balanced and enhanced protocol balance, which will benefit the patient. Approval of clinical trials in India within 30 days will expedite the trial process and give a boost to the drug development process in India. Early access to innovative pharmaceutical products is provided by new regulations that ensure ethical policies and protect patients' rights. These changes would increase sponsorship responsibilities and require more administrative controls to ensure compliance.

References

1. Pikee Saxena, Rohit Saxena. Clinical Trials: Changing Regulations in India. Indian J Community Med. 2014 Oct-Dec; 39(4): 197–202.
2. Drug and Cosmetic Act 1940 and Rules 1945. 2016 Available from: URL: https://cdsco.gov.in/opencms/export/sites/CDSCO_WEB/Pdf documents/acts_rules/2016DrugsandCosmeticsAct1940Rules1945.pdf
3. Rajashree Devarakonda. Current Clinical Trial Scenario of India: Challenges and Solutions. Pharma Bio World. July 2013; Page 16-20.
4. Schedule Y- CDSCO. 2019. Available from: URL: https://rgcb.res.in/documents/Schedule-Y.pdf
5. Aggregating clinical research regulations from around the world. National institute of allergy and infectitious disease. 2019. Available from: URL: https://clinregs.niaid.nih.gov/country/india#labeling_and_packaging
6. Lovely Joylen Castelino, Anoop Narayanan V, Swapnil Dylan Fernandes, Pankaj Kumar, Sandeep D S. Good Clinical Practices: An Indian Perspective. Research J. Pharm. and Tech 2018; 11(7): 3209-3215.
7. Sandeep Lahiry, Rajasree Sinha, Shouvik Choudhury, Ayan Mukherjee, Suparna Chatterjee. Paradigm shift in clinical trial regulations in India. 2018; Volume : 13, Issue : 1, Page : 51-55.
8. Clinical trials in India: Documents requirements. Available from: URL: https://morulaa.com/indian-medical-device-market/clinical-trials-in-india-document-requirements/
9. Bobby George. A New Dawn in the History of Clinical Research for India. IDMA Bulletin. 2019; Volume: 50, Issue : 17, Page: 8-14.
10. India: The New Drugs And Clinical Trial Rules, 2019. Available from: URL: http://www.mondaq.com/india/x/799018/Healthcare/The+New+Drugs+And+Clinical+Trial+Rules+2019.

CHAPTER 4.4

Safety Monitoring and Reporting on Clinical Trails

1. **Objective**

   This guideline replaces the 2009 level report: 'Safety monitoring and reporting for clinical trials involving therapeutic products' and reporting for clinical trials demonstrating current practice in the United States and the European Union. strengthens the system. This new guideline aims to address the widespread perception of stakeholders that Australia has placed an unnecessary burden on previous accommodating researchers and Human Research Protocol Committees (HREC) and has not actually contributed to patient safety.

2. **Purpose**

   This guide provides the collection, validation and analysis of adverse events and adverse reactions occurring in clinical trials involving test medical devices (IMPs) and test medical devices (IMDs) for trials conducted under clinical trial exemption (CTX) or medical testing. Refers to reporting. Information (CTN). Projects.

   The security monitoring and reporting requirements for IMP and IMD are broadly similar. However, to reflect the different terms and requirements of the respective Good Medical Practice Guidelines, the requirements for IMP and IMD are described separately in Part 1 and Part 2 of this document, respectively.

3. **Risk Monitoring for Security**

   The National Report on Ethical Behavior in Human Research (2007) (National Report) allows monitoring systems according to the risk, size and complexity of the experiment. The nature and extent of the participant's safety monitoring should be based on the assessment of the experimental intervention(s) associated with standard care and the level of knowledge about the IMP/IMD being evaluated. Sponsor plans for safety monitoring should be documented and regularly reviewed and revised during testing, while real-time analysis of safety data is performed.

Test sponsorship and current safety monitoring

The sponsor of a clinical trial is defined as 'the person, organization, or team responsible for securing an arrangement to initiate, manage and fund a study'. Many sponsor activities may be delegated to third parties, such as medical research institutions/centres, data security monitoring boards, or coordinating primary analysts.

The sponsor must be identified for all clinical trials. Although the definition of a test sponsor allows an individual to be designated as a sponsor, for non-commercial trials it is more appropriate for a company to assume that role rather than an investigator. It is also common for non-business partners to make joint arrangements to initiate, manage and finance group trials.

In such situations, it is important to ensure that all sponsored activities, including security monitoring and reporting, are explicitly assigned or excluded.

The ICH GCP and ISO 14155 sponsors are responsible for testing the current safety of the product under investigation. To ensure that a clinical trial has appropriate independent safety oversight, sponsors should generally use an independent team or

Independent person to review accumulated safety data (eg medical surveillance). When combining, data safety monitoring boards are best placed to perform experimental safety data analysis because they are in a unique position where they can blindly review safety information to evaluate treatments.

Encounter. Furthermore, they are often the only systems that can access emerging performance data for testing. Therefore, they have a clearer picture of changing the balance of risks and benefits within the trial.

These are the results of these reviews provided to HREC, investigators, agencies and regulatory authorities.

Sponsors shall, in the opinion of their safety groups or medical supervisors, be responsible for creating safety communications. Therefore, placing the sponsor at the center of the communication layer will ensure timely and orderly dissemination of information and link Australia to a common protocol review system with the rest of the world. In this model, sponsors report directly

HREC and investigators send any relevant information to their organization. Sponsors have the flexibility to delegate reporting responsibility to third parties, for example, to a coordinating center in a commercial trial.

Summary of Main Changes to Reporting Requirements [figure 1]

Change from 2009 Position Statement	Rationale
Removing the requirement to submit individual reports of adverse events (AEs), serious adverse events (SAEs), suspected unexpected serious adverse reactions (SUSARs), unanticipated serious adverse device effects (USADEs)and six monthly line listings to HRECs.	HREC are often not best placed to perform an analysis of these reports. The outcomes of the sponsor's analyses of accumulating safety data provide the HREC with more useful and useable information.
Removing the requirement to submit individual reports of AEs, SAEs, SUSARs/ USADEs and six monthly line listings to investigators to align with EU Regulation.	Updated/add ended investigator's brochures and spontaneous reports of significant safety issues provide investigators with the most relevant information on the use of the medicinal product or medical device.
Removing the requirement to submit individual reports of AEs, SAEs, *external* SUSARs/ USADEs and six monthly line listings to institutions.	Institutions are often not best placed to perform an analysis of these reports. The outcomes of the sponsor's analyses of accumulating safety data provides the institution with more useful and useable information.
Including the requirement for sponsors to provide HRECs with an annual safety report.	Provides HRECs with supports trial oversight, including a clear summary of the evolving safety profile of the trial and also evidence that the sponsor is conducting its ongoing safety monitoring appropriately.
Clarifying requirements and terminology for the reporting of significant safety issues.	Ensures that significant safety issues are communicated to all parties in a consistent manner and time frame.

4.4.1 Investigational Medicinal Product (IMP) Trails[1-5]

A. Definitions(IMPs)

The terminology associated with safety reporting is subject to global variation and companies conducting international trials may be required to use definitions outlined in their company policies. However, in order to promote consistency in Australia and a common understanding of safety reporting requirements, the following definitions for the categorization of safety events for IMPs should be adopted wherever possible.

Term	Description
Investigational Medicinal Product (IMP)	A pharmaceutical form of an active ingredient or placebo be ingtested clinical trial, including a product with a marketing authorization when used or assembled (formulated or packaged) in a way different from the approved form, or when used for an unapproved indication, a new patient group or when used to gain further information about an approved use. Note: This definition includes biological used as investigational medicinal products
BiologicaL	An item made from, or containing, human cells or human tissues, and that is used to treat or prevent disease or injury, diagnose a condition of a person, alter the physiological processes of a person, test the susceptibility of a person to disease, replace or modify a person's body part(s). Examples include: • Human tissue therapy products (e.g. skin, tissues, bone for grafting) • Processed human tissues(e.g. demineralised bone, collagen) • Human cellular therapy products (e.g. cartilage cells, cultured skin cells) • Immunotherapy products containing human cells • Genetically modified human cellular products.
Adverse Event (AE)	Any medical occurrence in a patient or clinical trial participant administered a medicinal product and that does not necessarily have a causal Relationship with this treatment.
Adverse Reaction (AR)	Any untoward and unintended response to an investigational medicinal product related to any dose administered. Comment: All adverse events judged by either the reporting investigator or the sponsor as having a reasonable possibility of a causal relationship to an investigational medicinal product would qualify as adverse reactions. The expression 'reasonable causal relationship' means to convey, in general, that there is evidence or argument to suggest a causal relationship. Note: The following are examples of types of evidence that would suggest a causal relationship between the investigational product and the adverse event: A single occurrence of an event that is uncommon and known to be strongly associated with drug exposure (e.g., angio edema, hepatic injury, Stevens-Johnson Syndrome) One or more occurrences of an event that is not commonly associated with drug exposure, but is otherwise uncommon in the population exposed to the drug (e.g., tendonrupture). An aggregate analysis of specific events observed in a clinical trial (such as known consequences of the underlying disease or condition under investigation or other events that commonly occur in the study population independent of drug therapy) that indicates those events occur more frequently in the drug treatment group than in a concurrent or historical control group.

Table *Contd...*

Term	Description
Investigator's Brochure (IB)	The document containing a summary of the clinical and non-clinical data relating to an investigational medicinal product that are relevant to the study of the product in humans
Product Information (PI)	The approved summary of the scientific information relevant to the safe and effective use of a prescription medicine. Note: In a trial in which the IMP is an approved product, the Product Information may replace the investigator's brochure. If the conditions of use differ from those authorized, the PI should be Supplemented with a summary of relevant clinical and non-clinical data that supports the use of the IMP in the trial. The Product Information should be used where available for each trial IMP adopted across Australian sites.

B. Safety Reporting Assessment Flowchart: IMP Trial [figure 2]

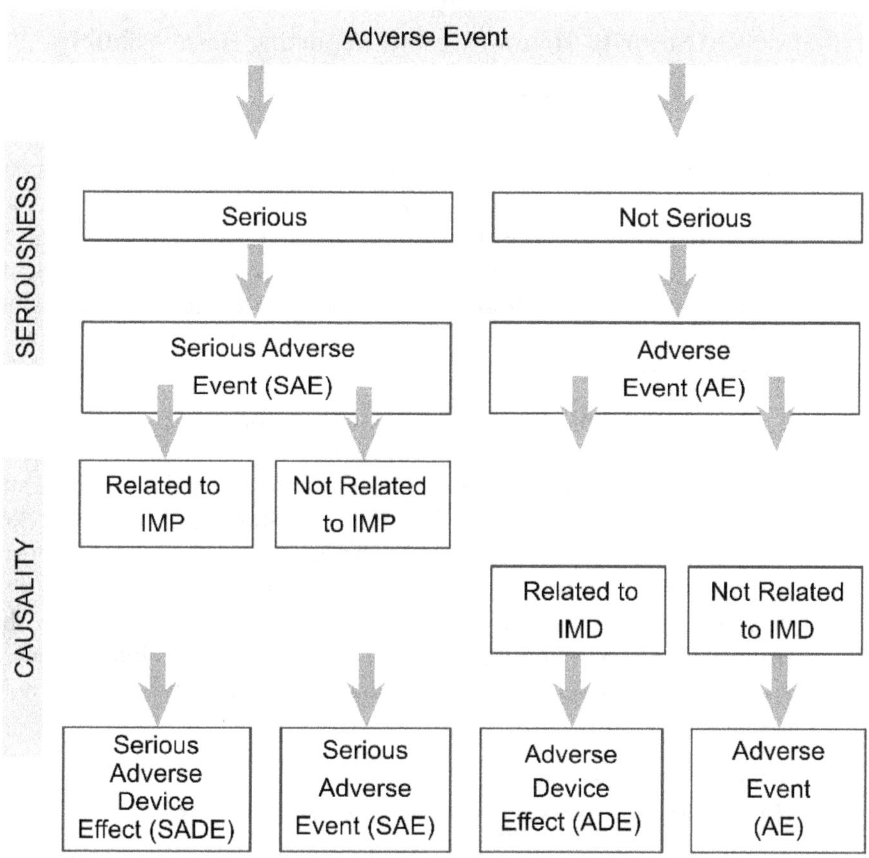

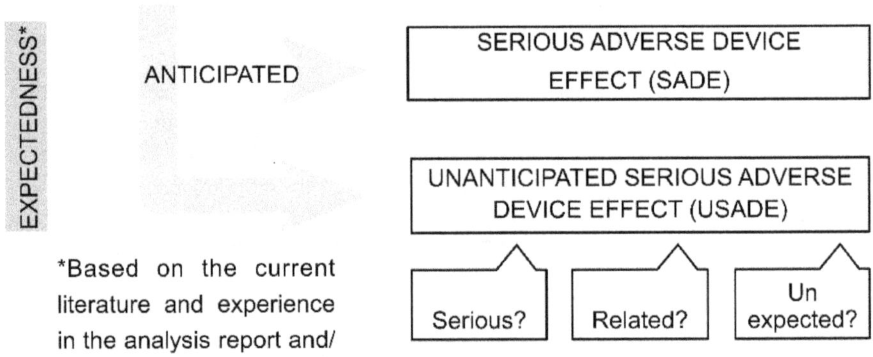

*Based on the current literature and experience in the analysis report and/ or contained in the Investigator's Brochure, Instructions for use or CIP

Adapted from the NIHR Clinical Trials Toolkit

C. Overview of Security Monitoring and Reporting Responsibilities

1. Sponsor's Responsibilities

Sponsors should establish safety monitoring procedures based on the risk, size and complexity of the proposed research. In experiments with a small number of participants, e.g. In phase I trials, risks are easily identified by closely monitoring adverse events, whereas in larger trials, risks are assessed by statistically comparing treatments. As a result, sponsors should identify the most appropriate provisions for current monitoring and be prepared to justify these provisions in the HREC review.

Sponsors should review all safety information reported by investigators and safety information from other sources. It acknowledges that all security data maintained by Commercial Sponsor is inaccessible to Commercial Sponsor; However, non-commercial sponsors will be responsible for reviewing all security information available to them. To increase the ability of non-commercial sponsors to meet their responsibilities, companies that provide medical supplies to other companies or obtain medical supplies from other companies must share safety information with each other. ,

Supporters need:

(a) Make sure the test protocol has clear clauses:

Risk Assessment and Management (if not in optional document) 9

- Definitions, procedures, responsibilities and reporting deadlines for safety reports

Any serious adverse event that does not require immediate reporting

(b) Keep detailed records of all reported adverse events and keep updated tables and/or tax lists

(c) When providing safety information to investigators and/or HREC, explain the impact of each report on patient safety, trial behavior, or trial documentation.

(d) Evaluate and classify safety reports received from investigators and report any unexpected serious adverse reactions to participants for administration of treatment products

For fatal or fatal SUSARs, immediately, but not later than 7 calendar days

Find the case with any follow-up information for an additional 8 calendar days

For all other SUSARs 15 calendar days after the case became known

Note 1: Sponsors must comply with global corporate policies that compel investigators to report individual SUSAR cases and six monthly tax lists to investigators; However, this procedure is not required for this guide. Sponsors may fulfill this obligation by posting these reports on the Portal or by e-mail. Confirmation of communication receipt may be requested when Sponsor confirms that the report has nothing to do with participant's safety or test conduct, but investigators are not required to print, review and file this report Is.

Note 2: When determining whether a SUSAR has occurred, Sponsor's reason assessment may conflict with Site Analyst's evaluation, and Sponsor may not downgrade Site Analyst's assessment (i.e. from 'inappropriate' to 'relevant' has been changed). In this case, if the investigator's decision triggers a SUSAR report, the investigator's and sponsor's opinions must be provided in any SUSAR reports sent to the regulatory authority.

Note 3: When reporting SUSAR to the regulatory authority, the blind must generally be approved by the sponsor.

To prevent dependence from entering, blindness should be maintained for all other persons involved in the conduct or administration of the experiment, including those responsible for data analysis and/or interpretation of the results.

I. Review the investigator's brochure at least once a year and update it as new and relevant information becomes available.

(e) Provide HREC and investigators with product information on any updates/additions to the investigator's brochure or, if appropriate,

Yes. Provide annual safety reports to HREC as well as a clear summary of the testing's growing safety profile. This report should allow HREC to assess whether current safety monitoring is being properly conducted and trial safety monitoring programs are being followed, and if necessary, to make new findings as testing progresses. should be taken into account.

Annual safety reports generally include the following:

Brief description and analysis of new and relevant findings

A brief review of the safety profile of IMP and its implications for participants, as well as all available safety data, and results of medical or non-medical studies relevant to IMP not listed in the Medical Products Register

Brief discussion of the effects of safety data on a trial's risk-benefit ratio

A description of the measures taken or proposed to reduce the risks

Note 1: Management summaries of safety information prepared for international regulators, such as the Development Safety Update Report (DSUR), can serve as an annual safety report (full DSUR not required) sent to HREC. The timing of the Annual Safety Report can be adjusted according to the reporting cycles of global organizations or combined with the Annual Progress Report sent to HREC.

Note 2: Annual safety reporting options where entry treatment is discovered are described in Section 2.5 of the ICH Guidance E2F: Developmental Safety Update Report.

(f) Ensure that all sponsorship responsibilities for safety monitoring and reporting (eg critical issues relating to reporting and regulation of SUSARs) are properly assigned or assigned.

Notify regulatory authorities, HREC and investigators of any significant safety issues that could adversely affect the safety of participants or could affect continued protocol acceptance or the conduct of trials. Critical security issues that meet the definition of immediate security action must be reported within 72 hours, and all critical security issues must be reported within 15 calendar days of being notified. Encourage or inform the sponsor of the issue. examples include:

A serious adverse event that could lead to investigations and necessitate a change in the behavior of the proceedings.

Risks to patient populations, such as invalidity of IMPs used to treat life-threatening disease.

An important safety discovery from a new full animal study (such as cancer)

Temporary suspension / termination of trial for safety reasons

Recommendations of the Data Security Monitoring Board relating to the safety of participants, such as increasing the frequency or severity of expected reactions

In one case events (eg toxic epidermal necrolysis, agranulocytosis, liver failure) may lead to immediate protective action.

Note 1: In most cases, critical security issues (SSIs) do not fall within the definition of SUSAR and are therefore not subject to the reporting requirements for SUSAR. SSI generally requires immediate safety action, correction, suspension, or other measures such as premature termination of testing. In addition, SSIs often make security-related changes to test documents. These changes should be submitted to HREC without any delay.

Note 2: Emergency Safety Measures (USM) are a type of critical safety issue in which the sponsor or test analyst acts promptly to prevent immediate danger to the health and safety of participants. As a result, USMs are often asked before the announcement of HREC.

If this initial contact is by telephone, a written notice must be sent by fax or email within 72 hours thereafter. Table 1 describes the types of actions to be taken as a result of SSI and the respective time frame for written notification.

Table 1 Sponsor Reports on Important Safety Issues.

Action	What is communicated	Recipients	Timelines and further review
Urgent safety measure (USMs	• Reasons for the urgent safety measure • Measures taken • Further actions planned	Cessation/ interruption of trial treatment) • Measures taken • Further actions planned	Notify the regulatory authority, investigators and the HREC Notify the regulatory authority investigators and the HREC Notify the regulatory authority, investigators and the HREC
Notification of anamendment	• Details of the significant safety issue • Further actions planned	Notify the regulatory authority investigators and the HREC	Without undue delay and no later than 15 calendar days of the sponsor becoming aware of the issue. Sponsors should submit to the HREC an amendment relating to any revised trial documentation, without undue delay
Temporary halt of a trial for safety reasons	• Reasons for the halt • The scope of the halt (e.g. suspension of recruitment or Cessation /interruption of trial treatment) • Measures taken • Further actions planned	Notify the regulatory authority, investigators and the HREC	Without undue delay and no later than 15 calendar days of the sponsor's decision to halt the trial. Where it is necessary to seek ethical review of related actions (e.g. informing participants or arranging continuing care and follow-up), a letter describing these actions should be submitted to the HREC within 15 calendar days of the temporary halt
Early termination of a trial for safety reasons	• Reasons for the early termination • Measures taken • Further actions planned	Notify the regulatory authority, investigators and the HREC	Without undue delay and no later than 15 calendar days of the sponsor's decision to terminate the trial. Where it is necessary to seek ethical review of related actions (e.g. informing participants or arranging continuing care And follow-up), a letter describing the sections should be submitted to the HREC within 15 calendar days of the early termination.

1. **Responsibilities of the Principal Investigator**

   Investigators should assess all local safety events and should act on any events as clinical care dictates. The role of the investigator with regard to safety reporting is to provide the sponsor with all relevant information so that an appropriate safety analysis can be performed.

   The Principal Investigator should:

   (a) capture and assess all AEs that occur at the site as required and in accordance with the protocol

   (b) report to the sponsor within 24 hours of becoming aware of the event:

   - all SAEs, except those that are identified in the protocol as not needing immediate reporting
   - any occurrences of congenital anomaly/birth defect arising from any pregnancy of a participant (or partner)
   - all urgent safety measure instigated by the site

   (c) report to the sponsor as specified in the protocol:

   (d) all safety critical events

   (e) any additional requested information relating to reported deaths

   (f) report to the institution within 72 hours of becoming aware of the event:

   (g) all significant safety issues

   (h) SUSARs arising from the local site.

2. **Responsibilities of the HREC**

   The sponsor, through their independent safety monitoring arrange-ments, has the primary responsibility for monitoring the ongoing safety of the investigational medicinal product. The HREC should be satisfied that the sponsor's arrangements are sufficiently independent and commensurate with the risk, size and complexity of the trial.

   The approving HREC should:

   (a) Assess the safety of proposed trials, including whether the evaluation of the anticipated benefits and risks is satisfactory and ensure that the sponsor has proportionate systems in place to mitigate and manage any identified risks

   (b) satisfy itself that the sponsor's ongoing safety monitoring arrangements are adequate, including the justification for appointing/not appointing a Data Safety Monitoring Board and any 'stopping rules' or criteria for with drawing individual participants from the trial.

(c) keep under review the adequacy and completeness of the informed consent process and documentation in the light of new information about risks and benefits

(d) assess whether changes to the risk-benefit ratio that are reported by the sponsor are compatible with continued ethical approval

(e) advise the regulatory agencies, investigators and their institutions of any decision to with draw approval

Note: While HRECs must keep approvals under review in light of safety information it receives, the responsibility for proactively monitoring the ongoing risk-benefit ratio of the trial remains with the sponsor at all times.

3. **Responsibilities of the Institution**

An institution's responsibilities and oversight of safety information in clinical trials will differ depending on whether they are hosting externally sponsored clinical trials or sponsoring locally lednon-commercial trials. In both cases they should help ensure that their site(s) understands and complies with sponsor requirements. Institutions should have oversight of any issues that may require management, such as disputes or litigation resulting from trials. Where the institution is also named as the trial sponsor, the institution will also assume the sponsor responsibilities set out in this document.

The Institution should:

(a) Assess whether any safety reports received impact on medico-legal risk, the responsible conduct of research, adherence to contractual obligations or the trial's continued site authorization and, where applicable, facilitate the implementation of corrective and preventative action

(b) Develop clear guidance for investigators detailing the require-ments for safety reporting and monitoring in clinical trials. This document(s) should cover the requirements for both externally sponsored clinical trials and, if applicable, internally sponsored investigator/initiated or collaborative group trials.

4. **Responsibilities of the Regulatory authority**

Clinical trials of unapproved therapeutic goods are conducted in Australia under either the Clinical Trial Notification (CTN) Scheme or the Clinical Trial Exemption (CTX) Scheme. Responsibility for the regulatory control of therapeutic goods in Australialies with the Therapeutic Goods Administration (TGA).

The CDSCO, TGA, EU, USFDA may:

(a) Conduct an audit of a clinical trial where necessary on safety grounds

(b) Stopatrial where that action is in the public's interest.

4.4.2 Investigational Medical Devices (IMD) Trials [1,2]

A. Definitions (IMDs)

The terminology associated with clinical trial safety reporting is subject to global variation and companies conducting international trials may be required to use definitions outlined in their company policies. However, it is recommended that the following definitions are adopted to promote consistency and a common understanding of safety reporting requirements. Where available, the definitions for IMDs have been sourced from ISO 14155 (2011): Clinical Investigation of medical devices for human subjects–Good Clinical Practice.

Term	Description
Adverse Device Effect (ADE)	Adverse event related to the use of an investigational medical device. Note: This definition includes adverse events resulting from in sufficient or inadequate Instructions for Use, deployment, implantation, installation, or operation, or any malfunction of the investigational medical device. This definition includes any event resulting from use error or from intentional misuse of the investigational medical device.
AdverseEvent(AE)	Any untoward medical occurrence, unintended disease or injury, or untoward clinical signs (including abnormal laboratory findings) in participants, users or other persons, whether or not related to the investigational medical device.
	Note: This definition includes events related to the investigational medical device or the comparator. This definition includes events related to the procedures involved.
	For users or other persons, this definition is restricted to events related to investigational medical devices.
Device	Deficiencies Inadequacy of a medical device with respect to its identity, quality, durability, reliability, safety or performance. Note: Device deficiencies include malfunctions, use errors, and inadequate labelling.
Investigational Medical Device(IMD)	Medical device being assessed for safety or performance in a clinical investigation Note: This includes medical devices already on the market, that are being evaluated for new intended uses, new populations, new materials or design changes.

Table *Contd...*

Term	Description
Investigator's Brochure (IB)	Compilation of the current clinical and non-clinical information on the investigational medical device(s) relevant to the clinical investigation.
Medical Device	Any instrument, apparatus, implement, machine, appliance, implant, software, material or other similar or related article: a. intended, by the person under whose name it is or is to be supplied, to be used for human beings for the purpose of one or more of the following: • diagnosis, prevention, monitoring, treatment or alleviation of disease • diagnosis, monitoring, treatment, alleviation of or compensation for an injury or handicap • investigation, replacement or modification of the anatomy or of a physiological process • supporting or sustaining life • control of conception • disinfection of medical devices, and b. That does not achieve its primary intended action in or on the human body by pharmacological, immunological or metabolic means, but that may be assisted in its intended function by such means.
Serious Adverse Device Effect (SADE) Serious Adverse Event (SAE)	An adverse device effect that has resulted in any of the consequences characteristic of a serious adverse event. a. Adverse event that: led to death Led to serious deterioration in the health of the participant, that either resulted in: • a life-threatening illness or injury, or a permanent impairment of a body structure or a body function, or • in-patient or prolonged hospitalization, or • medical or surgical intervention to prevent life-threatening illness or injury or permanent impairment to a body structure or a body function
	led to fetal distress, fetal death or a congenital abnormality or birth defect Note: Planned hospitalization for a pre-existing condition, or a procedure required by the Clinical Investigation Plan, without serious deterioration in health, is not considered a serious adverse event.
Significant Safety Issue (SSI)	A safety issue that could adversely affect the safety of participants or materially impact on the continued ethical acceptability or conduct of the trial
Unanticipated Serious Adverse Device Effect (USADE)	Serious adverse device effect which by its nature, incidence, severity or outcome has not been identified in the current version of the risk analysis report Note: Anticipated serious adverse device effect (ASADE) is an effect which by its nature, incidence, severity or outcome has been identified in the risk analysis report.

Table *Contd...*

Term	Description
Device Effect (USADE)	A measure required to be taken in order to eliminate an immediate hazard to a participant's health or safety.
Urgent Safety Measure (USM)	Note: This type of significant safety issue can be instigated by either the investigator or sponsor and can be implemented before seeking approval from HRECs or institutions.

B. Safety Reporting Assessment Flowchart: IMD Trials [figure 3]

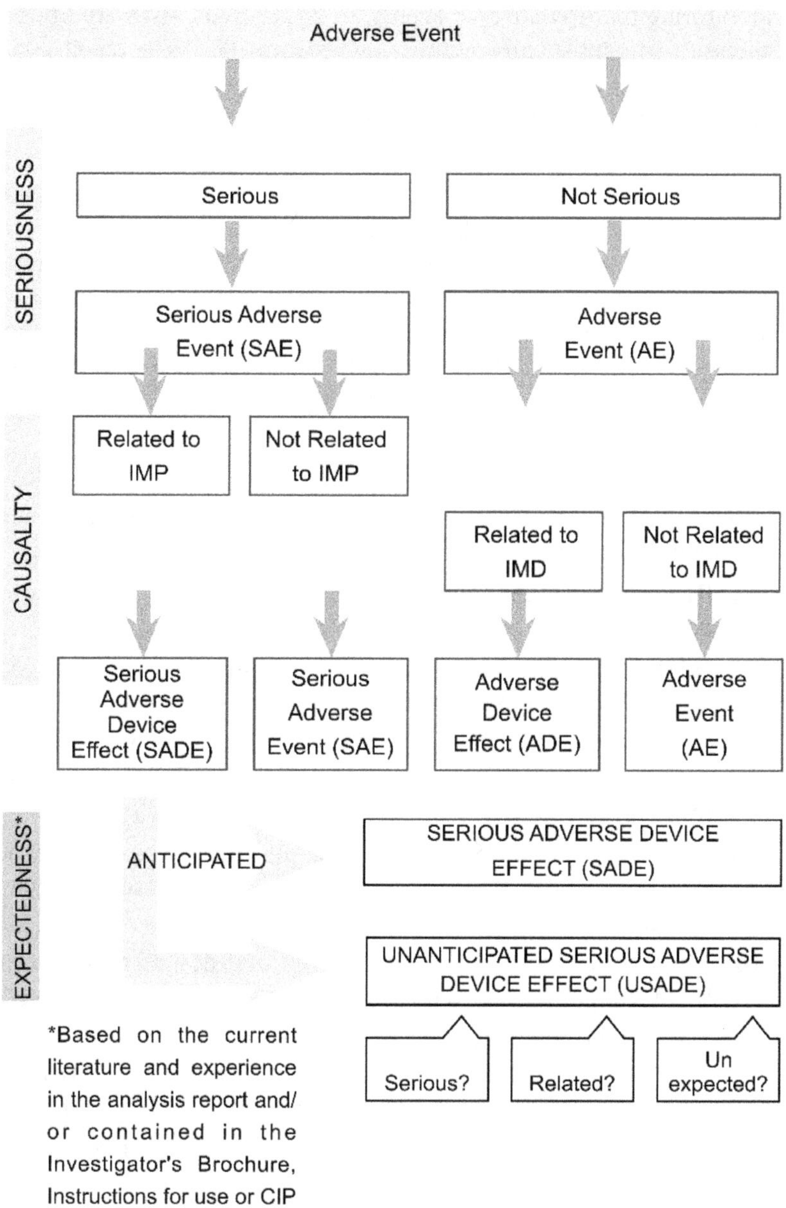

Adapted from the NIHR Clinical Trials Toolkit

C. Overview of Security Monitoring and Reporting Responsibilities

1. Sponsor's Responsibilities

Sponsors should establish safety monitoring procedures commensurate with the risk, size and complexity of the proposed research. In experiments with a small number of participants, e.g. In pilot or human experiments, hazards are most easily identified by carefully monitoring the first adverse events. In larger trials, risks are often better assessed by statistically comparing treatments. As a result, sponsors must identify the most appropriate provisions for current monitoring and be prepared to justify those provisions in the HREC review.

Sponsors should review all safety information reported by investigators and safety information from other sources. acknowledges that the entire security data maintained by the Commercial Sponsor is inaccessible to the Commercial Sponsor; However, non-commercial sponsors will be responsible for reviewing all security information available to them. To increase the ability of non-commercial sponsors to meet their responsibilities, companies that provide medical supplies or obtain medical supplies from other organizations must share safety information with each other.

Supporters need:

(a) Make sure the Medical Checkup Plan (CIP) has clear sections that describe:

Risk Assessment and Management (if not in the optional document)

- Definitions, procedures, responsibilities and reporting deadlines for safety reports

(b) Review the analyst's assessment of all adverse events and determine and document their severity and suitability for the investigative instrument.

(c) Examine all defects in the device and identify and document in writing whether they may cause serious adverse effects on the device.

(d) Maintain detailed records of all AE and device defects reported by investigators and maintain updated tables and/or tax lists

(i) When providing safety information to investigators and/or HREC, explain the impact of each report on patient safety, trial behavior, or trial documentation.

(e) Evaluate and classify information received from investigators and report all to USADE

What happens to Australian participants in medical product management:

For USADEs at risk or life-threatening, with any follow-up information for an additional 8 calendar days after the known 7 calendar days

For all other USADEs, 15 calendar days after the case became known

Note 1: Sponsor should not downgrade a Site Analyst's rating (i.e., change from 'Inappropriate' to 'Relevant') when it is determined that the Sponsor's due evaluation conflicted with the Site Analyst's rating to USADE Yes or No. In this case, if the investigator's decision triggers USADE's report, the opinions of both the investigator and the sponsor must be provided in any reports submitted to the regulatory commission.

Yes. Update the investigator's brochure or, if appropriate, follow instructions for use (IFU) and receive important new information.

(f) Provide instructions to HREC and investigators with investigator's brochures or any updates/additions for proper use

(i) Provide annual safety reports to HREC as well as a clear summary of the testing's growing safety profile. This report should allow HREC to assess whether current safety monitoring is being properly conducted and trial safety monitoring programs are being followed, and if necessary, to make new findings as testing progresses. should be taken into account.

Brief description and analysis of new and relevant findings

A brief discussion of the effects of safety data on the risk-benefit ratio for the trial

A description of the measures taken or proposed to reduce the risks

Note: The timing of the Annual Safety Report may correspond to reporting cycles of global organizations or may be aligned with the Annual Progress Report submitted to HREC.

(g) Ensure that all sponsorship responsibilities for safety monitoring and reporting (eg reporting critical safety issues to USADE and TGA) are properly assigned or assigned

Of. Notify TGA, HREC, and investigators of any significant safety issues that could adversely affect the safety of participants or could affect continued protocol acceptance or conduct of the trial. Critical security issues that meet the definition of immediate security action must be reported within 72 hours, and all other critical security issues must be reported by then.

15 calendar days, trigger or report the problem to the sponsor. examples include:

A serious adverse event, which may have been caused by investigative procedures and requires a change in the behavior of the proceedings

Risk to the patient population due to the ineffectiveness of the IMD used in the trial

Basic basic safety discovery of newly completed study using the same IMD

Temporary suspension / termination of trial for safety reasons

Recommendations of the Data Protection Monitoring Board are relevant to the safety of participants, such as increasing the frequency or severity of expected adverse effects of the device.

Note 1: Generally, critical security issues (SSIs) are not within the USADE definition and are therefore not subject to the reporting requirements for USADE. SSI generally requires immediate safety action, correction, suspension, or other measures such as premature termination of testing. In addition, SSIs often make security-related changes to test documents. These changes should be submitted to HREC without any delay.

Note 2: Emergency Safety Measures (USM) is an important safety issue in which the sponsor or test analyst acts promptly to prevent immediate danger to the health and safety of participants. As a result, USM is often sued before regulatory authority and reported to HREC. In these cases, it is strongly recommended that you contact regulatory authorities within 24 hours of the implementation of the sponsorship program.

If this initial contact is by telephone, a written notice must be sent by fax or email within 72 hours thereafter.

Table 2 Describes the types of actions to be taken as a result of SSI and the respective time frame for written notification. (Sponsor Reporting of Significant Safety Issues)

Action	What is communicated	Recipients	Timelines and further review
Urgent safety measure (USMs)	• Reasons for the urgent safety measure • Measures taken • Further actions planned	Notify regulatory authority, investigators and the HREC	Without undue delay and no later than 72 hours of the measure being taken. The HREC is not required to approve USMs but may consider whether any proposed actions are appropriate, such as the submission of an Amendment relating to revised trial documentation.

Table *Contd...*

Action	What is communicated	Recipients	Timelines and further review
Notification of an amendment	• Details of the significant safety issue • Further actions planned	Notify the regulatory authority, investigators and the HREC	Without undue delay and no later than 15 calendar days of the sponsor becoming aware of the issue. Sponsors should submit to the HREC an amendment relating to any revised trial document-tation without undue delay.
Temporary halt of a trial for safety reasons	• Reasons for the halt • The scope of the halt (e.g. suspension of recruitment or cessation /interruption of trial treatment) • Measures taken • Further actions planned	Notify the regulatory authority, investigators and the HREC	Without undue delay and no later than 15 calendar days of the sponsor becoming aware of the issue. Sponsors should submit to the HREC an amendment relating to any revised trial documentation without undue delay.
Early termination of a trial for safety reasons	• Reasons for the early termination • Measures taken • Further actions planned	Notify regulatory authority, investigators and the HREC	Without undue delay and no later than 15 calendar days of the sponsor's decision to halt the trial. Where it is necessary to seek ethical review of related actions (e.g. informing participants or arranging continuing care and follow-up), a letter describing these actions should be submitted to the HREC within 15 calendar days of the temporary halt.

1. **Responsibilities of the Principal Investigator**

Investigators should assess all local safety events and should act on any events as clinical care dictates. The role of the investigator with regard to safety reporting is to provide the sponsor with all relevant information so that an appropriate safety analysis can be performed.

The Principal Investigator should:

(a) Record every AE and observed device deficiency, together with an assessment and report to the sponsor as required by the clinical investigation plan

(b) Report to the sponsor without unjustified delay, all serious adverse events and device deficiencies that could have led to a serious adverse device effect

(c) Report to the sponsor within 24 hours any urgent safety measure instigated at the site

(d) Report to the sponsor pregnancies that occur while a participant is on a clinical trial as specified in the clinical investigation plan

(e) Follow-up any pregnancy until outcome (e.g. birth or spontaneous abortion) and report any incidents of congenital abnormality/birth defect as an SAE

(f) Supply the sponsor, upon sponsor's request, with any additional information related to the safety reporting

(g) Report to their institution without undue delay and no later than 72 hours of the Principal Investigator becoming aware of the event:

- All significant safety issues
- USADEs occurring at the site.

2. Responsibilities of the HREC

The sponsor, through their independent safety monitoring arrangements, has the primary responsibility for monitoring the ongoing safety of the investigational medical device. The HREC should be satisfied that the sponsor's arrangements are sufficiently independent and commensurate with the risk, size and complexity of the trial.

The approving HREC should:

(a) Assess the safety of the proposed trial and whether the evaluation of the anticipated benefits and risks is satisfactory, and ensure that the sponsor has proportionate systems are in place to mitigate and manage any identified trial risks

(b) Satisfy itself that the sponsor has adequate ongoing safety monitoring arrangements in place including the justification for appointing/not appointing a Data Safety Monitoring Board and any 'stopping rules' and criteria for with drawing individual participants from the trial

(c) Satisfy itself that the sponsor understands their obligation to report to the HREC anything that may adversely affect the safety of participants or the conduct of the trial, particularly amendments relating to changes made to the device design and manufacturing process, and other information that may alter risks and benefits

(d) Assess whether changes to the risk-benefit ratio that are reported by the sponsor are compatible with continued ethical approval

(e) Advise the regulatory authorities, investigators and their institutions of any decision to with draw approval

(f) Keep under review the adequacy and completeness of the informed consent process and documentation in the light of new information about risks and benefits.

Note: While HRECs must keep approvals under review in light of safety information it receives, the responsibility for proactively monitoring the ongoing risk-benefit ratio of the trial remains with the sponsor.

3. **Organizational Responsibilities**

The information security agency's responsibilities and management in clinical trials will vary depending on whether they conduct outsourced clinical trials or conduct locally conducted non-commercial trials. testing. In both cases they should help ensure that their site is understood and understood

Sponsor complies with requirements. Companies must also oversee any issues that require management, such as disputes or lawsuits that result from trials. If the Company is also designated as a Trial Sponsor, the Company will also accept the sponsorship responsibilities set forth in this document.

Company strictly:

(a) Evaluate whether a safety statement has an impact on the medical-legal risk at the test site, compliance with contract obligations or continued validation.

(b) Develop clear guidelines for investigators describing requirements for reporting and monitoring safety in clinical trials. This document(s) will cover the requirements for both externally sponsored clinical trials and, if applicable, internally sponsored investigator/onset or joint team trials.

4. **Responsibility for the management of therapeutic products**

Clinical trials of unauthorized therapeutic products are carried out in Australia under the Medical Trial Notification (CTN) scheme or the Medical Trial Exemption (CTX) scheme. Responsibility for regulating the regulation of medical products in Australia rests with the regulatory authorities of the Medical Administration.

regulatory authorities:

(a) Conduct a systematic examination of the medical examination necessary for security reasons

(b) Stop the investigation, that action is in public interest.

(c) notes

1. ISO 14155 (2011): Clinical Study of Medical Devices for Human Subjects - Good Medical Practice

2. Regulation of the European Parliament and the Medical Devices and Regulation Council (2001/83/EC, Regulation (EC) No. 178/2002 and Regulation (EC) No. 1223/2009/EEC - (Section 1.5.4) Evolving) of Medical Products test coordination)

References

1. Note for Guidance on Good Clinical Practice (ICHGCP)–Annotated with regulatory authorities Comments
2. Integrated Addendum to ICHGCP Current Step 2 version dated 11 June 2015
3. Regulation No 536/2014 on Clinical Trials on Medicinal Products for Human Use
4. The National Statement on Ethical Conduct in Human Research (2007), as amended.
5. Guidance for Industry and Investigators Safety Reporting Requirements for INDs and BA/BE Studies (FDA)

CHAPTER 4.5

Health Insurance and Portability and Liability Act

4.5.1 What is HIPAA?

The Health Insurance Portability and Accountability Act of 1996 (HIPAA or Kennedy-Kasabam Act [1] [2]) was passed by the 104th US Congress and passed into law by President Bill Clinton on August 21, 1996. It was mainly made, To modernize the flow of health care information, how to protect personally identifiable information from fraud and theft by healthcare and health care professionals, and to remove the limits of health insurance coverage. [3]

The action consists of five subjects

HIPAA Title I health insurance protects workers and their families when they lose or lose their jobs. [4]

Title II of HIPAA, also known as Administrative Simplification (AS) rules, requires the establishment of national standards for electronic health transactions and the establishment of national identities for providers, health insurance plans, and employers. [5]

Title III lays down guidelines for pre-tax medical expenses,

Title IV sets guidelines for health plans, and

Title V manages company-owned life insurance policies

Theme I: Access to Health, Portability and Renewal

Title I governs the availability and amounts of group HIPAA health plans and certain individual health insurance policies. It amended the Employees' Pension Income Protection Act, the Public Health Services Act and the Inland Revenue Code.

Title I - governs group health plan restrictions on coverage requirements and benefits for existing conditions. Group health plans may refuse to provide benefits related to conditions that existed before 12 months of enrollment in the plan or 18 months after enrollment is delayed. [6] I allow individuals to enroll in the program to reduce the duration of "credible coverage" before and after any "significant breaks" in coverage. [7] "Credible coverage" is defined relatively broadly and includes almost all group and individual health plans, including medical insurance and medical assistance. [8] A "significant difference" in coverage is defined as any 63-day period without any credit coverage. [9] This includes an exception, which allows employers to make a premium or co-pay for tobacco use or body mass index.

Title I [10] should also provide policies without exception for those (see above) who leave group health plans for more than 18 months, [11] unless individual policies are introduced. Or options for discontinued plans are not provided. As long as the insurer is in the market without exception regardless of health.

Some health care plans are not covered by Title I requirements such as long-term health plans and limited coverage plans such as dental or vision plans that are offered separately from a public health plan. However, if such benefits are part of a holistic health plan, HIPAA will still apply to such benefits. For example, if the new plan offers dental benefits, it must count towards continued coverage under the old health plan for any of its grace periods for dental benefits.

An alternative way to calculate continuing coverage that can be credited is available for a health plan under Title I. That is, 5 types of health care can be considered separately, including dental and vision insurance. Everything that isn't under those 5 categories must use the normal count (for example, a beneficiary can count with 18 months of normal coverage, but only 6 months of dental care, if the beneficiary doesn't have a public health plan) up to 6 months prior to the date of dental application). Because limited coverage plans are not included in HIPAA requirements, there is a unique case where an applicant in a general group health plan is unable to obtain a continuing credit coverage certificate for independent limited coverage. Dental-like plans used during the new plan's grace period to cover those coverages.

The hidden grace period is not valid under Title I (eg, "must be accident insured, beneficiary must be insured under the same health insurance contract"). Such subdivisions should not be operated through health scheme. Also, it needs to be rewritten so that they are HIPAA compliant. [12]

Title II: Prevention of Fraud and Abuse in Health Care; administrative simplification; medical liability reform

Title II of HIPAA establishes policies and procedures to maintain the confidentiality and security of personally identifiable health information, outlines a number of health care-related violations, and establishes civil and criminal penalties for violations. It also develops a number of programs to control fraud and abuse in the health care system. [13] [14] [15] [16] However, the most important rule of Title II is its administrative simplification rule. Title II The Department of Health and Human Services (HHS) must increase the efficiency of the health care system by developing standards for the use and dissemination of health care information. [16]

These rules apply to "notified companies" as defined by HIPAA and HHS. Closed companies include health plans, health care archives (such as billing services and community health information systems) and health care providers who send health care data in a controlled manner. of HIPAA. [17] [18]

In accordance with Title II requirements, HHS has issued five rules relating to administrative simplification: privacy rules, transaction and code package rules, security rules, unique identification rules, and enforcement rules.

5 Basic HIPAA Rules

Privacy rules

The Privacy Policy protects individuals' PHI and medical records with limitations and conditions on various uses and disclosures that may or may not be made without the patient's consent. This rule gives each patient the right to inspect and receive a copy of his record and to request corrections to his file. Typical forms that meet this rule are: Request for Access to Protected Health Information (PHI); Notice of Confidentiality Process (NPP) Form; Request Form for Accounting Disclosure; Requests for control of patient health care information; authorization for the application or disclosure form; and privacy complaint forms.

Safety rules

Defines and regulates safety regulations, standards, procedures and techniques relating to the protection of electronic PHI in storage, access and transmission. There are three levels of safety precautions. Discusses the allocation of administrative securities to the HIPAA Security Compliance Committee; Technical security handles the encryption and authentication methods used to control data access, and physical security handles the security of any electronic systems, data, or equipment within your facility and organization. Risk analysis and risk management protocols for hardware, software and transfers are subject to this rule.

Transaction rules

This rule discusses the transaction and code packages used in HIPAA transactions, including ICD-9, ICD-10, HCPCS, CPT-3, CPT-4 and NDC codes. These codes must be used correctly to ensure the safety, accuracy and security of medical records and PHI.

Rule of Rule Identifiers

HIPAA uses three unique identifiers for closed companies that use administrative and financial transactions regulated by HIPAA. These identifiers are: the National Provider Identifier (NPI), a 10-digit number used for healthcare providers locked in each HIPAA administrative and financial transaction; National Health Scheme Identifier (NHI), an identifier used to identify health plans and payers under Medical Care and Medical Services Centers (CMS); and the standard unique employer identifier, the Federal Employer Identification Number (EIN), which identifies and employs the company in HIPAA transactions.

Enforcement rules

This provision is taken from the provisions of the ARRA Hi-Tech Act for contraventions that occurred before or after the compliance date of February 18, 2015. It expands the rules under HIPAA Privacy and Security, increasing the penalties for any violations. This includes five key areas relating to the companies and business partners involved: the use of HIPAA security and privacy requirements; Establishing mandatory federal privacy and security breach reporting requirements; Creating new confidentiality requirements and accounting disclosure requirements and sales and marketing controls; Establish new criminal and civil penalties and enforcement procedures for non-compliance with HIPAA; and require that all new security requirements be included in all business associate contracts.

Title I: Tax Health Rules for Management of Medical Savings Accounts

Title II standardizes the amount each person can save in a pre-tax medical savings account. Since 1997, a medical savings account (MSA) has been available to employees under the High Exemption Scheme, which is funded by a small employer and the self-employed.

Title III: Application and Implementation of Group Medical Insurance Requirements

Title IV specifies the terms of group health plans relating to coverage for pre-existing conditions and changes the continuity of coverage requirements. It also clarifies coverage continuity requirements and includes a COBRA explanation.

Title V: Income Compensation for the Management of Tax Deductions for Employers

Title VI contains provisions relating to company-owned life insurance for employers paying company-owned life insurance premiums, which prevents the deduction of interest on life insurance loans, company grants or contracts related to the company. It also repeals the financial institution's rule on interest allocation rules. Finally, it amends the law relating to persons surrendering U.S. citizenship or permanent residency, expanding the assessed foreign tax against those who have surrendered their status in the United States for tax reasons, and as part of this the names of former citizens are being changed. Public registration by generating quarterly publications of selected persons abroad. [20]

(a) Purpose of HIPAA

Important The main objective of HIPAA:-

(i) To make the law easier for people to have health insurance

(ii) Protect the privacy and security of health care Information

(iii) To assist the health sector in controlling administrative costs.

(b) What is included in HIPAA?

1. Standardized electronic data transfer transactions and
   Code for all closed companies.
2. Standards for protecting data systems.
3. Privacy protection for personal health information.
4. Common national identifier for health care.

(c) Need of HIPAA?

In the year 2000, many newly diagnosed patients with depression received free samples of antidepressants in their mail.

It leaves the patient wondering how the pharmaceutical companies were informed about the patient's illness.

After a lengthy and thorough investigation, the doctor, the pharmaceutical company and the well-known drug chain were all accused of breach of confidentiality.

This is one of many reasons why the federal government should intervene and develop guidelines to protect patient privacy.

(d) About HIPAA

IP HIPAA is divided into two different categories. All of them:

- portability
- administrative simplification

1. Capability Portability

- This clause allows individuals to move their health insurance from one job to another so that their coverage is not reduced.

It also regulates health plans that require a person to move from one health plan to another with a pre-existing condition.

2. **Administrative Simplification**
   - This section aims to establish a set of standards for the receipt, transmission and maintenance of health care information.
   - Ensures the confidentiality and security of personally identifiable information.

(e) Management Requirements

Every company must appoint a Privacy Officer.

- Develop policies and procedures to guide HIPAA implementation, review and improvement. This includes action taken against persons who do not follow the guidelines.
- Provide education on HIPAA and organizational policies and practices.
- Develop a process for handling privacy complaints.

Make sure there is no retaliation against anyone who reports potential breaches in good faith.

- Take appropriate action to minimize any damages caused by the breach of privacy.
- Ensure there are procedures in place to demonstrate compliance with documentation and record keeping.

(f) Who should follow?

Person responsible for enforcing HIPAA rules and regulations. some examples:

health plan

Healthcare Clearing House

Healthcare providers who conduct certain financial and administrative transactions electronically.

4.5.2 HIPAA Overview

The Privacy Policy governs access to Protected Health Information (PHI).

The Security Protection Code defines ongoing administrative, technical and physical security practices to ensure the confidentiality, integrity and availability of ePHI.

The American Recovery and Re-Investment Act (ARRA) aims to establish secure electronic health records for all Americans by 2014.

Health Health Information Technology for Economic and Medical Health Law (HITECH)

ARRA/HITECH makes changes to HIPAA terms in 3 categories:

Notice of infringement

Business associate responsibilities

A punishment.

(a) Hitech and ARRA Rules

- HITECH is designed to encourage healthcare providers to use standardized health information technology and to protect personal health information.
- ARRA is a direct result of changes to HIPAA privacy, security and enforcement regulations and strengthens the confidentiality of health information and security protections. ARRA specifically addresses:

  Violation

  Electronic Health Record (EHR)

  Personal Health Record (PHR).

(b) Privacy rules

The Privacy Policy is designed to protect Individuals' Health Information (PHI) and allows individuals to:

1. Get a copy of their medical records.
2. Ask for changes to their medical records.
3. Learn and control how their PHI can be used.
4. Find out who got their PHI.
5. Send communication to an alternate location or alternate mode.
6. Register complaints and participate in investigations.

(c) Guidelines for Using and Exposing PHI

You may disclose information to the relevant authorities without the member's consent:

If required by law, order of court, etc.

Public Health Officials, FDA, etc.

domestic abuse or violence

assist law enforcement officers

report suspicious death

Provide workers' compensation information

assist in government activities

assist in disaster relief operations

to prevent serious danger to health or safety

for health management activities.

(d) Your responsibilities

what you need to do:

Disclose PHI - limit the information you share with anyone he or she wants to know ("minimum required" guideline)

Use PHI in accordance with HIPAA approved guidelines to access, calculate, edit and control PHI.

Access only the PHI needed to perform your job duties

Maintaining the confidentiality and security of subscription information at all times.

(e) HIPAA Patient Rights

HIPAA guarantees patients certain rights:

1. Right to Privacy,

   Right to confidential access to their health information Treatment, billing procedures and other health care activities (eg quality improvement)

2. The right to access and modify their health information upon request,

   Right to grant specific authorization to use their health Other than treatment, billing and other health information maintenance activities.

3. The right to be named in the directory of our patients,
4. Right to demand that persons do not disclose their presence in our facilities.

(f) Gram Required HIPAA Glossary

or Protected Health Information [PHI]

or closed companies [CE]

- Treatment, Payment and Health Care Activities [TPH]

Privacy Training Information [PT1].

(g) What does a closed company have to do with HIPAA?

- Inform patients about their privacy rights and how their information is used.
- Accept and implement privacy practices.
- Training employees to understand privacy practices.
- Appoint a privacy officer.
- Secure patient records with Secure Health Information [PHI].

(h) How do I protect my patient's privacy [figure 1]

Don't: ↓	Do: ↑
Tell anyone what you overhear about a patient.	Close doors in patient's rooms when discussing treatments.
Discuss a patient in public areas, such as elevators, hallways or cafeterias	Log off the computer when you are finished.
Look at information about a patient unless you need it to do your job.	Dispose of patient information by shredding or storing it in a locked container for destruction.
	Clear patient information off a your desk when your leave your desk.

- Safe computer and fax use
- Safeguards
    1. Physical Safeguard
    2. Technical Safeguard
    3. Administrative Safeguard.

(i) Compliance

- If you feel there has been a privacy violation, inform your instructor who will immediately assist you in contacting the Privacy Officer.
- Refer patients who have a privacy concern or complaint to the nurse in charge of the unit.

4.5.3 Summary

- All health information that specifically identifies an individual is considered confidential.
- Protecting the privacy of patient information is everyone's responsibility.
- Even though you are a student nurse, you are an active part of this program. Use patient information only to perform your responsibilities as assigned.
- Be aware! Don't intentionally or unintentionally disclose patient information. Help others to do the same.
- If you suspect any privacy violations or concerns, notify your instructor who will immediately assist you in contacting the Privacy Office.

References

1. *Atchinson, Brian K.; Fox, Daniel M. (May–June 1997).* "The Politics Of The Health Insurance Portability And Accountability Act" (PDF). Health Affairs. ***16** (3): 146–150.* doi:10.1377/hlthaff. 16.3.146. PMID 9141331. *Archived from* the original (PDF) *on 2014-01-16.* Retrieved 2014-01-16.
2. ^ "104th Congress, 1st Session, S.1028" (PDF). Archived (PDF) *from the original on 2012-06-16.*
3. ^ "HIPAA for Dummies".
4. ^ "Health Plans & Benefits: Portability of Health Coverage". *United States Department of Labor. 2015-12-09.* Archived *from the original on 2016-12-20.* Retrieved 2016-11-05.
5. ^ "Overview". *www.cms.gov. 2016-09-13.* Archived *from the original on 2016-11-02.* Retrieved 2016-11-05.
6. 29 U.S.C. § 1181(a)(2)
7. ^ 29 U.S.C. § 1181(a)(3)
8. ^ 29 U.S.C. § 1181(c)(1)
9. ^ 29 U.S.C. § 1181(c)(2)(A)
10. ^ (Sub B Sec 110)
11. ^ (Sub B Sec 111)
12. ^ "HIPAA for Healthcare Workers: The Privacy Rule". *2014.* doi:10.4135/9781529727890.
13. ^ 42 U.S.C. § 1320a-7c
14. ^ 42 U.S.C. § 1395ddd
15. ^ 42 U.S.C. § 1395b-5
16. ^ Jump up to:[a] [b] "42 U.S. Code § 1395ddd - Medicare Integrity Program". *LII / Legal Information Institute.* Archived *from the original on 2018-03-21.* Retrieved 2018-03-21.
17. ^ Jump up to:[a] [b] 45 CFR 160.103
18. ^ "What is the Definition of a HIPAA Covered Entity? - NetSec.News". *9 October 2017.* Archived *from the original on 6 May 2018.*
19. https://www.hipaaexams.com/blog/understanding-5-main-hipaa-rules/.
20. *Kirsch, Michael S. (2004). "Alternative Sanctions and the Federal Tax Law: Symbols, Shaming, and Social Norm Management as a Substitute for Effective Tax Policy". Iowa Law Review.* ***89** (863).* SSRN 552730.

CHAPTER 4.6

Informed Consent Process and Procedures

4.6.1 Definition

- A process by which a subject voluntarily confirms his or her willingness to participate in a particular trial, after having been informed of all aspects of the trial that are relevant to the subject's decision to participate.
- Informed consent is documented by means of a written, signed and dated informed consent form.
- The goal of the informed consent process is to provide people with sufficient information so that they can make informed choices about whether to begin or continue participation in clinical research.

4.6.2 Informed Consent Guidelines

1. **ICMR (Indian Council of Medical Research)**

   "Ethical Guidelines for Biomedical Research on Human Subjects" Published in 2000 and revised in 2006

2. **ICH**

   ICH Guidelines E6 section 4.8 under GLP (Good Clinical Practices).

4.6.3 Information Comprehension Voluntariness [Figure 1]

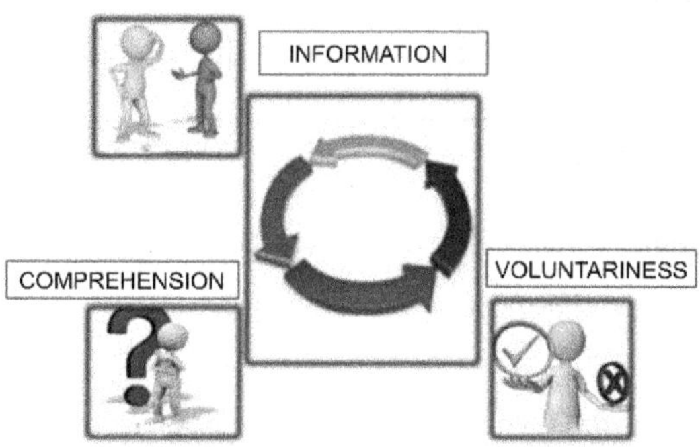

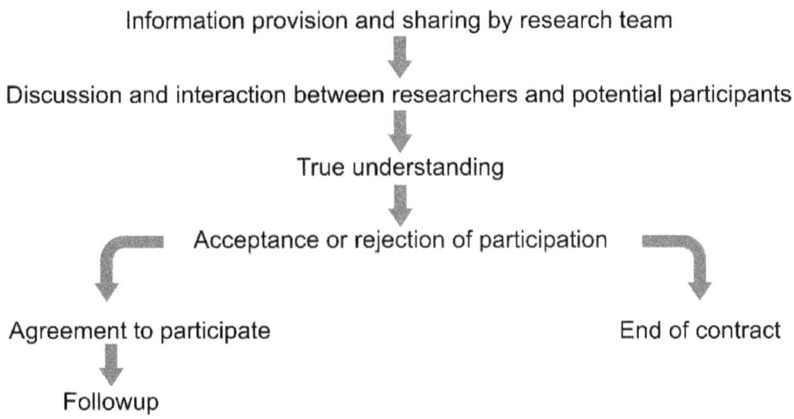

4.6.4 Approval Process

- Choose the correct environment and location to obtain permission
- Involve the required number of health workers.
- Involve family members in this process as needed.
- Confirm subject or legal authorized representative capable of doing.
- Make sure the object or LAR has sufficient grasp.
- Continue the approval process throughout the study.

4.6.5 Approval Process Plan

1. Identify barriers to learning participation and ways to overcome barriers
2. Identify meaningless words
3. Make a list of "Frequently Asked Questions".
4. Decide who will conduct the approval discussion
5. Decide where the approval debate will take place
6. Give enough time to explain the text on the topic.
7. Give enough time to read and reflect on the topic questions to answer.

4.6.6 Who can Sign the Informed Consent Form?

1. Subject or Legally Authorized Representative (LAR)
2. Person carrying out approval verification.
3. Fair Witness.

4.6.7 Informed Consent Form Elements

1. Essential Elements
   (a) A purpose
   (b) risk
   (c) profit
   (d) confidentiality
   (e) payment
   (f) Contact information
   (g) Voluntary participation.
2. Additional Components
   (a) Criteria for withdrawal.
   (b) Additional cost in subjects.
   (c) Report that there may be unforeseen risks.
   (d) Approximate number of study subjects.
   (e) Reports made through new discoveries.

4.6.8 ICF Component

(As per ICMR Guidelines, 2006)

1. Important information about research studies.
2. What is the study about, and why do we do it?
3. Benefits of participating in the study.
4. Potential risks of joining the study.
5. Certificate of Confidentiality.
6. What happens to the information collected after the inspection? Time has run out.
7. Compensation for being part of the course.
8. Possible costs of the course that may be part of the study.
9. Who can earn from the results of the study.
10. Option in any subject if they do not wish to participate study.
11. Initiative
12. Material Contact Information.
13. Study group contact information.
14. Approval: Name, Signature and Date
15. Parent or LAR: Name, Signature and Date.

References

1. Research Ethics and Compliance/ University of Michigan
2. Obtaining and Documenting Informed Consent/University of California, San Francisco.

CHAPTER 4.7

Pharmacovigilance

4.7.1 Introduction

Pharmacovigilance (PV) is the pharmacological science concerned with the detection, analysis, understanding, and prevention of side effects, particularly the long-term and short-term effects of drugs.

All medicines (medicines and vaccines) have side effects. It is important to monitor the known and unknown side effects of drugs and determine any new information regarding their safety profile.

- Pharmacovigilance looks at all available information to evaluate drug safety profiles

The benefits of pharmacovigilance medication should also be considered

Spontaneous reporting depends on the health professional.

4.7.2 Purpose and Objectives of Medicinal Awareness

Purpose:

Discover new information about drug-related risks

Purpose:

Improving patient care and safety

improving public health and safety

Promoting the safe, rational and appropriate use of medicines

Promote understanding, education and medical training in pharmacology awareness

4.7.3 How Pharmacovigilance Works? [figure 1]

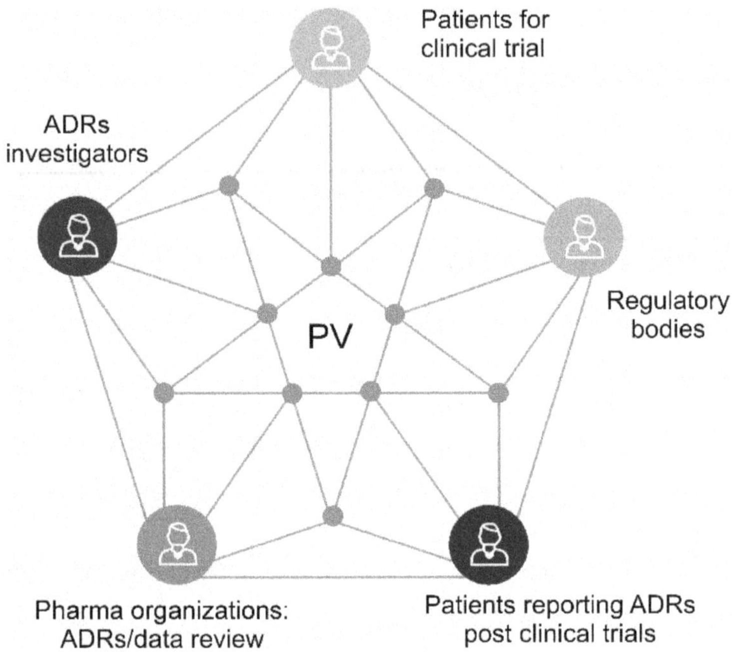

4.7.4 Adverse Drug Reactions Classifications [Table 1]

- which is noxious, unintended and which occurs A response at doses normally used in humans for Prophylaxis, Diagnosis or Therapy of disease, or for modification of physiological function…..(WHO 1972)

	Type A(Augmented)	**Type B(Bizarre)**
Pharmacologically predictable	Yes	No
Dose dependant	Yes	No
Frequency	Common	Rarer
Incidence	High	Low
Mortality	Low	High
Treatment	Adjust Dose	Stop the drug

4.7.5 Side Effect

Any unintended effect of a pharmaceutical product occurring at normal dosage which is related to the pharmacological properties of the drug. e.g. antihistamines producing sedation, anticholinergics producing dryness.

(a) Serious Adverse Effect

(b) Unexpected Adverse Effect

4.7.6 Phases of Product Development [Table 2]

			Clinical trials						
	Preclinical Testing	File IND at FDA	phase 1	phase 2	phase 3	File NDA at FDA	FDA		phase 4
Years	3-5		1	2	3		2-5	Total = 12 years	additional post marketing testing required by FDA
Test population	Laboratory and animal studies		20-80 healthy volunteeres	100-300 patient volunteers	1000-3000 patient volunteers		review process/ approval		
Purpose	asses safety and biological activity		determine safety and dosage	evaluate effectiveness and look for side effects	verify effectiveness, monitor adverse events from long term use.				
success rate	5000 compounds evaluated		5 enter trials				1 approved		

4.7.7 Pharmacovigilance and India

- India is a hub of Global Clinical trials & a destination for Drug Discovery & Development. However, whether patients in India receive safe drugs or not is still very much in question
- Rapid induction of NCEs and high tech Pharma products in the market throw up the **Challenges of monitoring Adverse Drug Reactions (ADRs)** overlarge multiethnic population base...

4.7.8 Who Should Report Safety Data?

- Physicians
- Pharmacists
- Pharmaceutical companies qualified persons – (Pharmacovigilance/ Regulatory manager)

- Investigational products (clinical trials)
- Post-approval reporting – Individual Case Safety Report (ICSR), Periodic Safety Update Report (PSUR)
- In many countries' patients are encouraged (but not obligated) to report side effects.

4.7.9 What to Report?

- It is important to report serious unexpected ADRs.
- Most cases of unexpected ADRs are associated with medicines newly introduced on the market.
- All suspected adverse reactions.
- Every single problem related to the use of a drug.
- ADRs associated with radiology contrast media, vaccines, diagnostics, drugs used in traditional medicine, herbal remedies, cosmetics, medical devices and equipment.

4.7.10 Four Common Drug Banned in other Countries but not in India

Drug	Year	Reason
Lumiracoxib	2008	Hepatotoxicity
Aprotinin	2008	Kidney and cardiovascular toxicity
Tegaserod	2007	Cardiovascular is chemic events
Ximelagatran	2006	Hepatotoxicity
Valdecoxib	2005	Dermatology adverse events
Pemoline	2005	Hepatotoxicity
Rofecoxib	2004	Thrombotic cardiovascular events
Levomethadyl	2003	Fatal arrhytmia
Rapacuronium	2001	Risk of fatal bronchospasm
Cerivastatin	2001	Rhabdomyolosis
Trovafloxacin	2001	Hepatotoxicity
Amineptine	2000	Hepatotoxicity, dermatological side effects, abuse potential
Cisapride	2000	Cardiac arrhythmias
Troglitazone	2000	hepatotoxicity

S.No.	Drugs	Used for	Reason for ban	Brand name
1	Nimesulide	Pain killer, fever	Liver failure	Nise, Nimulid
2	Phenylpropaolamine	Cold & cough	Stroke	D'cold, Vicks Action-500
3	Quiniodochlor	Anti-diarrheal	Damage to sight	Enteroquinol
4	Analgin	Pain-killer	Bone marrow depression	Novalgin

4.7.11 Importance of Pharmacovigilance

- Complete safety data (especially for unexpected and serious adverse events) can only be captured through pharmacovigilance
- It cannot be captured through clinical trials which are conducted in an "artificial environment."
  - In clinical trials
  - patients are not taking any other medications
  - do not have concomitant diseases
  - are taking the drug short-term (during the duration of the trials only) and
  - are not part of vulnerable groups (e.g., children, pregnant women, elderly, etc.).

4.7.12 Partners in Pharmacovigilance

- The WHO Quality Assurance and Safety: Medicines team
- The Uppsala Monitoring Centre (UMC)
- The National Pharmacovigilance Centers
  - Hospitals and Academia
  - Health Professionals
  - Patients
  - Other Partners.

4.7.13 Pharmacovigilance in Drug Regulation

Clinical Trial Regulation

(i) Collection of ADR

(ii) monitoring clinical data

(iii) reporting of clinical data

Post Marketing safety Monitoring.

4.7.14 THE Rapid

- The RaPID is a PV program it conduct public health program.
- It provide support to focal point.
- Focus on RaPID HIV, T.B, Malaria and other program.
- It is important to encourage and ensure reporting of ADR.
- It consists of various department for working various type of diseases.

4.7.15 1964: U. K. Starts Yellow Card System

- The Yellow Card Scheme is the main ADR reporting scheme in the UK and was introduced in 1964 after the thalidomide tragedy highlighted the urgent need for routine monitoring of medicines. It receives more than 20,000 reports of possible side effects each year.
  - True challenge lies in....˜ In recognizing at the earliest possible stage, the adverse effects that a drug may induce, so that the risk (unfavorable results) never becomes disproportionate to benefit (Favorable results).

4.7.16 At the Level of Clinicians

- My Doctor is a good doctor; He made me no iller than I was.......
- Willem Hussem (The Netherlands)1900 -1974
- Translation: Peter Raven
- There are no really safe biologically active drugs. There are only safe physicians.... Harold A. kaminetzsky1963.

- Active reporting of **ADVERSE DRUG REACTIONS** as forms are available freely e.g. Nimusulide
- European Medicine Evaluation Agency Bans **NIMESULIDE.**
  - Avoid Prescription errors Articles highlighting the rise in prescription errors.
    - 11. Students can start Pharmacy bulletins with help of Respected Principal & coordinators of an institution
    - (Australian Prescriber, USPDI).
    - **Aims of Drug Alerts....˜** The information resources should be designed to assist the health provider in their clinical choice of drugs, in an effort to reduce the incidence and severity of adverse effects & medication errors.

4.7.17 Drug Alert Leaflets

- FDA pulls anti parkinsonism drug of Pergolide from market
- EMEA bans Nimesulide
- Petitions to remove Cox2 inhibitors
- Cisapride under strict scrutiny
- Phenylpropanolamine risk of Hemorrhagic stroke.

4.7.18 Conclusion

It is expected that 50 – 75 % of medical errors are preventable. Think less about drug safety: more about patient safety Use and react to concerns Think less about regulating (incl. withdrawal) and automating data input: more about useful information output Think more about impact and consequences of decisions and non-decisions.

References

1. CSM & MCA. Pharmacovigilance. *Current Problems in Pharmacovigilance.* 1993. p. 1.
2. https://www.who.int/teams/regulation-prequalification/regulation-and-safety/pharmacovigilance

www.ingramcontent.com/pod-product-compliance
Lightning Source LLC
Chambersburg PA
CBHW070251260926
51849CB00001BA/139
* 9 7 8 9 3 9 5 0 3 9 5 7 4 *